www.wadsworth.com

wadsworth.com is the World Wide Web site for Wadsworth and is your direct source to dozens of online resources.

At *wadsworth.com* you can find out about supplements, demonstration software, and student resources. You can also send e-mail to many of our authors and preview new publications and exciting new technologies.

wadsworth.com
Changing the way the world learns®

Integrating Music into the Elementary Classroom

Fifth Edition

William M. Anderson

Joy E. Lawrence

Kent State University

Wadsworth
Thomson Learning™

Australia • Canada • Mexico • Singapore • Spain
United Kingdom • United States

Music Publisher: Clark Baxter

Senior Developmental Editor: Sharon Adams Poore

Assistant Editor: Cherie Hackelberg

Editorial Assistant: Jennifer Ellis

Print Buyer: Barbara Britton

Permissions Editor: Joohee Lee

Production Service: Gary Palmatier, Ideas to Images

Copy Editor: Elizabeth von Radics

Cover Designer: Gary Palmatier

Cover Photo: Nancy Sheehan/PhotoEdit

Cover Printer: Malloy Lithographing, Inc.

Compositor: Ideas to Images

Printer: Malloy Lithographing, Inc.

Printed in the United States of America

1 2 3 4 5 6 7 04 03 02 01 00

Library of Congress Cataloging-in-Publication Data
Anderson, William M.
    Integrating music into the elementary classroom / William M. Anderson, Joy E. Lawrence. — 5th ed.
        p. cm.
    Includes bibliographical references and indexes.
    ISBN 0-534-51751-X
        1. School music—Instruction and study. 2. Elementary school teaching. I. Lawarence, Joy E. II. Title.

    MT1 .A696 2000
    372.87'044—dc21

                                                    00-028206

For more information, contact
Wadsworth/Thomson Learning
10 Davis Drive
Belmont, CA 94002-3098
USA

For information about our products, contact us:
Thomson Learning Academic Resource Center
1-800-423-0563
http://www.wadsworth.com

International Headquarters
Thomson Learning
International Division
290 Harbor Drive, 2nd Floor
Stamford, CT 06902-7477
USA

UK/Europe/Middle East/South Africa
Thomson Learning
Berkshire House
168-173 High Holborn
London WC1V 7AA
United Kingdom

Asia
Thomson Learning
60 Albert Street, #15-01
Albert Complex
Singapore 189969

Canada
Nelson Thomson Learning
1120 Birchmount Road
Toronto, Ontario M1K 5G4
Canada

Preface

MOST ELEMENTARY SCHOOLS in the United States require that students receive instruction in music. Although large numbers of schools benefit from music specialists, responsibility for teaching music often falls to classroom teachers. Even in schools with formally trained music teachers, the amount of time these specialists spend with students is quite small compared with the total time students spend with their classroom teacher.

Most classroom teachers try to teach music (along with other subject areas), but many have a limited understanding of how music can be made to "fit" with the rest of the elementary program. Thus we see a need for a practically oriented book that shows how music can be taught and integrated into other areas of the elementary school curriculum.

Integrating Music into the Elementary Classroom, Fifth Edition, emphasizes the importance of enriching children's lives by making music a central part of the elementary school curriculum. This book provides guidelines for elementary teachers with limited experience as well as music specialists.

Integrating Music into the Elementary Classroom 5/e is comprehensive, covering music fundamentals as well as materials and methods for teaching music in the elementary classroom. It focuses on how children learn and presents popular, easy-to-use techniques for teaching singing, playing instruments, moving to music, creating music, and listening to music, as well as studying music from a multicultural perspective and relating music with the arts and other subject areas. Lesson plans are provided for kindergarten through grade six, along with more than 160 songs selected from various cultures and historical periods.

Integrating Music into the Elementary Classroom 5/e is unique in its focus on cultural diversity and integrating music with the entire elementary curriculum. It features:

- A contemporary approach based on national music standards
- Updated and expanded content
- Greater emphasis on technology, the Internet, and Web sites
- "For Your Journal" section at the end of each chapter
- A large number of lesson plans
- An accompanying CD of more than 40 songs
- A more artistically enhanced book

Acknowledgments

The authors wish to acknowledge the assistance of the following people in the preparation of this manuscript: Virginia Hoge Mead, Professor Emeritus of music education, Kent State University, for her help with Dalcroze eurhythmics; William D. Thomas, retired coordinator of vocal music, Cleveland Heights/University Heights schools, for his help in interpretative movement; Kathern Mihelik and Dr. Maria Foustalieraki for their help with the folk dances; Herbert Ascherman Jr., photographer, for his assistance with the photographs; Dr. Robert Schneider, vocal music teacher of Shaker Middle School, for his help in getting students and instruments for the photographs; and Dr. Keitha Hamann, Kent State University, for the accompanying recording. The personnel on the CD are: Keitha Lucas Hamann, Mary Lou Muckleroy, Carmen Roebke, Chrissy Devault, and Leslie Barnett, vocals; John Roebke and Keitha Lucas Hamann, piano; Carmen Roebke, Mary Lou Muckleroy, and Keitha Lucas Hamann, instruments; and Iris Dobson, Craig Adams, and Chuck Wright, recording technicians.

We would also like to thank the following reviewers for their comments: Patricia S. Poulter, Eastern Illinois University; Natalie Kreutzer, University of Idaho; Marie C. Miller, Emporia State University; Louise Patrick, Eastern Michigan University; Nancy Paxcia-Bibbins, Bridgewater State College; and Dr. Earlene Rentz, Baylor University.

Our special thanks to Clark Baxter, editor; Bob Kauser, permissions editor; Gary Palmatier, production manager; and Elizabeth von Radics, copy editor, for their insight, encouragement, and patience through the preparation of this book. Every effort has been made to trace the ownership of copyrighted material and secure the necessary permissions to reprint these selections. In the case of some selections for which acknowledgment is not given, extensive research has failed to locate the copyright owner. And, finally, a very special word of thanks to our families for their support through the lengthy endeavor of preparing this Fifth Edition.

William M. Anderson

Joy E. Lawrence

Contents

4 Teaching Music Through Singing   79

5 Integrating Songs with Other Subjects and Activities   135

6 Teaching Music Through Playing Classroom Instruments   211

*I*ntroduction

AS A TEACHER you are about to enter one of the most exciting domains of human experience—sharing with children what you know, cherish, and love so that the quality of their relationships with others will be richer, their perception of the world around them deeper, and their own lives more rewarding and fulfilled. This book is for you, the classroom teacher in the elementary school. It is you who will have daily contact with children in grades K through 6 at least 5 hours a day, 25 hours a week, 900 hours a year. The formal education of a child rests in your hands. Your enthusiasm is contagious, your beliefs in life's wonders inspire, your understanding comforts, and your knowledge and skill motivate and mold the intellectual and emotional growth of the children in your classroom.

Classroom teachers have an awesome task, with responsibility in a great many subject areas, including language arts, mathematics, science, social studies, physical education, art, and music. This book is based on the belief that *every* classroom teacher can accumulate knowledge and develop skills that will enable him or her *to lead a child in meaningful experiences with music of all peoples in America's diverse society*. Each of you has particular talents. Some of you sing well; others play instruments; still others may never have sung in a choir or played an instrument but enjoy listening and dancing to music. Some of you have traveled or read a great deal and would like to share with your students music and arts of other countries and peoples. Whatever your background, this book will help you build on your strengths to teach music and will expand your horizons so that you will be better equipped to integrate musical experiences into the elementary school curriculum.

The Importance of Music and Other Arts in the Elementary School

As you begin your study of music and develop materials for teaching, it will be helpful to ponder several questions that educators and parents often ask about the value of music and other arts in the general education of children: What is art? What is an arts experience? How does it differ from other experiences in life? Why is it important for children to have arts experiences?

At the outset it should be stated that there are many answers to the question *What is art?* When we talk about art, we are usually referring to music, painting, sculpture, dance, poetry, drama, and so on, rather than the sciences, such as physics, biology, and chemistry. An artwork expresses human feeling: excitement, relaxation, or joy. As the artist manipulates and arranges the media unique to a particular art (sounds in music, color and design in painting, and words in poetry), an expressive product emerges that we call a work of art (a musical composition, a painting, or a poem). The result is a projection of the personality and skill of the artist, a statement of the philosophy of the age in which it is produced, and an expression of a feeling or idea that transcends anything concerned with one individual or single period of time in history.

In studying works of art, we need to focus our attention on some basic criteria. The first of these is *craftmanship:* How carefully has the artist used materials (sounds, words, paint, or movement)? A second criterion is *creativity* or *imagination:* What has the artist done to create something fresh and new? How is the work *expressive?* Has the artist effectively captured a dimension of human feeling, and does this flow forth to the perceiver? As we select materials to be used in lessons for children, we will learn more about these criteria and how they can help us make decisions regarding our choice of artworks for use in the classroom.

Children experiencing art

The view taken in this book is that, in an arts experience, a person and a work of art are involved in intense interaction that creates a deeply satisfying sense of pleasure, heightened sensitivity to all dimensions of life, and a powerful feeling of self-worth and fulfillment. For instance, performances of Beethoven's Symphony No. 5 consistently stir the hearts and minds of audiences. No matter how many times one hears this piece, it always reaches out with fresh and distinctly new meanings. This is the unique quality of a true work of art, and it is precisely here where the arts experience differs from other types of experiences. The uniqueness of an artwork is its embodiment of human feeling and the potential it has of sharing this feeling with you and me. Such arts experiences are essential in the general education of every child, for through the arts the child develops his or her own expression of feelings and grows in the ability to understand and appreciate how artists throughout the world have expressed these same feelings, thus enriching the quality and the meaning of life.

In the words of Charles Fowler, an advocate for arts education, music and other arts:

- Teach us divergent, rather than convergent, thinking.
- Develop craftsmanship and the ability to apply aesthetics.
- Introduce us to perceptions and understandings that we could not acquire in any other way.
- Provide us with insight and wisdom that enlighten our understanding, making it deeper and more comprehensive.
- Facilitate human communication within and across cultures.
- Help us to define who we are and to articulate our own sense of being.
- Document our history, distinguishing our relationship to time by showing us as we were yesterday, as we are today, and as we can be tomorrow.
- Replenish our spirit and, by nurturing it, consoling it, and inspiring it, restore our humanity.[*]

In recent years the Harvard psychologist Howard Gardner has given particular support to the importance of music in the education of all children. Gardner contends that intelligence is a broadly based concept actually including various types of intelligences. He states that these *multiple intelligences* include linguistic and logical-mathematical (which we often see emphasized in schools) but also *musical,* spatial, bodily kinesthetic, interpersonal, and intrapersonal.[†] Gardner encourages teachers to provide a comprehensively balanced school curriculum that assists students in developing the potential of all of their intelligences.

Supporting Gardner's call for recognizing the importance of music in schools are a considerable number of new research studies that provide evidence of music's ability to stimulate brain activity and perhaps through music instruction to actually enhance certain cognitive abilities.[‡] These studies provide increasing evidence of the centrality of music in the education of all children and of the importance of classroom teachers' ensuring that musical study is an integral part of the school curriculum.

---

[*] Quoted in Jeffrey Patchen, "A Comprehensive Approach," *Music Educators Journal* 83, no. 2 (September 1996), p. 17.

[†] See Howard Gardner, *Frames of the Mind: The Theory of Multiple Intelligences* (New York: Basic Books, Harper Collins, 1993).

[‡] See "Recent Brain Research on Young Children," *Teaching Music* 6, no. 6 (June 1999), pp. 41–43, 54.

An Integrated Approach to Learning and Teaching

It is important for elementary school teachers to help students integrate knowledge across subject areas. Specialization is evident in a number of areas of the elementary curriculum, where there are teachers of reading, music, art, and physical education, and the daily schedule is organized around distinct segments such as mathematics and social studies. Although specialization has an important place, attention must also be directed toward fostering an integrated structure so that students develop some sense about how knowledge in one area relates to what is studied in another. If students are to learn to identify relationships among subject areas, they will need to learn from an interrelated perspective. We cannot assume that students will somehow assimilate information from various areas and then draw together the necessary integrated relationships on their own. In fact, students often do not see the most basic relationships among subject matter areas and thus must be shown how subjects are related. Teaching from such a perspective need not detract from specialized study, but it does require that teachers go beyond current practices and structure curricula based on relationships within and among subject matter areas.

Owen Franken/Corbis

Making music part of the classroom experience

Integrating music into a child's daily classroom experiences has many advantages. Foremost is that children can be taught to perceive ideas that are related. For example, they can discover that fundamental musical concepts—such as enlargement through repetition, contrast, and balance—are present in many subject areas. Further, as children study music and the visual arts as part of a social studies unit on a historical period or culture, they often develop a much clearer perspective of a particular time and its people. Many children have studied the period of Washington, Jefferson, and Franklin without realizing that several of the world's greatest composers (Haydn, Mozart, and Beethoven) lived during the same time and that the minuet, the third movement in symphonies of the classical period, was also a popular dance of the American colonists. Clearly, the primary focus of this book is to place music in an integrated learning environment, which we believe will contribute to meaningful and long-lasting educational experiences for children.

The Plan for This Book

It is important to design musical learning that focuses on multisensory experiences with music (learning through moving, seeing, and hearing music), as research has shown that children differ not only in the rate at which they learn but also in the way in which they learn best. Chapter 1 focuses on how children learn music, including those students with special needs. Chapter 2 suggests ways to design learning experiences appropriate to a variety of interests and levels of maturity. It also includes a segment on instructional technology.

Developing skill in understanding, performing, and interpreting music is possible for anyone willing to take the time to study, practice, and learn. Chapter 3 focuses on fundamentals of music. The classroom teacher requires knowledge and skill in the basic elements of music— melody, rhythm, texture, dynamics, tone color, and form—along with an understanding of how a composer uses these elements to express ideas, beliefs, and feelings. The chapter includes suggestions for activities for developing skills emphasized throughout the text: singing, playing instruments, listening, moving, creating music, and relating music to peoples, places, and cultures from many world traditions and historical periods. Music is basic to life, and meaningful experiences with it can enrich the quality of our lives as teachers as well as the lives of students.

To be confident in teaching music, a classroom teacher needs skill in teaching children to sing, play instruments, listen to music, express music through movement, and create music. Chapters 4 through 9 are devoted to developing these skills and also provide Orff, Kodály, and Dalcroze techniques and materials for teaching and integrating these approaches into the basic curriculum.

In chapter 10 the study of music in a multicultural context leads to a greater understanding of peoples, places, and cultures through singing, playing instruments, directed listening, and movement/dance.

Chapter 11 focuses on relating music and other areas of literary and visual arts, with the intent of helping students understand basic relationships between music and other art forms. The chapter includes suggestions for planning "integrative" programs suitable for open houses or similar events, as well as for creating "resource" units that make use of several arts.

The book concludes with an epilogue that features a plan for lifelong learning in music, with suggestions for preparing children to attend live concerts of music, criteria for purchasing recordings, and possibilities for making

Leading children into the world of music

music with friends outside of school. Appendices provide fingerings for the recorder and guitar chord tablature. Indexes are provided for the songs, listening examples, visual examples, literary examples, and two-chord and three-chord songs.

This book can be used both as a methods text for students preparing to be elementary classroom teachers and as a teaching resource in the classroom. Teachers are encouraged to keep this text available for reference and to use the many materials and teaching suggestions as they begin their careers.

We hope that as you complete this book, you will have gained a new perspective on integrating music into daily learning experiences and that your students will grow in knowledge, sensitivity, and understanding of themselves and their world.

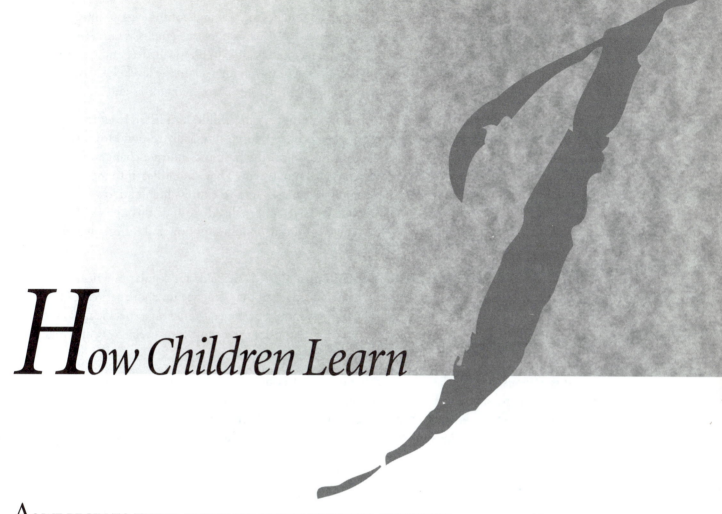

How Children Learn

As WE BEGIN TO THINK ABOUT TEACHING MUSIC TO CHILDREN, we must consider (1) ways children learn, (2) what principles are involved in the learning process, and (3) how we apply these principles to musical learning. Although many of the ideas presented in this chapter may apply to any subject area, our interest here is to relate them to the teaching of music and to integrated learning experiences with music.

Basic Types of Learning

Several basic types of learning should be considered when teaching music to children. The first of these may be categorized as *psychomotor learning*—that is, learning involving mental processes that control muscular activity. A second category of learning is *cognitive learning,* which deals with the acquisition of knowledge. A third category of learning is *affective learning,* which concerns itself with a *feeling* response to music.

PSYCHOMOTOR LEARNING

Students vary in their psychomotor learning abilities. Some children display considerable ability in singing, playing instruments, and moving to music, whereas others seem less responsive to such psychomotor learning activities. It is important for the teacher to nurture the musical potential of students regardless of their initial level of accomplishment.

Attention to developing psychomotor skills should begin early and continue as an integral part of the training children receive at more-advanced levels. For example, an emphasis on movement to music is based on the premise that children should be able to physically feel and respond to musical stimuli before being asked to identify such stimuli on a cognitive level. Such an approach to musical study clearly parallels the pedagogical principle of "sound before sight."

Psychomotor learning is particularly important in training children to listen to music. Directed listening should be approached by having children physically respond to musical sounds; for example, students should learn to follow the beat and indicate changes in tempo through clapping, marching, or other physical movement. They should learn to move in either twos or threes to demonstrate duple and triple meter, and to express high and low sounds with appropriate movements. Only after students have "internalized" sounds through movement and are able to respond accurately to musical stimuli should notation and other information about music be introduced.

An important aspect of psychomotor learning of music is the need for regular practice. Children seem to learn musical skills more effectively if they practice for short periods of time interspersed with intervals of rest. Thus efforts should be concentrated on a specific task (such as singing, playing an instrument, or listening to music) for a short time each day rather than for a long time once or twice a week.

It is obvious that the classroom teacher is in a better position to help students with skill development, since the formal music teacher may see students only once or twice a week. If children are to receive the frequency of training needed for optimum development of musical skills, classroom teachers must allow time in the daily schedule for such skill development.

COGNITIVE LEARNING

In terms of music, we ask children to learn about such things as elements of music, composers, style periods, and instruments. One of the most important concerns in cognitive learning is for information about music to be closely linked with actual musical experiences. Children need to have many experiences with sounds to understand musical information. For example, in teaching about 4/4 meter, the teacher may tell students that a quarter note receives one beat, a half note two beats, and a dotted half note three beats. Such information does not take on full meaning, however, until it is placed in an actual musical experience in which students clap or march as they count the beats in various note values.

One of the practical problems teachers must deal with in cognitive learning is that information must be in language that children can easily understand. Teachers must be particularly aware of the *level of language* to be used when presenting information to students at various grade levels. An effective way of dealing with problems of musical terminology is to use diagrams, symbols, or pictures. Often a child can more easily understand rondo form from a diagram, such as ● ■ ● ▲ ●, than from several minutes of words spoken by the teacher.

AFFECTIVE LEARNING

If music is to be important in children's lives, the teacher needs to be aware of how music expresses human feeling. Children should experience music in such a way that they are increasingly aware of how composers have used sound to express deep inner feelings, which, like ideas, have transcended peoples, places, and cultures of many different eras. For example, as students learn to move to the long, flowing melody in Smetana's *The Moldau* and learn the folk song on which it is based, they should experience the power and feeling generated by the minor tonality of this melody. In *affective learning* students experience through an art form inseparable mixtures of feelings that words cannot begin to express. This education in the *feeling* expressed in musical artworks becomes a cornerstone on which all musical teaching and learning are based.

Learning in Music Needs to Be Active

All learning needs to be *active:* Children need to respond to music by moving, singing, playing instruments, and creating. Linking information about music with actual musical sound encourages children to be actively involved with musical learning. Through such involvement they seem to assimilate and retain information more effectively and to exhibit greater interest and motivation to learn. For example, a teacher wishing to present rondo form to students must go beyond simply diagramming the form with letters *(ABACA)* on the chalkboard and telling students to listen for a recurring section of music *(A)* that alternates with contrasting sections of music *(B, C)*. Children need to sing or play the melodies of various sections, engage in some type of movement to the rhythm (clapping, marching, and so on), and perhaps place letters on a chalkboard to identify various sections of the form as they hear them.

Teacher-Centered and Child-Centered Learning

In considering various approaches to learning music, you will want to explore both teacher-centered and child-centered methods. The *teacher-centered approach* features the teacher primarily as a lecturer who presents material to the class by *defining* and *explaining*. For example, the teacher who wishes students to learn about duple meter approaches the topic by telling them that *duple* means "two," that in duple meter there are, therefore, two beats in a measure, and that the first beat normally receives the greater accent. The teacher may use musical examples to illustrate the definition, but in this approach students assume a rather passive role.

In contrast the *child-centered approach* to learning actively involves students in the learning process. In this approach the teacher presents students with a problem that needs to be solved. Under the teacher's guidance, students explore possible solutions through trial-and-error examination. The teacher guides students in their exploration, but the ultimate solution to the problem is largely student derived. For example, in presenting duple meter, the teacher first has students sing a song in duple meter, then has them clap the beat or conduct as they sing the song again, asks them if they can feel which beat receives the greater emphasis (first), and finally asks how the beats seem to group themselves. The teacher guides the students toward their ultimate understanding that the beats are grouped in twos (duple meter).

As you work with students at various age or grade levels, you will undoubtedly use both teacher-centered and child-centered approaches. Because students are more actively involved in the child-centered approach, however, teachers generally favor it, particularly in working with young children.

The Structure of Musical Learning

In structuring musical learning for the classroom, you need to (1) make what you teach meaningful, (2) organize material sequentially, (3) experience music before labeling it, (4) use a conceptual approach to learning, (5) use a multisensory approach to learning, (6) use a multicultural approach to learning, (7) provide reinforcement, and (8) teach for transfer.

1 MAKE WHAT YOU TEACH MEANINGFUL

You should emphasize activities that closely relate to things children perceive as interesting and meaningful. Some possibilities include capitalizing on children's interest in trains by having them listen to Villa-Lobos's "Little Train of the Caipira" or the bluegrass composition "Orange Blossom Special"; designing a unit of study on electronic music for those with interests in electronics and machines; or studying nature through such pieces as Beethoven's "The Storm" (Symphony No. 6, fourth movement) or Smetana's *The Moldau.*

2 ORGANIZE MATERIAL SEQUENTIALLY

One of the most important aspects of structuring musical learning in the classroom is to develop a successful sequence of activities. In developing plans for teaching music, you need to arrange learning experiences into a logical continuum, carefully linking each step with preceding and succeeding steps. Sequence may vary from classroom to classroom; that is, one teacher may develop a sequence of steps that proves successful in teaching certain musical concepts, whereas a second teacher who is teaching other students the same material may develop a different but equally logical sequence.

Often teachers develop several alternative plans for presenting material. In a classroom of twenty-five students, there will usually be children with a variety of academic and musical abilities and backgrounds. Some students may have had considerable experience with rhythmic activities, for example, whereas others may have had none. In presenting a rhythmic learning experience to such a class, the teacher needs to consider several alternatives in the sequence of events undertaken by the students.

3 EXPERIENCE MUSIC BEFORE LABELING IT

A young child may have many experiences with an apple—such as eating it, feeling that it is round, and seeing that it is green or red—long before being asked to label it with the word *apple.* Music should follow this same pattern of learning; that is, the child should have experiences with sounds by singing, playing instruments, listening to fast and slow tempos, or loud and soft dynamics before being asked to place these labels (*fast* or *slow, loud* or *soft*) on these musical events. Because music is the most abstract of all the arts—that is, it passes through time and exists only in the memory—actual experiences with musical sounds are essential before discussing any specific musical concept.

USE A CONCEPTUAL APPROACH TO LEARNING

Teachers have discovered that one of the most effective ways of helping students assimilate and retain information is through a conceptual approach to learning. Conceptual learning involves "students' developing the ability to give a common name or response to a class of stimuli varying in appearance."* Teachers using a conceptual approach focus learning on certain fundamental ideas considered basic to understanding music. These include concepts of melody, rhythm, texture, timbre, dynamics, and form. For example, melody as a fundamental concept in music involves a succession of pitches that are perceived as belonging together. Melodies may vary greatly with respect to their internal characteristics, such as differing number of pitches, various scales, movement principally by step or skip, variety of contour directions, and range. However different these internal characteristics may be, the central concept of melody is preserved as a meaningful succession of pitches.

Children develop a concept of melody through experiences with many types of melodies. It is important, therefore, that in the classroom students experience a wide array of melodies from various historical periods in Western music and from other musical traditions around the world. They should explore characteristics of melodies through singing, playing instruments, and listening. If learning experiences are carefully organized over a period of time, students will indeed develop a concept of melody and the many characteristics it may have.

As lessons are organized around the musical concepts of melody, rhythm, texture, timbre, dynamics, and form, it will be helpful to refer to the characteristics of each of these as outlined in chapter 3.

In addition to strictly musical concepts, analogous concepts are found in visual and literary arts. Among these are repetition and enlargement, contrast and variety, and balance (see chapter 11). Each of these concepts operates in a similar fashion but through different means in various art forms. Experiencing a concept through several art forms encourages integrated learning.

USE A MULTISENSORY APPROACH TO LEARNING

Students learn through a combination of their senses. Some learn more quickly through the visual sense, which is highly developed through watching television or playing video games. A chart or musical picture provides these children with something tangible to which to relate the music. The visual image remains even though the sound may end. Others may learn more quickly by moving to the music. For example, a child might perceive triple rhythm more quickly by moving in some fashion, such as tapping his or her thighs or swaying with the beat. Another child might learn just as quickly through the aural sense—that is, by hearing a melody a second time. People have different aptitudes and talents; the skillful teacher recognizes these differences and creates lessons that involve as many of the senses as possible.

---

*Janice T. Gibson, *Psychology for the Classroom* (Englewood Cliffs, N.J.: Prentice-Hall, 1976), p. 243.

6 USE A MULTICULTURAL APPROACH TO LEARNING

Music and the arts from different cultures contribute to our understanding of both others and ourselves. As the teacher creates lessons that involve singing and playing instruments from many musical traditions, students are encouraged to experience, respect, and appreciate the contributions of peoples, cultures, and eras different from their own. This may be true whether they are sharing music of a popular song, the black gospel tradition, or a Renaissance dance. In the United States, one of the goals of education is to broaden and appreciate our heritage of diversity. Music and other arts provide valuable insights and opportunities for such growth and development.

7 PROVIDE REINFORCEMENT

One of the most important tasks in the learning process is to provide reinforcement for learning. Children seek to be successful at whatever they undertake, and teachers need to construct music lessons that include effective rewards.

The focus of any system of rewards should be on positive reinforcement. Positive-reinforcement techniques should be applied consistently and in a variety of ways in every musical learning experience. The proper use of praise, for example, is a powerful way of encouraging students to repeat something they have done well. Reinforcement can often be as simple as a smile. Teachers often reward by granting privileges to students who successfully complete a task. These may be relatively simple, such as "Carlos, since you sang that part so well, you may now play the xylophone in this piece." Often the most effective types of reinforcement are those selected by the child. Children always have favorite things they like to do. Be sensitive and observant and use these things as rewards for accomplishments in the classroom.

Use reinforcement techniques during music lessons to reward both musical accomplishments and good behavior. Cooperative student behavior is essential if children are to accomplish musical tasks, so you should design reward techniques to encourage productive student behavior and optimize musical learning.

One of the most important goals for music teaching is to have students learn for intrinsic as well as extrinsic rewards. The real excitement in learning about music occurs when students want to sing, play instruments, or listen to music because of the intrinsic rewards of the musical experience itself. Although you may initially feel a need to use a variety of extrinsic rewards, you should encourage students to study music just because of the pleasure it gives them. Intrinsic rewards are especially important because they stay with students long after formal school experiences have been completed.

8 TEACH FOR TRANSFER

An essential goal in structuring musical experiences for children is *transfer*. The teacher needs to make a concerted attempt to encourage students to relate and use what they have previously learned to what they are currently studying. For example, if in a previous lesson students identified the balance of ABA form in the song "We Wish You a Merry Christmas," we hope that in a succeeding lesson they will be able to transfer the concept of balance through ABA form to another piece of music.

Children should also be encouraged to transfer ideas learned about music to other studies and to settings outside as well as inside the school. For example, they should be able to recognize concepts such as repetition and enlargement, variety and contrast, and balance in the visual and literary arts and in everyday examples at school and at home. They should also have some sense of how music and composers in a particular time period are related to history, geography, and other subject areas. For example, when students listen to a piece by Mozart, they should locate Austria on a map of Europe and learn about Salzburg and Vienna, where he lived and worked. As students identify the dates when Mozart lived (1756–1791), encourage them to associate these dates with famous Americans who lived at the same time (Washington, Jefferson, and Franklin) and events that took place then (the signing of the Declaration of Independence and the American Revolution).

One of the principal advantages of teaching for transfer is that material will often take on a greater sense of meaning for children if they can see relationships with other learning experiences. Further, if children have learned material by using it in a variety of settings, they are more likely to remember the information.

Techniques for Applying Principles to Musical Learning

COOPERATIVE LEARNING

Cooperative learning involves organizing students into small groups to undertake together a particular learning experience. Students of varying abilities are asked to work with one another to solve problems, to study an issue, or to complete a project. For example, students in a general music class may be divided into several small groups to investigate the reasons for differences in tone quality among stringed, wind, and percussion instruments. Each group is asked to construct either a stringed, wind, or percussion instrument and create a short composition demonstrating its distinctive timbre. The small-group projects can then be shared with the entire class.

©Myrleen Ferguson/PhotoEdit
Cooperative learning

In cooperative learning it is felt that slower students benefit from the challenge of working with those more advanced and that advanced students profit from helping explain things to others. The teacher in a cooperative learning setting tends not to tell students "how" but rather acts as a resource and guide for each group of students.

MUSICAL EXPERIENCES FOR INCLUSIVE LEARNING

Many times classroom teachers need to adapt techniques or materials so that *inclusive learning* can take place. Children who are visually challenged, hearing challenged, or physically or mentally challenged require special music-learning techniques to be built into the lessons. A philosophy of aesthetic education, which emphasizes music as an expression of feeling and active involvement in the learning process, applies to students with special needs. Physically challenged persons who have excelled in musical skills are legion; for example, Itzak Perlman (who suffered the crippling effects of polio as a child but went on to develop into a distinguished

Owen Franken/Corbis

Inclusive learning

concert violinist) and Ray Charles (who is visually challenged but developed into an extraordinary jazz pianist) are two of the most famous.

This section of chapter 1 focuses on guidelines for adapting techniques and materials for use with students who have special challenges. It is important to remember that children who are candidates for inclusive learning are often very responsive to the arts. In fact, many of them find some of the greatest joy and satisfaction in musical and other arts experiences.

When working with a student who has some form of challenge, it is particularly important that the teacher focus on the individual's capabilities and build on them, while at the same time being an understanding person. The student who experiences a challenge is a human being with feelings, emotions, capabilities, and desires. It is our job as teachers to nurture and develop the positive aspects of a student's abilities, always focusing on what he or she *can* do rather than on what he or she *cannot* do. The appearance of the challenged student often does not indicate what his or her capabilities are.

Although special education has many divisions and a multitude of classifications, two general types are (1) normal intelligence but physically challenged, visually challenged, or hearing challenged, and (2) mentally challenged.

Generally, the same teaching materials and basic techniques can be used with various types of challenged students. Hands-on experiences with music are encouraged for all students. Differences occur in adapting experiences so that students who have some sort of challenge can function successfully. The following are some guidelines for inclusive learning in music.

Physically Challenged: Confined to a Wheelchair

- Provide ample space.
- Create alternative ways of responding to rhythm other than walking (moving hands or head, tapping fingers, playing classroom instruments).
- Cover percussion handles with heavy carpet tape to make them bigger and easier to grasp.
- Fasten instruments to wheelchairs with notebook binder rings so that students cannot drop them.
- Place books, charts, and instruments at level of wheelchair student.
- Ask student for ideas for adapting activities (physically challenged students are constantly adapting and often can suggest the best solution to problems).

Visually Challenged: Partial Sight or Total Loss of Sight

■ Keep the physical setup of the classroom the same (instruments, piano, chairs, and so on in the same place).

■ Use tactile devices, such as rough and smooth surfaces, to aid in playing instruments.

■ Develop spatial consciousness (location of black and white keys on the keyboard and frets on the guitar).

■ Adapt movement activities by setting steps to number sequences (such as four steps right, two steps forward, three steps left). Visually challenged students are highly sensitive to such directions and can often learn dance steps before their sighted peers.

■ Encourage visually challenged students to lead in ear-training games. Their hearing sense is generally much more acute than that of sighted students.

(Many of the music series books are available in large-print editions and Braille from the Library of Congress, Washington, D.C.)

Hearing Challenged: Partial Hearing or Total Loss of Hearing

■ If possible, hold class in a room with a wood floor so that students can feel the vibrations of the music.

■ Have students feel the vibrations of a drumhead and create an inner feeling of beat by following a leader's motions.

■ Place such students in the front of the class, where they can read your lips. Encourage them to "feel" the concept of high and low by placing their fingers on the throat of a companion student and having that student sing high and low pitches. Students with a hearing challenge can gain a sense of pitch through this approach. They should be encouraged and allowed to sing in class, even though they may not always sing "in tune."

■ The use of earphones may enable students with hearing aids to hear the music, thus opening a world of sound to them.

THE GIFTED STUDENT

■ They may or may not have speech problems (especially in grades K and 1).

■ They need to be challenged often.

■ They need to perform often for peers and for adults.

■ They may or may not have a long attention span.

■ They may focus on a single instrument or idea.

■ They require extraordinary patience and much love and understanding.

■ They can often work well alone.

■ They do not always relate well to other students.

Guidelines for Musical Experiences for the Gifted Student

- ■ *Vocal range:* Wide, usually an octave or more. Build confidence by asking students to sing syllable patterns, such as:

do mi sol do   sol do do mi do   mi sol do re do

- ■ *Melody:* Choose songs that are longer and have many intervals and skips. Melodies with repeated patterns are often the most successful with gifted children.

- ■ *Rhythm:* Provide opportunities for experiences with rhythms on a variety of complexity levels. The gifted student can frequently play or sing a complex rhythm accurately.

- ■ *Harmony:* Unlimited use of chords on the Omnichord or, if the student is bigger, the guitar or even the piano. A gifted student can often remember chord sequences.

- ■ *Word meanings:* The gifted student has a broad vocabulary and can give meaning to words. Choose songs that are above the chronological age of the student; for example, "This Old Man" would be too babyish for a talented first grader.

- ■ *Movement:* In the quest for an appropriate movement, the gifted student may help the physically or mentally challenged student. Helping someone else is often very good for the gifted student.

THE MENTALLY CHALLENGED STUDENT

- ■ They learn at a slower pace.
- ■ They often have difficulty with motor coordination.
- ■ They may have speech problems.
- ■ They need constant and immediate reinforcement.
- ■ They have a short attention span.
- ■ They are often self-centered.
- ■ They require extraordinary patience and much love and understanding.
- ■ They are often very affectionate.

Guidelines for Musical Experiences for the Mentally Challenged Student

- ■ *Vocal range:* Limited, usually within an octave and lower range. Build confidence in the lower range, followed by developing the upper range. Use simple syllable patterns, such as:

sol mi sol la sol   sol mi do   do mi sol   sol la sol mi

- ■ *Melody:* Choose songs with small intervals and avoid large skips. Melodies with repeated patterns are often the most successful.

- *Rhythm:*
  - Provide opportunities for experiences with rhythms on a variety of complexity levels. Allow extra time for the student to play an instrument. *Example:* While the rest of the class plays on beats 1, 2, 3, and 4, have the mentally challenged child play only on beat 1 or at the beginning of a line or phrase.
  - Allow the student to set the tempo of the rhythm and then follow the student. *Example:* Strum chords on the keyboard, Omnichord, or guitar as the student plays a drum.
  - Use two students to play a two-beat pattern on a drum. The rest of the class claps with them.
  - Encourage students to create patterns for others to follow.
- *Harmony:* Limited use of chords on the keyboard, Omnichord, or guitar. Identify chords with colors or use tactile materials (e.g., C chord = burlap, F chord = silk, G chord = velvet). Place chord names or symbols on charts and hang them around necks of students.
- *Word meanings:* Give special attention to word meanings and pronunciation. Choose songs that are suitable for the intellectual age rather than the chronological age of the student.
- *Movement:* Proceed from large to small motor movements. Design movement activities with emphasis on much repetition. Allow more time for the movement to occur (tempos may be somewhat slower).
- Assign or ask for talented volunteers to help mentally challenged students who may be mainstreamed. Be sure to change helpers often and have a student assistant assigned to one particular activity.

Do not talk down to students or use "baby" or "special" music; a Sousa march can draw the same strong rhythmic response from mentally challenged students as any others. Teachers, however, may need to modify their expectations regarding a coordinated physical response to the beat. Classroom teachers must assess each student's special needs and then devise ways to bring that student into the mainstream of activity. Musical experiences must involve *all* students, and the personal satisfaction is great for the teacher who sincerely tries to help a student overcome a challenge so that he or she can have success and pleasure with musical experiences.

Instructional Technology for the Classroom

Many types of instructional technology are found in schools today and can increase the effectiveness of music instruction in the classroom. These include compact disc (CD) players, cassette recorders, video players, television, overhead and slide projectors, and computers.

Compact disc players are now available in most homes and schools and provide an extraordinary level of sound quality through digital recording techniques. Digital recording techniques are also available on audiotapes, but many schools still have analog cassette players which nevertheless produce excellent-quality sound. Many children possess their own CD or cassette players, which can be used to supplement those in the classroom.

Looking for Information About Music on the Internet

Ask students to use the Internet to find information to share with the class or for a bulletin board:

- Find information about a composer; e.g., Johann Sebastian Bach or Wolfgang Amadeus Mozart

- Find information about a type of music; e.g., hiphop or jazz

- Find information about a musical instrument; e.g., bagpipes or sitar

- Find information about a performer; e.g., Louis Armstrong or Itzak Perlman

- Find information about a particular musical group; e.g., Canadian Brass or Mighty Clouds of Joy

- Find information about music from a particular country/geographical area; e.g., Balinese music or Japanese music

Video players are also frequently found in homes and schools. A large and increasing number of videos are available in music. There are videos demonstrating instruments of the band and orchestra, ballet and opera, and the musics of other cultures. Such videos are especially effective because students can *see as well as hear* the musical presentation.

Television continues to play a central role in school educational programs. Television programs of orchestras, operas, jazz, rock, and other popular styles of music occur frequently and can be used to effectively supplement lessons in the classroom.

Overhead and slide projectors, which have also been available in schools for many years, are still a very effective means of enhancing instruction through providing visuals for a particular music lesson. For example, teachers can project a transparency to help guide a listening lesson, or show slides to prepare students for listening to the music of a particular culture.

Computers now provide one of the most far-reaching instructional technology tools for the classroom. Many music publishers are now creating computer software for use in schools. Consult your local library or audiovisual center for the many catalogs, books, and magazines discussing particular music programs. Computer software programs can display music notation and provide sounds of different pitches. With the addition of MIDI (Musical Instrument Digital Interface), the computer can even become an instrument. Many schools now have synthesizers that can produce different pitches, tone colors, rhythms, and textures. Classroom teachers, particularly those with a bent toward electronics, can use these instruments for music as well as math and science projects.

Computers and synthesizers are especially helpful in providing individualized instruction. Many computer games can also reinforce music teaching in the classroom. One of the fastest-developing areas of computer use involves students accessing the Internet and the World Wide Web. Students can use search functions on the Web to look up information on a composer, a musical instrument, or a specific genre of music. Thus through computer technology, students now have almost instant access to information for classroom reports and projects. Access to such information is also invaluable to classroom and music teachers preparing lessons.

For Your Journal

In your journal or portfolio, make a section on how children learn music, and comment on the things you have learned in this chapter as they relate to the elementary classroom. Be sure to include the following items:

- Psychomotor learning
- Cognitive learning
- Affective learning
- Active versus passive learning
- Teacher-centered versus student-centered learning
- Making what you teach meaningful
- Experiencing before labeling
- Teaching concepts
- A multisensory approach to learning
- A multicultural approach to learning
- Reinforcement of learning
- Transfer of learning
- Cooperative learning
- Ways a gifted student in music may be kept interested when he/she may already know what you have to offer
- Ways you might adapt a music lesson for a student who is physically, visually, hearing, or mentally challenged
- The role of technology, and specifically the Internet, in music teaching

Guidelines for Teaching Music

Designing Integrated Learning Experiences with Music

As you begin to think about teaching music in an elementary school classroom, there are a number of things you need to consider. These include (1) identifying long- and short-term goals; (2) deciding on musical concepts; (3) developing specific objectives that are related to learning abilities of various age levels; (4) choosing interesting and appropriate musical materials and activities that can be integrated with other classroom experiences; (5) involving students in logical and sequential activities that will enable them to learn easily and effectively; (6) deciding on length and frequency of lessons that focus on musical ideas or concepts; (7) relating music and activities to the lives of the student; (8) involving students in multi-sensory activities that focus on seeing (visual), hearing (auditory), and moving (psychomotor); (9) including multicultural experiences for students; (10) using audiovisual materials to enhance the lesson; (11) bringing review and closure to the learning experience; and (12) assessing to ascertain if objectives have been met.

IDENTIFYING LONG- AND SHORT-TERM GOALS

The first task in teaching a music lesson is to formulate long- and short-term goals. Goals are generally concerned with what is desired in terms of musical interest and behavior over a period of time.

Long-term Goals

Students will develop an appreciation of jazz might be a long-term goal. Other long-term goals might be (1) to foster perceptive listening so that students will interact with the art of music with ever-increasing satisfaction and meaning, (2) to develop musical skills and understanding, and (3) to appreciate music of different styles and cultures. Note that these statements use such verbs as *develop, foster, appreciate, understand,* and *enjoy.* These statements represent the philosophy of the educator or the school system, and it is from these long-term goals that short-term goals and a variety of behavioral objectives are formulated.

Short-term Goals

Short-term goals are related to long-term goals but are attained in a specified time. Short-term goals generally indicate what needs to be accomplished in a particular week or lesson. Examples of short-term goals include: (1) using classroom instruments, students will create and perform a sound piece; or (2) using the solfège system of music reading, students will successfully sing songs appropriate to their age.

Teachers who take time to formulate long- and short-term goals tend to have a clear sense of direction about what students are to learn. Without goals it is easy for both teachers and students to wander aimlessly and haphazardly through a series of musical activities without much learning taking place.

2 DECIDING ON MUSICAL CONCEPTS

One of the first decisions a teacher makes about a music lesson is what concept or concepts to cover. A *concept* has been defined by Woolfolk and Nicolich as "a collection of experiences or ideas that are grouped together based on some common properties."*

Principal musical concepts include melody, rhythm, texture, dynamics, tone color or timbre, and form. Within each of these large concepts are components or smaller concepts. Thus duple meter is a component of rhythm, melodic direction is a component of melody, and ternary form (ABA) is a component of form. A more complete description of other musical concepts is found in chapter 3.

Concepts may stand alone. In other words, you can teach students how repetition of a specific rhythm pattern gives unity to a composition or how perceiving the direction of a melody (up or down) can add understanding to a listening experience. But generally, teaching a concept occurs as part of a lesson and contributes toward increased perception and understanding of the music. If instruction focuses on perceiving such concepts as loud-soft, fast-slow, and upward-downward in isolation, students will not link them to the expressiveness of music. When this happens, music loses its meaning.

---

*Anita Woolfolk and Lorraine Nicolich, *Educational Psychology for Teachers* (Englewood Cliffs, N.J.: Prentice-Hall, 1980), p. 596.

DEVELOPING OBJECTIVES **3**

As you plan specific lessons, state clear objectives as often as possible in terms of observable behavior (through seeing, hearing, moving, and so on). In other words, state your objectives so that you can observe students demonstrating what they have learned. For example, "Students will demonstrate an understanding of AB form by using sheets of colored paper to outline the formal design in the song 'Home on the Range' (page 47)." Other objectives might be "Students will use alphabet cards to identify the ABACA sections of Mozart's Horn Concerto in E-flat (third movement, Rondo)" or "Students will demonstrate their understanding of rests by clapping their hands on the appropriate rests in the song 'If You're Happy.'"

Following are some long-term goals that reflect expectations of various grade levels. You will need to develop short-term goals and specific objectives for individual classes.

Preschool/Kindergarten

Students will:

1. Sing short songs in tune, with good breathing habits and tone quality.
2. Perform rhythms with a steady beat.
3. Perform music expressively.
   a. Loud-soft
   b. Fast-slow
   c. Legato-staccato
4. Respond to expressive qualities of music through movement.
   a. Duple meter and triple meter
   b. Strong accents and changing accents
   c. Steady beat
   d. Changing dynamics
5. Play simple rhythmic-melodic patterns on classroom instruments.
6. Sing, play, move, and create music expressive of individual imaginations.

Grades 1 and 2

Students will:

1. Sing short songs in tune, with good breathing habits and tone quality.
2. Distinguish between high and low, fast and slow, and instrumental tone colors.
3. Identify expressive use of repetition and contrast in simple songs and short listening examples.
4. Express through creative movement such musical concepts as:
   a. Steady beat
   b. Accent
   c. Gradually getting louder or softer
   d. Staccato
   e. Legato
5. Engage in singing games.
6. Play simple rhythmic-melodic patterns on classroom instruments.
7. Read and create simple music notation.

Grades 3 and 4

Students will:

1. Sing short songs in tune, with good breathing habits and tone quality.
2. Sing simple rounds and descants in tune.
3. Sing songs expressive of text.
   a. Legato and staccato
   b. Dynamics
   c. Phrasing
4. Analyze music in terms of elements.
   a. Melodic phrases
   b. Tone colors
   c. Formal structure
5. Read or create simple music notation.
6. Engage in singing games and dances.
7. Play simple melodies and rhythmic accompaniments on classroom instruments.

Grades 5 and 6

Students will:

1. Sing songs in tune, with good breathing habits and tone quality.
2. Sing songs in two and three parts.
3. Demonstrate rhythmic sense through:
   a. Identifying simple-to-complex rhythms (both verbally and aurally)
   b. Playing rhythms in 2/4, 3/4, 6/8, mixed meter
4. Play simple harmonic accompaniments on guitar, keyboard, or Omnichord.
5. Play simple melodies and descants on melody bells or recorder.
6. Identify music from other parts of the world according to its use of melody, rhythm, texture, tone color, and formal structure.
7. Develop musical leadership by taking part in musical plays.
8. Read and write music notation.

4   CHOOSING APPROPRIATE MUSICAL MATERIALS AND ACTIVITIES

As you prepare lessons to teach to children, one important consideration will be to choose musical materials and design activities that (1) are within the capabilities of a particular class, (2) are interesting and fun, and (3) can be integrated into other classroom subjects and experiences. Always emphasize active involvement of students in musical experiences such as singing, playing instruments, and moving to music.

An important difference that you must recognize is between "presenting" and "teaching." *Presenting* is generally teacher centered, whereas *teaching* focuses on the child. This book provides many suggestions for ways to involve children in successful musical experiences. Chapter 3, which focuses on the fundamentals of music, will help you gain and develop your musical skills so that teaching and learning music is rewarding for both you and your students.

TEACHING AND LEARNING IN LOGICAL SEQUENCE

Children learn best when ideas progress logically from simple to complex. As you plan lessons, consider what should come first, second, third, and so on. For example, you can introduce a song by performing it (or playing a recording of it), and then teach students the melody, words, and rhythms by using the rote, rote-note, or note approach.

A second technique you need to develop is presenting the same idea in many different ways. For example, to teach students the rhythm of a specific song:

- Ask students to play the beat (2/4 meter) on the drums.
- Have students experience the strong and weak beats by tapping thighs and clapping hands.
- Have one student play the strong beat on a tambourine and another play the weak beat on the claves.
- Ask students to speak the words in the rhythm of the song, accenting the first beat of each measure.
- Use a rhythm chart with notes or some type of graphic to help students see the beat.

Any or all of these ideas can be used in a logical sequence of events that proceed from the introduction of a song or larger composition to a deeper understanding of the piece.

DECIDING ON LENGTH AND FREQUENCY OF LESSONS

The length of lessons will depend on the age and grade level of the students. In general, younger children will need to have shorter lessons than older students, who have longer attention spans. For kindergarten through third grade, a lesson length of 20 to 25 minutes is recommended. Lessons for students in grades 4 through 6 may be 30 to 40 minutes. The decision about lesson length, however, needs to be carefully tailored to each particular class of students.

When planning, determine the approximate number of minutes needed for each segment of the lesson—for example, 5 minutes for introductory slides and discussion, and 10 minutes for singing a song and adding accompaniment. Such guides ensure that the various segments of the plan receive their fair share of time. Further, both teachers and students will be kept on track and will not wander significantly from the major points of the lesson.

Frequency of lessons is another important consideration in organizing music instruction. In general, students need to have lessons scheduled close enough for continuity of learning to be maintained. Further, it is generally better to have frequent short lessons rather than long lessons with considerable time gaps in between. The frequency of lessons is also related to the age and grade level of the students. Younger students need to have instruction more frequently than do older students. All students seem to do best with some music instruction as part of each school day.

7 RELATING MUSIC TO STUDENTS' PERSONAL LIVES

Relating music to the personal lives of students often occurs in preliminary activities as well as in the lesson itself. Many times, preliminary activities will lead students to an understanding of the concept being taught. Preliminary activities normally call for teachers to present something familiar to students, with the idea of letting that experience act as a bridge to the principal part of the lesson. For example, if you are going to talk about contrast in music, the lesson might have preliminary activities that involve students in looking for contrast in the classroom—in clothing, in a poem, in a visual artwork, or in movement. When the concept is clear in the minds of students, you can then involve them in appropriate experiences with musical sounds.

8 DEVELOPING MULTISENSORY EXPERIENCES

Children often learn more effectively if several of their senses are involved, rather than just one. For example, in an age where television often dominates the lives of children, developing and using the visual sense becomes an important teaching method. A visual cue is often helpful because it does not go away; it remains where you put it, and the student can leave the room either mentally or physically and return to find the visual cue in the same place. On the other hand, music involves sound; it passes through time and is gone. Thus using the visual sense as well as the aural offers children increased opportunities for understanding and success. The tactile sense is of particular interest to students who have some form of visual challenge and provides opportunities to relate sounds with touch. You can compare smooth sounds to silk, or jagged or rough sounds to burlap or hickory bark.

9 INCLUDING MULTICULTURAL EXPERIENCES

Through television and a variety of printed material, we are becoming increasingly aware of the closeness of other peoples of the world. Many of the world's cultures are present in the United States, where hundreds of different ethnic groups make up the American cultural mosaic. Studying the multicultural musical environment both of the world and of our own country is a wonderful way for students to learn a variety of new kinds of music. It also provides a distinctive opportunity for students to broaden their understanding of other cultures and to develop sensitivity and tolerance toward one another.

10 DESIGNING AUDIOVISUAL MEDIA

You will want to use media such as slides, films and videos, transparencies, and recordings. These items should be carefully written into the appropriate places in the lesson plan, including such items as cassette index numbers and compact disc (CD) tracks.

11 BRINGING CLOSURE TO A LEARNING EXPERIENCE

Near the end of a lesson, schedule a summary or closing activity in which to pull together the separate parts of the lesson and give students a feeling of finality. Quite often such closure is accomplished by students performing a piece in its entirety after having worked on separate segments during the lesson.

ASSESSING LEARNING

Assessment tells you if the goals you identified in the lesson have been achieved; it tells you how effective you have been in your teaching. Often you will discover that you have been successful with some aspects of a presentation and not as effective with others. By systematically assessing students, you learn what changes need to be made in materials and teaching strategies to ensure that students make satisfactory progress in all areas of study.

For students, periodic assessment is crucial in letting them know how well they are progressing in their musical study. Children need a sense of accomplishment, and a regular program of assessment gives them needed feedback. One of the most helpful aspects of assessment for students is that they become aware of strengths and weaknesses—in effect discovering areas in which they excel and areas to which they need to give more attention.

You will want to assess students with respect to musical performance skills, perception and understanding of musical concepts, and acquisition and retention of information about music. In performance, assessment focuses on progress made in singing and playing instruments. For example, is there steady improvement in students' ability to sing on pitch and with good tone quality? Can students physically execute duple and triple meter? Are students able to satisfactorily accompany pieces using classroom instruments?

Perception and understanding of musical concepts can be assessed through such techniques as a listening test chart (see chapter 7), in which students are asked to discriminate between contrasting phenomena (loud and soft, duple and triple, violin and trumpet) as they listen to a piece of music. Understanding is often demonstrated by students actually *doing* something, such as creating a "sound composition" illustrating rondo form. Still another way of demonstrating perception and understanding is to ask students to identify a similar concept (such as unity through repetition) in art forms such as music, painting, and poetry.

You can give periodic quizzes to determine how well students have assimilated and retained information about music presented in class. In general, it is better to give short quizzes at frequent intervals than to wait for long periods of time and give lengthy tests.

National Standards in Music Education

One of the most important contemporary developments in music education has been the establishment of national standards for school music programs. These standards, which are outlined in several books by MENC: The National Association for Music Education, *National Standards for Arts Education* and *The School Music Program: A New Vision,* are designed "to provide a foundation for building a balanced, comprehensive, and sequential curriculum in music."* Nine basic national voluntary *content standards* have been set forth for school music programs:

---

* *National Standards for Arts Education* and *The School Music Program: A New Vision* are available from MENC: The National Association for Music Education, 1806 Robert Fulton Drive, Reston, VA 20191; telephone 1-800-336-3768.

Students should:

1. Sing, alone and with others, a varied repertoire of music.

2. Perform on instruments, alone and with others, a varied repertoire.

3. Improvise melodies, variations, and accompaniments.

4. Compose and arrange music within specified guidelines.

5. Read and notate music.

6. Listen to, analyze, and describe music.

7. Evaluate music and musical performances.

8. Understand relationships among music, the other arts, and disciplines outside the arts.

9. Understand music in relation to history and culture.

Use these general content standards as a guide in developing lessons for different grade levels. (For each of the content standards, a series of *achievement standards* have been established for various grade levels.) You may wish to refer to *The School Music Program: A New Vision* for more information on the specific achievement standards for pre-K, K–4, and 5–8 grade levels.

Writing Lesson Plans

As you begin to write a lesson plan to teach music, you need to ask yourself the following questions:

1. What is the activity?

2. Whom is the lesson for? (grade level)

3. What concepts do you want to teach?

4. What materials do you need? (to be completed last)

5. What do you want to do? (objectives)

6. How are you going to do it? (procedures)

    a. Preliminary

    b. Main content

7. How will you tie everything together? (closure)

8. Did you teach what you thought you were going to? (assessing both yourself and your students)

As in all lesson plans, detail is critical, especially at the beginning, so don't leave anything to chance. Following are some sample lesson plans to help you see how a typical lesson might be set up.

"FIVE LITTLE PUMPKINS"

Activity: Performing a song

Grade: 2

Concepts: Ascending and descending patterns

From *Singing and Rhyming* of OUR SINGING WORLD series. © Copyright, 1959, 1957, 1950, copyright renewed by Ginn and Company.
Used by permission of Silver Burdett & Ginn, Inc.

Objectives

Students will:

1. Identify the upward motion of the beginning pitches of musical phrases from *one* to *five* little pumpkins.

2. Play the pitches F G A B♭ C on the xylophone as each occurs.

3. Create appropriate motions to song using pumpkins as a guide.

4. Sing with good tone quality.

Materials

- Pictures of pumpkins or pumpkins from field
- Pumpkin note heads with numbers
- Xylophone
- Fence or gate

Procedures

Preliminary Activities

1. Ask children to sit on the floor around you.

2. Show pictures of pumpkins or show several live pumpkins that are similar in size.

3. Announce that "Today we are going to learn a song about pumpkins."

Main Content

1. Sing the song "Five Little Pumpkins." Indicate pitches with hands.

2. Discuss the five pumpkin faces identified in the song.

3. Assign children to groups representing the five pumpkins.

4. Perform the song a second time and ask each group of children to raise their hands when their particular pumpkin is named.

5. Read all the words of the song together.

6. Perform the song phrase by phrase, asking children to repeat by singing.

7. Ask children to point to the music chart as each pumpkin is referred to (figure 2.1).

Figure 2.1

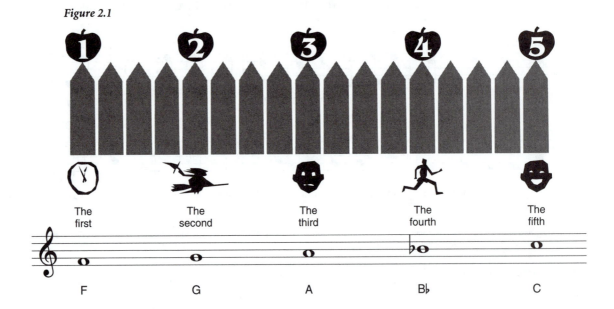

8. Have the class perform the song as a child plays the xylophone notes F G A B♭ C at appropriate times, noting that pitches are ascending.

9. Have the class perform the song as a child points to the appropriate pumpkin face.

10. Ask children to sing the words and music to "Ooo went the wind and out went the light, and the five little pumpkins rolled out of sight." Discuss which way "rolled out of sight" occurs (ascending or descending):

rolled___ out of sight.

11. Ask children to create a motion for "rolled out of sight."

12. Ask children to create motions for each musical phrase. For example, "five little pumpkins" could be five fingers; one finger = watch; two fingers = witch; three fingers = child doesn't care; four fingers = run; five fingers = ready for fun. The ending could be a swish with hands to snuff out the candle, then five fingers, hand over hand.

Closure

Have the class perform the entire song with motions.

Assessment

1. Do the beginning pitches of each phrase go up or down? (up)

2. What are the names of these pitches? (F G A B♭ C)

3. Do the last five pitches go up or down? (down)

4. Does the class perform the song with the correct pitches and rhythms?

5. Does the class perform the song with good tone quality?

Additional Integrative Areas

Reading, visual art, Halloween, mathematics, farming

"MAGIC PENNY"

Activity: Performing a song

Grades: 3–5

Concepts: Form: ABA
Rhythm: Syncopation
Harmony: Chords

Magic Penny

Key: D
Starting pitch: D
Meter: 4/4, begin on 1

Words and Music by Malvina Reynolds

Love is some - thing if you give it a - way, ___ give it a - way, ___ give it a - way,

Love is some - thing if you give it a - way, ___ you end up hav - ing more.   *fine*

It's just like a mag - ic pen - ny: Hold it tight and you won't have an - y;   *D.C. al fine*

Lend it, spend___ it and you'll have so man - y they'll roll all o - ver the floor. For

Words and music by Malvina Reynolds. Copyright © 1955, 1959, by Northern Music Company. Copyright renewed. Rights administered by MCA Music Publishing, New York, N.Y. Used by permission. All rights reserved. International copyright secured.

Objectives

Students will:

1. Diagram the form of "Magic Penny" using colored shapes.

2. Create movements that indicate the form (ABA).

3. Identify syncopated rhythms found in the song:

4. Sing with energy and clear diction.

5. Accompany the song with the following chords:

   D F♯ A

   G B D

   A C♯ E

   E G♯ B

Materials

- Song (or a recording: Fink/Marxer, *Collection for Kids,* Rounder Records, 8029)

- Keyboard, Omnichord, or guitar

- Resonator bells

- Tambourine

- Colored shapes

- Rhythm chart

- Master chord chart and individual chord charts: D F♯ A; G B D; A C♯ E; E G♯ B

Procedures

Preliminary Activities

1. Create some "magic" by "holding" and then hiding a magic penny.

2. Compare the magic penny of this song with giving love away. Help children discover that giving is also receiving.

Main Content

1. Play or sing the entire song (or use a recording).

2. Play or sing the entire song and select a child to hold up colored shapes for each section: ABA.

3. Sing or play the entire song and have children create a movement for part A and a contrasting movement for part B. Sing or play the song and ask children to perform the movements.

4. Teach the song phrase by phrase. Ask students to identify rhythms that repeat.

give it a - way, ___

5. Ask two or three children to play the syncopated rhythms on the tambourine when they hear them. (Syncopation is similar to a hiccup—the strong beat is *always* on the off beat.)

6. Lead the class in performing the song. Ask students how many times they sing/hear syncopation in lines 1 and 2. (7)

7. Lead the class in performing the song. Ask students how many times they sing/hear syncopation in lines 3 and 4. (5)

8. What is the total number of times that syncopation occurs? (19)
   - Part A = 7
   - Part B = 5
   - Part A = 7

9. Ask children to sing or play the entire song. Encourage them to sing with energy, clear diction, and good tone quality.

10. Introduce chords that can be played on resonator bells, Omnichord, or keyboard (see chapter 5). Invite students to play chords as indicated in the musical score (for older students use one bell per student):

    D = D F♯ A   A = A C♯ E

    G = G B D   E = E G♯ B

11. Practice the accompaniment while the rest of the class sings, reinforced by the syncopated pattern played on a tambourine.

Closure

Perform the entire song accompanied by the instrumental ensemble.

Assessment

1. What notes are used in the chords D, G, A, and E?

2. Identify the repeated rhythm pattern.

3. What does *syncopation* mean? Can students find and perform syncopated rhythms in the song?

Additional Integrative Areas

Mathematics, reading, magic

FAST AND SLOW MUSIC

Activity: Listening to music

Grades: 1–2

Concepts: Fast/slow

Objectives

Students will:

1. Visually identify objects that move fast and slow.

2. Demonstrate through body movements fast and slow, getting faster, and getting slower.

3. Verbally identify sounds that are fast and slow; sounds that move gradually faster and gradually slower.

4. Identify expressive uses of fast and slow, getting faster, and getting slower in the recorded music used.

Materials

- Recordings:
    - Saint-Saëns, "The Swan" from *Carnival of the Animals* (slow)
    - Rimsky-Korsakov, "Flight of the Bumble Bee" (fast)
    - Honegger, "Pacific 231" (fast/slow)
    - "Kalinka," Red Star Army Chorus (fast/slow) (Teldec CD 9031 77307-2, track 3)
- Cassette or CD player
- Pictures that suggest fast (auto racing, jogging, airplane taking off) and slow (turtle, person walking, leaf floating to the ground)
- Word cards (*fast, slow, getting faster, getting slower*)

Procedures

Preliminary Activities

1. Show pictures that suggest fast and slow.
2. Ask students to move their arms slowly, then faster; have them run and then slow down to a walk.
3. Ask students to dramatize a rosebud gradually opening or a candle melting down, a racehorse bursting through the starting gate or a football player running for a touchdown.

Main Content

1. Ask students to create slow sounds and then fast sounds. Experiment with sounds that start slowly and gradually get faster and fast sounds that gradually slow down.
2. Space students around the room. Ask them to move creatively as you play a fast or slow pattern on a drum. Invite individual students to take turns playing creative drum rhythms (fast-slow, getting faster–getting slower).
3. Play Saint-Saëns's "The Swan." Discuss the composer's choice of a slow tempo to represent a swan swimming on a pond.
4. Play Rimsky-Korsakov's "Flight of the Bumble Bee." Discuss the composer's choice of a fast tempo to represent a bumblebee flying past you.
5. Play Honegger's "Pacific 231." Ask students to place appropriate words on the chalkboard (fast, slow, getting faster, getting slower) as they listen to the music. After they have listened, discuss the composer's use of fast and slow to represent a train starting, traveling down the track, and then slowing down.
6. Play "Kalinka," performed by a Russian ensemble. Ask students to indicate where the music gets faster and slower.

Closure and Assessment

Play excerpts from "The Swan," "Flight of the Bumble Bee," "Pacific 231," and "Kalinka." Choose appropriate cards (with captions *fast, slow, getting faster,* and *getting slower*) and ask students to place them on the chalkboard as you play the selections. (Tape-record the selections so that they occur one after the other.)

Reminders for Planning and Teaching Lessons

- Visuals must be large enough to be seen from the back of the room. Do not use yellow or orange as a color for printed text; they cannot be seen on white paper. The same is true of black on blue or purple paper.

- Be sure that the lesson is appropriate in content and musical concepts for the maturity level of the students. A song with a very wide range, such as "The Star-Spangled Banner," is not suitable musically for young children. Many can't sing that high or that low.

- Remember that kindergarten, first-grade, and even second-grade students do not read well and need help in following a chart.

- You are a *leader* in teaching. Be involved in the lesson. Get the children involved in doing something, responding in some way.

- Be involved in the listening; don't just stand and gaze at the floor or look out the window.

- *Always use a mechanical source for the pitch of a song.* Otherwise, most of the time you will pitch the song too low, since adult voices are generally lower than children's voices.

- Be sure that you start the song on the pitch given. If the recorder is difficult for you, use a guitar, keyboard, or pitchpipe for the starting pitch.

- Avoid overusing colloquialisms, such as *OK* and *you guys.*

- Be accurate in teaching rhythm and melody.

- If you use a recording of a song, be sure to give the pitch and either mouth or sing the song along with the recording.

- Be sure that the lesson has sequence; don't "leapfrog" from one thing to another.

- Every lesson should have closure; avoid just stopping. Review to determine if you have achieved your objectives.

- Use terms accurately. For example, a *song* must have, or originally have had, words (if it is imbedded in a large piece). Everything else is a *composition* or a *piece*. In other words, Beethoven's Symphony No. 5 is not a song but a piece.

- Know how to work the audio equipment (cassette or CD player) before you begin the lesson.

- Recognize the cultural diversity that may be in your classroom and include music relevant to Native American, African American, Hispanic, Asian, or other students.

Some Options to Use When Teaching Music

If you do not play an instrument:

- Sing the song yourself.
- Play a recording.
- Ask a child to play the song on the piano or other keyboard instrument. (Many children take piano lessons and are delighted to have a reason to practice.)
- Ask a friend to tape-record the song (either melody, accompaniment, or both).

If you can't sing in a high register:

- Use a recorder or melody bells.
- Play a recording.
- Use a child to help you start the song.
- Indicate with your hand when the pitch should be high.
- Guide children to sing an octave higher than you sing (if you are a man).

If you have a poor sense of rhythm:

- Use a child to help you keep a steady beat.
- Use a metronome to help you practice the rhythmic and melodic patterns.
- Use a metronome in class to help keep the class together.

If you can't read music quickly or accurately:

- Teach songs that you have learned accurately by ear. (Save your music-reading practice for when you are alone.)
- Use recordings.
- Try to feel the contour of the melody with your hands; don't depend on the music notation.

If you have difficulty singing a song in tune:

- Use a recording.
- Play the song on melody bells or a recorder.
- Use small groups of children as your leaders.

If you feel insecure in finding the starting pitch and getting the children to sing together:

- Practice using melody bells or a recorder.
- Play the key note of the song (D for key of D major, F for key of F major, etc.).
- Play notes 1, 3, and 5 of the scale (e.g., C, E, and G in the key of C major). You may wish to sing the syllables *do, mi, sol* (1, 3, 5) to establish the tonality.
- Play the first two notes of the song.
- Sing the first two notes of the song.
- Establish the tempo and say, "Ready, sing."

If you don't know what to do when children won't sing:

- Be enthusiastic.
- Give clear directions.
- Select songs that need a lot of energy and are fairly fast.
- Select songs that are fun to sing.
- Select songs that have meaning to them and aren't just silly.
- Set an example by singing or playing the song.
- Add instruments as accompaniment (both harmonic—keyboard, Omnichord, or guitar—and percussion).
- Be sure the songs are within the children's vocal range.

Making Good Teaching Great Teaching

- Know what you can expect from children at each grade level. Know each child in your classroom. Care about them.

- Be an example. Students look up to you and seem to have a way of knowing whether you measure up to what they expect of you.

- Be energetic and industrious. Stay fresh and inspired. Never stop reading and learning. Burnout is a product of an uninspired person. Read! Attend conferences! Give above and beyond yourself. Remember: *The only things we really have are those we give away.*

- Learn to motivate both your students and the people you work with.

- Be a dedicated teacher. Never count your time, and remember that the student is the most important person in the classroom.

- Give freely of your love and your time.

- Be the best musician you can be. Learn about music by performing it and attending concerts. There is no substitute for knowing what you are teaching.

- Be active in teaching organizations. Learn all you can from others.

- Use activity teaching. Students learn by doing.

- Use top-quality music in your classroom. High-quality music and materials are the foundation of good teaching.

- Use first-rate supplementary materials. Develop a library of visuals that will enhance your teaching.

- Use a variety of musical styles: jazz, folk, electronic, blues, and so on.

- Build your classroom teaching skills and a program that is educationally sound.

- Be a firm, fair, and kind disciplinarian. Remember that you are the leader and that you determine what happens in your classroom. Everything begins at the top—and that means you.

- Reward all good work. Don't make your awards necessarily competitive. Keep it simple—maybe a smile from the teacher or a star on a good paper. Remember that praise is the very best reward.

- Show that you care about each student (even those who try your patience). Be sincere and interested in each life.

- Believe in the value of what you are doing. It is an anchor when the going gets rough.

For Your Journal

In your journal or portfolio, make a section on guidelines for teaching music and write a short summary based on ideas you learned from this chapter, including long- and short-term goals, musical concepts, developing objectives, choosing appropriate materials and activities, teaching and learning in logical sequence, deciding on the length and frequency of lessons, relating music to students' personal lives, developing multisensory experiences, including multicultural experiences, using audiovisual media, bringing closure to a learning experience, and assessment. Include a brief discussion of the national standards for music teaching. Drawing on the examples given, design your own lesson plan for teaching a musical concept.

*F*undamentals of Music: Understanding How Sounds Are Organized in a Musical Composition

MUSIC IS AN AURAL ART FORM consisting of the organization of sounds in time. An understanding of music begins with the perception of its basic elements, which include melody, rhythm, texture, tone color, dynamics, and form. This chapter explains some of the basic characteristics of these elements and provides musical examples. You are encouraged to *experience* the characteristics of the elements through actual performance. When you finish this chapter, you should be able to perform or listen to short musical compositions and describe them in terms of their basic elements.

Experiences with Melody

A *melody* is a succession of musical sounds that are perceived as belonging together. Melodies are familiar to all of us. We sing, whistle, and play melodies from the time we are little children. Whereas the rhythm or beat of a piece of music may dominate our physical response to it (toe-tapping, nodding), we generally recognize a composition by its melody. As you give close attention to the features of melodies discussed here, you will increase your understanding and experience greater pleasure in performing and listening to music.

A MELODY IS BASED ON A SET OF PITCHES

Pitch refers to the highness or lowness of a sound. By playing various pitches on the piano, resonator bells, or guitar, you can soon tell which are high and which are low.

A MELODY MOVES BY STEPS AND SKIPS

The distances between pitches are called *intervals.* Intervals between the tones of some melodies may be small, whereas in other melodies the distances between the various pitches can be quite large. Some melodies move basically by steps; others primarily by skips.

"JOIN INTO THE GAME"

Activity: Performing a song

Grade: 1

Concept: Melody moves by steps

Join into the Game

Words and Music by Paul Campbell

Key: C
Starting pitch: G
Meter: 3/4, begins on 3

Phrase 1

Let ev - 'ry - one clap hands like me. (clap hands)
Let ev - 'ry - one whis - tle like me. (whistle)

Phrase 2

Let ev - 'ry - one clap hands like me. (clap hands)
Let ev - 'ry - one whis - tle like me. (whistle)

REFRAIN
Phrase 3

Come on and join in - to the game;_____ (clap hands)
Come on and join in - to the game;_____ (whistle)

Phrase 4

You'll find that it's al - ways the same. (clap hands)
You'll find that it's al - ways the same. (whistle)

"REVEILLE"

Activity: Performing a song

Grades: 2–3

Concept: Melody moves by skips

Reveille

Key: G
Starting pitch: D
Meter: 2/4, begins on "and" of 2

U.S. Army Bugle Call

I can't get 'em up, I can't get 'em up, I can't get 'em up in the morn - ing; I

can't get 'em up, I can't get 'em up, I can't get 'em up at all!

A MELODY HAS SHAPE

Melodies may go up or down. If you look at the first section of "Row, Row, Row Your Boat" and "Joy to the World," you'll notice that the general direction of the first song is upward, whereas the general direction of the second is downward. Perform these two lines and listen to the melody going up or down.

Row, Row, Row Your Boat

Key: C
Starting pitch: C
Meter: 6/8, begins on 1

Row,   row,   row   your boat   gent - ly down   the   stream.

Joy to the World

Key: C
Starting pitch: C
Meter: 2/4, begins on 1

Joy   to   the   world!   the   Lord   is   come

Melodies sometimes move in terraces, starting at a low pitch and ascending in graduated levels, or beginning at a high pitch and descending in graduated levels.

Perform "The Farmer in the Dell" and trace in the air the terraced melody moving from low to high in the first half of the song.

The Farmer in the Dell

Key: G
Starting pitch: D
Meter: 6/8, begins on 6

England

1. The far-mer in the dell,_____ The far-mer in the dell, Hi! ho! the der-ry oh, The far-mer in the dell._____

Some melodies operate like a pendulum, undulating above and below one or several basic pitches.

Perform "Hickory Dickory Dock" and draw the movement of the melody on paper.

Hickory Dickory Dock

Key: F
Starting pitch: A
Meter: 6/8, begins on 1

J. W. Elliott

Hick-o-ry dick-o-ry dock, The mouse ran up the clock, The clock struck one, the mouse ran down, Hick-o-ry dick-o-ry dock.

A MELODY HAS RANGE

As you trace melodies, you will discover that the distance from the lowest to the highest note is sometimes large and other times small. The term *range* is used to describe these distances. Some melodies have a small range, whereas other melodies have a large range.

Perform "The Star-Spangled Banner" and identify the wide pitch range (low A♭ to high E♭); then perform "Old MacDonald Had a Farm" and identify its narrow pitch range (D to B).

The Star-Spangled Banner

Key: A
Starting pitch: A♭
Meter: 3/4, begins on 3

Music by John Stafford Smith
Text by Francis Scott Key

Old MacDonald Had a Farm

United States

Key: G
Starting pitch: G
Meter: 4/4, begins on 1

A MELODY IS MADE UP OF PHRASES

Melodies often have several sections, set off from each other by a slight pause or point of rest. These subsections, called *phrases,* function in similar fashion to a phrase in a sentence.

Perform "Shenandoah" and listen to the phrases. Outline the phrases by moving your hand from left to right in the air as you perform the piece. Select different-colored objects and, as each phrase occurs, place one object on a flannelboard. Point out that each object (color) represents a phrase in the melody.

Shenandoah

Key: D
Starting pitch: A
Meter: 4/4, begins on 4

American Sea Chantey

Oh, Shen-an-doah,___ I long to see you,___ A - way,___ you roll-ing riv-er,___ Oh,

Shen-an-doah,___ I long to see you. A - way, we're bound a-way___ 'Cross the wide Mis - sou-ri.

A MELODY MAY BE BASED ON A SCALE

Melodies are often based on scales, which are arrangements of pitches in an order from low to high. The two most common scales in Western music are *major* and *minor*.

Major Scale

Activities

1. Place the pitches of the following major scales on a chalkboard. Write the note names beneath each note. Have students sing the scales with a neutral syllable, such as "Loo," and then with note names. Ask students to take turns playing the scales on melody bells.

C major scale

Loo_____
C D E F G A B C

F major scale

Loo_____
F G A B♭ C D E F

G major scale

Loo_____
G A B C D E F♯ G

2. Point out that the distinctive quality of the *major scale* is due to its particular pattern of whole and half steps. Place a diagram of a keyboard on the chalkboard. Point out that the keyboard has twelve tones consisting of seven white keys (without any duplication of pitches) and five black keys. Between some notes, such as C and D, is an intervening black key; between others, such as E and F, there is none. If a black key intervenes between two consecutive white keys, the interval is described as a *whole step*. If no key occurs between two consecutive pitches, such as E to F (or C to C♯), the interval is described as a *half step*. The scale shown below has the following whole- and half-step pattern: W-W-H-W-W-W-H. It is described as a *major scale*. All major scales, regardless of the pitch on which they start, have the same pattern of whole and half steps.

3. Have students sing songs based on major scales, such as "Sweet Betsy from Pike," "Home on the Range," and "It's a Small World."

Sweet Betsy from Pike

American

Key: C major
Starting pitch: C
Meter: 3/4, begins on 3

Oh don't you re - mem - ber sweet Bet - sy from Pike, Who crossed the broad prai - ries with her hus - band, Ike, With two yoke of ox - en, an old yel - low dog, A___ tall Shang - hai roos - ter, and one spot - ted hog?

Home on the Range

Key: F major
Starting pitch: C
Meter: 6/8, begins on 6

Traditional

1. Oh, give me a home where the buf-fa-lo roam, Where the deer and the an-te-lope play;___ Where sel-dom is heard a dis-cour-ag-ing word, And the skies are not cloud-y all day.___

B *Chorus*

Home, home on the range,___ Where the deer and the an-te-lope play;___ Where sel-dom is heard a dis-cour-ag-ing word, and the skies are not cloud-y all day.___

It's a Small World

Key: G major
Starting pitch: B
Meter: Cut-time (2/2), begins on 2

Words and Music by Richard M. Sherman and Robert B. Sherman
Arr. by C. A. R.

DESCANT

It's a world of laugh-ter, world of tears; it's a
There is just one moon, one gol-den sun; and a

MELODY

1. It's a world of laugh-ter, a world of tears; it's a world of
2. There is just one moon and one gol-den sun; and a smile means

world of hopes, a world of fears. There's so much we share, it's
smile means friend-ship, ev-'ry-one. Though the moun-tains and

hopes and a world of fears. There's so much that we share that it's
friend-ship to ev-'ry-one. Though the moun-tains di-vide and the

time we're a-ware. It's a small world af-ter all. _____
o-ceans are wide. It's a small world af-ter all. _____

time we're a-ware. It's a small world af-ter all. _____
o-ceans are wide. It's a small world af-ter all. _____

REFRAIN

It's a small world af-ter all. It's a small world af-ter all.

It's a small world af-ter all, it's a small, small world. _____

Minor Scale

In addition to the major scale, the other most common scale in Western music is the *minor scale*. The minor scale differs from the major scale in the pattern of whole and half steps. In the following D minor scale, for example, the pattern of whole and half steps is W-H-W-W-H-W-W.

D minor scale

In many songs written in a minor key, the seventh degree of the scale will be raised (sharped) a half step. In the scales below, notice that G, the seventh degree, is raised (sharped); when a minor scale has the seventh raised, it is known as a *harmonic minor scale*.

A minor scale (harmonic minor)

Activities

1. Place the pitches of the D minor and A minor scales on the chalkboard. Write note names beneath each note. Have students sing the scales with a neutral syllable and then with note names. Ask students to take turns playing the scales on melody bells.

2. Perform the following songs based on minor scales.

Wayfaring Stranger

United States

Key: D minor
Starting pitch: D
Meter: 3/4, begins on "and" of 2

1. I'm just a poor way-far-ing strang-er, A-trav-'ling through this world of woe; But there's no sick-ness, toil nor dan-ger in that bright world to which I go. I'm go-ing there to see my fath-er, I'm go-ing there no more to roam; I'm just a-go-ing o-ver Jor-dan, I'm just a-go-ing o-ver home.

Go Down, Moses

Spiritual

Key: A minor
Starting pitch: E
Meter: 4/4, begins on 4

1. When Is-rael was in E-gypt's land, Let my peo-ple go. Op-pressed so hard they could not stand, Let my peo-ple go. Go down, Mos-es, 'Way down in E-gypt's land;__ Tell__ old Phar-aoh, Let my peo-ple go.

Pentatonic Scale

In addition to the seven-tone major and minor scales, melodies also consist of other types of scales, such as the five-tone, or *pentatonic,* scale, which is extremely common in the music of China and Japan as well as American folk music. Students can experience a pentatonic scale by playing the five black keys on the piano keyboard or by singing "Old MacDonald Had a Farm" (page 44).

Pentatonic scale

Activities

1. Play a pentatonic scale on the white keys of the piano, the pitches C D F G A.

2. Create a melody on a xylophone using only the pitches C D F G A. You may wish to play some pitches more than once, or you can extend the melody higher or lower using the same pitches. The melody will sound more interesting if you place it in a meter.

3. Perform the well-known Korean song "Ahrirang." It is based on the following pentatonic scale:

Arirang

Folk Song from Korea
English Words by Alice Firgau

Key: Pentatonic (C D F G A)
Starting pitch: C
Meter: 3/4, begins on 1

Ah - ri - rang, ah - ri - rang, ah - ra - ri - yo.

O - ver the hills of Ah - ri - rang.

Voic - es call me from far a - way.

I must fol - low I can - not stay.

A MELODY MAY CONTAIN ACCIDENTALS

You sometimes encounter the term *accidental*. Accidentals are notes (sharps, flats, or naturals) that are not in the key of the song but are added for a particular effect. For example, in the song "I Like It Here," which is in the key of B♭ major, the notes E-natural, F-sharp, and G-sharp are not part of the key but are used to make the melody more interesting.

I Like It Here

Words and Music by Clay Boland

Key: B♭
Starting pitch: F
Meter: 2/2, begins on "and" of 1

I like the U - nit - ed States of A - mer - i - ca,
I am so luck - y to be in A - mer - i - ca,

I like the way we all live with - out fear;
And I am thank - ful each day of the year,

I like to vote for my choice, speak my mind, raise my voice,
For I can do as I please, 'cause I'm free as the breeze,

1. Yes, I like it here.
2. like it here.

I'd like to climb to the top of a moun - tain so high,

Lift my head to the sky and say how grate - ful am I

For the way that I'm liv - ing, I'm work - ing and giv - ing

And help - ing the land I hold dear, Yes,

I like it, I like it, I like it here.

A MELODY HAS A KEY

If you wish to play or sing a melody, it is necessary to identify the key. If there are no sharps or flats, the song is in the key of C major or A minor.

Major Keys

There are two ways of determining the major key if a song has sharps in the key signature:

1. You can identify the farthest sharp to the right (or a single sharp if there is only one) and move up a half step. The key will be named for that pitch.

2. You can identify the last sharp and then simply name the next letter of the alphabet.

In the example below, either method gives you the key of G major.

If there are flats in the key signature, you can identify the major key by simply (1) identifying the flat before the last, or (2) counting down four lines and spaces from the farthest flat to the right. If there is only one flat (B♭), you use the second method and count down four lines and spaces to F. (Be sure to count the last flat as one.)

Minor Keys

Minor keys are related to major keys. The relative minor begins three half steps below the "home tone" of the major key. For example, the song "Zum Gali Gali" is in the key of E minor, which lies three half steps below G major. Note that both E minor and G major have the same key signature of one sharp.

Activities

1. Sing or play the song "Frère Jacques," which is written in the key of G major.

Key of G major

Frère Jacques

Key: G major
Starting pitch: G
Meter: 4/4, begins on 1

Round

Frè - re   Jac - ques,   Frè - re   Jac - ques,   dor - mez   vous,   dor - mez   vous?
Are   you   sleep - ing,   are   you   sleep - ing,   Broth - er   John,   Broth - er   John?

Son - nez les ma - ti - nes,   Son - nez les ma - ti - nes,   din,   dan,   don,   din,   dan,   don.
Morn - ing bells are ring - ing,   morn - ing bells are ring - ing,   ding,   ding,   dong,   ding,   ding,   dong.

2. Sing or play "Zum Gali Gali," which is written in E minor.

Key of E minor

Zum Gali Gali

Key: E minor
Starting pitch: E
Meter: 2/4, begins on 1

Israeli Folk Song

Zum ga - li ga - li, ga - li,   Zum ga - li ga - li,   Zum ga - li ga - li, ga - li,   Zum ga - li ga - li.

1. Pi - o - neers work   hard on the land;____   Men and wom - en   work hand in hand.
2. As they la - bor   all day____ long,____   They____ lift their   voice in____ song.

3. Sing or play "Home on the Range," which is written in F major (see page 47).

Key of F major

4. Sing or play "O Hanukkah," which is written in D minor (natural). (*Note: S'vivonim* means to spin the dredyl; *levivot* are potato pancakes. Some versions of the song replace this line with "Shining tops to play with and pancakes to eat.")

O Hanukkah

Jewish Folk Song

Key: D minor
Starting pitch: D
Meter: 4/4, begins on "and" of 4

O Ha-nuk-kah, O Ha-nuk-kah, come light the me-no-rah. Let's have a par-ty; we'll all dance the ho-rah. Gath-er round the ta-ble; we'll give you a treat, S'vi-vo-nim to play with, le-vi-vot to eat. And while we are play-ing, The can-dles are burn-ing low. One for each night, they shed a sweet light To re-mind us of days long a-go. mind us of days long a-go.

Reprinted from *Gateway to Jewish Song* by Judith K. Eisenstein, published by Behrman House, Inc., 1261 Broadway, New York, N.Y.

5. Many times composers label their pieces as being in a major or minor key, meaning that they are based on a particular major or minor scale. To hear what this means in terms of the sound of a piece, listen to excerpts from each of the following:

■ Major key: Mozart's Horn Concerto No. 3 in E-flat Major, K. 447, Rondo

■ Minor key: J. S. Bach's "Little" Fugue in G Minor

Experiences with Rhythm

Rhythm refers to the organization of musical sounds in time.

RHYTHM HAS A BEAT

1. Play a recording of "Stars and Stripes Forever" by John Philip Sousa. Call attention to the strongly felt beat in the music. Ask students to clap to it.

2. Sing or play Brahms's "Lullaby" and ask students to sway gently from side to side as if they were attempting to put a baby to sleep. Call attention to the weakly felt beat in the music.

3. Discuss the different moods expressed by music with a strongly felt beat and music with a weakly felt beat. (For example, strong beat conveys feelings of action and excitement; weak beat conveys feelings of peacefulness and restfulness.)

4. Select popular music by such groups as La Bouche, Los del Rio, or No Mercy and listen to such songs as "Macarena," "Sweet Dreams," and "It's All Coming Back to Me Now," as well as "The Power of the Dream" sung by Céline Dion (from Summer Olympics, 1996). Other popular songs contain strong and weak beats.

RHYTHM HAS TEMPO

1. The speed with which the beat recurs in music is called *tempo.* Compare the relatively fast tempo of "Stars and Stripes Forever" with the much slower tempo of Brahms's "Lullaby."

Lullaby

Key: C
Starting pitch: E
Meter: 3/4, begins on 3

Johannes Brahms

Lul - la - by and good - night with___ ros - es be - dight,___ with___ down o - ver - spread is___ ba - by's wee bed; Lay thee down now, and rest, May thy slum - bers be blest; Lay thee down now, and rest; May thy slum - bers be blest.

2. Listen and compare the tempos of "The Elephant" and "Birds" in Saint-Saëns's *Carnival of the Animals.*

3. Sing or play a familiar song, such as "America the Beautiful," and experiment with musical effects created by performing at different tempos (slow, medium, and fast).

4. Sometimes the tempo gradually gets faster or slower. Listen to Honegger's "Pacific 231," a musical composition about a train. Notice the gradual increase in tempo at the beginning of the composition as the train starts up and the gradual decrease in tempo near the end of the piece as the train slows down.

RHYTHM HAS METER

As the beat recurs in most music, certain pulses are emphasized or accented. The accenting of specific pulses establishes a pattern of strong and weak beats called *meter.* The patterns of beats are divided into measures by bar lines. In the meter signature, the top number indicates the number of beats in a measure, and the bottom number indicates the type of note receiving a single beat. In "Hot Cross Buns," for example, the time signature of 2/4 indicates that there are *two* beats in a measure and that the quarter note receives *one* beat.

Hot Cross Buns

Key: G
Starting pitch: B
Meter: 2/4, begins on 1

England

Hot cross buns, hot cross buns, One a pen-ny, two a pen-ny, hot cross buns.

Activities

1. In much music the meter is organized in groups of either two beats (duple meter) or three beats (triple meter). Place the following terms on the chalkboard:

   duple = 2

   triple = 3

2. Have students chant the following in duple meter:

Ar - thur, Ar - thur has a quar - ter   Jen - ny, Jen - ny has a pen - ny.

   ■ Have them chant the above and play a drum or clap on the strong beats.

   ■ Have them slap their thighs on beat 1 and clap on beat 2.

3. Have students chant the following in triple meter:

| Da | - vid | and | Jon | - a | - than | like | to | play | golf | a | - gain |

| Le | - roy | and | Chris | - to | - pher | play | on | the | hock | - ey | team |

■ Have them chant the above and play the drum or clap on the strong beats.

■ Have them slap their thighs on beat 1 and clap on beats 2 and 3.

4. Ask students to sing "Hot Cross Buns" and then "America," clapping the duple and triple meters, respectively.

America

Key: F
Starting pitch: F
Meter: 3/4, begins on 1

Traditional
Words by Samuel Francis Smith

My coun - try! 'tis of thee, Sweet land of lib - er - ty,

Of thee I sing; Land where my fa - thers died,

Land of the Pil - grims' pride, From ev - 'ry___ moun - tain - side

Let___ free - dom ring!

5. Some music does not have any meter at all. Such sounds may be organized according to the text (as with Gregorian chants) or duration of a musical idea (such as Varèse's *Ionization*).

6. In music of some cultures, *polyrhythms* may occur—that is, a number of highly contrasting rhythms performed at the same time. Experiment with the following example of African polyrhythm by dividing the class into five sections and having each perform one of the rhythmic lines over and over. (Have students count from one to twelve and clap on the appropriate notes.) When they perform all five lines simultaneously, they will have created polyrhythm.

Bruno Nettl, *Folk and Traditional Music of Western Continents*, 2nd ed., © 1973. By permission of Prentice-Hall, Inc., Englewood Cliffs, New Jersey.

RHYTHM MAY HAVE SYNCOPATION

Sometimes in music, beats or portions of beats that would normally be unaccented are instead accented. This is called *syncopation*.

1. Ask students to clap and count the following pattern, emphasizing the strong portion of the beat:

2. Ask students to clap and count the following pattern, emphasizing the weak portion of the beat:

3. Repeat 2 above, tying together the second and third eighth notes in each measure:

4. Ask students to clap and count the above rhythm with the tied eighth notes now written as quarter notes. Have them recite "Syn-co-pah" as they clap.

5. Sing the song "Five Little Frogs" and call attention to the syncopated rhythm.

6. Write out the first line of "Five Little Frogs" on the chalkboard or on a transparency; circle the syncopated rhythm.

Five Little Frogs

Key: C
Starting pitch: G
Meter: 4/4, begins on 1

Words by Louise Binder Scott
Music by Virginia Pavelko

1. Five green and speck-led frogs Sat on a speck-led log,

Eat - ing some most de-li-cious bugs. *(Yum, yum!)*

One jumped in - to the pool, Where it was nice and cool,

Then there were four green speck-led frogs *(Glub, glub!)*

2. Four green and speckled frogs . . .
   Then there were three green speckled frogs. *(Glub, glub!)*

3. Three green and speckled frogs . . .
   Then there were two green speckled frogs. *(Glub, glub!)*

4. Two green and speckled frogs . . .
   Then there was one green speckled frog. *(Glub, glub!)*

5. One green and speckled frog
   Sat on a speckled log,
   Eating some most delicious bugs. *(Yum, yum!)*
   He jumped into the pool,
   Where it was nice and cool,
   Then there were no green speckled frogs. *(Glub, glub!)*

RHYTHM PATTERNS MAY REPEAT

Often a musical composition contains repeated rhythmic patterns. These help tie together or unify a piece of music.

1. Have students sing "Five Little Frogs" and clap the rhythm of the song.

2. Ask students to identify the rhythmic patterns that repeat. Write them on the chalkboard.

3. Have students clap the above rhythm or play it on a drum.

4. Sing the song again, listening carefully to the repeated patterns.

5. Play several minutes of Beethoven's Symphony No. 5, first movement. Ask students to count the number of times they hear the opening four-note rhythm pattern.

6. Word rhythms often match the musical rhythms. Have students recite the lyrics of "America" to the following musical rhythm:

$$\frac{3}{4}$$

My coun - try! 'tis of thee,

7. Perform only the rhythm to part 1 (up to the chorus) of "Erie Canal." Then perform only the rhythm to part 2 (chorus). Be sure to keep a steady beat (use *doo* or *tah*).

Erie Canal

Key: D minor, chorus in F major
Starting pitch: A
Meter: 2/2, begins on "and" of 2

United States

I've got a mule, her name is Sal, Fif-teen miles on the E-rie Ca-nal. She's a good old work-er and a good old pal, Fif-teen miles on the E-rie Ca-nal. We've hauled some barg - es in our day. Filled with lum-ber coal and hay, And we know ev-'ry inch of the way From Al-ban-y___ to___ Buf-fa-lo.___

Chorus

Low bridge, ev-'ry-bo-dy down, Low bridge, 'cause we're com-ing to a town; And you'll al-ways know your neigh-bor, You'll al-ways know your pal, If you've ev-er nav-i-gat-ed on the E-rie Ca-nal.

READING RHYTHMS

Music notation was created (and has evolved over the centuries) to show both the pitch of the sound (whether it is high or low) and how long it is supposed to continue (duration). Musicians have created a series of symbols to represent how long a sound is to last. Figure 3.1 illustrates this system. Each of these notes has a name based on the idea of a "whole."

Figure 3.1. Symbols of duration: music notation

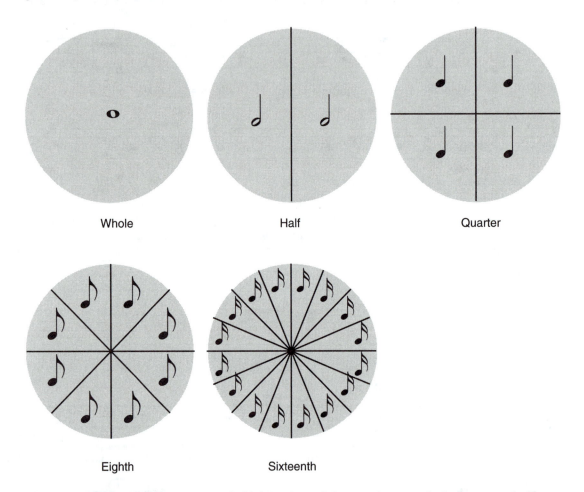

In figure 3.1 each symbol represents half the value of the previous symbol; thus, two half notes equal one whole note (♩ + ♩ = o); two quarter notes equal one half note (♩ + ♩ = ♩); two eighth notes equal one quarter note (♪ + ♪ = ♩); and two sixteenth notes equal one eighth note (♪ + ♪ = ♪).

A dot (·) after a note is a symbol that lengthens that note by half its value. Thus, if a half note is to receive a duration of two counts, a dot placed next to it indicates that it will now receive three counts.

Here are some examples for you to try. Remember that 4/4 meter indicates that there are four beats to a measure and that a quarter note (♩) receives one count.

1. Bongo drums or woodblock:

2. Conga drum or claves:

3. Maracas or hand drum:

4. Ratchet (twirl) or tambourine:

Music would be very dull if we heard only sound and no moments of silence. Silences in music are called *rests,* and there is a rest equal to every note. Examine the following table and notice the shapes of the various rests.

Duration of Notes	*and Rests*
o Whole note	▬ Whole rest
♩ Half note	▬ Half rest
♩ Quarter note	❩ Quarter rest
♪ Eighth note	⁊ Eighth rest
♬ Sixteenth note	⁊ Sixteenth rest

Here are some other examples to try (instruments listed or of your choice):

1. Bongo drums:

2. Conga drum:

3. Maracas:

4. Ratchet (twirl):

You may also create your own rhythm.

Experiences with Texture

Texture refers to the number of lines of music being performed and to the relationships among different musical lines.

TEXTURE MAY BE MONOPHONIC

1. Sing "America" together in unison without accompaniment. Because there is just one musical line, the texture is described as *monophonic* (*mono* = one; *phonic* = sound).

2. Think of other examples of monophonic texture, such as a boy or a girl singing a song while walking down the street alone, or a single bird singing while sitting on a tree branch.

TEXTURE MAY BE HOMOPHONIC OR HARMONIC

When melodies are accompanied by chords, the texture is described as *homophonic* or *harmonic*. In music, harmony is created when more than one pitch sounds at the same time. It most often occurs in the chordal structure of a musical composition.

Normally, musicians speak of harmony as occurring within the framework of a major or minor scale. You have already experienced major and minor scales and melodies. *Chords* can be constructed on every scale degree by arranging pitches a third apart above the principal pitch. For example, in the C major scale, the chords are as follows:

Chords most often consist of three pitches. Some chords, however, have four pitches. Such a chord is called a *seventh chord,* because the distance between its lowest and highest notes is seven scale degrees:

Activities

1. Accompany "Merrily We Roll Along" by playing the chords on the resonator bells, tone chimes, handbells (be sure to snap your wrist when playing the tone chimes or handbells), keyboard, Omnichord, or guitar.

Merrily We Roll Along

Key: C major
Starting pitch: E
Meter: 4/4, begins on 1

Traditional

Mer - ri - ly we roll a - long, roll a - long, roll a - long.

Mer - ri - ly we roll a - long o'er the dark blue sea.

2. Play the chords C (C E G) and G₇ (G B D F) to accompany "My Hat."

My Hat

Key: C major
Starting pitch: G
Meter: 3/4, begins on 3

Germany

My hat, it has three cor-ners;____ Three cor - ners has my hat;____ And

had it not three cor-ners,____ It would not be my hat.____

3. Play the chords G (G B D), C (C E G), and D₇ (D♯ A C) to accompany "Yankee Doodle" (page 479).

TEXTURE MAY BE POLYPHONIC

When music has two or more different lines being sung or played at the same time, the texture is described as *polyphonic*.

1. Sing "Row, Row, Row Your Boat" as a three-part round (class divided into three sections). Notice that when everyone is singing, there are three different lines of music.

Row, Row, Row Your Boat

Key: C
Starting pitch: C
Meter: 6/8, begins on 1

Traditional

2. Listen to the opening section (exposition) of Bach's "Little" Fugue in G Minor, particularly noticing the several different lines of music.

Experiences with Tone Color

Musical tones are distinguished from each other by the quality of their sounds. In music this is called *tone color* or *timbre* (pronounced "tam-ber").

TONE COLOR VARIES WITH THE TYPE AND SIZE OF MATERIAL PRODUCING THE SOUND

1. Explore ways to produce different sounds; for example, strike two sticks together, shake pebbles in various-sized cans, blow air across different sizes of pop bottles.

2. Listen to each sound and describe it with words.

3. Make a list on the chalkboard of all the different qualities of sounds you make. Notice that the tone color varies with the type and size of the material producing the sound.

Exploring Tone Colors

1. Sing the song "The More We Get Together."

2. Create an accompaniment, first with tone colors created by mouth, for example:
   a. Oom-pah-pah.
   b. Oom-ss-ss.
   c. Oom-deedle-eet.

3. Perform as an accumulative song, that is:
   a. Begin with Oom-pah-pah.
   b. Add Oom-ss-ss.
   c. Add Oom-deedle-eet.
   d. Add the melody of "The More We Get Together."

4. Create an accompaniment with the different tone colors of classroom percussion instruments, for example:
   a. Use bongo drums with Oom-pah-pah.
   b. Use sand blocks with Oom-ss-ss.
   c. Use a tambourine with Oom-deedle-eet.

5. Sing as an accumulative song as in step 2.

The More We Get Together

TONE COLOR VARIES WITH DIFFERENT TYPES OF INSTRUMENTS

Musical instruments can be classified on the basis of the quality of their sounds. For example, on *stringed instruments,* the distinctive sound is produced by vibrating strings, which are set in motion by being either bowed or plucked. *Wind instruments* produce their distinctive sounds with a vibrating air column, which is set in motion by vibrating a reed, "buzzing the lips," or simply blowing across a notch or other opening. On *percussion instruments* the sounds are produced by striking the instruments with either the hand or a mallet or by striking several objects together.

Activities

1. Find instruments at home or at school, or make your own instruments for the class to listen to and classify.

2. Listen to some examples of musical instruments from throughout the world and describe their distinctive tone colors. Include some electronic instruments such as those found in current popular music.

TONE COLOR VARIES WITH DIFFERENT TYPES OF VOICES

Singers can also be classified according to the tone color or quality of the musical sounds they produce.

Activities

1. Listen to different vocal tone colors produced by individuals in your class, taking turns singing a familiar song.

2. Listen to recordings of women and men singing. Think of some words to describe the different tone colors of women's and men's voices (women's voices are generally lighter and thinner than the heavier, fuller sounds of men).

3. Play recordings of singers from different areas of the world (such as Africa, China, and India) and discuss differences in tone color.

Experiences with Dynamics

The term *dynamics* describes the degree of softness or loudness in music. Different dynamic levels are used by composers to help express various moods in music and to provide variety or contrast in musical works.

DYNAMIC LEVELS MAY BE SOFT OR LOUD

1. Sing the American spiritual "Steal Away," exploring soft and loud dynamic levels. Note that this song was sung by slaves on plantations and that it focuses on an afterlife with the words "I don't have long to stay here." Notice how the mood of the piece changes with different dynamic levels for various sections of the lyric. For example, sing softly the words "I don't have long to stay here" and loudly the words "He calls me by the thunder; The trumpet sounds within-a my soul."

2. Use a megaphone (or make one out of cardboard). Talk into the small end for the sound to be louder, or talk into the large end for the sound to be softer.

DYNAMIC LEVEL MAY GRADUALLY GET LOUDER (CRESCENDO) OR SOFTER (DECRESCENDO)

1. Explain that a composer indicates "to get louder"—a *crescendo*—or "to get softer"— a *decrescendo*—with similar symbolic shapes:

Draw the shapes on the chalkboard.

2. Sing "Steal Away" again, this time adding the suggested crescendos and decrescendos.

3. Create a short piece of music with classroom instruments, using different dynamic levels to provide variation or contrast.

Experiences with Musical Forms

The term *form* refers to how a composition is put together. Most forms are based on repetition and contrast.

REPEATED MUSICAL IDEAS UNIFY COMPOSITIONS, AND CONTRASTING IDEAS PROVIDE VARIETY

Some of the most common musical forms are binary, ternary, rondo, fugue, and theme-and-variation.

Binary Form

As the name implies, musical compositions in *binary* form have two principal sections: The first is often labeled A and the second, B.

Activities

1. Sing "Home on the Range" (page 47) and listen and look for the two contrasting sections, A and B.

2. Diagram the form by having students place sheets of red (A) and blue (B) paper on the board.

3. Using transparent plastic in two colors, cut circles to fit over the fronts of flashlights. Listen to "Johnny B. Goode" (Chuck Berry, *His Best*, vol. 1, UNI/Chess Records Asin B000005KQI). Have half of the students shine flashlights with one color on the ceiling as they hear the verse, and have the other half shine flashlights with a different color on the ceiling for the chorus.

Ternary Form

In many musical compositions, an A section of music is followed by a B section, and then there is a return to the A section. In effect, such compositions consist of three sections, and the form is described as *ternary*.

Activities

1. Sing "We Wish You a Merry Christmas."

2. Diagram the form with colored paper.

3. Explain that repeating the A section helps tie together or unify the piece. The B section is designed to provide contrast or variety.

We Wish You a Merry Christmas

Key: A
Starting pitch: E
Meter: 3/4, begins on 3

English

Rondo Form

A larger form based on the repetition of a musical idea is the *rondo*. A rondo can be diagrammed in the following way:

Theme	Contrasting Idea	Theme	Second Contrasting Idea	Theme
A	B	A	C	A

Activities

1. Using a drum to keep the beat, ask students to walk around the room. On a signal, they should change the way they walk (backward, sideways, on tiptoe, on their heels, etc.). On a second signal, they should return to the way they walked at the beginning. On a third signal, they should walk a different way.

2. Repeat, having one student hold colored cards marked A B A C A. As each card is held up, students walk in the appropriate fashion.

3. Listen to the third movement of Mozart's Horn Concerto No. 3 in E-flat Major, having the students make up movements to follow the form. Diagram the form on the board with sections of colored paper and letters.

Paper	Letters	Musical Idea
Red	A	Horn with orchestral accompaniment playing pulsating, driving theme
Blue	B	Contrast provided by smooth, lyrical theme played by horn with orchestral accompaniment
Red	A	Return to pulsating A theme
Green	C	Lyrical, contrasting section
Red	A	Pulsating theme from beginning

Fugue Form

The *fugue* is another musical form based on repetition and contrast. The first section of the fugue is known as the *exposition*. In the exposition the *subject* (musical idea) is stated in one musical line and then imitated in other musical lines. For example, in Bach's "Little" Fugue in G Minor, the melody begins in the soprano line and then imitatively repeats in the alto, tenor, and bass lines.

Following the exposition, segments of contrasting musical ideas known as *episodes* alternate with periodic returns of the subject. The episodes are particularly important in providing variety in the musical work. The repetition of the subject from time to time helps tie the musical composition together and provides a sense of unity.

Activity

Play a recording of Bach's "Little" Fugue in G Minor. Follow the diagram of events in the composition (see the table below). If you wish, have students provide a visual response to their listening experience by asking half of the class to raise their hands whenever they hear the subject, and the other half to raise their hands whenever they hear the episodes.

"Little" Fugue in G Minor

J. S. Bach

Listening Guide to Bach's "Little" Fugue in G Minor

Call Number	Measures	Events
1	1–21	Exposition, main melody (subject) repeats three more times (in alto, tenor, and bass lines)
2	22–24	Episode, section designed to offer variety, contrast
3	25–30	Subject with selected voices in other melodies called counterpoint
4	31–32	Episode
5	33–36	Subject with selected voices in counterpoint
6	37–40	Episode
7	41–45	Subject with selected voices in counterpoint
8	46–49	Episode
9	50–54	Subject with selected voices in counterpoint
10	55–62	Episode
11	63–68	Subject with selected voices in counterpoint; conclusion

Theme-and-Variation Form

In *theme-and-variation* form, the theme is generally stated at the beginning. Thereafter it is repeated over and over, but with changes each time for contrast.

Activities

1. Explore the theme-and-variation form through the following:

   a. Have students draw circles on the chalkboard or on paper and then create many different ways (variations) of changing the circle.

   b. Have students print their names in at least eight different ways (using a different color, a different shape, a different size, curved lines, straight lines, etc.).

2. Sing the song "Simple Gifts." Explore ways of creating variety in the song by singing it faster or slower, louder or softer.

3. Listen to "Variations on Simple Gifts" from Aaron Copland's ballet *Appalachian Spring*. This orchestral selection, which is based on the "Simple Gifts" melody, is cast in theme-and-variation form. Listen carefully to see if you can identify ways in which the composer changes each appearance of the tune.

Listening Guide to Copland's *Appalachian Spring,* "Variations on Simple Gifts"

Theme	"Simple Gifts" Played on the Clarinet
Variation 1	Variation (contrast) in tone color with "Simple Gifts" in oboe and bassoon
Variation 2	Variation (contrast) in tone color with "Simple Gifts" in stringed instruments; theme augmented
Variation 3	Variation (contrast) in tone color with "Simple Gifts" in trumpet
Variation 4	Variation (contrast) in tone color with "Simple Gifts" in clarinet and bassoon
Variation 5	Variation (contrast) in tone color and texture with "Simple Gifts" in the full orchestra

a. Place pictures of the following instruments on the bulletin board:

Clarinet

Oboe

Bassoon

Strings (violin, viola, cello, bass)

Trumpet

Full orchestra

b. Ask students to pretend that they are playing a clarinet, violin, or trumpet. Have them hum the tune of "Simple Gifts" as they "play" their imaginary instruments.

c. As students listen to Copland's "Variations on Simple Gifts," have them point to pictures of instruments used in each variation.

For Your Journal

In your journal or portfolio, make a section on fundamentals of music and comment on the things you have learned in this chapter as they relate to the elementary classroom. Be sure to include the following items: melody, rhythm, texture, tone color, dynamics, and form. Include specific musical examples to illustrate each.

Teaching Music Through Singing

FROM A VERY YOUNG AGE, children express their feelings through play chants and sound patterns that they experience alone or share with other children. Because singing is an intimate, highly expressive experience, it is an important way for a child to convey happiness, love, dreams, joy, and sadness.

Songs provide a rich storehouse of musical and literary treasures. Folk songs tell us of the ways peoples from other cultures, times, and places have lived and worked, whereas art songs may describe such things as a waterfall or a butterfly. Hymns, chorales, and spirituals provide opportunities to express feelings of awe, inspiration, praise, and thanksgiving.

Children should sing for sheer fun and pleasure in a variety of recreational activities, such as games, folk songs and dances, and musical plays. They should also learn musical concepts such as melody, rhythm, and form through the pieces that they perform.

Characteristics of the Child Voice and Children's Song Interests

Teachers need to understand children's vocal characteristics and song interests to set realistic musical expectations and develop appropriate teaching strategies.

The singing voice of a young child (boy or girl) is relatively high, light in both quality and volume, and often limited to an octave or less in *range* (lowest note to highest note). A clear,

Children singing

flutelike quality is desirable and should be promoted. Many children in today's television- and movie-oriented society have been greatly influenced by pop singers, and some will try to imitate their sounds. The teacher should encourage and nurture the beauty of the child voice, however, not an imitation of the adult voice.

Major differences develop between a girl's voice and a boy's voice as they mature through childhood. Initially, the girl's voice is light and thin and has a slightly translucent quality. As she matures, she is capable of creating a bigger sound but retains the same light quality. When a girl enters adolescence, her voice becomes breathy, and she often temporarily loses the ability to sing high notes. By the age of fifteen, she begins to develop the mature voice of a woman, and at this time the true soprano and alto qualities start to emerge.

A boy's voice is similar to a girl's until the age of nine, when it begins to develop the fullness and power we associate with such musical groups as the Vienna Boys' Choir. A boy's voice reaches its peak of clarity and brilliance *just before it begins to change.* American boys tend to want to sing lower than their European counterparts, and it is not unusual for a young boy, speaking in a high unchanged voice, to announce that he would like to sing bass. Allowing a boy to sing low before he is vocally ready is not advised. We need to acknowledge his wish to be grown-up yet suggest that he sing the "lower" part of the song, as opposed to the "lowest."

It is generally agreed that, if they are to be confident singers as adults, children must learn to match pitches and sing short musical phrases before the age of nine. By the age of nine, a child is becoming much more sensitive and self-conscious about singing alone. The ability to sing in tune and to sing increasingly complex melodies depends on carefully constructed singing experiences that follow the basic physical development of the child.

A child's vocal range varies a great deal. Contributing factors include natural talent, maturity, and musical experience.

The appropriateness and interest of songs also varies with the talent and interests of students. Most of the songs in the basal series books have been found to work well throughout the United States in a variety of teaching situations. A teacher should also consider whether a particular song can enhance lessons in other areas, such as social studies, language arts, or science.

As you gain experience in analyzing and teaching songs to children of different ages, you will want to refer frequently to the following outline of musical expectations.

PRESCHOOL AND KINDERGARTEN (AGES FOUR AND FIVE)

Vocal Characteristics and Abilities

■ Voices are small and light.

■ Children are generally unable to sing in tune.

■ Singing range is D–A for most; D–D for some.

■ Children can sing play chants and easy tonal patterns.

Come   and play   with   me_____

■ Children can sing short melodies in major, minor, or pentatonic scales.

■ Children can sing melodies with one note to a syllable.

■ Children can sing with an awareness of a steady beat.

■ Children can sing repeated rhythmic patterns accurately.

■ Children can sing softly and loudly.

■ Children can sing melodies with or without a simple accompaniment.

Song Interests

Preschool children like songs that tell a story. Consider how many nursery rhymes are little dramas: "Jack and Jill," "Little Jack Horner," and "Polly, Put the Kettle On." Little children enjoy songs that give them an opportunity for natural expression. When they act out "Three Little Kittens Who Lost Their Mittens," they really become the little kittens. They are very much at home in the land of make-believe. Children also like songs that deal with familiar experiences: bedtime and wake-up songs; helping songs; and songs about friends, family, animals, the seasons, and special occasions.

EARLY PRIMARY: FIRST AND SECOND GRADES (AGES SIX AND SEVEN)

Vocal Characteristics and Abilities

- Most voices are light and high; a few may be low.

- Many children are still unable to sing in tune at age six.

- By age seven most children will be able to sing at least short phrases in tune and will begin to sing alone.

- Children can understand high and low pitches.

- Children can sustain a single pitch.

- Range expands from five to six consecutive pitches (D–B) to a full octave (D–D).

- Children understand the difference between a playground-shouting voice and a singing voice.

- Children begin to understand the importance of breath in singing.

- Children can sing melodies in major, minor, and pentatonic scales.

- Children can sing call-and-response songs, as well as songs in two- or three-part form.

- Children sing with attention to dynamics and changes in tempo.

- Children can sing rhythmically, accenting strong beats and performing simple syncopation.

- Children can sing from simple music notation.

- Children can sing melodies with simple harmonic or rhythmic accompaniment.

Song Interests

At six and seven, children enjoy songs about animals, community, friends, action (with movement or creative motions), pretending, folk games from around the world, and special occasions.

INTERMEDIATE: THIRD AND FOURTH GRADES (AGES EIGHT AND NINE)

Vocal Characteristics and Abilities

- Most children can sing a song in tune.

- Girls' voices continue to be very light and thin.

- Boys' voices begin to develop the rich resonance of the mature boy soprano-alto voice.

- Some children can sing rounds, partner songs, canons, and descants. There is little use of alto or lower parts.

- Some children have much more control over expressive qualities of singing, such as legato, dynamics, and sustained phrases.

- Some children are capable of singing melodies or parts from music notation.

- Some children can harmonize parts or chords by ear, such as thirds and sixths.

- Some children can sing songs with more-complex rhythms.

Song Interests

At eight and nine, children enjoy songs about early America (Native Americans, Pilgrims), transportation, geography (New England, the West, the South), the circus, planets, and people and songs that express emotions. Songs from other lands (such as Mexico, Africa, China, and Japan) are appealing because of their contrasting styles.

UPPER ELEMENTARY: FIFTH AND SIXTH GRADES (AGES TEN AND ELEVEN)

Vocal Characteristics and Abilities

- Unchanged voices remain clear and light; boys' voices become more resonant.

- Some children show greater ability to sing in two and three parts.

- Some children have a heightened rhythmic sense and respond to music with strong rhythms.

- Many children tend to imitate the quality and style of pop singers.

- Some voices begin to change—that is, boys' voices become lower, and girls' voices become very breathy.

- Some children can read simple music notation.

Song Interests

Children enjoy songs related to adventure, work, transportation, history, and feelings such as happiness, sadness, and love, as well as songs from other cultures and countries. Children also enjoy folk songs from America, songs about places or events, and contemporary popular songs. They like to harmonize and accompany songs with classroom instruments, especially guitar, keyboard, Omnichord, and recorder. They are enthusiastic about dramatics and producing musical plays.

Techniques for Teaching Children to Sing

Although many children can sing naturally, others require guidance and help in learning to use the head voice, singing in tune, and developing good tone quality.

CREATING AN ENVIRONMENT FOR SINGING EXPERIENCES

There are many ways to help children achieve readiness for singing. Songs sung to them by a parent, teacher, or friend provide an effective model for them to follow. Recordings of children's voices found in the many music series books, as well as recordings of children's choirs, should be used during the day, both before and during class periods. Children learn to reproduce tonal sounds by imitation. Hearing songs repeatedly will help them relate to pitch, melody, and rhythm. In other words, children should be surrounded with interesting songs and many models of good singing.

IMPROVING POSTURE

Because the body is the "instrument" for singing, it must be held upright; that is, a child must sit or stand with shoulders erect, head up, and spine straight. Create games and draw analogies to improve posture. For example:

1. Ask the children to reach for an imaginary bar above their heads and to pull their bodies upward toward it. They should then relax and put their arms down to their sides.

2. Have the children pretend they are puppets and have collapsed on the floor. Then have them pretend that they are being pulled up with a string attached to the backs of their necks. (Children can take turns being puppets and puppeteers.)

3. Have them pretend that they are inflated balloons just ready to leave the ground.

TEACHING GOOD BREATHING HABITS TO SUPPORT THE TONE

Most children who cannot sing in tune, or in their head voice, have not developed the ability to support a tone with their breath. As they learn to "feel" the pitches, they will be better able to "match" the pitches. Have students imitate you in the following exercises.

1. Sip air as if through a soda straw and release it with a hissing sound. Be sure to keep the sound steady and not like a radiator that has sprung a leak.

2. Sip air as if through a soda straw and let the air out on a high "Ooo" sound, descending to a low sound. Use this same technique to imitate sirens.

3. Pretend that your finger is a lighted candle. Fill your lungs with air and blow gently on the "candle" so that the "flame" flickers but does not go out.

4. Inhale quickly, as if you see a fumble on the one-yard line by your favorite football team.

5. Lean over from the waist, letting your arms dangle. Breathe deeply, expanding the ribs. Straighten up and exhale slowly and steadily.

FINDING THE HEAD VOICE

Children who cannot sing in tune share a common problem: They are unable to manipulate their voices so that they can match the musical sounds they hear. Before a child can sing comfortably, he or she must learn how it feels and sounds to use the *head voice.*

One way of helping children find their head voice is to strengthen the concept of different "voices." Try the following game:

> Teacher: Let's see if you can use your different voices. First, listen to me . . . "This is my whispering voice."
>
> Child answers (in a whisper): This is my whispering voice.
>
> Teacher: This is my talking-low voice.
>
> Child: This is my talking-low voice.
>
> Teacher: This is my talking-high voice.
>
> Child: This is my talking-high voice.
>
> Teacher: This is my yelling voice.
>
> Child: This is my yelling voice.
>
> Teacher (on a single pitch): This is my singing voice.
>
> Child (same pitch): This is my singing voice.

A second approach is to help children discover speech inflection. Start with speaking small phrases, such as Gradually develop these phrases into tonal intervals, like the following (either sing or play pattern on melody bells):

{Musical notation in 3/4 time, F major key signature}

Good morn - ing. How are you?

A third approach involves imitating familiar sounds, such as the swooping up and down of a siren or the calls of the bobwhite, cuckoo, and cardinal.*

---

* Additional songs and ideas may be found in *One, Two, Three . . . Echo Me!* by Loretta Mitchell (West Nyack, N.Y.: Parker Publishing, 1991), pp. 1–28. Especially useful are the ideas for using puppets to teach the difference between singing and speaking.

DEVELOPING THE ABILITY TO MATCH TONES

The ability to match tones is directly related to breathing techniques, ear training, a relaxed jaw, and singing with energy. Most children have sung childhood chants, such as:

Come on ov-er to my house

You can use similar chants to help them learn to match tones.

Activities

1. Using a few pitches (such as G E A, in the chant illustrated above), create question-and-answer games. Because most adults sing too low for children, it is wise to use a pitch pipe, recorder, or melody bells to give the starting pitch or the beginning melodic phrase. If possible, avoid using the piano; the tone is too heavy for young voices and they have trouble matching it. If a child cannot sing the response in the key in which you play or sing it, try to match his or her range and work from there.

Where is Jim-my? I'm here.

What hol-i-day is com - ing? Val-en-tine's Day is com - ing.

2. Using two toy telephones, create a telephone game. Play or sing a chant, such as, "Hello, how are you?" Have the child answer, "Hello. I'm fine," for example.

3. In the song "Listen to the Wind" (see next page), invite children (grades K–1) to match tones on the pitches C and A on the word *Who-ee:*

Who - ee

Note that *who* is the easiest sound for children to sing and is most effective in developing the head voice. Playing these two pitches on resonator bells, melody bells, or recorder enables the child to hear the pitch he or she is trying to match. (See chapter 6, "Teaching Music Through Playing Classroom Instruments" for a detailed discussion and suggested activities.) Many times even a young child can play these two pitches on the bells. You may need to mark the proper pitches with colors to aid in identification.

Listen to the Wind

Key: F
Starting pitch: C
Meter: 3/4, begins on 1

German Folk Tune: *Cuckoo*
Words by Joy E. Lawrence

Who - ee! Who - ee! hear___ the wind, Who - ee! Who - ee! hear___ the wind,
Pit - ter pat - ter goes___ the rain, Pit - ter pat - ter goes___ the rain,

Comes down the chim - ney, Goes up the chim - ney, Who - ee! Who - ee!___ hear___ the wind.
Here on the win - dow, There on the win - dow, Pit - ter pat - ter___ goes___ the rain.

You may wish to add the following percussion accompaniment to the song:

Drum:

Rhythm sticks:

4. "Hello, There!" (see next page) is an easy tone-matching song that is especially appropriate for kindergarten children, many of whom have played "echo" in the woods or in a cavern of some kind. Here the teacher sings, and the children "echo" to help with the tone-matching process. Have the children sit in a circle as you sing the song. (You may want to place tape on the floor to aid the children in forming a circle.) Choose one child to cover his or her eyes and sit in the center and another child to be the echo. The child who is "it" tries to identify the child who sings the echo after the teacher. Continue the game by taking turns with a new child being "it" and a second child singing the echo.

Hello, There!

Key: C
Starting pitch: G
Meter: 2/4, begins on "and" of 2

Traditional

5. In "Going on a Picnic," ask children (grades K–1) to be creative in deciding what to take. Reinforce the two pitches (F and C) as they occur, by playing them on a keyboard or resonator bells.

Going on a Picnic

Key: F
Starting pitch: F
Meter: 4/4, begins on 1

Words and Music by Lynn Freeman Olson

DEVELOPING THE CONCEPTS OF HIGH AND LOW

A basic skill in tone matching is to develop the concepts of high and low.

Activities

1. Show pictures that illustrate the concepts of high and low, such as a plane and a car, a child stretching upward and one kneeling down, or a bird in a tree and a dog lying on the ground.

2. Create a variety of movements indicating low to high and high to low. For example, children could stand and stretch arms high, then stoop low to feel the ground:

I am down low. Now I'm up high.

3. Ask the children to be puppets on a string and pretend that their voices are being lifted up. Use a marionette to illustrate. Have different children "work" the voices of each other.

4. Have the children sing "Ooo" as they pretend that they are watching their favorite baseball player hit a home run. Voices should rise as the ball goes into the upper stands.

5. For those who have difficulty hearing their own voice, give the following direction: Cup one hand behind your ear and place the other hand in front of your mouth. (This makes an echo chamber.) Sing "Ooo" into your hand so that it sounds high and then low.

6. Repeat the following simple chant several times:

Dog-gie down low, Bird-ie up high.

Change keys each time, gradually getting higher.

7. Turn a xylophone so that the lowest pitches are to the left and the highest pitches are to the right. Play low C followed by high C. Play the full scale from bottom to top (C D E F G A B C) and then top to bottom (C B A G F E D C). Ask children to sing the ascending scale with syllables *(do re mi fa sol la ti do)*. Ask the class if they sang high or low when they began. Compare singing the scale with a plant growing up tall. On a chalkboard or chart, place eight pictures of a plant or tree developing from seed to full maturity. Point to pictures as the children sing the scale.

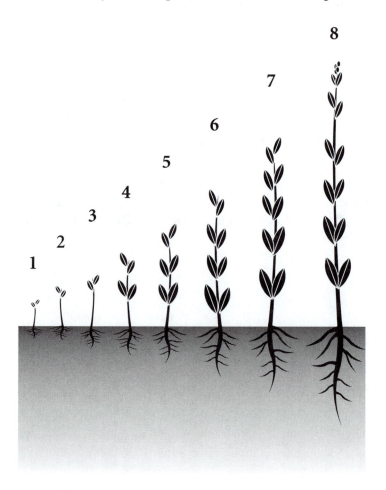

DISCOVERING PATTERNS

All pieces of music have patterns that repeat. These patterns may be melodic, rhythmic, or harmonic. Teaching children to identify these patterns and then perform them shortens the time required for them to learn to sing songs or to listen perceptively to a larger musical composition.

Activities

1. Examine repeated patterns on fabric or wrapping paper.

2. Show pictures with patterns that occur more than once.

3. Sing the well-known English song "Looby Loo" (see next page). Point out the two rhythm patterns that are repeated. Have one child play the first rhythm pattern on a classroom percussion instrument such as rhythm sticks:

Pattern I

Have another child play the second pattern on another instrument such as a triangle. Be sure to choose instruments with different tone colors.

Pattern 2

Ask the children to count how many times each pattern is played. (Pattern 1 is performed six times, including the D.C. repeat, whereas pattern 2 is performed four times. Notice that exact repetition occurs twice, with the third and fourth times slightly altered.)

Put the following scale pattern on the chalkboard or a chart and point to the notes as the class sings the verse, to show how the song moves upward. These syllables correspond to the notes on the staff of F G A B♭ C. (Showing a scale pattern helps children know which way to make their voices go—up or down.)

do re mi fa sol
F   G   A   B♭ C

In "Looby Loo" the chorus is different from the verse both in melody and in rhythm. Give students flashlights with colored transparencies in them, and have children with one color "dance" their flashlights on the ceiling for the rhythm of the chorus and children with another color "dance" their flashlights for the verse. Of course, most kindergarten children will want to act out the words of the song and create additional verses of their own. This provides an easy link to rhyming and teaching the use of words in a language arts lesson.

Looby Loo

English Singing Game

Key: F
Starting pitch: F
Meter: 6/8, begins on 1

Here we go loo - by loo, Here we go loo - by light. Here we go loo - by loo

All on a Sat - ur - day night. _____

1. I put my right hand in, _____ I take my right hand
2. I put my left hand in, _____ I take my left hand
3. I put my right leg in, _____ I take my right leg
4. I put my left leg in, _____ I take my left leg

out – _____ I give my hand a shake, shake shake, And turn my - self a - bout. Oh,
out – _____ I give my hand a shake, shake shake, And turn my - self a - bout. Oh,
out – _____ I give my leg a shake, shake shake, And turn my - self a - bout. Oh,
out – _____ I give my leg a shake, shake shake, And turn my - self a - bout. Oh,

4. Play or sing other songs with repeated rhythm patterns and have the children clap the pattern or play it on percussion instruments.

The repeated pattern in the song "Jack-o'-Lantern," for example, is:

This pattern occurs six times. Clap the pattern or play it on classroom percussion instruments as an ostinato.

Use a drum to keep the steady beat:

Teach the words and melody of the song by imitation.

Jack-o'-Lantern

Key: D
Starting pitch: D
Meter: 3/4, begins on 3

German Folk Song
Words by Lois Holt

1. Jack - o' - lan - tern, jack - o' - lan - tern, You are such a fun - ny sight.
2. You were once a yel - low pump - kin Grow - ing on a stur - dy vine.

As you sit there in the win - dow, Look - ing out at the night.
Now you are a jack - o' - lan - tern. See the can - dle - light shine.

Preparing to Teach a Song

Follow these steps when preparing to teach a song:

1. Choose an appropriate song for a specific class or grade level. (Refer to pages 81–83 for musical expectations and song interests of various maturation levels.)

   a. Choose a song within a child's vocal capability (range and rhythm).

   b. Choose a song with an interesting and appropriate text.

   c. Choose a song that may increase the child's perception and understanding of music as an expressive art form.

   d. Choose a song that can be integrated with other activities (when possible).

2. Analyze the musical materials of the song—that is, range of melody, rhythmic patterns, formal structure, harmony, and expressiveness of text (see the sample analysis that follows).

3. Decide on what musical concepts to emphasize, such as skips, rhythmic/tonal patterns, or repetition.

4. Decide on what vocal techniques the class needs to work on, such as good breathing, using the head voice, tone matching, or posture.

5. Determine the approach you will use to teach the song (rote, rote-note, note). In the sample analysis that follows, "Tinga Layo" will be taught using the rote-note approach for grades 3–4.

6. Determine how you might integrate the song into other classroom activities, such as movement and social studies.

7. Prepare a lesson plan.

ANALYSIS: "TINGA LAYO"

Permission given by Facultad de Artes—Universidad de Chile. Juan Amenabar Ruiz, Vice-Decano.

Expressiveness of Text

The song should be sung moderately fast with lots of energy. It is important to observe both legato ("Tinga Layo") and staccato ("Run, little donkey, run!") as you sing.

Melody

- There are two phrases in the refrain:

  Tinga Layo! Run, little donkey, run!
  Tinga Layo! Run, little donkey, run!

- There are two short phrases and one long phrase in the verse:

  My donkey yes
  My donkey no
  My donkey stop when I tell him to go!

- The range of the melody is from C to C.

- The melody basically moves stepwise, with larger skips occurring in the verse.

- The melody is in the key of C major.

Rhythm

- The meter is duple: 2/4.
- The tempo is moderately fast.
- The meter is the same throughout.
- Repeated rhythm pattern occurs in measures 3 and 7.

Formal Organization

The song is organized in an ABA pattern.

Texture (Harmony)

The song can be accompanied on the keyboard, Autoharp, or Omnichord. Classroom percussion instruments can be used to create variety and interest.

Chords are C, F, G_7; or transpose to key of D (D, G, A_7).

LESSON: "TINGA LAYO"

Activity: Teaching a song

Grades: 3–4

Concepts: Expressiveness/energy in singing, rhythm in patterns

Objectives

Students will:

1. Sing with good tone quality.
2. Sing with accurate pitches and rhythms.
3. Identify rhythm patterns by sound and notation.
4. Accompany song on keyboard, Omnichord, or guitar and classroom percussion instruments.

Materials

- Song
- Keyboard, Autoharp, Omnichord, or guitar
- Classroom percussion instruments
- Rhythm chart
- Chord chart

Procedures

1. Emphasize the need for energy in singing. Review several breathing exercises:

    a. Sip through a straw and vocalize "Ooh" downward.

    b. Breathe and blow out two candles, one close to you and one at a distance.

2. Play or sing "Tinga Layo" for the class.

3. Play or sing the song again and ask the children to tap their thighs and clap on beats 1 and 2 (duple meter). Repeat, using a drum or tambourine for meter beats.

4. Sing or play the first two phrases of the song. Accompany yourself on a chording instrument. Ask students to clap the melodic rhythm (the words) and accent as you do. Sing the first two phrases again and have students sing. Emphasize the need for good breathing and energy in singing.

5. Sing or play the verse and have students repeat after you.

6. Demonstrate the following rhythm:

    Using a rhythm chart, ask students to clap the rhythm.

7. Repeat, using a drum or maracas to play the rhythm pattern.

8. Ask students to find how many times the "musical picture" occurs in the song (four times if you include the repeat).

9. Ask the class to read both the English and Spanish words of the song. Read with expression—or example, legato for "Tinga Layo" and staccato on "Run, little donkey, run!"

10. Introduce the chords C, F, and G_7 (on a keyboard, Autoharp, or Omnichord) or D, G, and A_7 (on a keyboard, Autoharp, or guitar). Provide each student with a chord chart showing where the chords are located on a guitar (see appendix B).

    Practice singing the song and pushing down an imaginary chord bar (any one will do for this exercise) and strumming at the beginning of each measure. When students can sing and strum at the same time, ask selected students to accompany the song, using only a single chord wherever it occurs. For example, one student might play C, a second, F, and a third, G_7. As skill increases, each student will be able to play all three chords to accompany the song.

Closure

1. Sing "Tinga Layo" accompanied by a chording instrument (keyboard, Omnichord, or guitar) and rhythm instruments. Emphasize again the importance of posture, good breathing, energy, legato and staccato singing, and the crisp rhythm of:

2. Extend use of the song into movement activities and listen to other examples of calypso music.

Assessment

1. What are some reasons why you need energy to sing?

2. Can you demonstrate duple meter? Triple meter?

3. Can you identify some rhythmic patterns that occur in the song "Tinga Layo"?

Leading a Song

Before you develop techniques for teaching children to sing songs, you need to be able to *lead* a song. As with all musical skills, this requires practice. The more you do it, the more comfortable you will be standing before a class and leading them in a song. You first need to analyze the song to determine the following:

- Whether you sing or play the melody accurately or should use a recording
- The starting pitch and how to find it on an instrument or with your voice
- The meter of the song (duple or triple)
- On what beat the song begins and on what beat to say "sing"
- What the text of the song is about and how it can be performed expressively (e.g., smoothly, loudly, softly, with or without accents)
- How to end the song together

The following guidelines for leading a song will contribute to your success and will also improve the singing of your students.

1. Check the posture of students and be sure that they are looking at you. Assume a posture that reflects the mood of the song.

2. Sing the song, perform it on an instrument, or use a recording to establish the key, tempo, dynamic level, and mood. Perform the entire song unless students already know it. Be sure that you reflect energy and pride in your performance, whether you are actually playing or singing the song or using a recording.

3. Return to the starting pitch or pitches and play or sing them for the class. Then say "1, 2, ready, sing," or "1, 2, sing," depending on the meter and whether the song begins on an upbeat. Be sure that the speed (tempo) of your "1, 2, . . ." is the same as the tempo of the song—not too fast and not too slow. It is important for students to begin with the first word rather than drift in along the way.

4. Lift your arm to indicate your breathing so that students will also breathe and sing together. Remember: Good breathing, a lot of energy, and the desire to produce a pleasing sound are major factors in achieving good singing. The act of singing is *physical,* not mystical.

5. Give students a signal with your hand when they are to sing. You are *leading* a song, not just singing along with them. If you use a recording, be sure that you know the introduction well and that you can count the beats accurately.

Figure 4.1. Conducting patterns

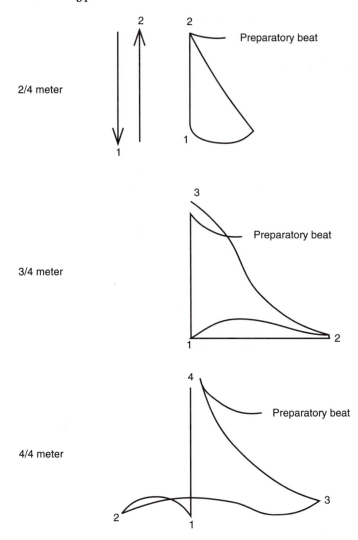

2/4 meter

2

2   Preparatory beat

1

1

3/4 meter

3

Preparatory beat

1   2

4/4 meter

4

Preparatory beat

2   1   3

6. Use the conducting patterns in figure 4.1 to keep the singing together. Be sure that the downbeat is always on l.

7. You may also consider "mapping" the melody—that is, raising or lowering your hands with the melody. Be sure that the style of the gesture fits the mood of the song.

8. So that they end together, give a clear signal to stop students at the end of the song.

9. Look at the students and be supportive. Praise students if they did well, but don't say "good" when the singing was poor. Give them specific suggestions for improvement and then try the song again.

10. Use imagination when leading a song. If students miss the meaning of the song and just sing along, try different ways of singing so that students can express themselves with different moods.

11. Show pride in what you are doing. Become an actor or actress. Leave your troubles outside the classroom. Enjoy the music and make it fun. Both you and your students will enjoy it.

12. Practice leading the following song, suitable for grades 3–5.

Jingle Bells

Pierpont

Key: G
Starting pitch: D
Meter: 2/4, begins on 1
Introduction to tempo: (2 measures) 12 / ready sing

Dash - ing through the snow in a one - horse o - pen sleigh, O'er the fields we

go, Laugh - ing all the way. Bells on bob - tail ring mak - ing spi - rits

bright. What fun it is to ride and sing a sleigh - ing song to - night.

Jin - gle bells, jin - gle bells, jin - gle all the way! Oh, what fun it

is to ride in a one - horse o - pen sleigh!____ Jin - gle bells, jin - gle bells,

jin - gle all the way! Oh, what fun it is to ride in a one - horse o - pen sleigh!

Teaching Songs to Children

There are many ways to teach songs. The three discussed here are rote (both nonconceptual and conceptual), rote-note, and note. You will find many ideas in the basal series textbooks. Most of these are not structured in perfect order for either you or your class, and you will find that adapting the activities may be the most suitable for your teaching skills and style. You may also wish to combine various methods with different songs. Remember that a multisensory approach, in which students hear, see, and physically respond, is one of the most effective.

Teaching students to read music is not very different from teaching them to read poems or stories. Teachers sometimes say, "But I don't read music," as if that is a permanent condition. You can learn to read music, and so can your students. The more songs you teach, the more confident and proficient you will become. Although the saying *Practice makes perfect* may not be totally true, it is a fact that practice can improve one's musical skill.

TEACHING A SONG BY ROTE (NONCONCEPTUAL)

When you teach a song by rote, students learn through imitation. There are no materials in the hands of students; they learn the tune, rhythms, and words through aural memory. Short songs are usually taught in their entirety (whole-song approach); longer songs require teaching single sections or phrases, putting the sections together, and then singing the entire song. The following activities are intended simply to teach the song.

1. Teacher plays or sings the entire song.

2. Perform the song phrase by phrase and have children imitate each phrase in turn. Use your hands to "map" the melody, which gives children a visual reference that indicates whether their voices should be high or low and whether the duration is long or short.

3. Ask children to imitate the motions or actions you perform as you sing the song. Relate your actions to the words of the song so that they become cues to remembering the words. This method is appropriate for children in early childhood classes or primary grades.

4. As you perform the song several times, have children create movements or a game. Often students can perform the song quite soon, because they have heard it many times.

5. Perform the song and leave out a little motion, pattern, or word. Ask students to fill it in at the proper time.

6. As students listen to a performance of the song, ask them to arrange, in order, pictures or charts specified in the song.

7. Students perform the entire song.

Guidelines for Teaching Songs to Children

As you teach songs to children, it is important to remember the following:

1. All children can experience some degree of success in singing activities.

2. If a child cannot match a pitch, it doesn't mean that the child cannot *hear* any difference in pitch; it probably means that the child doesn't know what it *feels* like to match a pitch. Conduct tone-matching activities regularly and frequently.

3. Good singing, like good speech, requires controlled breath.

4. Good singing, like good speech, requires clear diction and articulation.

5. Choose songs with a limited range for young children and beginning singers.

6. Pitch songs for the children, not for the teacher. Generally, an adult voice is much lower than a child's voice. Use a mechanical source to find the pitch (a pitch pipe, recorder, keyboard, autoharp, or Omnichord). Transpose melodies that are too high or too low. (See page 218 for specific activities involving transposition.)

7. Choose a variety of songs representative of different moods, tempos, tonalities, forms, rhythms, and melodies.

8. Choose songs representative of different cultures—both Western and non-Western. Include folk, art, patriotic, fun, ethnic, popular, and children's songs.

9. Choose songs "for the moment" (popular) as well as songs of permanent value.

10. It will be helpful if you can answer the following questions when deciding to use a particular song:

    a. Is it musically expressive? Does it have a sense of completeness and beauty?

    b. Is the melody easily singable? Does it have a comfortable singing range? Are the intervals between notes easily singable?

    c. Is the rhythm interesting?

    d. Is there sufficient repetition and contrast to make the song interesting?

    e. Are the text and length of the song appropriate for a child's maturity and musical abilities?

    f. Do the words appropriately fit the melody and rhythm?

    g. Does the song fit the objectives for the lesson? For example, if your aim is to develop an awareness of ascending and descending melodies, the song must have these characteristics.

NONCONCEPTUAL ROTE LEARNING

Activity: Singing the song "Michael Finnegan"

Grades: 3–4

Concepts: Rhythm: Duple meter
Harmony: Chords F, C
Melody: Repeated phrases

Michael Finnegan

Children's Game Song

Key: F
Starting pitch: C
Meter: 2/4, begins on upbeat

Silver Burdett Music © 1981. By permission of Silver Burdett Company.

Objectives

Students will sing the song expressively with:

1. Good tone quality.
2. Correct pitches.
3. Correct rhythms.
4. Correct words.

Materials

■ Recorder or melody bells, keyboard or Omnichord, or a recording of the song

Procedures

1. Sing or play (recorder, melody bells, keyboard, Omnichord, or recording) the first verse.

2. Read the words to verse 1. Ask students to identify words that rhyme: *Finnegan, chinnegan, in again, begin again.*

3. Discover rhythm patterns that are repeated:

4. Sing or play the song again. This time ask children to clap the meter with you. It is in duple meter with two pulses per measure.

5. Sing each phrase and ask students to imitate. (There are four phrases; repeat each as necessary.)

6. Sing again combining phrases 1 and 2, then 3 and 4.

7. You are now ready to have students sing the entire song. Do the following in order:

    a. Play the F major triad (to set the tonality or key feeling): F A C A F.

    b. Play the first two notes of the song: C, F.

    c. Think about the tempo of the song (remember to keep the same tempo). Play four F major chords on the keyboard or Omnichord and at the same time say, "1, 2, 1, sing." (Note that the song begins on an upbeat.)

8. Follow the same procedure to teach each verse.

Closure

Sing the song and accompany on appropriate instruments.

Assessment

1. Identify those melodic phrases that are the same.

2. Name the words that rhyme. Where do you find them?

3. What does 2/4 mean?

4. Create a pattern and clap it in duple meter. Create a second pattern and clap it in triple meter.

5. Play an F chord on a chording instrument.

TEACHING A SONG BY ROTE (CONCEPTUAL)

In teaching a song by rote with a conceptual emphasis, you focus on some aspect of the song, such as ascending or descending melody, duple meter, beat, or repetition of melodic or rhythmic pattern. Although no notation as such is used, students participate in many activities of an imitative nature. For example, you might clap the duple meter of the song, accenting the first beat. Or you might have students raise their hands when the melody goes up, and lower their hands when the melody goes down. The following teaching strategies focus on a particular concept.

■ **Rhythm:** Focus the students' attention on an aspect of rhythm. For instance, you could clap a rhythm pattern from the song and ask the children to echo it. This could be extended to saying the words or playing the particular rhythm on a classroom percussion instrument.

■ **Pitch:** Focus the students' attention on an aspect of pitch. You could "map" the melody, indicating where it goes high or low or has long or short durations. Tone matching might be included as you ask students to imitate a high pitch or a short pitch pattern. You could also ask students to sing the melody patterns or play them on resonator bells or xylophone.

- **Dynamics:** You could sing the song inappropriately and ask students what purpose loud and soft serves. They can discover which dynamics are most suitable for a particular song or phrase.

- **Form:** Focus the students' attention on an aspect of form. Guide students in discovering the form of the song, such as AB or ABA. Some of the activities in the following sample lesson plan will help students discover which sections of the song are the same and which are different. Perceiving how a song is put together can contribute to speed in learning.

CONCEPTUAL ROTE LEARNING

Activity: Singing the song "Michael Finnegan"

Grades: 2–4

Concepts: Rhythm: Duple meter
             Harmony: Chords F, C

Objectives

Students will:

1. Sing with good tone quality.

2. Sing with correct melody and rhythms.

3. Identify and perform duple meter.

4. Accompany the song on a chording instrument using the F and C chords.

Materials

- Keyboard instrument, Autoharp, Omnichord, or guitar
- Classroom percussion instruments

Procedures

1. Perform the song "Michael Finnegan" in its entirety.

2. Read the words to verse 1. Ask students to identify words that rhyme: *Finnegan, chinnegan, in again, begin again.*

3. Ask students to identify rhythm patterns that are repeated. Have students echo you as you chant them:

4. Sing the words to the song phrase by phrase. (There are four phrases.) Ask students to sing each phrase after you.

5. Sing or play the song again. This time ask students to clap the meter with you. (It is in duple meter with two pulses per measure.)

6. Assign half of the class to sing the song while the other half claps the duple meter, accenting the first beat. Switch assignments and sing through again. Add percussion instruments such as rhythm sticks or claves.

7. Play the two accompaniment chords (F, C) on the keyboard, Autoharp, or Omnichord. Ask an individual student to play these chords.

Closure

Have the class sing "Michael Finnegan" accompanied by a keyboard instrument, Autoharp, or Omnichord and percussion instruments.

Assessment

1. Identify those melodic phrases that are the same.

2. Name words that rhyme and find them in the music.

3. Name, play, and sing the melodic/rhythmic pattern.

4. What does duple meter mean? What does triple meter mean? Which is in the time signature of this song? How do you know?

5. Why would you choose the chords F and C to play and accompany this song?

TEACHING A SONG BY ROTE-NOTE

Teaching a song by the rote-note method involves not only imitating what is heard but also recognizing short melodic or rhythm patterns. You can combine media such as flash cards or posters with the playing or singing of melodic and rhythmic patterns to introduce experiences with music notation.

ROTE-NOTE LEARNING

Activity: Singing the song "Michael Finnegan"

Grades: 2–4

Concepts: Melody: Repetition of phrases and pitches

Objectives

Students will:

1. Recognize repeated phrases of the melody.

2. Recognize repeated pitches of the melody.

Materials

- Accompanying instrument (keyboard, Autoharp, Omnichord, or guitar)
- Charts with repeated patterns
- Colored strips of paper
- Coloring materials
- Copies of song

Procedures

1. Sing or play the song "Michael Finnegan."

2. Use colored strips of paper to represent each phrase—for example, use red for phrase 1, "There was an old man named Michael Finnegan"; yellow for phrase 2, "He had whiskers on his chinnegan"; red for phrase 3, "He pulled them out but they grew in again"; green for phrase 4, "Poor old Michael Finnegan. Begin again." Ask students which phrases are repeated (1 and 4).

3. Use copies of the song so that students can mark the music with colors. Ask them to mark the music with colors that correspond to the strips of paper.

4. Compare the notation of the contrasting phrases. What is different? What is similar? What is the same?

5. Play the five repeated pitches in the first measure of the song (F F F F F). Call attention to their being the same. Play the four repeated pitches in the second phrase (G G G G). Repeat procedure for the third (F F F F) and fourth (F F F F F F F) phrases.

6. Sing or play the song again. Give the starting two pitches (C and F) and ask students to sing the song, tracing in the air the outline of the melody as they sing.

Closure

Play or sing "Michael Finnegan" again.

Assessment

1. Invite students to raise their hands as they sing, when they hear four or more pitches that are the same.

2. Ask them to locate these repeated pitches on their copies of the song.

3. Have students locate phrases of the song where the pitches are not the same.

TEACHING A SONG BY NOTE: THE KODÁLY APPROACH

Teaching a song by note means to teach students to read the music notation. This requires preparation in understanding and conceptualizing the abstract symbols that represent the various elements in music, such as melody, rhythm, and harmony. In teaching most songs to elementary-age children, you will rely heavily on the rote or rote-note approach, but you should introduce the reading of music notation at an early age.

It is important that a child's experience with the sounds of music precede contact with visual symbols. Symbols of music notation take on meaning only when they can be connected to a tonal or rhythmic grouping that has been sung or played. The approach to music reading in this book is based on the Kodály system of tonal and rhythm syllables as practiced in American schools. It is an adaptation of a method of music education developed by the Hungarian composer/educator Zoltán Kodály (1882–1967), who created a method based on the Hungarian language and folk music. The method stresses good singing and music literacy—the ability to read music. And though rhymes and children's game songs are important, body movement is also an effective means of learning.

The Kodály approach focuses on a balance of singing, listening, playing, moving, thinking, and creating. In the Kodály method, pitch discrimination and the concepts of high and low are taught first. Hand signs (adapted from John Curwen's approach in England) contribute to learning music through a combination of eye (seeing), ear (hearing), and body (moving). The philosophy of the Kodály approach is as follows.

- All people capable of lingual literacy are also capable of musical literacy. Learning to read music, like learning to read words, is a taught skill. Knowing how to read this language increases the quality of life itself.

- Singing is the best foundation for musicianship. Singing is as natural an activity as speaking. It is through singing that musical knowledge can be internalized.

- To be most effective, music education must begin with the very young child. It is in his or her early years that a child acquires discrimination in pitch as well as language.

- The folk songs of a child's own linguistic heritage constitute a musical "mother tongue" and therefore should be the vehicle for all early instruction. The natural patterns of rhythm and melody are found in folk music of all cultures. Through folk music, children can gain a sense of identity with the present and continuity with the past.

- Only music of the highest artistic value, both folk and composed, should be used in teaching. All music used with children should have intrinsic value, for it is from this heritage that the child will learn to value good music.

- Music should be at the heart of the curriculum—a core subject used as a basis for education. Music contributes to all phases of a child's development: emotionally, intellectually, physically, and aesthetically.

The tools of the Kodály method are (1) the tonal syllables *do, re, mi, fa, sol, la, ti, do;* (2) hand signs; and (3) rhythm duration syllables.

The first tool, tonal syllables, is based on tonality, and one purpose of this approach is to develop the ear to hear and perform tonal patterns (see figure 4.2).*

Figure 4.2. Tonal syllables: Movable do

---

* Lawrence Wheeler and Lois Raebeck, *Orff and Kodály Adapted for the Elementary School,* 3rd ed. (Dubuque, Iowa: Wm. C. Brown, 1985).

Figure 4.3. Curwen-Kodály hand signs

The second tool of the Kodály approach is the use of hand signs. Originally developed by John Curwen in England in 1870, and somewhat modified for use in Hungarian schools, these hand signs have become an invaluable teaching aid (see figure 4.3).

The third tool of the Kodály method is rhythm duration syllables. Rhythm is taught by patterns and by relative durations over the beat. The rhythm syllables (see figure 4.4) are used widely in North America.*

---

* For a detailed discussion of Kodály methodology, see Robert E. Nye and Vernice T. Nye, *Music in the Elementary School,* 6th ed. (Englewood Cliffs, N.J.: Prentice-Hall, 1992), and Lois Choksy et al., *Teaching Music in the Twentieth Century* (Englewood Cliffs, N.J.: Prentice-Hall, 1986).

Figure 4.4. Chart of Kodály's rhythm duration syllables

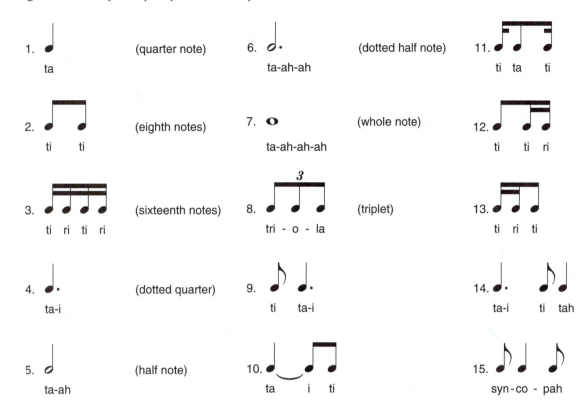

READING MUSIC NOTATION

Activity: Singing the song "Michael Finnegan"

Grades: 3–5

Concepts: Tonal syllables *(do, re, mi, fa, sol, la, ti, do)*

Rhythm syllables: ti-ti   ti-ri-ti-ri

Objectives

Students will:

1. Sing the song by reading the correct pitches using tonal syllables.

2. Sing the song by reading the correct rhythms using rhythm syllables.

3. Sing the song with energy and enthusiasm.

Materials

- Charts with tonal syllable patterns such as *do mi sol, mi re do, sol do, re sol do,* and *ti la sol*

- Chart with tonal scale

- Chart with rhythm syllables

- Keyboard, Omnichord, or guitar; and resonator bells

Procedures

1. Discuss the value of reading music and compare it to reading words. For example, reading music saves time and allows the student to learn many more songs. Reading music also provides the student with a skill that can enhance all musical experiences and activities.

2. Review the meter (2/4) and the key (F major).

3. Sing the F major scale from *do* to *sol* (not the full octave). Practice singing the intervals using charts showing the patterns of the song.

4. Create a game using any combination of *do, re, mi, fa, sol.* Appoint a student as leader and have the rest of the class echo. Use resonator bells or xylophones in place of singing if you wish.

5. Play or sing the song and have students clap the meter beats (1 2 1 2).

6. Introduce rhythm patterns by playing or singing the following for students and having them imitate:

7. Introduce rhythm syllables used in the song:

8. Place the following patterns on charts and ask students to read them using rhythm syllables:

9. Place a copy of the song on a transparency and ask students to read the rhythm using syllables.

10. Sing the F major scale *(do re mi fa sol la ti do)* and then the descending scale *(do ti la sol fa mi re do).*

11. Practice singing tonal syllables from the chart. Locate similar patterns in the song.

12. Sing the song using tonal syllables.

13. Speak the words of the song in rhythm.

14. Sing the entire song from notation.

15. Emphasize the need for singing with good tone color, enthusiasm, and energy.

Closure

Sing the song using tonal syllables and then sing it using rhythm syllables. Finally, sing the song using words.

Assessment

1. In the song "Michael Finnegan," where is *do?* Where is *re, mi, fa, sol?*

2. In the song "Michael Finnegan," what are the rhythm syllables for eighth notes? For sixteenth notes?

3. What advantage do you have when you know tonal syllables? Rhythm syllables? How do they help you learn a song?

4. In the song "Michael Finnegan," what tonal syllables are used?

5. What is the difference between singing a song with a lot of energy and singing one just because the teacher tells you to do it?

SINGING ADDITIVE SONGS

An *additive song* is one that has several verses, each of which piggybacks on the previous verse, for example, "The Twelve Days of Christmas" (see page 112).

Teaching Part Singing

Singing in parts adds an exciting dimension to musical experiences. It is important, however, that a child be able to sing a simple song in tune before trying to sing harmony; thus, part singing is seldom attempted before third grade. Each of the following approaches or songs can be used singly or in combination with a variety of age levels to teach this important skill.

LINING OUT A SONG

Lining out is a technique for learning a song in which each line is presented by a leader and then repeated by a group. If the note at the end of each phrase is sustained (with the voice or an instrument), lining out is a good first step in developing part singing. This is appropriate for grades 3–6.

1. Sing the song phrase by phrase, each time sustaining the pitch of the last note. Ask students to imitate each phrase after you sing it.

2. Divide the class in half and ask one half to begin the song and the other half to answer.

The Twelve Days of Christmas

English Carol

Key: F
Starting pitch: C
Meter: 4/4 (duple), begins on 4

1. On the first day of Christ - mas my true love sent to me: A par - tridge___ in a pear tree.

2. On the sec - ond day of Christ - mas my true love sent to me: Two tur - tle doves and a par - tridge___ in a pear tree.

3. On the third day of Christ - mas my true love sent to me: Three French___ hens, two tur - tle doves, and a par - tridge___ in a pear tree.

4. On the fourth day of Christ - mas my true love sent to me: Four col - ly birds, three French___ hens, two tur - tle doves, and a par - tridge___ in a pear tree.

5. On the fifth day of Christ - mas my true love sent to me:

Five gold-en rings, four___ col-ly birds, three French hens,

two___ tur-tle doves, and a par-tridge___ in a pear tree.

End (Fine)

Go back to the sign and sing to the end (Del Segno al Fine)

6.–12. On the sixth day of Christ-mas my true love sent to me: 6. Six geese a-lay-ing, *(seventh, etc.)*

7. Seven swans a-swimming,

8. Eight maids a-milking,

9. Nine drummers drumming,

10. Ten pipers piping,

11. Eleven ladies dancing,

12. Twelve lords a-leaping,

Old Texas

American Cowboy Song

Key: G
Starting pitch: D
Meter: 2/4, begins on "and" of 1

I'm goin' to leave _____ old ___ Tex - as now; _____

I'm goin' to leave _____ old ___ Tex - as

___ They've got no use _____ for the long - horn cow. _____

now; _____ They've got no use _____ for the long - horn cow.

2. They've plowed and fenced

   My cattle range,

   And the people there

   Are all so strange.

3. I'll take my horse, and I'll take my rope,

   I'll hit the trail upon a lope,

   Say "adios" to the Alamo,

   And turn my face toward Mexico.

SINGING CANONS

A *canon* is a contrapuntal (imitative) musical composition sung by two or more groups in which the melody is imitated exactly and completely by the successive voices, though not always at the same pitch. The song "Salamanca Market"* (which is based on the pentatonic scale: *do, re, mi, sol, la*) is a "canon" song.

---

*The Salamanca Market is in the city of Hobart, Tasmania, an island off the coast of Australia. The market was named after the British general Arthur Wellesley Wellington's victory over France at Salamanca, Spain, in 1812.

Salamanca Market

Words and Music by Mary Goetze

Key: C
Starting pitch: C
Meter: 2/4 (duple), begins on 1

From Macmillan *Share the Music* 3 (1995), pp. 152–53. Reprinted by permission of McGraw-Hill Companies.

SINGING DIALOGUE SONGS OR ECHO SONGS

Dialogue, or *echo*, songs use repetitive phrases in a second voice. "Go, Tell It on the Mountain" is suitable for grades 3–6. "The Keeper" is appropriate for grades 5–6.

Go, Tell It on the Mountain

Spiritual

Key: F
Starting pitch: A
Meter: 4/4, begins on 1

The Keeper

Key: D
Starting pitch: A
Meter: 4/4, begins on 4

English Folk Song

VERSE

A keep-er would a - hunt-ing go, And un-der his cloak he car-ried a bow,

All for to shoot at a mer-rie lit-tle doe, A - mong the leaves so___ green, O!

CHORUS

1. Jack-ie boy! Sing ye well? Hey down, Der-ry, der-ry down! A -

2. Mas - ter? Ver-y well! Ho down! A -

mong the leaves so___ green, O! To my hey, down, down!

mong the leaves so___ green, O! To my ho down, down!

Hey down, Der-ry, der-ry down! A - mong the leaves so___ green, O!

Ho down! A - mong the leaves so___ green,___ O!

(Chorus only)

SINGING CALL-AND-RESPONSE SONGS

A *call-and-response song* is usually one in which a part is sung by a leader, who is answered by people singing the chorus. The two parts may come together, creating harmony at the close, as in the following example, "Tina Singu."

Tina Singu

Song from Lesotho

Key: F
Starting pitch: C
Meter: 4/4 (duple), begins on 1

Sotho: Ti - na sing - u le - lu - vu tae - o. Wat - sha, wat - sha, wat - sha,
Pronunciation: ti na sing u lɛ lu vu tae o wat sha wat sha wat sha

Ti - na, Ti - na sing - u le - lu - vu tae - o.
ti na ti na sing u lɛ lu vu tae o

Wat - sha, wat - sha, wat - sha. wat - sha, la la la la la
wat sha wat sha wat sha wat sha la la la la la

Reprinted by permission of McGraw-Hill Companies.

ADDING DESCANTS

A *descant* is a melody that is sung or played above the primary melody. A simple descant can be created by using the individual notes of the song's chords with an occasional "passing" tone. In the following song, "Did You Ever See a Lassie?" a basic descant has been created from the fifth (C) and third (A) of the F chord, and the fifth (G) of the C7 chord. You may also wish to add chord roots to the song "It's a Small World."

Did You Ever See a Lassie?

Key: F
Starting pitch: F
Meter: 3/4, begins on 3

German Folk Song
Arr. by Joy E. Lawrence

The descant in "Did You Ever See a Lassie?" has been created from the following chords. The bottom pitch is the root. (See chapter 6 for a more detailed discussion and suggestions for instruments.)

It's a Small World

Key: G
Starting pitch: B
Meter: 2/2, begins on 2

Words and Music by Richard M. Sherman and Robert B. Sherman
Arr. by Joy E. Lawrence

1. It's a world of laugh-ter, a world of tears; it's a world of
2. There is just one moon and one gold-en sun; and a smile means

hopes and a world of fears. There's so much that we share, that it's
friend-ship to ev-'ry-one. Though the moun-tains di-vide and the

time we're a-ware. It's a small world, af-ter all._____
o-ceans are wide. It's a small world, af-ter all._____

REFRAIN

It's a small world, af-ter all. It's a small world af-ter all.

It's a small world, af-ter all, it's a small, small world._____

Chords

Descant created from these chord roots

Percussion pattern

Claves

Triangles

You can also create harmony by singing the verse and chorus at the same time, as you would do in a partner song.

He's Got the Whole World in His Hands

Key: D
Starting pitch: A
Meter: 4/4, begins on "and" of 3

Spiritual

He's got the whole world___ in His hands___ He's got the

whole world___ in His hands___ He's got the whole world___

in His hands___ He's got the whole world in His hands.___

2. He's got the wind and rain in His hands. (3 times)
   He's got the whole world in His hands.

3. He's got you and me brother in His hands. (3 times)
   He's got the whole world in His hands.

4. He's got everybody in His hands. (3 times)
   He's got the whole world in His hands.

Descant (created from chord roots)

Percussion

Drums

Shaker
(Rattle)

ADDING COUNTERMELODIES

A *countermelody* is a second melody, which may be above or below the main melody.

1. Start by having students sing the melody of "Oh, Be Joyful."

2. Play the two countermelodies on the facing page. You may use a recorder, melody or resonator bells, or a xylophone.

3. Ask the class to sing the melody as you play the countermelody.

4. Sing each countermelody with the suggested words. Ask individual students to reinforce on the instruments.

5. Play and sing the entire song, adding the accompaniment ensembles.

You may wish to perform the song in the following order:

1. Verses 1 and 2 sung in unison, accompanied by keyboard or Omnichord.

2. Verse 1 sung a second time with countermelody 1 sung or played on a keyboard, resonator bells, or a xylophone. Omnichord plays chords.

3. Verse 2 sung a second time with countermelody 2 sung or played on a keyboard, a recorder, resonator bells, or a xylophone. Omnichord plays chords.

4. Instrumental interlude played by instrumental ensemble only. Omnichord plays chords.

5. Verse 3 sung in unison with instrumental ensemble accompanying. Omnichord plays chords.

Oh, Be Joyful

Key: C
Starting pitch: C
Meter: 4/4, begins on 1

From Gaudeamus Hodie
Words and Music by Natalie Sleeth

1. Oh, be joy-ful, Oh, be ju - bi-lant, Put your sor - rows far a - way.
2. We will sing a song of friend - ship, We will raise our voic - es strong.

We re - joice and sing to - geth - er this hap - py day.
We'll re - joice and sing to - geth - er the whole day long.

Countermelody 1

Oh, be joy - ful, Oh, be joy - ful on this day.

Countermelody 2

Oh, be joy - ful, Oh, be joy - ful, Oh, be joy - ful, put your sor-rows a - way.

Bells or recorders

SINGING OSTINATO CHANTS

An *ostinato* is a repeated melodic or rhythmic pattern. "The Cuckoo" is suitable for grades 4–5. "Zum Gali Gali" is appropriate for grades 4–6.

The Cuckoo

Key: G
Starting pitch: B
Meter: 3/4, begins on 3

Austrian Folk Song
Ostinato: Joy E. Lawrence

1. O I went to Pe - ter's flow - ing spring Where the wa - ter's so good, And I
2. Af - ter Eas - ter come sun - ny days That will melt all the snow; Then I'll
3. When I've mar - ried my maid - en fair, What then can I de - sire? O a

heard there the cuck - oo As she called from the wood.
mar - ry my maid - en fair, We'll be hap - py, I know.
home for her tend - ing And some wood for the fire.

REFRAIN

Ho - li - ah, Ho - le - rah - hi - hi - ah, Ho - le - rah cuck - oo! Ho - le - rah - hi - hi - ah

Ho - le - rah cuck - oo! Ho - le - rah - hi - hi - ah, Ho - le - rah cuck - oo! Ho - le - rah - hi - hi - ah - ho!

OSTINATO

Ho - le - rah cuck - koo - koo, Ho - le - rah cuck - koo - koo, Ho - le - rah cuck - coo - coo - Ho - le - rah cuck - koo - koo,

Ho - le - rah cuck - koo - koo, Ho - le - rah cuck - koo - koo, Ho - le - rah cuck - koo - koo Ho.

1. Have the class sing the song.

2. Accompany on keyboard, Autoharp, Omnichord, or guitar while the class sings the song.

3. Chant the word rhythms of the ostinato. Ask the class to imitate.

4. Sing the ostinato on pitches. Ask the class to sing the ostinato.

5. Have half of the class sing or play the ostinato while the other half sings the refrain.

Rhythm ostinato

Zum Gali Gali

Key: E minor
Starting pitch: E
Meter: 2/4, begins on 1

Israeli Folk Song

1. Sing or play the ostinato used in "Zum Gali Gali."

2. Play the E minor chord on a keyboard, Autoharp, Omnichord, or guitar while the class sings the ostinato.

3. Perform the song with accompaniment. Have part of the class sing the ostinato while the rest sing the melody.

4. Add the following rhythms on drum, claves, and tambourine:

SINGING ROUNDS

A *round* consists of exact imitation of a given melody sung one or two measures later. Singing rounds can help a child begin to comprehend the concept of harmony. There are several steps to follow for such singing to be successful:

1. The melody must be learned very well.

2. As children sing the song, play the melody as a round (that is, beginning a measure or two later). Use melody bells or a recorder, which will enable the children to hear the melody as a second part while singing.

3. Choose the best singers to sing the second part of the round. Encourage them to be on their own.

4. Do not try a three- or four-part round until children are secure with two parts.

Sing the following rounds. Begin with two parts, gradually adding a third or fourth part. "Kookaburra" is appropriate for grades 3–4; "Dona Nobis Pacem" is appropriate for grades 4–6.

Australian Folk Song

Key: D
Starting pitch: A
Meter: 2/4, begins on 1

Kook - a - bur - ra sits on an old gum tree,___ Mer - ry, mer - ry king of the bush is he.___

Laugh, kook - a - bur - ra, laugh, kook - a - bur - ra, Gay your life must be.

Dona Nobis Pacem

Key: F
Starting pitch: F
Meter: 3/4, begins on 1

Traditional

SINGING PARTNER SONGS

The creation of a *partner song* involves the following considerations.

1. The two songs must be about the same length.

2. The two songs must be in the same key.

3. The meter must be the same; that is, both songs need to be in duple or triple meter.

4. The words may or may not be similar, but partner songs work best together when the text of one complements that of the other.

Following are two partner songs. See if you can determine how the guidelines fit. Students will find that they can sing them together when they know both songs well.

Cielito Lindo

Partner: "My Bonnie"
Key: B♭
Starting pitch: F
Meter: 3/4, begins on 1
Combines an ostinato on the verse with the partner song on the chorus

Mexican Folk Song

Bring back my señ - or - i - ta.

Bring back my señ - or - i - ta.

If

you will go___ down to Mex - i - co___ you will

Bring back my señ - or - i - ta.

meet a hap - py señ - or - i - ta.___

Bring back my señ - or - i - ta.

All Night, All Day

Partner: "Swing Low, Sweet Chariot"
Spiritual
Key: F
Starting pitches: C, A
Meter: 4/4, begins on C and A

All night, all day, An - gels watch - ing o - ver

Swing low, sweet char - i - ot,___ com - in' for to car - ry me

me, my Lord.___ All night, all day,

home! Swing___ low, sweet char - i - ot,___

An - gels watch - ing o - ver me. 1. Now I lay me
2. If I die be -

com - in' for to car - ry me home!

down___ to sleep, An - gels watch - ing o - ver me, my Lord.___
fore___ I wake,

Com - in' for to car - ry me home.

For Your Journal

In your journal or portfolio, make a section on singing. Be sure to include:

- Differences in vocal characteristics and abilities of children in preschool and kindergarten (ages 4 and 5), grades 1 and 2 (ages 6 and 7), grades 3 and 4 (ages 8 and 9), and grades 5 and 6 (ages 10 and 11)

- Differences in song interests in preschool and kindergarten (ages 4 and 5), grades 1 and 2 (ages 6 and 7), grades 3 and 4 (ages 8 and 9), and grades 5 and 6 (ages 10 and 11)

- Techniques for teaching children to sing

- Steps in preparing to teach a song

- How to lead a song

- Teaching a song by rote, rote-note, and note

- Teaching part singing, including lining out a song; singing canons, dialogue or echo songs, and call-and-response songs; adding descants and countermelodies; and singing ostinato chants, rounds, and partner songs

*I*ntegrating Songs with Other Subjects and Activities

MUSIC SHOULD BE AN INTEGRAL PART of a child's daily life. One of the unique opportunities that the classroom teacher enjoys is introducing many musical experiences into the day's activities. Songs can be used to develop physical coordination; teach phonics; provide opportunities for creative dramatics; contribute to a greater understanding and appreciation of peoples, places, and cultures; and bring new meanings to the study of history. Holidays such as Halloween, Thanksgiving, Christmas, and Hanukkah have traditionally used songs to express feelings appropriate to the celebration. Other areas in the elementary curriculum that lend themselves to the use of music include the study of animals, learning about community helpers, and expressing ideas about nature (spring, summer, autumn, and winter).

The following integrative categories are of special interest to elementary-age children:

- Action
- Animals
- Circus
- Social studies
  - Geography
  - History (famous people/events)
- Holidays
  - Rosh Hashanah (Jewish New Year)
  - Halloween
  - Thanksgiving, Sukkot, and Shavuot

- Hanukkah
- Christmas
- Kwanzaa
- New Year's Day
- Martin Luther King Jr. Day
- Chinese New Year
- Valentine's Day
- Presidents' Day—George Washington and Abraham Lincoln
- Saint Patrick's Day
- Patriotic songs of the United States of America
- Getting acquainted
- Human relationships and emotions
- Language arts
- Mathematics
- Science
- Seasons
  - Spring
  - Summer
  - Autumn
  - Winter
- Transportation

Representative songs have been selected for many of these categories, and materials and suggestions for planning lessons are provided. You are encouraged to create your own lessons from the suggestions that follow each song. The authors recognize that additional holidays are celebrated by various groups and we urge the classroom teacher to develop appropriate activities that highlight these special days.

You will find lists of additional songs as well as CD-ROMs and videos at the end of each integrative unit. These have been selected for a variety of grade levels and abilities. You are encouraged to teach these songs, which can be found in the basal music series of your school, to add to the list of integrative categories, and to devise other interesting ways to include songs in the classroom.

Integrative Category: Action

"THE HOKEY POKEY"

Grades:	K–1
Integrative area:	Action/coordination
Concepts:	Melody: Narrow range
	Rhythm: Steady beat, duple meter, repeated patterns

The Hokey Pokey

Key: G
Starting pitch: D
Meter: 4/4, begins on "and" of 3

American Folk Song

Moderately and rhythmically

You put your
{ right hand in, _____
left hand in, _____
right foot in, _____
left foot in, _____
whole self in, _____ }
You take your
{ right hand out, _____
left hand out, _____
right foot out, _____
left foot out, _____
whole self out, _____ }
You put your

{ right hand in _____
left hand in _____
right foot in _____
left foot in _____
whole self in _____ }
And shake it all a - bout. And then you do the ho - key po - key and you

turn your - self a - bout; And that's what it's all a - bout. Hey!

Objectives

Students will:

1. Sing the song with good tone quality.
2. Indicate their knowledge of a narrow melodic range.
3. Clap the steady beat.
4. Clap in quadruple meter.
5. Perform repeated rhythmic and melodic patterns.
6. Perform appropriate movements.

Materials

- Chart showing narrow and wide ranges
- Individual charts: D E F♯ G and sample keyboard (either a cardboard keyboard, a piano, or an electronic keyboard)
- Chart showing a steady beat
- Chart showing the following repeated rhythm pattern:

(2 times)

- Drum and tambourine

Procedures

1. Warm up voices by using techniques for developing the head voice (see p. 85).

2. Sing the song or play a recording. Ask students to clap the steady beat as they listen.

3. Sing the song or play a recording and ask students what word they might say or sing for the highest note.

4. Show the chart that indicates a narrow range of sound. Match with the appropriate word.

5. Play D and G on the xylophone and show children that these pitches are close together, meaning that this music has a narrow range.

6. Select students to hold each letter and ask other students to count the number of letters in between. Use this visual to reinforce the sound of a narrow range.

7. Sing or play a recording of the song again. Ask students to clap the steady beat and accent the first and third beats. Be careful with the syncopation.

8. Perform the song again. Ask students how many times they can hear the following rhythm pattern:

    (10)

9. Ask students to sing the song, and select one student to play the repeated pattern on the tambourine.

10. Have students stand and imitate your motions as you sing the song or play a recording.

Closure

Ask students to form a circle and, as they sing the song, do the motions suggested by the words. Accompany on the drum (steady beat) and tambourine (repeated pattern).

Assessment

1. Review the concept of narrow range by asking students to define the term and point to it on the appropriate chart.

2. Ask a student to illustrate steady beat and quadruple meter by clapping.

3. Ask a student to play on the tambourine the rhythm pattern that was repeated.

4. Ask students what motions were referred to in the words of the song.

5. While still in the circle, ask children to sing the song and do the motions. Ask two children to accompany on drum and tambourine.

"IF YOU'RE HAPPY"

Grades:	K–1
Integrative areas:	Action: Movement, coordination
Concepts:	Melody: Steps-skips, repetition
	Rhythm: Quadruple
	Tone color: Rhythm sticks, drum

If You're Happy

Key: F
Starting pitch: C
Meter: 4/4, begins on 4

Traditional

Suggestions for Lessons

1. Have children act out the directions in the song.

2. Discuss things we do when we're happy (smile, clap hands, and so on). Identify many words that describe happiness.

3. Play the game "Simon Says" to encourage the use of right and left ("Simon says, raise your right hand," and so forth).

4. Add rhythm instruments (rhythm sticks, drum) to accompany the song.

More Songs: Action

- "Che Che Koolay" in Silver Burdett *Music* 3, p. 34; Silver Burdett *Music* 2, p. 55
- "How D'ye Do and Shake Hands" in Silver Burdett *Music* 3, p. 144; Holt, Rinehart and Winston *Music Book* 1, p. 4
- "Little Red Caboose" in Silver Burdett Ginn *World of Music* K, p. 72
- "Little Tommy Tinker" in Macmillan *Music and You* 2, p. 231
- "One Finger, One Thumb" in Macmillan *Music and You* K, p. 109; Silver Burdett Ginn *World of Music* K, p. 120
- "Shake My Sillies Out" in Silver Burdett Ginn *The Music Connection* 1 (2000), p. 292

Integrative Category: Animals

"MY BIG BLACK DOG"

Grades: K–1

Integrative areas: Improvisation, creativity, movement, coordination, farm, chickens, dramatics, vocabulary

Concepts: Melody: Steps and skips
                     Tempo: Moderate
                     Rhythm: Steady, mostly quarter and eighth notes

My Big Black Dog

Key: F
Starting pitch: F
Meter: 4/4, begins on 4

English Play Song

Materials

- Picture of dogs
- Recording of song (optional)

Objectives

Students will:

1. Identify melodic steps and skips.

2. Decide on an appropriate tempo.

3. Identify walking notes (quarter notes) and running notes (eighth notes).

4. Sing with energy and correct words, pitches, and rhythms.

Procedures

1. Show pictures of various kinds of dogs, ending with a picture of a big black dog.

2. Ask whether anyone in the class has a big black dog.

3. Where would you find chicks? (On a farm)

4. What is the difference between a "crack" and a "fence"?

5. Sing the song or play a recording.

6. Teach the song by rote—using your hand to indicate skips.

7. Ask students which words and music are the same. ("Whoever took my big black dog")

8. Have students sing the song with you or with the recording.

9. Guide students in creative motions for the following phrases:
   a. Big black dog
   b. Bring him back
   c. Big chicks over the fence
   d. Little chicks through the crack

10. Ask half the class to sing the song; ask the other half to do the motions. Then have them change roles.

Closure

When the students know the song and motions very well, ask them to do both.

Assessment

1. Is the song mostly steps or skips?

2. What are some words that skip with the music? ("Whoever took my big black dog")

3. How would you decide how fast to sing the song?

4. Do you sing mostly quarter notes (walking) or eighth notes (running)?

5. What is the song about? Who is the main character?

"THE ELEPHANT"

Grades:	1–2
Integrative areas:	Zoo study, circus study, dramatics, visual art, vocabulary
Concepts:	Melody: Low register, mostly steps
	Tempo: Slow/fast, contrast
	Form: ABA

The Elephant

Key: A
Starting pitch: C#
Meter: 4/4, song begins on "and" of 4

Words and Music by Hap Palmer

From HAP PALMER'S FAVORITES, published by Alfred Publishing Co., Inc. Copyright © 1971, 1976 HAP-PAL MUSIC INC.

Objectives

Students will:

1. Identify the low register of the song as distinct from a high register.
2. Identify the frequency of steps with occasional skips.
3. Perform appropriate tempos: slow, fast.
4. Define the meaning of ABA form.

Materials

- Pictures of elephants, lions, birds
- Charts with words: *elephant, lion, bird, jungle, rumble, hunter* (Be sure children can read words)
- Recordings of Saint-Saëns's *Carnival of the Animals* and Debussy's "Jimbo's Lullaby" from *The Children's Corner Suite*
- Chart or transparency with song
- Cards marked *A, B,* and *A*
- Omnichord, autoharp, or keyboard

Procedures

1. Show pictures of elephants. Discuss their size and slow movements.
2. Play the recording of Saint-Saëns's "The Elephant" from *Carnival of the Animals*. Discuss the character of sound that the composer selected to represent an elephant. Follow the same procedure with Debussy's "Jimbo's Lullaby" from *The Children's Corner Suite*.
3. Sing the song or play a recording. Identify other animals mentioned in the song (tigers, lions, birds).
4. Teach the melody by imitation (rote) as follows. Hold up appropriate vocabulary card as needed.
   a. The elephant moves very slowly, oh so very slowly. He doesn't like to move too fast, because he is so big and fat. (Cards: *elephant, slowly, fast, big, fat*)
   b. But should he see a tiger or spy a mean old hunter, he will start to run and shake the ground, and make them all fall down. (Cards: *tiger, hunter, shake, fall*)
   c. Rumble, rumble, rumble, hear the jungle rumble. Rumble, rumble, rumble, hear the jungle rumble. (Cards: *rumble, jungle*)
   d. Trees shake and sway as the birdies fly away; lions run and hide with their babies by their side. (Cards: *trees, birdies, lions, babies*)

   Sing (a) and (b) a second time.
5. Sing the song or play a recording. Ask students to identify whether the song is mostly high or mostly low.
6. Sing the song or play a recording. Ask students to identify where the song gets faster and slower. What words indicate the faster tempo of the song?
7. Ask students to sing the song with you. While all sing, ask half the class to stand on the slow part and the other half to stand on the fast part.
8. Ask students to sing the song again, and in the first phrase identify which words move by steps and which move by skips. Follow the same procedure for subsequent phrases.

9. Indicate with cards marked *A, B,* and *A* that the song has three sections. Sing or play a recording of the song. Ask students to indicate when the A section begins and when the B section begins by pointing to the appropriate card.

Closure

Sing the entire song accompanied by keyboard, Autoharp, or Omnichord.

Assessment

1. Ask students which words are in the low register.

2. Ask students to identify where the music moves by steps or skips (words).

3. Ask students to identify where the music goes fast and where it goes more slowly.

4. As you perform the song, ask students to identify by pointing to the appropriate card when the song is in the A section, when it is in the B section, and when it is in the A section again.

"SIX LITTLE DUCKS"

Grades:	K–1
Integrative areas:	Dramatics, movement, visual art, science, vocabulary
Concepts:	Rhythm: Steady beat, duple meter
	Melody: Large skips

Key: F
Starting pitch: A
Meter: 4/4, begins on 1

Traditional American

Suggestions for Lessons

1. Dramatize "Six Little Ducks" with movements.

2. Draw pictures of ducks in a pond or walking toward a pond. Show pictures of baby ducks and a mother duck.

3. Discuss characteristics of ducks, such as the facts that they swim, have wings, have webbed feet, and so on. Combine with a science unit on animals found around water, such as frogs and fish.

4. Create stick puppets to represent the ducks. Dramatize the song.

"COUNTING UP THE DINOSAUR"

Grades:	1–4
Integrated areas:	Language arts, social studies, mathematics
Concepts:	Repetition and contrast
	Steps and skips
	Notation: ♩ ♫ ♩
	Rhythm patterns: 𝄴 ♩ ♫ ♩ ‖

Counting Up the Dinosaur

Key: B♭
Starting pitch: B♭
Meter: 2/2, begins on 1

Words and Music by David Eddleman

One di - no - saur, two di - no - saur, three di - no - saur,
Eight di - no - saur, nine di - no - saur, ten di - no - saur, e -

four di - no - saur, five di - no - saur, six di - no - saur,
leven di - no - saur, twelve di - no - saur, thirteen di - no - saur,

First Ending

sev - en di - no - saur or more.

Objectives

Students will:

1. Describe a dinosaur.

2. Count the dinosaurs. (15)

3. Pronounce each of the following and identify by sight:

   a. Stegosaurus

   b. Dinosaur

   c. Brontosaurus

   d. Tyrannosaurus Rex

4. Identify more than one ending and the coda.

5. Sing B♭ (= 1) C (= 2) D (= 3) C (= 4) B♭ (= 5) A (= 6) B♭ (= 7)

6. Sing "fourteen dinosaurs" up the scale and "fifteen dinosaurs" up a different scale.

7. Identify steps and skips by ear and by sight.

8. Identify by ear and by sight the six rhythms that repeat in the refrain: $\frac{2}{2}$ ♩ ♫ ♩

Materials

- Pictures of dinosaurs and other prehistoric animals. (Look up information on and pictures of dinsoaurs on the Internet.)

- Charts with words: *Stegosaurus, Dinosaur, Brontosaurus, Tyrannosaurus Rex*

- Keyboard, Autoharp, or Omnichord

- Transparency of song lyrics

- Overhead projector

Preliminary Experiences

1. Ask students to discuss who "Barney" is on TV.

2. Show pictures and discuss dinosaurs: when they lived, what they ate, how big they were, what family they belonged to, and so on.

Procedures

1. Show pictures of the animals on the charts and ask students to link the word with the proper picture.

2. Sing the song (first verse only).

3. Show the different endings and the coda in the musical score.

4. Sing the song again while pointing out the endings and coda.

5. Use hand signals to indicate where the melody goes down; sing the refrain.

6. Say the words of the refrain and ask students to imitate.

7. Ask students to sing the refrain.

8. Ask students to identify the half notes that go up and down (B♭, C, D, C, B♭, A). Sing the refrain again.

9. Sing the coda yourself.

10. Ask students to sing the coda with you.

11. Ask students to sing the refrain and coda. (Follow the directions for "Leading a Song" p. 97.)

12. Sing the song and ask students to join in the refrain with proper ending and then the coda.

13. Place transparency of song on an overhead projector and ask students how many times the same melody occurs. (two measures—two times)

14. Ask students to identify by pointing to lines in the verse that have the same rhythm. (1, 2, 3, 4)

15. Read the words of the first verse together and then sing. Read the words of the second verse together and then sing. Do for each verse.

Closure

Sing the song through (all the verses and the refrain).

Assessment

1. Students will describe dinosaurs.

2. Students will pronounce the words from the chart: *Stegosaurus, Dinosaur, Brontosaurus, Tyrannosaurus Rex.*

3. Ask students to count the number of dinosaurs in the song.

4. Ask students to identify the two endings and how they are different.

5. Ask students to define a coda.

6. Ask students to show how the refrain goes up and down by half notes.

7. Ask students to identify steps and skips by sight and by ear.

8. Ask students to identify the rhythm pattern that repeats in the refrain and the one that repeats in the verse.

More Songs: Animals

- "All the Pretty Little Horses" in Silver Burdett *Music* 3, p. 48; Holt, Rinehart and Winston *Music Book 2,* p. 79

- "Animal Farm" in Macmillan *Music and You* 3, p. 144

- "Barnyard Song" in Macmillan *Music and You* 2, p. 52; Holt, Rinehart and Winston *Music Book* 2, p. 120

- "The Cat" in Holt, Rinehart and Winston *Music Book* 2, p. 36; Silver Burdett Ginn *World of Music* 2, p. 110

- "Doggie Doggie" in Macmillan *Share the Music* 1 (1995), p. 286

- "Donkey, Donkey" in Macmillan *Share the Music* 2 (1995), p. 120

- "Ducklings" in Macmillan *Music and You* 1, p. 216, and K, p. 187

- "Frog in the Bog" in Holt, Rinehart and Winston *The Music Book* 2, p. 118

- "Frog in the Pond" in Silver Burdett Ginn *World of Music* K, p. 130

- "Grizzly Bear" in Silver Burdett Ginn *The Music Connection* 1 (2000), p. 5

Integrative Category: Circus

"CIRCUS PARADE"

Grades:	3–5
Integrative areas:	Creative dramatics, visual art
Concepts:	Rhythm: Quadruple meter; 4/4, steady beat
	Melody: Skips, contour, contrasting second melodic phrase, accidental (F♯)
	Form: Two-part: AB

Circus Parade

Key: C
Starting pitch: G
Meter: 4/4, begins on 3

Words and Music by Milton Kaye

1. Oh, here comes the cir-cus band, Ta-ra-ra-ra, ta-ra-ra-ra-ra. Here comes the

cir-cus band, Ta-ra-ra-ra-ra-ra! Zing! Zing! Zing! Zing!

Ta-ra-ra-ra, Ta-ra-ra-

ra. Oh, how much I love the cir-cus, Ta-ra-ra! Boom! Boom!

Reprinted by permission of Milton Kaye.

Objectives

Students will:

1. Perform the song while clapping or tapping a steady beat.

2. Identify the use of an accidental (F♯) throughout song, both visually and aurally.

3. Demonstrate an understanding of the contrasting second melodic phrase through singing or playing an instrument.

4. Identify the two sections of the song (verse and refrain) through charts (AB).

Materials

- Pictures of circuses

- Written score of song for each student or transparency of song for use with an overhead projector

- Xylophone, resonator bells, and drums

- Individual cards in two colors and marked *A* and *B*

- Charts showing steady beat and the word *quadruple* (for older children)

Procedures

1. Show pictures of a circus and a circus band.

2. Discuss the events, people, and animals found in a circus.

3. Sing or play a recording of "Circus Parade." Ask students to clap a steady beat, accenting the first beat as they listen.

4. Ask students to circle each F♯ on their copies, or ask a student to circle the F♯ on the transparency.

5. Point out that the F♯ is only a half step below G, and that is very close. Sing or play the distance from G to F♯. Ask how many times this pattern occurs in the song. (six times)

6. Have students read the words from their scores or from a chart or transparency (for students who can read).

7. Sing or play a recording of the song. Ask students to sing the verse and top melody of the chorus.

8. Read the verse of the song with Kodály rhythm syllables: Ta-ah = ♩, Ta = ♪, Ti = ♪, Ta-ah-ah-ah = 𝅝, Ta-i = ♩. Ask students to listen to the melody as you sing or play a recording. Sing the verse of the song and the refrain (top melody only), using rhythm syllables.

9. Ask the class to sing the entire song with words.

10. Ask a student to play on the xylophone or resonator bells the four pitches that make up the descending melodic phrase: F E D C. These are found in the refrain. The rest of the class should map the direction of these pitches with their hands.

11. Ask students to sing the top line and selected students to play the contrasting melody on instruments.

12. Use a drum for the last "Boom, boom." Sing the refrain again, using xylophone and resonator bells for the descending melody and the drum for the final two notes.

Closure

Ask the class to sing the song with instruments used at appropriate places.

Assessment

1. Sing or play a recording of the song. Ask students which chart shows a steady beat and whether they tap two or four beats in each measure.

2. Show a chart of the interval G–F♯ and ask a student to demonstrate the sound of these two pitches by singing or playing an instrument.

3. Ask students to locate G–F♯ in their musical scores. Discuss how many times this pattern appears.

4. Sing or play a recording of the song and ask students which charts they might use to diagram the form (AB) or (ABA).

More Songs: Circus

- ■ "Carousel" in Holt, Rinehart and Winston *Exploring Music* 2, p. 64
- ■ "Circus" in Macmillan *Share the Music* 2 (1995), p. 311
- ■ "Circus Band" in Holt, Rinehart and Winston *Exploring Music* 7, p. 134
- ■ "Circus Parade" in Silver Burdett Ginn *World of Music* 2, p. 14
- ■ "He's a Clown" in Silver Burdett Ginn *World of Music* 3, p. 172

Integrative Category: Social Studies—Geography

"GATATUMBA"

Grades:	3–6
Integrative areas:	Culture, vocabulary, dramatics
Concepts:	Rhythm: Steady beat, mostly eighth notes
	Melody: Narrow range, repeated phrases
	Harmony: Mostly thirds

Gatatumba

Key: C
Starting pitch: G
Meter: 2/4, begins on 2

Spanish Folk Song
Arr. Francis Girard
English Version Rosemary Jacques

Hur - ry, hur - ry, Ga - ta - tumba, Bring the tam - bour - ine and drum. Hur - ry,
Ga - ta - tum - ba, tum - ba, tum - ba, Con pan - de - ras y so - najas, Ga - ta -

hur - ry, Ga - ta - tumba, All is read - y, won't you come? Hur - ry,
tum - ba, tum - ba, tum - ba, No te me - tas en las pajas, Ga - ta -

hur - ry, Ga - ta - tumba, Strike the bell and let it ring. Hur - ry,
tum - ba, tum - ba, tum - ba, To - ca el pi - to y el ra - bel. Ga - ta -

hur - ry, Ga - ta - tumba, Ev - 'ry - bod - y wants to sing!
tum - ba, tum - ba, tum - ba, Tam - bo - ril y cas - ca - bel.

The Spanish words of "Gatatumba" are pronounced as follows:

Ga-ta-tum-ba, tum-ba, tum-ba,
Gah-tah-toom-bah toom-bah toom-bah

Ga-ta-tum-ba, tum-ba, tum-ba,
Gah-tah-toom-bah toom-bah toom-bah

Con pan-de-ras y so na-jas,
Kohn pahn-deh-rahs ee soh-nah-hahs

To-ca el pi-to y el ra-bel.
Toh-kahl pee-toh yehl rah-behl

Ga-ta-tum-ba, tum-ba, tum-ba,
Gah-tah-toom-bah toom-bah toom-bah

Ga-ta-tum-ba, tum-ba, tum-ba,
Gah-tah-toom-bah toom-bah toom-bah

No te me-tas en las pa-jas,
Noh teh meh-tahs en lahs pah-hahs

Tam-bo-ril y cas-ca-bel.
Tahm-boh-reel ee kahs-kah-behl

Instrumental ensemble

Bass xylophone

Recorder (as a drone)

Drum (throughout)

Suggestions for Lessons

1. Locate Spain on a world map. Notice its relationship to surrounding areas (southern Europe, bounded by sea).

2. Discuss which Spanish instruments could be used to accompany the song (guitar, castanets).

3. View pictures of Spanish dress, cathedrals, and dances.

4. Discuss the use of the Spanish language in the United States (southern and southwestern states).

"ROLL ON, COLUMBIA"

Grades: 4–6

Integrative areas: Geography, science

Concepts: Rhythm: Steady beat, 3/4 meter, repeated patterns
                     Melody: Moves mostly by steps, narrow range
                     Texture/harmony: Descant on top provides harmony; harmony mostly in thirds or sixths; chords: F, B♭, C₇
                     Form: Two sections: verse and refrain, AB

Roll On, Columbia

Words by Woody Guthrie
Music based on "Goodnight, Irene" by Huddie Ledbetter and John Lomax

Key: F
Starting pitch: C
Meter: 3/4, begins on 1

1. Green Doug-las fir where the wa-ters cut through, Down her wild
2. Oth-er big riv-ers add pow-er to you: Yak-i-ma,
(3.) Bon-ne-ville now there are ships in the locks. The wa-ter has
(4.) on up the riv-er is the Grand Cou-lee Dam: The big-gest thing

moun-tains and can-yons she flew, Ca-na-di-an North-west to the
Snake, and the Klick-i-tat, too. San-dy, Wil-lam-ette, and the
ris-en and cov-ered the rocks. Ship-loads a-plen-ty are
built by the hand of a man To run the great fac-t'ries and

o-cean so blue, Roll on, Co-lum-bia, roll on.
Hood Riv-er, too
soon past the docks,
wa-ter the land.

3. At
4. And

REFRAIN
Countermelody

Roll-ing a-long, roll-ing a-long, roll-ing a-long, Co-lum-bia, roll on. Your

Roll on, Co-lum-bia, roll on. Roll on, Co-lum-bia, roll on. Your

pow-er is turn-ing our dark-ness to dawn. Roll on, Co-lum-bia, roll on, roll on.

pow-er is turn-ing our dark-ness to dawn. Roll on, Co-lum-bia, roll on.

Suggestions for Lessons

1. Review the location of the Columbia River and the function of the Grand Coulee Dam. (Look up information about the Columbia River and Grand Coulee Dam on the Internet.)

2. Perform the rhythm of the song by clapping a steady beat and accenting the first beat of each measure (triple meter).

3. Play or sing the harmony (countermelody) found in the refrain.

4. Ask students to read pitches using solfège or rhythm syllables.

More Songs: Social Studies—Geography

- "Crescent Moon" (China) in Silver Burdett Ginn *World of Music* 5, pp. 76–77
- "Deep in the Heart of Texas" in Silver Burdett Ginn *The Music Connection* 3 (2000), p. 132
- "Going to Boston" in Macmillan *Music and You* 5, p. 15
- "Hawaiian Rainbows" in Silver Burdett Ginn *World of Music* 2, p. 40
- "Land of the Silver Birch" (Canada) in Silver Burdett Ginn *World of Music* 5, pp. 80–81
- "Laredo" in Silver Burdett Ginn *World of Music* 5, pp. 72–73
- "Lone Star Trail" in Silver Burdett Ginn *World of Music* 2, p. 17
- "My Home's in Montana" in Macmillan *Music and You* 3, p. 48; Silver Burdett Ginn *World of Music* 3, p. 20; Silver Burdett Ginn *World of Music* 6, p. 88
- "On Top of Old Smokey" in Holt, Rinehart and Winston *The Music Book* 5, p. 97
- "Rio Grande" in Silver Burdett Ginn *World of Music* 5, pp. 6–7
- "San Francisco" in Macmillan *Share the Music* 5 (1995), pp. 182–83

Integrative Category: Social Studies—History

"SHENANDOAH"

Grades: 4–6

Integrative areas: Transportation, geography, social customs, visual art

Concepts: Rhythm: Mixed meter, syncopation
                   Melody: Wide range
                   Dynamics: ⬦

Key: D
Starting pitch: A
Meter: 4/4, begins on 4

Traditional

1. O Shen - an - doah,____ I love your daugh - ter, A - way____ you roll - ing ri - ver, For her I've crossed the roll - ing wa - ter, A - way____ we're bound a - way,____ A - cross the wide____ Mis - sour - i.____

2. The trader loved this Indian maiden,
   Away, you rolling river,
   With presents his canoe was laden.
   Refrain.

3. O Shenandoah, I'm bound to leave you,
   Away, you rolling river,
   O Shenandoah, I'll not deceive you.
   Refrain.

4. O Shenandoah, I long to hear you,
   Away, you rolling river,
   O Shenandoah, I long to hear you.
   Refrain.

Suggestions for Lessons

1. Ask students where the highest note is (D) and where the lowest note is (A). Circle them on a transparency. Ask students whether this is a wide or a narrow range.

2. Perform the song or use a recording. Ask students to read the words.

3. Teach the song by rote, using the phrase method. Ask students to sing the entire song.

4. After the class has sung the song, ask on what words there is syncopation (*daugh-ter, ri-ver, wa-ter, Mis-sour-i*). Circle these words on the transparency.

5. Sing the song again with emphasis on syncopation.

6. Study the Shenandoah Valley region and trace the Shenandoah River. (Look up information about the Shenandoah River on the Internet.) Note the distance to the Missouri River and discuss the hazards of taking such a trip by wagon train.

7. Present images, draw pictures, or create a diorama of wagon trains as they moved westward and crossed the Missouri River.

More Songs: Social Studies—History

- "Chester" in Holt, Rinehart and Winston *The Music Book* 5, p. 67
- "Columbus Sailed with Three Ships" in Macmillan *Music and You* K, p. 44
- "George Washington" in Macmillan *Music and You* K, p. 156
- "Greatest American Hero" in Silver Burdett Ginn *World of Music* 5, p. 105
- "In My Merry Oldsmobile" in Silver Burdett Ginn *World of Music* 5, pp. 58–59
- "Johnny Has Gone for a Soldier" in Silver Burdett Ginn *World of Music* 5, p. 26

Integrative Category: Holidays

ROSH HASHANAH (JEWISH NEW YEAR)

The Jewish New Year is called Rosh Hashanah and is celebrated in September or October. It begins at sundown and lasts ten days. The *Kiddush,* a prayer, is recited before the evening meal. Various foods are given symbolic meanings. The holidays conclude with Yom Kippur, a sacred day of remembrance and forgiveness.

Suggestions for Lessons

1. Put the words *Rosh Hashanah* and *Yom Kippur* on charts so that students can see them. Discuss the meanings of these two words and what they symbolize.

HALLOWEEN

Halloween is one of our oldest festive holidays. Its origin dates back to long before the Christian era. It was held on what is now the last day of October. Giant fires were lit in honor of the sun god, whose spirit, so it was believed, deserved recognition and honor for the important role it played in growing crops. The ceremony was a solemn, devout religious rite around the roaring flames of the fire.

It was not until the Middle Ages that ghosts and witches were introduced into the Halloween celebration, which was now celebrated on All Hallow's Eve, the night before the Christian festival established in memory of the saints and called All Saints' Day. All sorts of pranks and mischievous antics were performed. The pranksters continued their mysterious ghostly deeds until midnight. When the midnight church bells would ring, ushering in the holy day, the Halloween celebrations ceased. Over the years the customs of Halloween celebrations have changed from time to time and place to place. Today we celebrate with costumes and parties.

"THE WITCH RIDES"

Grades:	K–1
Integrative areas:	Dramatics, movement
Concepts:	Rhythm: Duple meter
	Melody: Wide range, repeated pitches, ascending/descending

The Witch Rides

Key: D minor
Starting pitch: D
Meter: 6/8, begins on 6

Music by Grace M. Meserve
Verses I and 3 by Grace M. Meserve
Verses 2 and 4 by Mary Joy

1. The witch is on her broom - stick, Rid - ing ver - y fast.
2. See the ghosts come float - ing, White a - gainst the sky.
3. The skel - e - ton is danc - ing On his bo - ny toes;
4. See the fun - ny gob - lins Danc - ing down the street,

Oo_____ Oo_____ Hal - low - e'en at last._____
Oo_____ Oo_____ They go drift - ing by._____
Tip - ping, tap - ping, On and on he goes._____
Knock - ing, knock - ing, Cry - ing, "Trick or treat."_____

Reprinted by permission of Silver Burdett.

Suggestions for Lessons

1. Dramatize "The Witch Rides" by galloping on phrases 1, 2, and 4. Stop on "Oo, Oo" and tip the imaginary broomstick down on the second beat of the measure.

2. Ask students to map the melody in the air as they hear it.

3. Play the steady beat (two beats to a measure) on rhythm sticks.

4. Add creative verses to the song.

"LET'S MAKE A JACK-O'-LANTERN"

Grades:	1–3
Integrative areas:	Visual art, candles, creative dramatics
Concepts:	Rhythm: Repetition, steady beat

Let's Make a Jack-o'-Lantern

Key: F
Starting pitch: C
Meter: 4/4, begins on "and" of 3

Words and Music by Daniel S. Hooley
Piano Accompaniment by Kryste Andrews

1. Let's make a jack-, jack-, jack - o' lan - tern; I'll show you
2. In - side we'll put, put, put a can - dle To make a

how, how, how it's done. You sim - ply scoop out a lit - tle yel - low
shine, shine, shin - ing light. We'll make a fine jack - o' - lan - tern for our

pump - kin, And cut a pump - kin face for fun.
win - dow, To grin at peo - ple in the night.

Reprinted by permission of Daniel S. Hooley.

Suggestions for Lessons

1. Using pumpkins, make several jack-o'-lanterns. Scoop them out and cut faces.

2. Place candles in the jack-o'-lanterns. Turn out the lights so the jack-o'-lanterns can glow.

3. Place the jack-o'-lanterns around the classroom.

More Songs: Halloween

- "Dry Bones" in Silver Burdett Ginn *The Music Connection* 4 (2000), pp. 78–79
- "Halloween" in Macmillan *Share the Music* 1 (1995), p. 241
- "Halloween Night" in Macmillan *Share the Music* 3 (1995), p. 268
- "How Did You Know" in Silver Burdett Ginn *World of Music* 2, pp. 200–201
- "On Halloween" in Silver Burdett Ginn *World of Music* 2, p. 198
- "Pick a Pumpkin" in Macmillan *Share the Music* 2 (1995), p. 261
- "There Once Was a Witch" in Silver Burdett Ginn *World of Music* 2, p. 299
- "Watch Out" in Silver Burdett Ginn *The Music Connection* 4 (2000), p. 208
- "What Will You Be on Halloween?" in Macmillan *Share the Music* K (1995), p. 228

THANKSGIVING, SUKKOT, AND SHAVUOT

There are many fall festivals that celebrate harvest time. Some of these are the American Thanksgiving and the Jewish Sukkot and Shavuot.

Thanksgiving is an American holiday on which people of all faiths give thanks in their own individual ways for freedom to work, play, and worship. It is usually associated with pumpkins, corn, and turkey, which were the chief foods used by the Native American Indians in Colonial times. It is also a time in which the classroom teacher will want to impress on children the founding of our country, the trials and hardships that brought the first settlers to our shores, and the rugged individualism that has characterized American society ever since. A celebration of thanksgiving for the people who survived that first winter in the American colonies, the holiday often focuses on the people known as Pilgrims.

The Jewish Sukkot is a celebration of a completed harvest. It is also known as the Feast of Tabernacles or the Feast of Booths. Many people build small structures out of leaves or branches in remembrance of their ancestors who wandered the desert. The Jewish Sukkot is a joyous celebration. Shavuot is another Jewish festival which celebrates the end of the harvest season and the beginning of the fruit season. It too is joyful and a time of sharing.

"MISTER TURKEY"

Grades:	K–1
Integrative areas:	Creative dramatics, visual art
Concepts:	Rhythm: Steady beat
	Melody: Short phrases, repetition
	Form: AA

Mister Turkey

Key: G
Starting pitch: G
Meter: 4/4, begins on 1

Music by Robert W. Gibb
Words by L. E. Ashley

See him strut-ting all a-round, Fat Mis-ter Tur-key!

Hear the gob-ble, gob-ble sound, Fat Mis-ter Tur-key.

From *Listen and Sing*, Copyright © 1943, 1936, by Ginn and Company (Xerox Corporation). Used with permission of Silver Burdett Ginn.

Suggestions for Lessons

1. Dramatize the song with appropriate actions—strutting, saying "gobble, gobble," and so on.

2. Draw pictures of turkeys.

3. Ask students to sing the song and to clap the duple meter.

"FIVE FAT TURKEYS"

Grades:	K–2
Integrative areas:	Number sequences, creative dramatics
Concepts:	Duple meter, steady beat, short phrases

Suggestions for Lessons

1. Dramatize the short story of the five fat turkeys.

2. Select a student to keep a steady beat with a drum.

3. Invite students to stand tall on the highest note (last line).

"OVER THE RIVER AND THROUGH THE WOOD"

Grades:	4–6
Integrative areas:	Social studies—history, geography; weather; visual art
Concepts:	Rhythm: Repetition Melody: Range of one octave Form: ABAC

Over the River and Through the Wood

Lydia Maria Childs

Key: C
Starting pitch: G
Meter: 6/8, begins on 1

1. O-ver the riv-er and through the wood, To grand-fath-er's house we go._____ The
2. O-ver the riv-er and through the wood and straight to the barn-yard gate,_____ We
3. O-ver the riv-er and through the wood, now soon we'll be on our way._____ There's

horse knows the way to car-ry the sleigh through the white and drift-ing snow._____
seem_____ to go so ver-y slow, and it's so_____ hard to wait._____
feast-ing and fun for ev-er-y-one, for this is Thanks-giv-ing day._____

O-ver the riv-er and through the wood, Oh, how_____ the wind does blow!_____ It
O-ver the riv-er and through the wood, now grand-moth-er's cap I spy._____ Hur-
O-ver the riv-er and through the wood, get on,_____ my dap-ple gray! The

stings the toes and bites the nose, As o-ver the ground we go.
rah for the fun! The pud-ding's done. Hur-rah for the pump-kin pie!
woods will ring with songs we sing, for this is Thanks-giv-ing day.

Suggestions for Lessons

1. Study pictures by Currier and Ives* of early rural American scenes. Focus on pictures of sleighs and winter scenes. Discuss or dramatize what it might have been like to ride in a sleigh. Ask children to bring replicas of sleighs that they might have at home, such as those often used as Christmas decorations.

2. Create scenes in art class that express the verses of the song.

3. Play and clap the duple pulse:

4. Identify the repeated pitches and rhythm patterns.

_____

* See Museum of New York, *100 Currier and Ives Favorites* (New York: Crown Publishers, 1978).

"WE GATHER TOGETHER"

Grades: 4–6

Integrative areas: Social studies—history; language arts—vocabulary

Concepts: Rhythm: Triple meter, repeated patterns ♩. ♪ ♩
                       Melody: Wide range
                       Dynamics: ⟨═ ═⟩

We Gather Together

Key: C
Starting pitch: G
Meter: 3/4, begins on 3

Netherlands
Trans. Theodore Baker

We gath-er to-geth-er to ask the Lord's bless-ing; He chas-tens, and
has-tens, His will to make known. The wick-ed op-press-ing, cease
them___ from dis-tress-ing. Sing prais-es to His name. He for-gets not His own.

By permission of G. Schirmer, Inc., New York.

Suggestions for Lessons

1. Read and study stories or pictures of the first Thanksgiving in America.

2. Discuss the role of Pilgrims, Native Americans, and traders.

3. Locate Plymouth, Massachusetts, on a map of the United States. Using an atlas, locate other cities in the United States that have the name *Plymouth*. Point out the coastal area of Plymouth, England, and discuss the use of English and Dutch names for American regions or cities, such as "New" England, and "New" York.

4. Dramatize the first Thanksgiving. Sing "We Gather Together" as students reenact the Pilgrims gathering around the table to celebrate an abundant harvest. Teach the meaning of such words as *chasten, oppressing, ordain, maintain, extol,* and *tribulation.* Emphasize the seeking of freedom from oppression, and freedom to worship, as reasons for coming to America.

5. Ask students to sing the song in its entirety.

More Songs: Thanksgiving, Sukkot, and Shavuot

Thanksgiving

- "Come Ye Thankful People Come" in Silver Burdett Ginn *World of Music* 5, p. 231; and Macmillan *Share the Music* 5 (1995), p. 296

- "For Thy Gracious Blessings" in Macmillan *Share the Music* 5 (1995), p. 297

- "Grandpa's Turkey" in Holt, Rinehart and Winston *The Music Book* 1, p. 186

- "Tallis Canon" in Silver Burdett Ginn *World of Music* 3, p. 20

- "Thanksgiving" in Silver Burdett Ginn *World of Music* 2, pp. 202–203
- "The Turkey Game" in Silver Burdett Ginn *The Music Connection* 1 (2000), pp. 138–39

Sukkot

- "Gather 'Round" in Macmillan *Share the Music* 3 (1995), pp. 271–72
- "Harvest Time" in Macmillan *Share the Music* 3 (1995), p. 272

Shavuot

- "Festival of First Fruits" in Macmillan *Share the Music* 3 (1995), p. 273

HANUKKAH

Hanukkah, Christmas, and Kwanzaa celebrations occur in December. Children should experience the beautiful music of these seasons. The Jewish celebration is very old, and Kwanzaa is very new, but all three reflect joy.

Hanukkah is a Hebrew word meaning "dedication." Known as the Feast of Lights, it is an eight-day celebration commemorating the rededication of the Temple at Jerusalem (165 B.C.) after the Maccabees had defeated the Syrian Greek armies. During the festival a candle is lit for each day. Hanukkah is celebrated with parties and the exchange of gifts. The menorah, a candelabra that holds the eight candles, may be found in many Jewish homes.

"HANUKKAH IS HERE"

Grades:	K–1
Integrative areas:	Cultural heritage; social studies—history
Concepts:	Rhythm: Duple meter, steady beat
	Melody: Narrow range, repeated phrases
	Tonality: Minor

Hanukkah Is Here

Key: D minor
Starting pitch: D
Meter: 4/4, begins on 1

Words and Music by Suzanne Clayton

1. Light the can-dles, light the can-dles, light the can-dles, Ha-nuk-kah is here.
2. Spin the drei-dl, spin the drei-dl, Spin the drei-dl, Ha-nuk-kah is here.
3. Dance the ho-ra, dance the ho-ra, Dance the ho-ra, Ha-nuk-kah is here.

Reprinted by permission of Suzanne Clayton, Pittsford Recreation ORFF.

Suggestions for Lessons

1. Ask a Jewish student to bring a menorah to class and tell how his or her family celebrates Hanukkah.

2. Draw menorahs in art class.

3. Discuss the use of Hebrew in Jewish worship. Invite a Jewish student to sing a song in Hebrew for the class.

"O CHANUKAH"

Grades: 3–5

Integrative areas: Cultural heritage; Hanukkah; social studies—history

Concepts: Melody: Repetition, steps and skips
                    Symbols: Use of repeat sign; first and second endings
                    Harmony: In thirds
                    Rhythm: Quadruple meter
                    Descant: Melodic and rhythmic repetition

O Chanukah

Key: D minor
Starting pitch: D
Meter: 4/4, begins on last half of 4

Jewish Folk Song
English Words by Judith Eisenstein

From *The Gateway to Jewish Song*, by Judith Eisenstein. Reprinted by permission of the author.

Alto glockenspiel or alto xylophone

More Songs: Hanukkah

- "Burn Little Candles" in Macmillan *Share the Music* 1 (1995), p. 255
- "Candles of Chanukah" in Silver Burdett Ginn *World of Music* K, p. 170
- "Hanukkah Is Here" in Macmillan *Share the Music* K (1995), p. 238; and Silver Burdett Ginn *The Music Connection* 1 (2000), p. 220
- "In the Window" in Silver Burdett Ginn *World of Music* 2, p. 206; and *The Music Connection* 2 (2000), p. 186
- "Joyous Chanukah" in Silver Burdett Ginn *World of Music* 2, p. 207; and *The Music Connection* 2 (2000), p. 187
- "Light the Candles" in Macmillan *Share the Music* 1 (1995), p. 254
- "My Dreidel" in Macmillan *Share the Music* K (1995), p. 239
- "On This Night" in Silver Burdett Ginn *The Music Connection* 1 (2000), p. 221
- "Who Can Retell?" in Macmillan *Share the Music* 5 (1995), p. 307

CHRISTMAS

Christmas is a time when Christians celebrate the birth of Jesus Christ. The scene often re-created is called the Nativity. Christmas Eve is a time of special music and pageantry in many Christian churches. Although there is much secular celebration, Christmas remains a religious holiday featuring the giving of gifts and a time when thoughts turn to peace on earth and goodwill toward men. Some of the most wonderful musical treasures we have found are in the Christmas carols from countries around the world.

"JOLLY OLD SAINT NICHOLAS"

Grades: K–2

Integrative areas: Creative dramatics, customs of Christmas

Concepts: Rhythm: Duple meter, mostly eighth notes, steady beat
                     Melody: Narrow range, repeated pitches, repeated phrases

Key: G
Starting pitch: B
Meter: 2/4, begins on 1

Carol

1. Jol - ly old Saint Nich - o - las, Lean your ear this way;___ Don't you tell a
2. When the clock is strik - ing twelve, When I'm fast a - sleep,___ Down the chim - ney
3. John - ny wants a pair of skates; Su - sy wants a dol - ly; Nel - lie wants a

sin - gle soul What I'm going to say;___ Christ - mas Eve is com - ing soon,
broad and black With your pack you'll creep;___ All the stock - ings you will find
sto - ry book; She thinks dolls are fol - ly. As for me, my lit - tle brain

Now you dear old man, Whis - per what you'll bring to me; Tell me, if you can.
Hang - ing in a row; Mine will be the short - est one; You'll be sure to know.
Is - n't ver - y bright; Choose for me, Dear San - ta Claus, What you think is right.

Suggestions for Lessons

1. Read the following story of Saint Nicholas: According to an old legend, Saint Nicholas was the Bishop of Myra in the fourth century. Because of his great love for children, he was designated the patron saint of children. There were many tales of his kindness to the poor and the gifts he took to them. The custom of giving gifts is carried on in our exchange of Christmas presents.

2. Have a child act as Saint Nicholas, with other members of the class whispering to him something special they would like for Christmas.

3. Dramatize the text of the song. For example, on "lean your ear this way," cup your ear; on "don't you tell a single soul," shake your finger; on "when I'm fast asleep," hold hands to ears, and so on.

"LAS POSADAS SONGS"

Grades: 3–4

Integrative areas: Creative dramatics, customs of Christmas

Concepts: Rhythm: Steady beat, duple and triple meter, repeated patterns
Melody: Repeated phrases, narrow range
Form: AB

Music Through the Day, © 1962. By permission of Silver Burdett Company.

Suggestions for Lessons

1. Describe Mexican customs of celebrating Christmas. Every night, during the weeks before Christmas, candlelit processions go from house to house, seeking lodging (posadas), as Mary and Joseph did in Bethlehem. Merrymaking follows the worship before the crèche (manger scene) and the breaking of the piñata, a decorated pâpier-maché animal or object filled with candy and nuts. Someone is blindfolded and the piñata is dangled out of reach of the person's stick. After the person swings wildly, the piñata is placed so that it can be broken, and everyone scrambles for its contents.

2. Dramatize the breaking of the piñata.

3. Create a piñata in art class.

4. Compare the Mexican custom of celebrating Christmas with customs from other parts of the world.

"DECK THE HALLS"

Grades: 3–6

Integrated Areas: Visual arts and history

Concepts: Rhythm: Quadruple meter, steady beat, repeated patterns
                  Melody: Repeated phrases, wide range, mostly steps
                  Tonality: Major
                  Form: AABA

Suggestions for Lessons

1. Study pictures from the time of Charles Dickens (1812–1870).

2. Create simple costumes and a "caroling" scene around a lamppost.

3. Discuss the use of *fa la la* as a refrain-type response in the song. Many joyful songs use nonsense syllables as a refrain.

"O COME, ALL YE FAITHFUL (ADESTE FIDELES)"

Grades: 5–6

Integrative Areas: Language arts—Latin; visual art

Concepts: Rhythm: Steady beat, duple
                     Melody: Wide range, mostly steps, long phrases
                     Form: AB

O Come, All Ye Faithful (Adeste, Fideles)

Key: G
Starting pitch: G
Meter: 4/4, begins on 4

Arr. by John Francis Wade
Trans. F. Oakley

Suggestions for Lessons

1. Explain that during the Middle Ages, Latin was the only accepted language in the Christian Church. Introduce students to singing Latin with the verse found in "Adeste, Fideles" ("O Come, All Ye Faithful").

   Pronunciation key for Latin words:

   a = "ah"   ae = "ay"

   i = "ee"   u = "oo"

   e = "eh"   g = soft *g*

2. Dramatize the song with students taking the role of monks.

3. Create a stained-glass window and cathedral atmosphere.

4. Perform the song phrase by phrase.

5. Teach the song phrase by phrase.

6. Ask students to sing the song.

More Songs: Christmas

- ■ "A Holly Jolly Christmas" in Macmillan *Share the Music* 4 (1995), pp. 288–89

- ■ "Children, Go Where I Send Thee" in Silver Burdett Ginn *The Music Connection* 3 (2000), pp. 214–15

- ■ "Christmas Is Coming" in Macmillan *Music and You* 4, p. 69; and Holt, Rinehart and Winston *Exploring Music* 2, p. 73

- ■ "Frosty the Snowman" in Silver Burdett Ginn *World of Music* 2, pp. 208–209

- ■ "Here Comes Santa Claus" in Silver Burdett Ginn *World of Music* 1, p. 197

- ■ "The Huron Carol" in Silver Burdett Ginn *World of Music* 5, p. 243

- ■ "Little Drummer Boy" in Holt, Rinehart and Winston *Exploring Music* 2, p. 80

- ■ "Rise Up Shepherd and Follow" in Silver Burdett Ginn *World of Music* 5, p. 238

- ■ "Rudolph, the Red-Nosed Reindeer" in Silver Burdett Ginn *The Music Connection* 3 (2000), pp. 206–207

- ■ "Silver Bells" in Macmillan *Share the Music* 5 (1995), pp. 318–19

- ■ "Sleep Well, Little Children" in Silver Burdett Ginn *The Music Connection* 3 (2000), p. 208

KWANZAA

Kwanzaa is a holiday observed by many African Americans. It was created in 1966 by Dr. Maulana Karenga and is based on African harvest celebrations. Kwanzaa is a joyous occasion.

The word *Kwanzaa* means "first fruits" in the Swahili language, which is used in many parts of Africa. *Kwanzaa* has seven letters, signifying the seven principles of Kwanzaa: unity, self-determination, collective work and responsibility, cooperative economics, purpose, creativity, and faith. The celebration lasts from December 26 to January 1 and is similar to the Jewish celebration of Hanukkah, which lasts eight days but varies as to the day it starts.

Each evening a candle is lit and one of the seven principles is discussed. The candleholder is called the *kinara*. On the last day, there is feasting and dancing called the *karamu*.

The following song, suitable for grades 4–6, "Lift Every Voice and Sing," is frequently sung during Kwanzaa. You may also wish to sing the Kwanzaa song "Harambee" (*The Music Connection* 3 (2000), Silver Burdett Ginn, p. 229).

"LIFT EVERY VOICE AND SING"

Grades:	4–6
Integrative areas:	Cultural heritage; social studies—history
Concepts:	Rhythm: ♫ ♩. ; ♩. ♩ ♪
	Melody: ⌢
	Tonality: Key of G

Lift Every Voice and Sing

Key: G
Starting pitch: F
Meter: 6/8 in duple (two groups of 3's), begins on 4 (if counting six counts to a measure) or on 2 (if in duple)

Music by Rosamond Johnson
Words by James Weldon Johnson

In Macmillan *Share the Music* 5 (1995), p. 324. Reprinted by permission of McGraw-Hill Companies.

Suggestions for Lessons

1. Discuss the meaning of Kwanzaa and why it is a celebration. Look up information on the Internet: *www.official kwanzaawebsite.org* and *www.meekwanzaakit.com.*

2. Discuss why we use an African celebration in America.

3. Have students select percussion instruments such as are found in Africa—drums, rattles, and bells—and create an ostinato that will go with the song.

4. Write the form of the song on a transparency or chalkboard: A B C C' (minor mode) B.

5. Sing the two B sections (lines 3 and 4, lines 7 and 8).

6. Sing or play the two C sections, one being slightly different.

7. Sing the first two lines, noticing the similarity of rhythms.

8. Sing the entire song through.

9. Discuss the meaning of the song. Why do students think this is called the African American national anthem?

10. What can students do to be American yet still value the African culture?

11. Have students identify a person in the African American community who they think embodies the spirit of Kwanzaa. Invite this person to share his or her experiences and goals with the class.

NEW YEAR'S DAY

The Western New Year begins on January 1 with traditional festivities taking place on New Year's Eve. The Scots brought a tradition with them to the New World with the singing of "Auld Lang Syne," suitable for grades 2–6.

"AULD LANG SYNE"

Grades:	2–6
Integrative areas:	Cultural heritage; social studies—history
Concepts:	Rhythm: ♩. ♪ ♩ ♩
	Tonality: Key of F
	Form: AB

Auld Lang Syne

Key: F
Starting pitch: C
Meter: 4/4, begins on 4

Scotch Air
Words by Robert Burns

Suggestions for Lessons

1. Discuss the Scotch accent and the differences with American usage. Example: *gie's* means "to give," *o* means "of," *auld* means "old," and so on.

2. Draw or show a map of Scotland.

3. Invite some natives of Scotland to come to class and share with students both their language and their experiences of childhood.

4. Ask students which measures are the same.

5. Teach students to sing the song.

MARTIN LUTHER KING JR. DAY

"WE SHALL OVERCOME"

Grades: 3–6

Integrative areas: Social studies—history, social problems, nonviolent protest

Concepts: Melody: Mostly steps, legato, repetition
                      Form: AB

We Shall Overcome

Key: C
Starting pitch: G
Meter: 4/4, begins on 1

Civil Rights Song

Suggestions for Lessons

1. Review the events leading to the emergence of Dr. Martin Luther King Jr. as a civil rights leader. Look up information on, quotes from, and pictures of Martin Luther King Jr. on the Internet.

2. Read descriptions of the famous gathering at the Lincoln Memorial in 1963, and have students study the speech "I Have a Dream" given by Dr. King at this event.

I Have a Dream
. . . I say to you today, my friends, that in spite of the difficulties and frustrations of the moment, I still have a dream. It is a dream deeply rooted in the American dream. I have a dream that one day this nation will rise up and live out the true meaning of its creed: "We hold these truths to be self-evident, that all men are created equal." I have

a dream that my four children will one day live in a nation where they will not be judged by the color of their skin but by the content of their character.

I have a dream today. When we let freedom ring, when we let it ring from every village and every hamlet, from every state and every city, we will be able to speed up that day when all of God's children, black men and white men, Jews and Gentiles, Protestants and Catholics, will be able to join hands and sing the words of the old Negro spiritual "Free at last, free at last, thank God Almighty, we are free at last."

3. Discuss the appropriateness of the setting—the Lincoln Memorial. Show pictures of this well-known national monument.

4. Play a recording of Dr. King delivering this speech. Discuss with students the melodic flow of his vocal delivery and its roots in the gospel music of the African American church.

5. Dramatize the gathering of people from all over the United States and appoint a student to read the speech as the rest of the class hums and then sings "We Shall Overcome."

"MARTIN LUTHER KING"

Grades:	2–4
Integrative areas:	Social studies—justice, history, protest, leadership
Concepts:	Rhythm: Steady beat, 4/4 meter, repeated patterns
	Melody: Mostly steps, range within an octave
	Form: ABCA

Martin Luther King

Key: D major
Starting pitch: D
Meter: 4/4, begins on "and" of 3

Words and Music by Theresa Fulbright

Reprinted by permission of Theresa Fulbright.

Suggestions for Lessons

1. Ask students to discover the repeated words and rhythms as they view the song from a transparency or their books.

2. Discuss the meanings of such words as *peace, love,* and *freedom.* Place these words on cards.

3. Show pictures of Dr. Martin Luther King Jr. Discuss his role as a leader for freedom.

4. Use green, yellow, and red strips of paper to diagram the song. Discuss the significance of these colors to African American culture.

CHINESE NEW YEAR

The Chinese New Year occurs later than the Western celebrations, in January or February. The year's calendar is named for an animal—such as a dog, a rabbit, a rat, a dragon, and others—and is the second oldest calendar known to man, at 4,600 years old. The Chinese New Year is a long holiday that ends with the Lantern Festival, which occurs with the first full moon of the New Year. Sing the following two songs, which are representative of the Chinese New Year.

"GO A TIN"

Grades:	1–3
Integrative areas:	Cultural heritage; social studies—history
Concepts:	Rhythm: Quadruple: ♩ ♩ ♩ 𝄽

Go A Tin

Starting pitch: A
Meter: 4/4, begins on 1

Taiwanese Folk Song
English Version by MMH

English: Lan - tern bright, lan - tern bright,
Taiwanese pronunciation: go a tin go a tin

Light the_____ way, my_____ lan - tern bright.
aai ge_____ iai gya_____ go a tin

In Macmillan *Share the Music* 2 (1995), p. 281. Reprinted by permission of McGraw-Hill Companies.

"CHINESE NEW YEAR"

Grades:	1–3
Integrative areas:	Cultural heritage; social studies—history
Concepts:	Rhythm: ♫♩♪
	Melody: Pentatonic (C, D, E, G, A)
	Form: ABAC

Chinese New Year

Starting pitch: C
Meter: 6/8, begins on 1

Words and Music by Low Siew Poh

From Silver Burdett Ginn *The Music Connection* 2 (2000), p. 196.

Suggestions for Lessons

1. Use bells and drums for accompaniment.

2. Ask students to play the last two measures of line 4 as an interlude between verses.

3. Note that although the song is written in 6/8 meter, it is in duple with three eighth notes to a single beat.

4. Discuss the use of fireworks and parades in the Chinese culture.

5. Create a dragon and have a parade. Children may sing or use recorded Chinese music.

6. If your school has a large and diverse Asian population, explore the many songs and activities associated with the variety of New Year celebrations.

VALENTINE'S DAY

"SOMEBODY LOVES ME"

Grades:	K–2
Integrative areas:	Friendship, visual art
Concepts:	Rhythm: Syncopation, repetition, quadruple meter, rests (percussion only)
	Melody: Repetition, range

Somebody Loves Me

Words and Music by Gaynor Jones

Key: C
Starting pitch: C
Meter: 4/4, begins on 1

Reprinted and recorded by permission of Gaynor Jones Lowe.

Alto glockenspiel

Percussion: drum or shaking instrument

"I MADE A VALENTINE"

Grades:	K–l
Integrative areas:	Visual art, friendship
Concepts:	Meter: Triple meter
	Melody: Repetition, melodic contour

I Made a Valentine

Key: D
Starting pitch: D
Meter: 3/4, begins on 1

Music by Lynn Freeman Olson

I made a val-en-tine bor-dered in white; I planned it care-ful-ly; cut it just right.

Look at the fan-cy dec-o-ra-tions I drew All on the val-en-tine I made for you.

Suggestions for Lessons

1. Read one of the many stories about the origin of Valentine's Day: Saint Valentine was a Roman priest who made friends with children. The Romans imprisoned him when he refused to worship their gods. Children missed their friend and tossed loving notes between the bars of his cell window. In A.D. 496 Pope Gelasius named February 14 Saint Valentine's Day, and the custom of sending messages of love and friendship spread throughout Europe and America.

2. Make valentines in art class to give to parents and friends.

3. Create short rhymes in language arts that focus on love and friendship.

More Songs: Valentine's Day

- "Be My Valentine" in Silver Burdett *Music* 2, p. 148
- "Best Friends" in Silver Burdett Ginn *World of Music* 2, p. 182
- "Mail Myself to You" in Macmillan *Share the Music* 1 (1995), pp. 272–73
- "Valentine, Valentine" in Holt, Rinehart and Winston *The Music Book* 2, p. 152
- "You and Me" in Silver Burdett Ginn *World of Music* 2, p. 186

PRESIDENTS' DAY: GEORGE WASHINGTON

"COLUMBIA, THE GEM OF THE OCEAN"

Grades:	4–6
Integrative areas:	Social studies—history, government, freedom/independence; language arts—vocabulary; visual art; listening
Concepts:	Rhythm: 4/4 meter, repeated patterns: ♪♪ ♩ Melody: Octave skips, accidentals, descending scale melody

Columbia, the Gem of the Ocean

Key: F
Starting pitch: C
Meter: 4/4, begins on 4

United States

O Co-lum-bia, the gem of the o-cean, The home of the brave and the free,___ The
shrine of each pa-triot's de-vo-tion, A world___ of-fers hom-age to thee. Thy___
man-dates make he-roes as-sem-ble, When___ lib-er-ty's form stands in view, Thy
ban-ners make tyr-an-ny trem-ble, When___ borne___ by the red, white and blue! When___
borne by the red, white and blue! When___ borne by the red, white and blue! Thy___
ban-ners make tyr-an-ny trem-ble, When___ borne___ by the red, white and blue.

"OLD COLONY TIMES"

Grades:	4–6
Integrative areas:	Social studies—history, government, freedom/independence; language arts—vocabulary; visual art; listening
Concepts:	Rhythm: Fermata, quadruple meter Melody: Mostly steps, narrow range, repetition phrases Form: AB

Old Colony Times

Key: F
Starting pitch: C
Meter: 4/4, begins on 4

American Song

1. In good old Col-o-ny times When we were un-der the king, Three
2. The first, he was a mil-ler, And the sec-ond, he was a weav-er, And the
3. Now the mil-ler, he stole corn, And the weav-er, he stole yarn, And the
4. The mil-ler got drown'd in his dam, The weav-er got hung in his yarn, And the

ro-guish chaps fell in-to mis-haps Be-cause they could not sing Be-
third, he was a lit-tle tail-or, Three ro-guish chaps to-geth-er.
lit-tle tail-or stole broad-cloth for to keep these three rogues warm. Be-
dev-il clapp'd his claw on the lit-tle tail-or With broad-cloth un-der his arm.

cause they could not sing, Be-cause they could not sing, Three

ro-guish chaps fell in-to mis-haps, Be-cause they could not sing.

Suggestions for Lessons

1. Show pictures of Mount Vernon, home of George Washington. Explain that it is open to the public as a national monument.

2. Study the Revolutionary War period and the events that led to George Washington's election as the first president of the United States. Look up information and pictures on the Internet.

3. Display *Washington Crossing the Delaware* by Currier and Ives.* Observe the use of vertical and horizontal lines to create stability, and also the red, white, and blue colors.

*See Museum of New York, *100 Currier and Ives Favorites* (New York: Crown Publishers, 1978), p. 43.

4. Show a picture of *George Washington* (the sculpture) by Greenough. Note how he has been cast as a Roman statesman.

5. Read the words to "Columbia, the Gem of the Ocean." Discuss the meaning of such words as *Columbia, gem, shrine, patriot, homage, mandate,* and *tyranny.* Relate the name *Columbia* to the American space shuttle *Columbia.*

6. Discuss the relationship of the United States to England before the Revolutionary War. Dramatize the song "Old Colony Times."

7. Read stories about George Washington:

   ■ Suzanne Hilton, *The World of Young George Washington* (New York: Walker Publishers, 1987).

   ■ May Yonge McNeer, *The Story of George Washington* (Nashville: Abingdon, 1973).

   ■ Robert M. Quackenbush, *I Did It with My Hatchet: A Story of George Washington* (New York: Pippin Press, 1989).

8. Sing the section that has a fermata.

9. Note repetition in refrain.

PRESIDENTS' DAY: ABRAHAM LINCOLN

"ON SPRINGFIELD MOUNTAIN"

Grades:	4–6
Integrative areas:	Social studies—history, geography, politics, Civil War; poetry; visual art
Concepts:	Rhythm: Triple meter, rhythm patterns: ♩ ♩ ♫ Tempo: Slow Melody: Melody centers around G and D (*do* and *sol*), many skips

On Springfield Mountain

American Folk Song

Key: G
Starting pitch: D
Meter: 3/4, begins on "and" of 2

On Spring-field Moun-tain there did dwell A love-ly youth, I knew him well. Too roo-de-nay too roo-de-noo, Too roo-de-nay too roo-de noo.

"BATTLE HYMN OF THE REPUBLIC"

Grades: 4–6

Integrative areas: Social studies—history, geography, politics, Civil War; poetry; visual art

Concepts: Rhythm: Duple meter, strong beat, repetition of rhythm patterns: ♪♩
Melody: Wide range, mostly steps, a few skips
Dynamics: Loud
Form: AB

Battle Hymn of the Republic

Key: B♭
Starting pitch: F
Meter: 4/4, begins on 4

Music by William Steffe
Words by Julia Ward Howe

Mine eyes have seen the glo - ry of the com - ing of the Lord; He is tramp - ling out the vin - tage where the grapes of wrath are stored; He hath loosed the fate - ful light - ning of His ter - ri - ble swift sword; His truth is march - ing on.

Chorus

Glo - ry, glo - ry hal - le - lu - jah! Glo - ry, glo - ry hal - le - lu - jah! Glo - ry, glo - ry hal - le - lu - jah! His truth is march - ing on.

Suggestions for Lessons

1. Read the essay "Abe Lincoln Grows Up" by Carl Sandburg.* Discuss how the writer portrays Abraham Lincoln as a boy and the spirit and background of the man who became the sixteenth president of the United States.

2. Read the Gettysburg Address. Have students study the events that led to this occasion. Dramatize the event by asking a student to read the speech while the rest of the class sings "Battle Hymn of the Republic."

*Johnson, Sikels, and Sayers, *Anthology of Children's Literature*, 4th ed. (Boston: Houghton Mifflin Co., 1970), pp. 1067–71.

3. Show slides of the Lincoln Memorial in Washington, D.C. Point out that this monument is modeled after the famous Parthenon in Athens, Greece. Discuss the power and stillness represented in the figure of Lincoln.

4. Listen to *Lincoln Portrait* by Aaron Copland. Identify the theme from "On Springfield Mountain." Sing the song in class.

5. Read stories about Abraham Lincoln:

   ■ Russell Freedman, *Lincoln: A Photobiography* (New York: Clarion Books, 1987).

   ■ Carol Greene, *Abraham Lincoln: A President of a Divided Country* (Chicago: Children's Press, 1989).

   ■ Jim Hargrove, *Abraham Lincoln: The Freedom President* (New York: Ballantine, 1989).

   ■ Rebecca Stefoff, *Abraham Lincoln, 16th President of the United States* (Ada, Okla.: Garrett Educational Corporation, 1989).

6. Look up information on and pictures of Abraham Lincoln on the Internet.

7. Teach the song phrase by phrase.

8. Sing the song in its entirety.

More Songs: Presidents' Day

■ "Abraham Lincoln" in Silver Burdett Ginn *World of Music* 4, p. 119

■ "George Washington" in Macmillan *Music and You* K, p. 156

■ "George Washington" in Macmillan *Share the Music* K (1995), p. 246

SAINT PATRICK'S DAY

Saint Patrick was born in Great Britain, but was taken to Ireland as a slave in the 1400s. He subsequently escaped to France, where he studied for the priesthood. Returning to Ireland in 1432 as a Christian missionary, he is credited with converting Ireland to the Christian faith and came to be known as its patron saint. March 17 is his feast day and is a national holiday in Ireland. Many people in the United States "become Irish" for the day as the celebration has continued with parades, speeches, and revelry.

The song that follows, "Macnamara's Band," was written by an Irishman and is often played by a bagpipe band. The bagpipe has a bag that is inflated with air from the piper's mouth, and this air makes the reed sound. Pipers can inhale without stopping the sound. The melody has a separate pipe that is fingered and one or more drone pipes that accompany the melody with a single pitch or chord. "Macnamara's Band" is suitable for grades 3–6.

"MACNAMARA'S BAND"

Grades:	1–3
Integrative areas:	Cultural heritage; social studies—history
Concepts:	Rhythm: Repetition of ♩ ♪ ♩ ♪
	Melody: Steps and some skips
	Tonality: Key of F

Macnamara's Band

Key: F
Starting pitch: C
Meter: 6/8 (but is usually sung in duple meter), begins on 4 (if in 6/8 meter—otherwise, on 2 in duple meter)

Music by Shamus O'Connor
Words by John J. Stamford

Verse

1. Oh! me name is Mac - na - mar - a, I'm the lead - er of the band,_____
2. Right_____ now we are re - hears - in', for a ver - y swell af - fair,_____
3. Oh! my name is Un - cle Yul - lus and from Swe - den I have come,_____
4. Oh! I wear a bunch of sham - rocks and a un - i - form of green,_____

Al - though we're few in num - bers we're the fin - est in the land.
The an - nual cel - e - bra - tion, all the gen - try will be there.
To play with Mac - na - mar - a's band and beat the big bass drum,
And I'm the fun - niest look - ing Swede that you have ev - er seen.

We play at wakes and wed - dings and at
When Gen - 'ral Grant to Ire - land came he
And when I march a - long the street the
There's O' - Bri - ens and Ry - ans and Shee - hans and Mee - hans, they

ev' - ry fan - cy ball,_____ And when we play to
took me by the hand,_____ Says he, "I nev - er
la - dies think I'm grand,_____ They shout, "There's Un - cle
come from Ire - land,_____ But by Yim - min - y I'm the

fu - ner - als we play the march from Saul.
saw the likes of Mac - na - mar - a's band."
Yul - lus play - ing with an I - rish band."
on - ly Swede in Mac - na - mar - a's band.

Refrain

Oh! the drums go bang, and the cym - bals clang, and the horns they blaze a -

way;_____ Mc - Car - thy pumps the old ba - zoon while I the pipes do play;

And, Hen - nes - sey Ten - nes - see too - tles the flute, and the mu - sic is some - thin' grand;_____ A cred - it to old Ire - land is Mac - na - mar - a's band.

Suggestions for Lessons

1. Form a "Macnamara's band" from rhythm instruments.

2. Use the F of the handbell, resonator bells, or tone chimes as the drone.

3. Play or sing the refrain and ask students to play when they think their instrument is called.

4. Ask students to read the words of the verses and discuss the meanings of *wakes, gentry, General Grant, shamrock, O'Brien,* and *Swede.*

5. Play or sing the verses and ask students to play and/or sing on the refrain.

6. Divide the class and ask one half to sing and the other half to play on the refrain.

7. Play or sing the verse and notice that the melody of the first two lines is the same as the melody of the last three lines, but the rhythm is different.

8. Ask students to sing the song and play instruments with you or with a recording.

Integrative Category: Patriotic Songs of the United States of America

Patriotic songs of the United States express the hopes, desires, and feelings of pride American people have for their country and its heroes. Such songs embody the history and feelings of the American people as they have struggled through wars, famine, depression, and victories to build a better life for themselves and their children. These songs have become favorites because they appeal to people in a direct but simple manner and because there is a vitality that inspires us generation after generation.

"I LIKE IT HERE"

Grades:	4–6
Integrative areas:	Patriotism, freedom
Concepts:	Melody: Accidentals, half and whole steps
	Rhythm: Duple meter, steady beat
	Symbols: Repeat sign, first and second endings

I Like It Here

Words and Music by Clay Boland

Key: B♭
Starting pitch: F
Meter: 2/2, begins on "and" of 1

1. I like the U - nit - ed States of A - mer - i - ca,_____ I like the
2. I am so luck - y to be in A - mer - i - ca,_____ And I am

way we all live with - out fear._____ I like to vote for my choice,___
thank - ful each day of the year._____ For I can do as I please,___

____ speak my mind, raise my voice. Yes, I like it here.
____ 'cause I'm free as the breeze. Yes, I

like it here._____ I'd like to climb to the top of a moun - tain so high, ___

Lift my head to the sky___ and say how grate - ful am I_____ For the

way that I'm liv - ing, I'm work - ing and giv - ing And help - ing the land I hold

dear._____ Yes, I like it, I like it, I like it here.

Suggestions for Lessons

1. Have students play a drumbeat on their knees as they listen to and then sing the song.

2. Read the poem "I Hear America Singing"* by Walt Whitman:

I Hear America Singing

I hear America singing, the varied carols I hear,
Those of the mechanics, each singing his as it should be blithe and strong,
The carpenter singing his as he measures his plank or beam,
The mason singing his as he makes ready for work or leaves off work,
The boatman singing what belongs to him in his boat, the deck hand singing on the
    steamboat deck,
The shoemaker singing as he sits on his bench, the hatter singing as he stands,
The wood-cutter's song, the ploughboy's on his way in the morning, or at noon intermission
    or at sundown,
The delicious singing of the mother, or the young wife at work, or the girl sewing or washing,
Each sings what belongs to him or her and to none else,
The day what belongs to the day—at night the party of young fellows, robust, friendly,
Singing with open mouths their strong melodious songs.

More Songs: Patriotic Songs

- "America," p. 59
- "America the Beautiful" in Silver Burdett Ginn *World of Music* 3, p. 189
- "Fifty, Nifty, United States" in Holt, Rinehart and Winston *The Music Book* 5, p. 4;
  and Macmillan *Share the Music* 5 (1995), p. 286–87
- "Johnny Has Gone for a Soldier" in Silver Burdett Ginn *The Music Connection* 5
  (2000), p. 194
- "Pledge of Allegiance to the Flag" in Holt, Rinehart and Winston *The Music Book* 5, p. 1
- "The Star-Spangled Banner," p. 43
- "We'll Find America" in Holt, Rinehart and Winston *Exploring Music* 7, p. 7
- "Yankee Doodle," p. 479

---

*Walt Whitman, *The Complete Poems of Walt Whitman*, edited by Francis Murphy (New York: Penguin Books, 1986), p. 47.

Integrative Category: Getting Acquainted

"HOW DO YOU DO?"

Grades:	K–1
Integrative areas:	Talking to others, self-image
Concepts:	Melody: Repetition of phrases, narrow range
	Rhythm: Duple meter, steady beat, repetition of rhythmic patterns
	Form: AABA

How Do You Do?

Key: F
Starting pitch: C
Meter: 2/4, begins on "and" of 2

Folk Tune from Germany
Words Adapted

1. As I was walk - ing down the street,
2. Now when I'm walk - ing down the street,

I saw the peo - ple walk - ing;
And met some friends out walk - ing,

And when they met some - one they knew,
I smile at them, and they smile too,

They start - ed in a - talk - ing:
And then we start a - talk - ing:

"How do you do?" "How do you do?"
"How do you do?" "How do you do?"

And when they met some - one they knew,
And ev - 'ry - one is smil - ing, too,

They start - ed in a - talk - ing.
And ev - 'ry - one is talk - ing.

Used by permission of D.C. Heath and Company.

Suggestions for Lessons

1. Discuss what you say when you meet someone new. Examples include "How do you do?" "Pleased to meet you," and so on.

2. Discuss what you say when you make a new friend. Examples include "How about coming over to my house?"

3. Play a game. Teacher picks a child and sings, "How are you today?"

Child answers by singing, "I am fine today." (Can be improvised also.)

4. Use a song pattern to call the roll and ask the child to sing a response with his or her own name. Examples:

5. Sit in a circle and sing a question, then point to a child in the circle who must sing an answer. This same game can be played with teams, with points given to the teams that sing correctly.

6. Begin teaching the song by rote with line 5: "How do you do?"

7. Ask a child to play the xylophone whenever the class sings "How do you do?"

8. Sing the verse and stop on "walking," asking students what the word should be. Continue through the song, stopping at the end of each phrase ("walking," "a-talking").

9. Point out that the first two lines repeat, then the class sings "How do you do?" and lines 6 and 7 repeat.

Integrative Category: Human Relationships and Emotions

"MAGIC PENNY"

The music for "Magic Penny" is on page 32.

Grades: 3–4

Integrative areas: Getting along with others, love, developing positive self-image, aspiration

Concepts: Rhythm: Syncopation, repetition of patterns, duple meter
Melody: Repetition of phrases, wide range
Form: ABA

Suggestions for Lessons

1. Discuss the text of the song "Magic Penny." Ask students for examples of those feelings of pleasure they experience when they have shared something with someone else.

2. Create a class project in which students share with those less fortunate, such as reading to older persons who have lost their sight, or sending get-well cards to a child in the hospital.

More Songs: Human Relationships and Emotions

- "Happiness" in Macmillan *Music and You* 6, p. 264
- "Loneliness Song" in Macmillan *Music and You* 5, p. 65; and Holt, Rinehart and Winston *The Music Book* 5, p. 210
- "Look to the Rainbow" in Silver Burdett Ginn *World of Music* 3, p. 159
- "The Ups and Downs of Friendship" in Silver Burdett Ginn *The Music Connection* 3 (2000), pp. 32–33
- "You Can't Buy Friendship" in Silver Burdett Ginn *World of Music* 2, pp. 194–95

Integrative Category: Language Arts

"OLD MACDONALD HAD A FARM"

The music for "Old MacDonald Had a Farm" is on page 44.

Grades:	K–2
Integrative areas:	Linking sight and sound, effect of accumulation in music and in poetry, creativity, word/phrase sequencing
Concepts:	Rhythm: Mostly ♩ and ♪ notes, repetition of patterns Melody: Short phrases, repetition of pitches, narrow range Harmony: Chords: G, C, D₇

Suggestions for Lessons

1. Have each child choose a particular animal or sound and remember where it is in the verse sequence.

2. Read poems that use the same type of sequencing, such as "The House That Jack Built" or "The Twelve Days of Christmas." Discuss the effect of such a technique (it lengthens the poem or song, increases its complexity, and so on).

More Songs: Language Arts

- "Mister Frog Went A-Courtin'" in Silver Burdett Ginn *World of Music* 2, p. 18
- "Who Built the Ark?" in Silver Burdett Ginn *World of Music* 2, p. 52
- "Turn, Turn, Turn" in Silver Burdett Ginn *World of Music* 5, pp. 62–63

Integrative Category: Mathematics

"FIVE LITTLE FROGS"

Grades:	K–3
Integrative areas:	Nature, numbers, number relationships
Concepts:	Rhythm: Duple meter, syncopation, repetition Melody: Direction of phrases

Five Little Frogs

Key: C
Starting pitch: G
Meter: 4/4, begins on 1

Words by Louise Binder Scott
Music by Virginia Pavelko

1. Five green and speck-led frogs
2. Four green and speck-led frogs
3. Three green and speck-led frogs
4. Two green and speck-led frogs
5. One green and speck-led frogs

Sat on a speck-led log

Eat-ing some most de-li-cious bugs. (Yum, yum!)

1.–4. One jumped in-to the pool,
5. He jumped in-to the pool,

Where it was nice and cool.

1. Then there were four green speck-led frogs.
2. Then there were three green speck-led frogs.
3. Then there were two green speck-led frogs.
4. Then there was one green speck-led frogs.
5. Then there were no green speck-led frogs.

(Glub, glub!)

Suggestions for Lessons

1. Dramatize the words of "Five Little Frogs."

2. Chart repeating phrases with colors.

3. Map the direction of the melody.

4. Emphasize breath for octave skips.

5. Use fingers or charts showing *5, 4, 3, 2, 1* to indicate the number of frogs remaining.

6. Emphasize subtracting one from each set of frogs.

More Songs: Mathematics

- "Counting Song" in Macmillan *Music and You* 1, p. 213; and Silver Burdett Ginn *World of Music* 2, p. 31

- "The Twelve Days of Christmas" in Macmillan *Music and You* 5, p. 266

Integrative Category: Science

"FOLLOW THE DRINKIN' GOURD"

Grades: 4–6

Integrative areas: Astronomy, Civil War (Underground Railroad)

Concepts: Rhythm: Duple meter, syncopation, triplets
Melody: Repetition of phrases, narrow range
Form: AB

Follow the Drinkin' Gourd

Key: E minor
Starting pitch: E
Meter: 2/2, begins on "and" of 2

Spiritual
Arr. by Paul Campbell

1. When the sun comes back and the first quail calls,_____
2. Now the river bank'll make_____ a mighty good road;_____ The
3. Now the riv - er ends_____ be - tween two hills;_____

Fol - low_____ the Drink - in' Gourd.___ Then the Old Man is a wait - in' for to
dead trees - 'll show you the way. And the left_____ foot,_____ peg - foot,_____
Fol - low_____ the Drink - in' Gourd.___ And_____ there's an - oth - er riv - er on the

car - ry you to free - dom,_____ Fol - low the Drink - in' Gourd.
trav - el - in'_____ on, Just you fol - low the Drink - in' Gourd.
oth - er_____ side, Just you fol - low the Drink - in' Gourd.

REFRAIN

Fol - low_____ the Drink - in' Gourd,_____ Fol - low_____ the Drink - in' Gourd,___ For the

Old Man is a wait - in' for to car - ry you to free - dom, Fol - low the Drink - in' Gourd.

Suggestions for Lessons

1. Study the origins and placement of selected constellations in the galaxy, such as the Big Dipper and Orion.

2. Visit a local planetarium to learn more about astronomy.

3. Create charts showing some of the most common constellations and stories about them. Discover at what seasons of the year they are most visible.

4. Use a compass to demonstrate the magnetic pull to the north. Show students the location of the North Star and the Big Dipper. Discuss ways that a traveler could find his or her way home without a compass.

5. Have students read stories about the Civil War and the Underground Railroad. Be certain that they do not confuse this with a bona fide train. Explain that the North Star and Big Dipper showed slaves the way to freedom.

6. Place the words on a chart. Have students read the words to each verse of the song. Explain what each means.

7. Listen to a recording of (or sing) "Follow the Drinkin' Gourd." Have students read the words as they listen.

8. Teach the song, starting with the chorus, followed by the verses. Pay particular attention to the repetition of the syncopated rhythmic pattern.

9. Sing the entire song through.

More Songs: Science

- "Aquarius" in Holt, Rinehart and Winston *Exploring Music* 7, p. 177
- "Clouds" in Silver Burdett *Music* 4, p. 55
- "Moon Is Coming Out" in Macmillan *Music and You* 1, p. 225

Integrative Category: Seasons

More Songs: Seasons

Spring

- "April Showers" in Silver Burdett Ginn *World of Music* 6, p. 251
- "At the Spring" in Silver Burdett Ginn *The Music Connection* 4 (2000), p. 86
- "If All the Raindrops" in Silver Burdett Ginn *The Music Connection* 2 (2000), p. 75
- "Rain Song" in Silver Burdett Ginn *The Music Connection* 4 (2000), p. 40
- "Springtime" in Macmillan *Share the Music* 2 (1995), p. 290
- "Springtime Has Come" in Silver Burdett Ginn *The Music Connection* 2 (2000), p. 9

Summer

- "In the Good Old Summertime" in Macmillan *Share the Music* 3 (1995), pp. 304–305
- "Take Me out to the Ballgame" in Macmillan *Share the Music* 2 (1995), pp. 130–31; and Silver Burdett Ginn *The Music Connection* 3 (2000), pp. 22–23

Autumn

- "Autumn Leaves" in Macmillan *Share the Music* K (1995), p. 222
- "Autumn Leaves Now Are Falling" in Holt, Rinehart and Winston *Exploring Music* 1, p. 40
- "Gather 'Round" in Macmillan *Share the Music* 3 (1995), p. 270–71

Winter

- "Let's Play in the Snow" in Macmillan *Share the Music* 1 (1995), p. 249
- "Mitten Song" in Macmillan *Share the Music* K (1995), p. 237
- "North Winds Blow" in Macmillan *Share the Music* 1 (1995), p. 248
- "Winter Fantasy" in Silver Burdett Ginn *The Music Connection* 4 (2000), pp. 212–13
- "Winter Wonderland" in Silver Burdett Ginn *The Music Connection* 3 (2000), p. 202

Integrative Category: Transportation

"ERIE CANAL"

The music for "Erie Canal" is on page 63.

Grades:	4–6
Integrative areas:	History, geography, visual art, poetry, vocabulary, science
Concepts:	Rhythm: Duple meter, syncopation, repetition of patterns
	Melody: Repetition of phrases, many skips
	Tonality: Minor/major
	Form: AB

Suggestions for Lessons

1. Present the following background on the Erie Canal: The Erie Canal, authorized in 1817 and completed in 1825, connected Lake Erie (Buffalo) and the Hudson River (Albany). A 363-mile waterway, it was of immense significance in the development of commerce in the United States. This cheap, all-water route provided transportation for agricultural produce from the west to the east and manufactured products from the east to the "new" west. The canal teemed with boats and barges as pioneers swarmed to find new lands. Songs of the mule skinners who drove the mules along the towpath as they hauled the flat-bottom boats echoed through the countryside both day and night. Because low bridges occurred at frequent intervals along the canal, the mule skinners would shout a warning to the passengers on the boat so that they could duck. This song is about a mule skinner and his mule, Sal. It tells of the produce carried and the friendliness of the passengers.

2. Study the canal as a means of transportation. Use encyclopedias and the Internet for references. Locate Albany and Buffalo on a map of New York and determine how long the canal was. Find Lake Erie and place it in relation to the other Great Lakes. When was the Erie Canal considered part of the "new" west? (1825) Discover when other cities in this area (Cleveland, Cincinnati, and Columbus, Ohio) were founded. What was the Western Reserve? Have students learn about other canals, such as the Panama Canal, the Canal at Corinth (Greece), and the Suez Canal.

3. Using the dictionary, explore the meanings of such words as *barge, mule skinner,* and *navigation.*

4. Listen to the two parts of the song: Part A is in the minor mode, and part B is in a major mode. Part B is also called the *chorus.*

5. Teach the song, starting with the chorus (part B). Note the repetition of the rhythm, ♪♪, then teach the verses.

"THE JOHN B. SAILS"

Grades:	4–6
Integrative areas:	History, geography, vocabulary, visual art, science
Concepts:	Rhythm: Duple meter, syncopation, ties
	Melody: Narrow range, repetition of phrases
	Harmony: Mostly thirds and sixths
	Chords: G, C, D_7

The John B. Sails

Calypso Folk Song from the Bahamas

Key: G
Starting pitch: D
Meter: 4/4, begins on 4

1. Oh, we came on the sloop John B. My grand-fath-er and me, A-
2. The first mate he got sad, Feel-in' aw-f'ly bad, Then he
3. The poor cook he got fits, And throw 'way all the grits, Then he

round Nas-sau Town we did roam. Walk-in' all night
Captain come a-board, took him a-way. Please let me a-lone
took and eat up all of the corn. Please let me go home.

Just see-in' the sights, Well, I feel so break-up, I want to go home.
And let me go home, Well, I feel so break-up, I want to go home.
I want to go home, Well, this is the worst trip Since I was born.

REFRAIN

So hoist up the John B. sails, See how the main-s'l sets,

Send for the Cap-tain a-shore, Let me go home. Please let me go home,

I want to go home. Well, I feel so break-up, I want to go home.

Silver Burdett, VI. © 1981. Silver Burdett Company. Used by permission of Silver Burdett Company.

Suggestions for Lessons

1. Read several sea chanties (also spelled "shanties"), such as "Yeo, Heave Ho." Discuss the meaning of the words used, such as *capstan* and *anchor*.

   ### Yeo, Heave Ho
   Yeo, heave ho! 'Round the capstan go—
   Heave, men with a will, Tramp, and tramp it still!
   The anchor must be weighed, The anchor must be weighed.
   Chorus:
      Yeo ho! Heave ho!
      Yeo ho! Heave ho!
   Yeo, heave ho! Cheerily we go,
   Heave, men with a will, Tramp, and tramp it still
   The anchor grips the ground, The anchor grips the ground.
   Chorus:
      Yeo ho! Heave ho!
      Yeo ho! Heave ho!
   Yeo, heave ho! raise her from below,
   Heave, men, with a will,
   Tramp, and tramp it still;
   The anchor's off the ground
   And we are outward bound.
   Chorus:
      Yeo ho! Heave ho!
      Yeo ho! Heave ho!
   Yeo, heave ho! round the capstan go,
   Heave, men, with a will,
   The anchor now is weighed, The anchor now is weighed.
   Chorus:
      Yeo ho! heave ho!
      Yeo ho! heave ho!

2. Write your own poem or short story about sailing ships.

3. Listen to a recording of sea chanties: *Sea Shanties*, RCA Victor LSC 2551 (Robert Shaw).

4. Listen to *Windjammer* by Morton Gould (original sound track for the film *Windjammer*, Columbia CL 1158).

5. Study how various artists have expressed their feelings about sailing and sailing ships, and show the following scenes by Currier and Ives:*
   - *The Clipper Yacht "America"*
   - *Clipper Ship "Nightingale"*
   - *The Wreck of the Steam Ship "San Francisco"*
   - *Summer Scenes in New York Harbor*

6. Locate the Bahama Islands on a map. Discuss the meanings of *calypso* and the cultural background of the Bahamian people. Identify Latin American instruments, such as maracas, claves, and bongo drums, that seem appropriate to accompany the song.

7. Present the principles of sailing in science class. Compare the terminology with that found in traditional sea chanties. Children could also study fishing activities of sailing vessels, such as whaling and fishing for mackerel, porpoise, smelt, herring, cod, and flounder.

---

*See Museum of New York, *100 Currier and Ives Favorites* (New York: Crown Publishers, 1978).

"I'VE BEEN WORKING ON THE RAILROAD (DINAH)"

Grades:	2–5
Integrative areas:	History, geography, social change, passenger/shipping, visual art, poetry
Concepts:	Rhythm: Duple meter, steady beat, repetition patterns:

Melody: Short phrases, repetition of phrases
Tonality: Major
Form: AB

I've Been Working on the Railroad (Dinah)

Traditional

Key: G
Starting pitch: G
Meter: 4/4, begins on 1

I've been work-ing on the rail-road all the live-long day;

I've been work-ing on the rail-road to pass the time a-way.

Don't you hear the whis-tle blow-ing? Rise up so ear-ly in the morn.

Don't you hear the cap-tain shout-ing, "Di-nah, blow your horn!"?

Di-nah won't you blow, Di-nah won't you blow, Di-nah won't you blow your horn?_____

Di - nah won't you blow,   Di - nah won't you blow,   Di - nah won't you blow your   horn?

Some - one's in the kitch - en with   Di - nah,   Some - one's in the kitch - en, I   know,____

Some - one's in the kitch - en with   Di - nah,   Strum - ming on the old ban - jo.

Fee   fie   fid - dle - ee - i - o,   Fee   fie   fid - dle - ee - i - o,____

Fee   fie   fid - dle - ee - i - o,   Strum - ming on the old ban - jo.

"CASEY JONES"

Grades: 4–6

Integrative areas: Trains, history

Concepts: Rhythm: Duple, steady beat, repetition of rhythm patterns, syncopation
                     Melody: Repetition of phrases, range from B♭ to D
                     Form: Verse and refrain: AB

Casey Jones

Words by T. Lawrence Seibert
Music by Eddie Newton

Key: B♭
Starting pitch: B♭
Meter: 4/4, begins on 1

1. Come, all you round - ers, if you want ___ to hear ___ A story ___ a - bout ___ a ___ brave en - gi - neer, And Ca - sey Jones ___ was the round - er's name. On a six - eight ___ wheel - er, boys, he won ___ his fame. The call - er called Ca - sey at a half ___ past four. Ca - sey kissed his ___ wife ___ at the sta - tion door. He mount - ed to the cab - in with his or - ders in his hand, And he took his fare - well trip ___ to the Prom - ised Land.

2. Put in your wa - ter and ___ shov - el your coal. Put your head out ___ the win - dow, watch them driv - ers roll. I'll run her till ___ she leaves the rail, 'Cause I'm eight hours ___ late ___ with the west - ern mail. He looked at his watch, ___ and his watch ___ was slow. He looked at the wa - ter, and the wa - ter was low. He turned ___ to the fire - man, and then ___ he ___ said, "We're ___ goin' to reach ___ Fris - co, but we'll all be dead."

3. Ca - sey pulled up ___ at ___ Re - no hill. He toot - ed for the cross - ing with an aw - ful shrill. The switch - man knew ___ by the en - gine's moans That the man at the throt - tle was ___ Ca - sey Jones. He pulled up with - in ___ two ___ miles of the place, And ___ Num - ber ___ Four ___ stared him in ___ the face. He turned ___ to the fire - man, said, "Boy, you bet - ter jump, 'Cause there's two ___ lo - co - mo - tives that's a - go - in' to bump."

REFRAIN

Ca - sey Jones___ mount - ed to the cab - in Ca - sey Jones,___ with his
Ca - sey Jones,___ Goin' to reach___ Fris - co. Ca - sey Jones,___ But we'll
Ca - sey Jones,___ Two___ lo - co - mo - tives, Ca - sey Jones,___ That's a -

or - ders in his hand. Ca - sey Jones___ Mount - ed to the cab - in, And he
all___ be___ dead. Ca - sey Jones,___ Goin' to reach___ Fris - co, We're___
go - in' to bump," Ca - sey Jones,___ "Two___ lo - co - mo - tives that's a -

took his fare - well trip___ to the Prom - ised Land.
goin' to reach___ Fris - co, but we'll all___ be dead.
two___ lo - co - mo - tives that's a - go - in' to bump."

Suggestions for Lessons

1. Review what is known about the character Casey Jones. He was known for the speed at which he could make a train travel and for the wonderful sound he could get out of the train whistle. Some stories tell us that the people who worked in the fields near the railroad track could tell when Casey was at the throttle by the sound of the whistle.

2. Review the difference between a diesel and a locomotive. Show pictures of each.

3. Discuss the meaning of a ballad (story) and read the words of the song as a story.

4. Teach the syncopated patterns by playing and singing the rhythm patterns.

5. Use colored charts for repeating phrases.

6. Create an overlay for the overhead projector with repeated phrases in "Casey Jones."

7. Dramatize the story as students sing the song.

8. Invite students to bring in toy trains (steam locomotives, diesels). Discuss how train travel has changed over the past one hundred years.

9. View pictures of trains and train travel:
   - Claude Monet, *The Saint-Lazare Railroad Station*
   - Currier and Ives, *The "Lightning Express" Trains**

10. Listen to musical compositions about trains, such as Villa-Lobos, "Little Train of the Caipira"; Honegger, "Pacific 231"; Miller, "Chattanooga Choo-Choo"; and "Orange Blossom Special."

11. Read the following poem by David McCord about a train.

Song of the Train†

Clickety-clack,

Wheels on the track,

This is the way

They begin the attack:

Clickety-clack,

Click-ety-clack,

Click-ety, clack-ety,

Click-ety

Clack

Clickety-clack,

Over the crack,

Faster and faster

The song of the track:

Clickety-clack,

Clickety-clack,

Clickety, clackety,

CLACKETY

Clack.

Riding in front,

Riding in back

EVERYONE hears

The song of the track:

Clickety-clack,

Clickety-clack,

clickety, CLICKETY,

Clackety

CLACK.

---

*Museum of New York, *100 Currier and Ives Favorites* (New York: Crown Publishers, 1978), p. 57.

†David McCord, *Far and Few* (New York: Little, Brown, 1952).

More Songs: Transportation

Ships

■ "Cape Cod Chantey" in Macmillan *Music and You* 5, p. 251; and Silver Burdett Ginn *World of Music* 4, p. 29

■ "Gallant Ship" in Holt, Rinehart and Winston *Exploring Music* K, p. 129

■ "Sailboat in the Sky" in Silver Burdett Ginn *The Music Connection* 3 (2000), p. 176

Trains

■ "Clickety Clack" in Macmillan *Music and You* K, p. 184

■ "Down at the Station" in Macmillan *Share the Music* K (1995), p. 142

■ "Engine, Engine, Number Nine" in Macmillan *Share the Music* 1 (1995), p. 281; and K, p. 112

■ "Paddy Works on the Railway" in Silver Burdett Ginn *The Music Connection* 4 (2000), p. 118

■ "Rock Island Line" in Silver Burdett Ginn *The Music Connection* 4 (2000), p. 140

■ "Wabash Cannonball" in Silver Burdett Ginn *World of Music* 5, pp. 14–15

Airplanes

■ "I'm Flying Home" in Silver Burdett Ginn *The Music Connection* 2 (2000), pp. 120–21

Automobiles

■ "Car Song" in Macmillan *Share the Music* K (1995), pp. 120–21; Silver Burdett *Music* 1, p. 34; and Silver Burdett Ginn *World of Music* 1, p. 16

■ "Little Blue Truck" in Macmillan *Share the Music* K (1995), p. 124

For Your Journal

In your journal or portfolio, make a section on integrating songs with other subjects and activities and give illustrative examples.

Teaching Music Through Playing Classroom Instruments

STUDENTS ARE USUALLY ENTHUSIASTIC about performing music on instruments, and you will generally find them highly motivated and very responsive. As with singing, playing instruments involves students directly in making music, spontaneously or from a musical score, alone or with a group. Experience is often the best teacher; students learn to listen attentively both to the music they are playing themselves and to the music performed by the total ensemble. Individual players come to rely on others and to respect their roles in the creative process of performing music together.

Development of motor coordination is essential in playing classroom instruments. Through such activities many students improve the effective use of their arms, hands, fingers, legs, and feet.

Classroom instruments function in a variety of ways. Some are used to play melodies (recorder, melody bells, xylophone, and glockenspiel), others to play harmony (keyboard, guitar, Autoharp, and Omnichord), and still others to play both melody and harmony (keyboard, handbells, tone chimes, and resonator bells). The many percussion instruments, such as drums, tambourines, claves, and triangles, are used to play rhythms.

As students learn to play instruments, they should develop the following skills.

- The ability to choose appropriate instruments for such musical concepts as:
  a. Steady beat
  b. Differences in dynamics
  c. Musical form
  d. Pitch and melody

- The ability to discriminate and select appropriate rhythm instruments for various types of music

- An awareness of the expressive potential of different instruments

- The ability to select and play instruments that can add to the expressiveness of music through accompaniment

Teachers need to learn the physical and musical characteristics of some of the most common classroom instruments and develop basic playing skills that will enable them to demonstrate these instruments and guide students in playing them.

The following guidelines will contribute to students' successful experiences with playing instruments:

1. Provide many aural experiences before using instruments.

2. Provide many opportunities for immediate success.

3. Reinforce each playing skill before going on to a new one.

4. Give *all* students an opportunity to play instruments.

5. Use instruments on a regular basis.

6. Encourage students to improvise.

7. Use instruments in musical ways.

8. Keep directions simple.

9. Avoid giving out all of the instruments at once.

10. Avoid asking students to "experiment" in creating sounds indiscriminately.

11. Avoid letting students mistreat instruments.

12. Avoid allowing students to "abuse" music by unmusical playing or behavior.

13. Ask students to "play" the instrument, not "hit" the instrument.

Careful attention to these guidelines will reward both you and your students with musically satisfying experiences.

This chapter focuses on a general description and the functions of melody, harmonic, and percussion instruments and techniques for teaching students to play them. It deals with selecting an appropriate instrument, playing rhythm accompaniments to songs, developing a rhythm ensemble, making your own instruments, and integrating instrumental experiences into the classroom. The chapter concludes with sample lessons.

Melody Instruments

A *melody* instrument is any instrument that can produce enough different pitches to play a melody. Classroom instruments that meet this criterion are piano and electronic keyboards, melody bells, resonator bells, xylophone, glockenspiel, metallophones, handbells, tone chimes, and recorder. The functions of these melody instruments include (1) playing melodies, (2) playing ostinato melodic patterns, and (3) playing descants and harmony parts.

PIANO AND ELECTRONIC KEYBOARDS

The piano and electronic keyboards (such as those made by Casio, Yamaha, and Suzuki) are used primarily for playing melodies and simple accompaniments.

When you play the piano, depressing the keys causes hammers to strike strings. You can sustain the sound by depressing the right damper pedal, which raises the felt pads (called *dampers*) from the strings and allows them to continue to sound. When you release the pedal, the dampers return to the strings and stop the sound. When playing the following simple exercises and tunes, try to play a pitch on the piano and then press downward on the pedal. Remove your finger from the key and listen to it continue to sound. Then release the pedal with your foot and notice that

Piano

Electronic keyboard

the tone stops. Careful use of this pedal will allow you to play melodies smoothly. Too much pedal—that is, playing a melody with the pedal depressed throughout—will cause the tones to blur together. A little experimentation will make this principle clear to you.

Although an electronic keyboard is laid out in the same way as on the piano, it offers a variety of tone colors to choose from. That is, the electronic keyboard can sound somewhat like a harpsichord, a piano, an organ, a violin, and so on. In this way electronic keyboards differ dramatically from the piano.

The Form of the Keyboard

Because the "form" of the keyboard (pattern of black and white notes) is also found on melody and resonator bells, you will want to become familiar with it. (See the keyboard template at the back of the book.)

Position yourself at the center of the keyboard. You will notice white keys and black keys grouped into twos and threes. This pattern is repeated throughout the keyboard:

Each white key has a letter name that corresponds to a line or space on the staff. Thus, the pitch name E represents the white key E on the keyboard. The piano keyboard is divided into a series of eight pitches to the octave; there are eight octaves. The lowest pitch (to your left) is A. Play this note and then move up the keyboard, playing only the white notes. The pitches are A, B, C, D, E, F, and G; then you start over again.

The octave A, B, C, D, E, F, G, A is divided into twelve semitones, or half steps. Raising a pitch a half step is called a sharp (♯) (for example, F, F♯), and lowering it a half step is called a flat (♭) (for example, G, G♭). Notice in the following example that a single black note may have two names (for example, F♯ and G♭). This is called *enharmonic.*

The pitch to the left of the two black keys in the center of the piano keyboard is called *middle C.* Place your right thumb on A (below middle C), followed by your third finger on A♯. Play the chromatic scale (half steps), alternating finger and thumb with each pitch. Next, play from A to B. Notice that this is a whole step (A♯ is in between). Play from C♯ to D♯. Notice that this is a whole step with D in between. Locate and play other half and whole steps.

Middle C

Fingering

To play a melody on a keyboard, you need to use the correct fingers. Follow these steps, and you will soon be able to play a melody:

1. Place your right hand on the keyboard with your thumb on middle C.

2. Curve your fingers above the keys, cupping your hand slightly as if over an orange, with the wrist flat.

3. Raise your thumb and "drop" it to the bottom of the key. Do not try to "push" the key down. The pitch should sound bright and clear.

4. Follow this same procedure with each of your five fingers playing successive pitches.

5. Now play the following exercise with your right hand, using the fingers indicated:

   ■ thumb = 1

   ■ index = 2

   ■ middle = 3

   ■ ring = 4

   ■ little = 5

6. Now place your hand so that the thumb is on G and the fifth finger is on D. Repeat the above pattern with your hand in this position.

Now you are ready to play the following melodies. To ensure correct rhythm, be sure to count the beats out loud as you play.

Mary Had a Little Lamb

Key: G
Starting pitch: B
Meter: 4/4, begins on 1

Sara J. Hale

Good News

Key: G
Starting pitch: B
Meter: 4/4, begins on 2

Spiritual

Good news, Chariot's comin'. Good news, Chariot's comin'.

Good news, Chariot's comin'. Don't leave me behind.

Lightly Row

Key: G
Starting pitch: D
Meter: 2/4, begins on 1

Germany

Lightly row, Lightly row, O'er the shining waves we go.

Smoothly glide, smoothly glide on the silent tide.

Michael, Row the Boat Ashore

Key: C
Starting pitch: C
Meter: 4/4, begins on 3

Spiritual

Michael, row the boat ashore, Hallelujah. Michael,

row the boat ashore, Hallelujah.

Transposition

Sometimes it is necessary to transpose a piece of music from one key to another. This often occurs because of a need to lower the pitch level of a song to make it easier to sing or to play.

The following song is shown first in the key of G major and then transposed down one whole step to the key of F major.

The Farmer in the Dell

England

Key of G

The far - mer in the dell,_____ The far - mer in the dell,

Hi! ho! the der - ry oh, The far - mer in the dell._____

Key of F

The far - mer in the dell,_____ The far - mer in the dell,

Hi! ho! the der - ry oh, The far - mer in the dell._____

Notice that the chordal accompaniment is also transposed.

G major

G   D7

F major

F   C7

Sing and accompany the song first in G major and then in F major.

MELODY BELLS

A set of *melody bells* consists of a series of chromatically tuned metal bars mounted horizontally on a frame in the form of a keyboard. The smaller set contains pitches that range from C to G. Larger sets consist of two complete octaves. The lower pitches are to the left, and the higher pitches are to the right.

Twenty-five-note chromatic bells

Melody bells

Eight-note diatonic step bells

Step bells

A smaller set of melody bells constructed vertically as "steps" encompasses only one octave (eight notes) without sharps or flats. The pitches go higher as the bells go "up the ladder." Many use a different color tone bar for each pitch.

Melody bells are played with a short stick with a mallet head made of wood, rubber, string, or yarn. The choice of mallet head determines the tone quality. A hard mallet will produce a bright, loud tone, whereas a soft mallet will produce a quiet, mellow tone.

To play melody bells, grasp the mallet with your thumb and one or two fingers. Keep your wrist flexible and strike the bell near the center, letting the mallet rebound instantly. If you hold the stick too tightly, the tone will lack resonance and brilliance.

Have students practice striking the bells, holding the mallets in either hand until they can alternate L-R-L-R-L-R as they move up or down a melody pattern. It is important for students to develop the technique of playing with two mallets. A little practice will reward the student with a musically satisfying sound.

RESONATOR BELLS

Resonator bells are tuned metal bars mounted individually on a block of wood or plastic that serves as its own resonator. When played as a melody instrument, resonator bells function in the same fashion as melody bells. Because they are not fastened to one another, however, individual bells can be removed and can also be used to play harmony as well as melodies.

Resonator bells

Xylophone

XYLOPHONES

Xylophones are pitched instruments made from tuned wooden bars mounted individually on a frame. They do not have black bars (keys) like keyboards or melody bells but generally have the B-flat and F-sharp accidentals. You can purchase other accidentals to make it possible to play in several keys. Xylophones are especially useful in playing ostinato melodies, harmonic patterns, and descants. They are available as soprano, alto, and bass instruments.

You play xylophones with the same technique as melody bells, but with soft instead of hard mallets.

GLOCKENSPIELS

Glockenspiels, whose tones are clear and brilliant, are similar to melody bells in that they are tuned metal bars mounted horizontally on a frame. Like xylophones, glockenspiels do not have sharps or flats; but the tone bars are removable, and you can purchase and add the B-flat and F-sharp accidentals. You can also add other accidentals to play melodies in several keys. Glockenspiels are generally played with wooden or rubber mallets. There are both alto and soprano glockenspiels.

Glockenspiel

Metallophones

METALLOPHONES

Metallophones are large diatonic instruments that include the chromatics B-flat and F-sharp. The tone bars are of aluminum and are tuned for perfect pitch and harmonics. They provide a full and resonant sound to the ensemble. The soprano and alto metallophones are smaller than the large metallophone, which has a deep bass sound.

HANDBELLS

A set of *handbells* cast by Schulmerich, Malmark (American), Petit and Fritzen (Holland), or Whitechapel (England) is a fine addition to the classroom collection. They can have 25 chromatic bells (two octaves), 37 bells (three octaves), or 49 to 61 bells, which may be added one at a time.

Music can be played as a single melody or for harmony, or a particular piece that involves melody and harmony can be played.*

Handbells may be combined with other instruments, such as recorder, flute, Omnichord, or Orff instruments.

Handbells

Tone chimes

TONE CHIMES

These have a variety of names, including choir chimes by Malmark and tone chimes by Suzuki. Like handbells, these are chromatic, but they are lightweight, durable, and have a clarity of sound. They come in chromatic sets of 25 (two octaves) or 37 (three octaves). Additional tone chimes may be purchased singly or as an octave set.

RECORDER

The *recorder* has become increasingly popular as a melody instrument in elementary classes. It has a clear, pure tone that blends well with young voices. Any song is a potential recorder piece, and many music series books provide simple ostinato patterns and descants that can be played on either the soprano or alto recorder.

The two kinds of recorders—baroque and German—are identified by their fingering patterns. You can determine which kind your recorder is by comparing the size of the fourth fingerhole with the fifth. If the fifth hole is larger than the fourth, it is a baroque recorder and you

*The reader is referred to the American Guild of English Handbell Ringers (AGEHR) for further information; see *www.agehr.org.*

Recorder

should use baroque fingering (as in this book). If the fourth hole is larger than the fifth, it is a German recorder and you must use German fingering. Recorder instruction texts generally provide both fingerings.

Children age nine and older are most successful at playing recorders. Younger children do not yet possess the finger dexterity and coordination to play this instrument. The photo at left shows the correct way to place the instrument in the mouth.

Observe the following suggestions when playing the recorder.

1. Place the tip of the mouthpiece between your lips and in front of your teeth. Never place the mouthpiece between your teeth.

2. Blow gently.

3. Whisper the sound "too" or "doo" into the mouthpiece. Avoid a "whoo" sound. Use the tongue to stop or release the air.

4. Begin with a few pitches and gradually add notes. Avoid songs that contain middle C until students have perfected the technique of covering the holes tightly. (Middle C is a difficult pitch to play on the recorder.)

Fingering

The fingers of the left hand control the upper tone holes, while the fingers of the right hand cover the lower holes.

1. The thumb of the left hand has three positions:
   a. Covers the thumbhole
   b. Does not cover the thumbhole
   c. Covers only half of the thumbhole

2. The bottom two holes have double openings so that the player can play C-sharp and D-sharp.

3. You play pitches by covering the holes completely with your fingers. The slightest leak will create the wrong pitch or a high-pitched squeal. Minimize finger movements, because the higher you raise your fingers, the greater the possibility that a hole will become uncovered.

4. A simple thumb rest can be made by taping a piece of eraser to the back of the recorder. This provides for greater stability in holding the instrument.

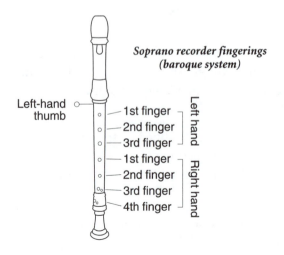

*Soprano recorder fingerings
(baroque system)*

Left-hand thumb

1st finger
2nd finger
3rd finger } Left hand

1st finger
2nd finger
3rd finger
4th finger } Right hand

Experiences

1. Introduce the recorder to students by having them play the following pitches:

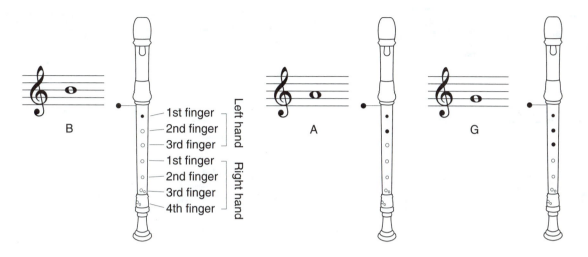

2. Sing "Hot Cross Buns" (page 58) and then play it by ear on the recorder.
   Play "Au Clair de la Lune" from notation:

Au clair de la lu – ne, Mon a - mi Pier - rot.

3. Use the same three pitches to create a simple descant to "America" (page 232).

4. Compose and perform additional tunes using these three pitches. Use titles such as "BAG" or "GAB," which reflect the occurrence of these three pitches in the tune.

5. Gradually add the following pitches:

6. Try playing some simple melodies, such as the "Ode to Joy" theme from Beethoven's Ninth Symphony (facing page), "Jolly Old Saint Nicholas" (page 169), and "Merrily We Roll Along" (page 67).

Ode to Joy (Ninth Symphony)

Key: G
Starting pitch: B
Meter: 4/4, begins on 1

Ludwig van Beethoven

USING MELODY INSTRUMENTS IN THE CLASSROOM

Students should be encouraged to use classroom instruments to play familiar songs and simple melody patterns by ear. Short childhood chants are effective for developing the ear and for vocal tone matching. As children sing the chants, they should match them on melody bells, handbells, resonator bells, or tone chimes.

Rain, Rain

Rain, rain, go a - way, Come a - gain some oth - er day.

Starlight, Starbright

Star - light, star - bright, First star I see to - night.

Wish I may, Wish I might Have the wish I wish to - night.

Golden Bells

Folk Song from China

Key: Pentatonic
Starting pitch: A
Meter: 4/4, begins on 1

Hear the gold-en bells sound a-cross the wa-ters blue.

Gen-tle winds that blow sing their sweet_ song for you;

Oo___ Oo___

Sing their sweet song for you. Oo___

From *New Dimensions in Music,* Book 4 © 1970 American Book Company. Reprinted by permission of D. C. Heath and Company.

Drums

Finger cymbals

Xylophones

(8 times)

(8 times)

(Lines 1 and 2)

(4 times)

One of the advantages to using melody or resonator bells is that the letter names of the notes are stamped on each tone bar; thus students can be guided to relate a letter name with each pitch. Because it is difficult to read music and play melody bells at the same time, however, teachers should encourage children to improvise melodies and play songs by ear. Descants and ostinatos can be taught from notation but are best performed from memory.

Melodic Ostinato

An *ostinato* is a repeated pattern that occurs throughout a composition. Select one of the following patterns to play on the xylophone or glockenspiel to accompany "Row, Row, Row Your Boat" (page 68). The ostinato should be played initially by ear only, and later from music notation.

1.

2.

The song "Colorful Boats" (page 414) is composed on the following pentatonic (five-note) scale. Play the following melodic ostinato or have students create their own. Any combination of pitches may be used.

Pentatonic scale

Melodic ostinato

Play or sing "Good News" (page 217), "Lightly Row" (page 217), "Mary Had a Little Lamb" (page 216), or "Sweet Betsy from Pike" (next page), adding the suggested accompaniments. You may wish to create your own rhythm pattern and choose different instruments.

Sweet Betsy from Pike

Traditional

Key: C
Starting pitch: C
Meter: 3/4, begins on 3

Oh, don't you re - mem - ber sweet Bet - sy from Pike Who crossed the broad
prai - ries with her hus - band, Ike, With two yoke of ox - en, an
old yel - low dog, A___ tall Shang - hai roost - er and one spot - ted hog.

Descant: Glockenspiel

Bass xylophone/metallophone (Notice that these are written in the treble clef.)

Using Melody Instruments to Play Harmony

Resonator bells can be used to play simple chords as harmonic accompaniments. Individual students can be assigned a single note of the chord, such as D, F, or A; thus, three students can play at the same time. Sing the following songs accompanied by chords played on the resonator bells, handbells, or tone chimes.

The Peddler (Korobushka)

Key: D minor
Starting pitch: A
Meter: 2/4, begins on 1

Russian Folk Song
English Words Adapted by Linda Williams

1. Treas - ures have I in my Ko - ro - bush - ka,___
2. Cost - ly and fine are the wares I bring you,___
3. Treas - ures have I in my Ko - ro - bush - ka,

Can you hear the ped - dler's cry?
Love - ly la - dy, feast your eye!
Bring your ko - pecks, come and buy!

REFRAIN

Though you see me in rags and tat - ters I
You may dance to the ba - la - lai - ka___

wear a smile up - on my face.
wear - ing sa - tin, silk, and lace.

Chords   A7   Dm   Gm

America

Key: G
Starting pitch: G
Meter: 3/4, begins on 1

Arr. Henry Carey
England c. 1690–1743

My coun - try, 'tis of thee, Sweet land of lib - er - ty, of thee I sing. Land where my

fath - ers died, land of the pil - grim's pride. From ev - 'ry___ moun - tain side Let___ free - dom ring.

Chords

G   C   D7

This Old Man

Key: F
Starting pitch: C
Meter: 2/4, begins on 1

Nursery Rhyme

This old man, he played one, he played nick nack on my thumb, With a

nick nack, pad - dy wack, give the dog a bone, this old man came roll - ing home.

Chords

F   C7

Other types of harmony that can be played on melody instruments include descants (a second contrasting melody), rounds, and simple alto or tenor harmony parts. After experimenting with different melody instruments, choose the one that is most satisfying to you and that produces the best musical result for each of the following:

- Descants
  "Did You Ever See a Lassie?" (page 120)
  "It's a Small World" (page 121)

- Rounds
  "Dona Nobis Pacem" (page 129)
  "Row, Row, Row Your Boat" (page 68)

- Simple harmony
  "Swing Low, Sweet Chariot" (page 377)
  "Hahvah Nahgeelah" (page 366)
  "The John B. Sails" (page 202)
  "I've Been Working on the Railroad" (page 204)

Harmonic Instruments

Instruments such as the Autoharp,* Omnichord, and guitar are referred to as *harmonic* instruments, as they can be used to play harmonies or drones as accompaniments to songs or to provide an introduction, an interlude, or a coda (ending) to a composition.

THE AUTOHARP

The *Autoharp* is a small stringed instrument that is easy to carry and to play. It has a range of nearly four octaves, which can be divided into three registers: low, medium, and high. The sounds of each register can be used to create a variety of rhythmic and tonal effects.

---

*Autoharp is a registered trademark of Oscar Schmidt
International, Inc., Garden State Road, Union, New Jersey.

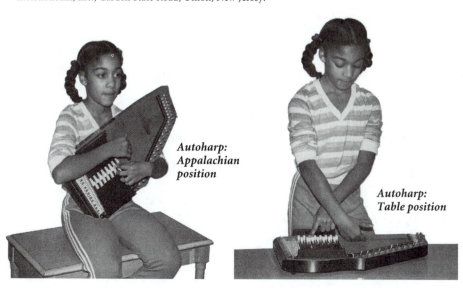

*Autoharp:
Appalachian
position*

*Autoharp:
Table position*

*Autoharp:
Lap position*

Low register   Middle register   High register

The Autoharp can be played with one pick in a lap or table position or the upright "Appalachian style" position. By using a set of finger picks in the upright position, you can play melodies as well as chords.

The Autoharp may have 12, 15, 21, or more chord bars. This discussion is limited to the 15-bar Autoharp, which is diagrammed as follows:

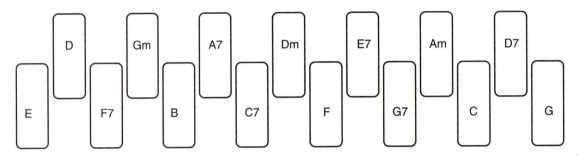

Each bar carries a chord name. When you press the chord bar, the pitches (strings) that are not part of that chord are blocked off by felt strips; thus, the only pitches that sound are the ones that are part of that chord. Experiment by pressing the C chord bar. While it is depressed, pluck each string. You will discover that only C, E, and G will sound; however, they will sound in more than one octave, which gives a rich texture to the tone when you strum. Press the chord bar firmly for the duration of the strum, or the pitches will not be blocked off and the sound will "run together."

Place the instrument on a table with the longest strings closest to you. Press the C chord bar with your left index finger, cross over with your right arm, and strum your pick across the strings from low (closest to you) to high (away from you). You should grasp the pick loosely between your thumb and index finger. Play several chords while keeping a steady beat. Place the third finger of your left hand on the G_7 chord bar and your ring finger on the F chord bar. Now play the following harmony pattern:

(Strum)　　／ ／ ／ ／　　／ ／ ／ ／　　／ ／ ／ ／　　／ ／ ／ ／
　　　　　　C C C C　　F F F F　　G_7 G_7 G_7 G_7　　C C C C

You can obtain different sound qualities by changing the material of the pick (such as using a plastic card, an eraser, or coins) or by strumming the right end (short strings) or left end (long strings) of the instrument.

By moving your left index finger to the right and up, you can play a D_7 chord. Directly to your right is the G chord. Practice various combinations until you feel comfortable.

　　／ ／ ／ ／　　／ ／ ／ ／　　／ ／ ／ ／　　／ ／ ／ ／
　　G G G G　　C C C C　　D_7 D_7 D_7 D_7　　G G G G

　／ ／ ／ ／　　／ ／ ／ ／　　／ ／ ／ ／　　／ ／ ／ ／　　／ ／ ／ ／　　／ ／ ／
　C C C C　　D_7 D_7 D_7 D_7　　G G G G　　C C C C　　F F F F　　C G_7 C

Try accompanying the song "Galway Piper" on the Autoharp by using two chords: D and A_7.

Galway Piper

Key: D
Starting pitch: D
Meter: 4/4, begins on 1

Traditional Irish Folk Song

Lively

D ... A7
Ev - 'ry per - son in the na - tion,___ Of a great or hum - ble sta - tion,___

D ... A7 ... D
Holds in high - est es - ti - ma - tion, Pip - ing___ Tim___ of___ Gal - way. Loud - ly___ he can play or low.

A7 ... D ... A7 ... D
He can___move you fast or slow, Touch your___hearts or stir your toe, Pip - ing___Tim of Gal - way.

Alternating playing in the low and high registers of the Autoharp adds variety and interest to the accompaniment. Play and sing "The Cuckoo" (page 126), playing the first beat in the low register and the second and third beats in the upper register.

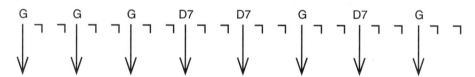

Follow this chord diagram:

G G G D₇   D₇ G G D₇   D₇ G   *(Repeat)*

G D₇ D₇ G   G D₇ D₇ G

Play the following songs. Try holding the Autoharp upright and also placing it in the lap or table position. Experiment with various strum patterns.

- ■ "This Old Man" (page 232)
- ■ "Jolly Old Saint Nicholas" (page 169)
- ■ "We Wish You a Merry Christmas" (page 73)
- ■ "Gatatumba" (page 153)

Tuning the Autoharp

It is important that the Autoharp be kept in tune. Like all musical instruments, the Autoharp is affected by weather and atmospheric conditions, so frequent tuning is necessary. If you have trouble hearing chords, ask a music teacher or perhaps a teacher who plays piano or guitar to help you.

One of the more difficult ways of tuning an Autoharp is to match each pitch with that of the piano. Because the piano is often out of tune, the result may be less than pleasing. A better way is the following:

1. Begin with an F major chord. Find the pitches F, A, and C. Tune them to a set of tuned bells or a pitch pipe. Use the hammer provided to tighten the string and raise the pitch; loosen it to lower the pitch. If you have trouble finding the right tuning peg, trace your finger along the string. Once the F major chord is in tune, you are ready to tune other chords.

2. Press the C major chord bar and tune the C chord (C, E, G). Remember that you have to tune all the pitches throughout the Autoharp, not just the three in the middle register.

3. Continue as above with the G major chord bar, followed by:

   - D_7 F# strings to be tuned
   - $B\flat$ B♭ strings to be tuned
   - E_7 G# strings to be tuned
   - A_7 C# strings to be tuned
   - $E\flat$ E♭ strings to be tuned

4. Touch up as needed.

THE OMNICHORD

The *Omnichord* (or *Q chord*) is characterized by marked chords that you can press down and play. It can play rhythms or can automatically execute chord combinations with a rhythm or walking bass line. You can use the Omnichord by playing chords only. The Omnichord is self-contained with a built-in amplifier and is completely portable.

There are many major, minor, and seventh chords on the Omnichord, as well as such preset rhythm patterns as waltz, march, and rock. Separate tempo and volume controls are provided for both chords and rhythms. The performer, however, must be careful to release each chord completely before moving to a different one or the chords will not change.

The electronic component enables you to select from the following tone colors: piano, guitar, banjo, organ, flute, chimes, brass, vibes, and synthesizer.

The SonicStrings, a unique feature of the Omnichord, encompass four full octaves. These SonicStrings play pitches of the chord selected. Thus, if the student plays a C major chord, the SonicStrings can also be strummed to sound the pitches C, E, and G at more than one octave.

Omnichord

THE GUITAR

The *guitar* is a popular instrument with children, and, by third grade, many have physically matured enough to hold it and begin to play simple chords.

There are many different types of guitars, including Hawaiian, twelve-string, folk, classical, steel-string, and electric. The two types of guitars most used in the classroom are the classical guitar with nylon or gut strings, and the steel-string flattop guitar.

Contemporary rock groups use electric guitars. Both classical and steel-string guitars are acoustic (not amplified). The basic difference is in the tone quality, the classical nylon-string guitar having a more mellow quality and the steel-string flattop guitar having a bright and brassy sound. Because nylon strings are easier on the fingers, the classical guitar is usually recommended for beginners.

The basic function of the guitar in the classroom is to accompany songs. The guitar can provide an introduction, interlude, or ending to a song. The guitar's great advantages are that there are only six strings to tune and, because many students may own guitars, more instruments may be available for use in the classroom. A guitar player can move freely around the classroom. This chapter provides an introduction to basic guitar skills that will enable you to accompany songs. Materials are limited to the use of eight chords (as used in the keys of D, G, E, and E minor). For detailed discussions and more-advanced techniques, consult one of the many excellent publications that teach one how to play the guitar.

The six strings of the guitar are E A D G B E. The following diagram shows the matching pitches on the piano keyboard:

String name E A D G B E

String number 6 5 4 3 2 1

Tuning the Guitar

Tune the open strings to a piano that is in tune. If no piano is available, use a pitch pipe and tune the lowest string (E). Notice that the strings of the guitar are numbered from the highest pitch—1—to the lowest pitch—6. Guitar pitches are notated one octave higher than they actually sound. The pitch of each string is adjusted by turning the tuning peg. To lower the pitch, turn a peg toward you; to raise the pitch, turn it away from you. The diagram at right shows which strings are controlled by each tuning peg.

By following the steps listed on the facing page, you will be able to tune a guitar accurately. The diagram below shows the finger positions you will use.

1. After you have tuned the bass E string, place your second finger (left hand) on that same string at the *fifth* fret. Match the next string (A) to that pitch. The open fifth string is now A.

2. Place your finger on the A string at the *fifth* fret. Match the next string (D) to that pitch.

3. Place your finger on the D string at the *fifth* fret. Match the next string (G) to that pitch.

4. Place your finger on the G string at the *fourth* fret. Match the next string (B) to that pitch.

5. Place your finger on the B string at the *fifth* fret. Match the next string (E) to that pitch.

Now that you have tuned the guitar, you can try some simple chords. Chords are created by placing one or more fingers on designated frets. Place your index finger (1) on the third string, first fret; second finger on fifth string, second fret; and third finger on fourth string, second fret. Strings 1, 2, and 6 are open. Strum the E major chord.

Place your second finger on the fifth string, second fret, and your third finger on the fourth string, second fret. Strings 1, 2, 3, and 6 are open. Strum the E minor chord.

Each fret on the neck of the guitar represents a half step in the chromatic scale. Pluck the highest string (E). Now place your index finger on the string between the metal strips (frets) and pluck the string. You will now hear F. Move your finger up each fret and you will hear the pitch go up by half steps.

Follow the same procedure for each string and listen for the half steps.

Playing the Guitar

There are three basic positions for playing the guitar:
(1) classical style, in which the player is seated and places a
foot on a small stool or platform; (2) folk style, in which the
player is seated and balances the guitar on a crossed leg; and
(3) standing, where the player uses a neck strap. Regardless
of the position you choose, the back of the guitar should
remain flat against your body. Avoid tipping it downward
to see the strings more clearly, thus creating an "Autoharp"
playing effect. In addition, do not allow the neck of the
guitar to drop below the horizontal position.

*Classical-style
position*

*Folk-style
position*

*Standing
position*

To play the guitar, you need to know how to strum with your right hand and form chords with your left hand. The notation, called *tablature,* indicates which strings are to remain open and which strings are to be fretted. An *X* indicates that the string is not sounded, whereas an *O* indicates that the string is open. The circle on the fretboard indicates where the fingers are to be placed. Left-hand fingers are identified as follows:

① = index finger

② = middle finger

③ = ring finger

④ = little finger

The thumb is not used in playing the guitar. You must use the tips of your fingers to press down the strings. They should be close above the frets that stop the string but should not touch the frets. Here are the diagrams for the other chords used in this book. (See Appendix B for a complete chord chart.)

G major *D major*

G C D₇ D G A₇

Strum Patterns

The *sweep strum* is created by a downward motion of the thumb across all the strings. It can be used on accented beats as well as unaccented beats. The *brush strum* is created by using the backs of the fingernails across the strings. It is used on unaccented beats. A combination of sweep and brush strums can be used for duple meter (sweep-brush) and triple meter (sweep-brush-brush). The *pluck-sweep strum* involves plucking the root of the chord and strumming on the remaining chords. It is often done with a plastic pick.

Guitar capo

Using a Capo

A *capo* (capotasto) is a device that clamps over the strings of a guitar and holds them down tightly at a new pitch level, instantly transposing a song into a higher key. When the capo is in place, chord fingerings are the same but the sounds are at a new pitch level. For example, if the capo is installed on the second fret (one whole step higher) and a D chord is played, it will sound like an E chord. If the capo is put on the third fret, chords will sound one and a half steps higher. Thus, if you know two chords in the key of D major, D and A₇, you could place the capo on the third fret and play in the key of F. The two chords would now sound as F and C₇ using the same fingering. Experiment with key changes by placing the capo on the appropriate fret to match the key in which you wish to play.

Playing Song Accompaniments

1. Play and sing "Shalom, Chaverim" accompanied by one chord (E minor). (Another one-chord song you might play is "Zum Gali Gali" on page 127.)

Shalom, Chaverim

Key: E minor
Starting pitch: B
Meter: 4/4, begins on 4

Israeli Folk Song

Sha - lom, cha - ve - rim! Sha - lom, cha - ve - rim, Sha - lom, Sha - lom! Le

hit ra — ot, le hit ra — ot, Sha - lom, sha - lom.

2. Practice changing back and forth from the G chord to the D₇ chord (see previous page). Then try accompanying "Clementine," "La Raspa" (page 244), or "Old Texas" (page 114).

Clementine

Key: G
Starting pitch: G
Meter: 3/4, begins on 3

United States

Oh, my dar - lin', oh, my dar - lin', Oh, my dar - lin' Clem - en - tine, You are

lost, and gone for - ev - er, Dread - ful sor - ry, Clem - en - tine.

La Raspa

Mexico

Key: G
Starting pitch: D
Meter: 4/4, begins on "and" of 4

Now work of the day is done, And un-der the set-ting sun The
The band plays a live-ly beat, A - mi-gos, a - mi-gas meet, And

mu - sic calls ev - 'ry one To come join in all the fun.
soon cou - ples fill the street With sounds of their danc - ing feet.

Their voic - es are lift - ed in hap - py song, No - bod - y has a care; And

peo - ple re - joice that the night is long, Laugh - ter is ev - 'ry - where.

3. Use the C and G chords to accompany "Mary Ann."

Mary Ann

Key: C
Starting pitch: E
Meter: 4/4, begins on 1

Calypso

All day, all night Ma - ry Ann,_____ Down by the sea - shore sift - ing sand._____

Ev - en lit - tle chil - dren join in the band_____ Down by the sea - shore sift - ing sand._____

4. Use the D and A₇ chords to accompany "He's Got the Whole World in His Hands" and "Six Little Ducks" (page 145).

He's Got the Whole World in His Hands

Key: D
Starting pitch: A
Meter: 4/4, begins on "and" of 3

Spiritual

He's got the whole world___ in His hands,___ He's got the whole world___ in His hands,___

He's got the whole world___ in His hands,___ He's got the whole world in His hands.___

5. Use the G, C, D, and D₇ chords to accompany "Muffin Man."

Muffin Man

Key: G
Starting pitch: D
Meter: 4/4, begins on 4

England

Oh, do you know the muf – fin man, the muf – fin man, the muf – fin man? Oh,

do you know the muf – fin man that lives in Dru – ry Lane?

6. Practice the following progression (D, A₇, D), using the pluck-sweep strum until it is smooth, and then play "Down in the Valley" using this technique.

Down in the Valley

Key: D
Starting pitch: A
Meter: 3/4, begins on 1

Traditional

1. Down in the val – ley, val – ley so low,_____
2. Hear the wind blow, love, hear the wind blow,_____

Hang your head o – ver, hear the wind blow._____
Hang your head o – ver, hear the wind blow._____

Note: You can transpose this song into the key of G and use the chords G and D₇.

Percussion Instruments

A third group of classroom instruments, *percussion* instruments, are used primarily to provide rhythmic accompaniments to songs. These instruments can also be used in ensembles and to play original musical compositions. They are divided into woods, metals, and skins.

Although most percussion instruments are commercially available, later in this chapter we include suggestions for the innovative teacher who wishes to make such instruments. Before using percussion instruments in the classroom, you should have a thorough knowledge of the types of musical effects that can be produced by each instrument. In the sections that follow, you will find brief descriptions of frequently used instruments, directions for playing them, and some functions they might serve.

WOODS

Wood percussion instruments include rhythm sticks, claves, woodblocks, maracas, sand blocks, and the güiro.

Rhythm Sticks

Description: Sticks with both a smooth surface and a ribbed surface. They are usually 12 inches in length and are round.

Function: Beat, meter, special effects.

Playing: Hold one stick in each hand and strike them together. They may also be scraped (over the ribbed surface). Sticks may also be used to tap other objects, such as a desk, chair, book, or drum.

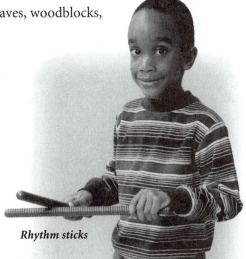

Rhythm sticks

Claves

Description: Cylindrical hardwood blocks (pronounced "*clah*-vays"). They are generally about 6 inches long and 1 inch in diameter and are made from resonant material.

Function: Rhythms (particularly Latin American), beat, syncopation.

Playing: Hold one clave loosely in a partly closed hand and strike the clave held in the other hand. Tap out the rhythm.

Claves

Woodblock

Woodblocks

Description: Hollow blocks of wood that create an interesting *clip-clop* sound.

Function: Beat, meter, syncopation, special effects.

Playing: Strike blocks with a hard mallet.

Maracas

Maracas

Description: Dried gourds whose seeds have dried, making a crisp, swishing sound.

Function: Rhythm patterns, Latin American music, syncopation.

Playing: Usually played in pairs by shaking.

Sand blocks

Sand Blocks

Description: Small blocks of wood covered with varying grades of sandpaper. Handles for each are attached.

Function: Meter, beat, swishing effects.

Playing: Rub two blocks together.

Güiro

Güiro

Description: An elongated wooden instrument with resonating holes and a serrated surface that is scraped with a stick to produce the sound (pronounced "gwee-*ro*").

Function: Used to accentuate rhythms in Latin American music.

Playing: Hold instrument in one hand while scraping the serrated surface with a stick held in the other hand.

METALS

Metal percussion instruments include cymbals, finger cymbals, triangles, tambourines, jingle bells, and jingle sticks.

Cymbals

Cymbals

Description: Discs of brass with a depression in the center of each.

Function: Accents, crescendos, climax.

Playing: (1) Strike together in a slicing manner and "stop" sound against the body; (2) strike together and let sound continue on, such as in a cymbal crash; (3) hold on to cymbal and play with a soft mallet.

Finger Cymbals

Description: Tiny replicas of large cymbals.

Function: Special effects, soft accompaniment patterns.

Playing: Touch the rim of one with the rim of another, rather than trying to clap them together.

Finger cymbals

Triangle

Description: A steel rod bent in the form of a triangle with one angle open. It is suspended on a string and played by striking it with a metal stick.

Function: Meter, accents, sustained sound, special effects.

Playing: Hold triangle by string and tap with metal striker. Be sure not to touch triangle with your hand, or the sound will be muted or stopped.

Triangle

Tambourine

Tambourine

Description: A miniature drum with small metal discs attached to the wooden rim. The discs vibrate when the instrument is struck or shaken.

Function: Sustain sounds, accents, special effects, meter.

Playing: Shake, tap with a hand on the drumhead (if there is one), tap the side of the rim with a hand.

Jingle bells

Jingle Bells

Description: Bells mounted on sticks, leather straps, or small frame.

Function: Rhythmic effects in Native American music; sleigh ride, beat, meter.

Playing: Shake or wear around wrists or ankles.

Jingle sticks

Jingle Sticks

Description: Two metal discs attached to a stick.

Function: Meter, sustained sounds, beat, special effects.

Playing: Tap the wooden handle against the palm of the hand.

SKINS

The *skin* percussion instruments, so called because they are based primarily on striking stretched skins, include the hand drum, bongo drums, and conga drum.

Hand Drum

Hand drum

Description: Metal band covered with a head made of leather or plastic. The head is struck from one side only.

Function: Meter, beat, accents, tempo.

Playing: Strike with a hard or soft mallet, a stick, or the hands.

Bongo drums

Bongo Drums

Description: Two small drums of different pitches— one high, the other low. The head may be a membrane or plastic.

Function: Often used in Latin American music to play syncopated rhythms.

Playing: Place bongos between the crossed legs of the seated player. Use fingertips and palms of hands to strike the heads. Striking the center of the drumhead and the rim produces different pitches and timbres.

Conga drums

Conga Drum

Description: A tall, barrel-type drum with a membrane head. It has a deep, resonant tone quality. The drum may be placed directly on the floor, in stands, or suspended from the shoulder by a strap.

Function: Used in both Latin American and African music for rhythm accompaniments.

Playing: Strike with fingertips, palms of hands, or even elbows. Striking the center of the drumhead, the rim, and the shell produces different pitches and timbres.

How to Select an Appropriate Instrument

The ability to play a musical instrument is directly related to a student's physical growth and coordination. Some questions to be considered in the choice of instruments include the following.

- What degree of eye-ear physical coordination is required? Playing melody bells from written notation requires a high degree of skill and coordination (ages ten to eleven), whereas playing a two- or three-note melodic pattern by ear or by letter or number is a task young children (ages five to nine) can handle.

- Is a large hand required? Many chords on the guitar require a large hand and the ability to stretch the fingers. A student must also be big enough to hold the instrument.

- What instruments use large muscle movements? Such instruments as drum, tambourine, cymbals, and rhythm sticks are appropriate for use by young students (ages five to seven).

- Can students move their fingers quickly from one chord bar to another while strumming chords on an Omnichord (ages nine to eleven)?

- Have students developed sufficient eye-finger dexterity and coordination to play the recorder? Their hands must also be large enough to cover all the fingerholes (ages nine to eleven).

Just as a composer must decide on the instruments to use in a composition, so teachers must guide students in selecting and playing instruments appropriate to the expressiveness of the music. The following questions will serve as guidelines in determining this selection:

- Is there an ethnic (such as an Asian or a Latin American) influence in the music?

- What is the style of the music (march, waltz, calypso, rock)?

- Is the melody most expressive when played on a percussive instrument, such as melody bells or xylophone, or on a sustaining instrument, such as recorder or piano?

- Is a harmonic accompanying instrument (such as keyboard, Autoharp, Omnichord, or guitar) needed to maintain the tonality of the song?

- Can percussion instruments be used to create variety and interest through playing rhythm patterns or ostinatos?

- What is the nature of the text of the song? Does it portray, for example, a quiet mood, activity, or joyousness?

- What instruments can best be used to: (a) keep a steady beat; (b) express loud and soft; (c) show contrast in texture, mood, and tempos; or (d) illustrate musical form (such as AB, ABA, or rondo)?

Playing Rhythm Accompaniments to Songs

The following steps will contribute toward successful experiences in using percussion instruments to accompany songs.

1. Ask students to pat their thighs to keep the tempo beat (speed of song). Repeat using selected rhythm instruments such as rhythm sticks.

2. Ask students to pat their thighs and clap their hands in duple or triple meter. Add selected rhythm instruments and accent the first beat of each meter group.

3. Improvise patterns and ask students to imitate by clapping or playing instruments.

4. Ask students to improvise rhythm patterns on instruments within the meter beat pattern, such as triple meter:

5. Decide on patterns to use for a selected song. Choose appropriate instruments. Apply these steps to "Rock-a My Soul" (page 254), using the instruments indicated.

Rock-a My Soul

Key: D
Starting pitch: F♯
Meter: 4/4, begins on 1

Spiritual

Rock - a my soul___ in the bos - om of A - bra - ham, Rock - a my soul___ in the

bos - om of A - bra - ham, Rock - a my soul___ in the bos - om of A - bra - ham,

Oh, rock - a my soul. So high, can't get o - ver it, So low,

can't get un - der it, So wide, can't get a - round___ it, I must go in___ at the door.

Claves:

Hand drum:

Tambourine:

Developing a Rhythm Ensemble (Grades K–3)

You can organize a classroom percussion ensemble to perform a musical composition. The choice of instruments will depend on such musical characteristics as high-low, strong beat–weak beat, dynamics, and accents. Expressiveness may be further achieved by: (1) alternating the total ensemble with a smaller group of instruments; (2) alternating the total ensemble or a smaller group of instruments with a solo instrument; (3) contrasting different timbres (such as jingle sounds with wood sounds). Leadership skills may be developed by having individual students conduct the ensemble.

Rhythm ensemble

Students should listen to a selected composition many times. After each hearing, they should make decisions regarding their choice and use of instruments. The entire experience should be one of developing aural skill in hearing expressive changes in music. The following guidelines will assist you in this task.

1. Select a musical composition that has a strong rhythm and clear use of instruments.

2. Have students determine the meter (duple/triple).

3. Determine whether there are accents and if they are on the beat or off the beat (such as syncopation).

4. Decide on instrumentation that is expressive of the composition.

5. Create a playing guide (as appropriate to grade level).

Musical compositions that are effective with a rhythm ensemble include:

- Sousa marches
- Elgar, *Pomp and Circumstance,* March #1
- Mozart, Symphony No. 40 in G Minor (third movement: minuet)
- Bizet, "Farandole" from *L'Arlésienne Suite*
- Polkas: "Over the Waves," "Carnival of Venice," "Varsoviana"
- Grieg, "In the Hall of the Mountain King" from *Peer Gynt Suite*
- Schubert, *Marche Mílitaire*
- Many popular pieces

Methods and Materials for Integrating Instrumental Experiences into the Classroom

Playing instrumental accompaniments adds interest and variety to many songs and contributes toward perceptual and motor skills. The choice and use of appropriate instruments in musical experiences can enrich the study of history, geography, culture and people, poetry, feelings and moods, and holidays. Use the following suggestions as you plan your lessons.

LANGUAGE ARTS (GRADES 4–6)

Use classroom instruments to express ideas and sounds in poems or stories, as in the following two examples.

1. Select classroom instruments to express appropriate sounds in a Halloween story or poem, such as the following one by Kay Maves. Encourage students to be creative in their choice of playing techniques.

   ### Gargoyles*

   Gargoyles perch by day on the rooftops,
   With frozen stone smiles, and long, lolling mouths ajar,
   No movements no sound 'til dark, and then GARGOYLE!
   Zipping, slipping through the night air!
   Laughing, leering tearing through the quiet air!
   Scaring cats, chasing bats 'til dawn
   When each one flits to his rooftop
   And stares with his cold stone eyes at the busy streets
   Through the only bright day,
   And knows that night will come when GARGOYLE!
   Laughing, leering tearing through the quiet air!
   Scaring cats, chasing bats,
   Reeling, spinning, shrieking, grinning GARGOYLE!

2. Dramatize "Five Little Pumpkins" (page 29) and use music and text to determine rhythmic accompaniment and pitch relationships. Consider the following suggestions:

   a. Steady beat (rhythm sticks)

   b. Resonator bells (one for each pitch of the phrase):

   1 = F
   2 = G
   3 = A
   4 = B
   5 = C

   c. "Run and run and run" (play on melody bells):

   run and run and run.

---

* Kay Maves, "Gargoyles," *New Dimensions in Music* (New York: American Book Co., 1970), pp. 107–108. By permission of D. C. Heath & Co.

    d. "Ooo went the wind" (glissando on xylophone)

    e. "*Out* went the light" (woodblock)

    f. "Rolled out of sight" (jingle sticks)

3. Read the story of *Peter and the Wolf.** Select classroom instruments to represent each character. Decide on a rhythm, melody, or playing technique. Follow up by listening to Prokofiev's *Peter and the Wolf.* Discuss the composer's choice and use of instruments.

4. Read the story *Little Toot* by Hardie Gramatky.† Select classroom instruments to represent the various boat sounds and types of boats. Use them to dramatize the story.

5. Read a children's story of your choice and select musical instruments to represent each character. Decide on a rhythm, melody, or playing technique for each.

SCIENCE: SOUND (GRADES 4–6)

1. Explore concepts of sound through classroom instruments.

    a. Place the terms *sound, vibration, pitch,* and *frequency* on the chalkboard. Select a drum; as you strike the head, have the students place their hands against the side of the instrument. They will feel and hear the *sound* produced by the *vibration* of the instrument. Explain that the vibration of the instrument produces the *pitch,* the highness or lowness of musical sounds. Select some instruments, such as the Omnichord, that produce both high and low sounds. Ask individual students to play them; then discuss why high or low sounds are produced (discovering that high sounds are produced by short strings or small instruments and low sounds by long strings or large instruments). Demonstrate how high-to-low pitches can be produced by lengthening an instrument. Have a student play a clarinet or flute first with just the mouthpiece and then add sections of the instrument, gradually lengthening the pipe and lowering the pitch. Pitch is directly related to the frequency of vibration. Sound vibrations move back and forth in a cycle; the number of cycles of vibration per second is known as the *frequency.* Some instruments produce sounds of low frequency or pitch, whereas other instruments produce sounds of high frequency or pitch.

    b. Explore various types of sounds by making your own musical instruments. Try for both high and low sounds. Also explore how sounds change depending on which material the musical instrument is made of. The sidebar on the following page provides suggestions for making your own instruments.

---

* Johnson-Sickels-Sayers, *Anthology of Children's Literature* (Boston: Houghton Mifflin, 1970), p. 261.

† Hardie Gramatky, Ibid., pp. 81–82.

How to Make Your Own Musical Instruments

Cymbals

Materials: Lids of pans

Directions: Make a hole in the lids with a nail and fasten a spool or piece of wood for the handle.

Triangle

Materials: Steel rod bent into a triangle
blunt-end bolt

Directions: Strike bent rod with the blunt-end bolt.

Hand Drum

Materials: A quart or gallon can
Two pieces of canvas or leather
3 to 5 yards of heavy cord
Enamel or lacquer and brush
Leather punch

Directions: Remove the ends of the can and smooth the edges. Paint the can. Cut two pieces of rubber or leather about 4 inches larger in diameter than the can. Punch the same number of holes in each piece at least 1 inch from the edge. Place the two pieces of canvas or leather over the ends of the can and lace them together. Tie a cord securely around the ends of the drum and adjust the lacing until you get the desired sound.

Jingle Bells

Materials: 6-inch dowel
Three jingle bells
Two tacks
3-inch leather or plastic strap
Four pieces of thin wire

Directions: Punch holes in the strap and fasten the bells to the strap with the wire. Tack the strap to the dowel (use small tacks to avoid splitting the wood) or drill a hole through the wood and anchor the strap securely with the wire.

Claves

Materials: 1-inch dowels of hardwood, which give clear tone when tapped together: beech, mahogany, walnut, cherry, ash, or sycamore

Directions: Cut dowels into 6-inch lengths. Apply several coats of varnish or hard wax.

Rhythm Sticks

Materials: Hardwood dowels $3/8$ inch to $5/8$ inch in diameter

Directions: Cut dowels into 12-inch lengths. Carve ridges on one side and paint rods in bright colors.

Woodblock

Materials: Small wooden box (such as a cigar box)

Directions: Fasten lid tightly onto hollow box. Strike box with stick or mallet.

Maracas

Materials: Ball of plasticine
Dowel
Tissue paper and newspaper
Paste or glue
Peas, buttons, rice, or pebbles

Directions: Shape the desired size of plasticine on a length of dowel. Apply small pieces of damp tissue paper and add small pieces of pasted newspaper. Build up layers of white or colored newspaper. When ball is dry, cut in half, and remove plasticine. Join the two halves together and glue. Drop a few hard objects into the shell and replace the dowel. Secure with strips of paper and paste. When dry, paint the maraca with bright colors.

Sand Blocks

Materials: 3-inch square blocks of wood, $3/4$ inch to 1 inch thick
Sandpaper

Directions: Cover blocks of wood with various thicknesses of sandpaper (to get the desired effect). Add handles made from empty spools of thread or cabinet knobs.

African Rattle

Materials: Large gourd or papier-mâché shell mounted on a dowel
Buttons
Knotted string

Directions: Fasten buttons on knotted string and form into loose net. Mount on the outside of the gourd or shell.

2. Provide classroom materials as stimuli for group discussion, special-credit projects, and hands-on activities. The following materials are available from the Friendship House, 29313 Clemens Rd., Suite 2G, Box 450978, Westlake, OH 44145-0623; 1-800-791-9876; *www.friendshiphouse.com:*

   - "Let's Learn Music" — 17" × 22" posters, #600
   - "101 Bulletin Boards from the Music Classroom" — #1245
   - "Make Your Own Instruments from Around the World" — activity book and cassette, #1205
   - "Making Simple Musical Instruments" by Bart Hopkin — #887
   - "Music Crafts for Kids"— activity book, #830
   - "Giant Vinyl Floor Keyboard" — 24" × 54", #781

SOCIAL STUDIES—HISTORY: MEDIEVAL/RENAISSANCE (GRADES 4–6)

1. Create a simple dance to a medieval Ductia (bowing, stepping forward, stepping backward, moving in a circle). Add a hand drum and tambourine for a percussion accompaniment. (See *A Medieval Christmas,* MCA Classics 1986 CD.)

SOCIAL STUDIES—GEOGRAPHY: AMERICAN WEST (GRADES 4–6)

1. Select songs that describe activities of the American cowboy, such as roping, branding, herding cows, or eating around a campfire. Some possibilities are:
   - "Home on the Range"
   - "Red River Valley"
   - "Get Along Little Dogies"
   - "Old Paint"
   - "Night Herding Song"
2. Add guitar, keyboard, or Omnichord accompaniment to each.
3. Introduce the harmonica and have selected students accompany the singing by ear.

Sample Lessons

DYNAMICS

Activity: Experiencing dynamics through playing instruments

Grades: 1–3

Concept: Dynamics: Loud/soft

Objectives

Students will:

1. Increase their perception of the expressive use of dynamics by playing classroom instruments.

2. Demonstrate an understanding of dynamics by their choice and expressive playing of classroom instruments.

Teacher Preparation

1. Listen to *The Rhythm Makers* "Loud and Soft" (Tom Thumb Records Co.* CD T303).

2. Prepare a chart with symbols:

   - *f*   forte   loud
   - *p*   piano   soft
   - crescendo $<$
   - decrescendo $>$
   - accents

Materials

- Recording "Loud and Soft"
- Chart with symbols

Procedures

1. Engage students in an echo game:

   TEACHER: Cup hands and call "Hello . . ."

   STUDENTS: "Hello"

   TEACHER: "Are you there?"

   STUDENTS: "Are you there? Are you there? Are you there?" (each time softer)

---

*Rhythms Production, Whitney Building, Box 34485, Los Angeles, CA 90034.

2. Echo-clap the following rhythms:

TEACHER (loudly) ♩ ♫ ♩ ♩

STUDENTS (softly) ♩ ♫ ♩ ♩

TEACHER (loudly) ♫ ♩ ♫ ♩

STUDENTS (softly) ♫ ♩ ♫ ♩

3. Play or sing the echo song "Hello There!" (page 88). Ask students to respond by:

   a. Singing an answer using tonal syllables

   b. Playing an answer on melody or resonator bells

4. Explore playing a single instrument loudly and softly.

5. Discover instruments that make loud sounds and those that make soft sounds.

6. Choose large cymbals and a pair of finger cymbals. Play an echo game: One child taps the large cymbal with a soft mallet; a second student answers by tapping the finger cymbals (on rim only). Apply to the words, such as "Hello," in the song.

7. Invite children to choose instruments that could make a loud sound (drum, cymbals, woodblock) and those that might make a soft sound (sand blocks, jingle sticks). Divide class into two groups. Assign loud instruments to group 1 and soft instruments to group 2. Loud instruments will play on first "Hello," soft instruments on second "Hello." Practice the rhythm:

Loud: ♪| ♫ ¿|

Soft: ⁊| ¿ ⁊ ♪| ♫

8. Have children listen to "Loud and Soft." Play instruments as directed (be sure students do not bang or hit the instrument to make it loud):

   ■ Group 1   Louder instruments
   ■ Group 2   Softer instruments

   Proceed by alternating sets of instruments throughout the piece. Children without instruments participate with group 1 (loud—clapping hands) or group 2 (soft—tapping fingers).

Assessment

1. Observe whether students play loudly or softly at appropriate time while listening to "Loud and Soft."

2. Play "Kalinka" and ask students to raise their hands as the music gets louder and bow their heads as the music becomes or starts softer. (Help students understand that loud does not always equal fast and soft does not always equal slow.)

REPETITION AND CONTRAST

Activity: Playing instruments

Grades: 2–3

Concepts: Repetition
            Contrast

Objectives

Students will:

1. Identify contrasting melodies by playing selected instruments.

2. Demonstrate an understanding of form by creating a rhythm accompaniment involving contrasting timbres for each section.

3. Increase their ability to hear repetition and contrast of musical ideas in music.

Materials

- Songs: "We Wish You a Merry Christmas" (page 73)
  "Home on the Range" (page 47)

- Recordings: Mozart, *Eine Kleine Nachtmusik*, Rondo
  Alpert, "Spanish Flea"*

- Geometric forms

- Classroom instruments:
  Group 1: Drum, tambourines, sticks
  Group 2: Triangles, jingle sticks, finger cymbals, jingle bells

- Bulletin board with pictures of the instruments

Procedures

1. Provide a large table with two signs: *Heavy, Light.*

2. Explore the contrasting timbres of instruments. Each student plays and places an instrument in front of the appropriate sign. After all are in place, invite several students to play one instrument from each section. Ask the class to decide whether the instrument is in the right place or ought to be with the other group.

3. Play a game in which all of the instruments are placed at the rear of the classroom. Each student has an "Instrument Sheet." (Pictures could also be placed on a chalkboard or bulletin board.) A selected student chooses and plays an instrument from the back of the room. Students circle the instrument on their worksheet or point to a picture on the board.

4. Select four students to play drum, tambourine, sticks, and cymbals in the following rhythm:

---

* Herb Alpert and the Tijuana Brass, *Greatest Hits*, A&M Records CD 3267.

5. Select four students to play the triangle, jingle sticks, finger cymbals, and jingle bells in the following rhythm:

6. Compare the sounds created by the two groups of instruments in 4 and 5 above.

7. Listen to Herb Alpert's "Spanish Flea." Play a steady beat on the hand drum for the main theme. Have students select categories of instruments to use for the contrasting theme (sticks, woodblock, claves; jingle bells, jingle sticks, tambourine, triangle; hand drum, conga drum, bongo drums, snare drum).

8. Select a single instrument to play the main theme and other instruments to play the contrasting sections. Practice playing the following rhythm and changing on cue:

9. Listen to "Spanish Flea" and accompany with the instruments. Alternate heavy and light instruments for the contrasting sections. Invite a student with a keen musical sense to be the director of the ensemble. Involve all of the students in playing the instruments. Provide the leader with a conductor's baton.

Closure

1. Listen to Mozart's *Eine Kleine Nachtmusic,* Rondo, and accompany with heavy or light instruments the main melody and the contrasting melodies. Involve all of the students in playing the instruments. Either the teacher or a student may conduct with a baton.

2. Select instruments to play the contrasting sections of "We Wish You a Merry Christmas" (page 73); one possibility would be jingle sticks (A), claves (B), jingle sticks (A).

Assessment

1. Identify the contrasting melodies when they occur in Mozart's *Eine Kleine Nachtmusic,* Rondo, by raising hands.

2. Identify the main melody of the Rondo by raising hands.

3. Create an ABA form by playing contrasting instruments.

4. Create an AB form by playing contrasting instruments.

For Your Journal

In your journal or portfolio, make a section on playing classroom instruments in the elementary school. Give some examples of how you would integrate instrumental experiences into the classroom. Comment on how you would select appropriate instruments and include information on:

- *Melody instruments* (piano and electronic keyboards, melody bells, resonator bells, xylophone, glockenspiel, metallophones, handbells, tone chimes, and recorder)
- *Harmonic instruments* (Autoharp, Omnichord [or Q chord], and guitar)
- *Percussion instruments* (woods [rhythm sticks, claves, woodblocks, maracas, sand blocks, and güiro], metals [cymbals, finger cymbals, triangle, tambourine, jingle bells, and jingle sticks], and skins [hand drum, bongo drums, and conga drum])

Finally, comment on how you would add a rhythmic accompaniment to a song, develop a rhythm ensemble, and make some of your own musical instruments.

*T*eaching Music Through Listening

IN OUR SOCIETY radio and television, home stereos, and portable players surround us with music. Sometimes music serves as a background of sound while we wait in an office, ride in an elevator, or shop in a mall. At other times, such as when attending a concert, ballet, or opera, we must listen carefully to enjoy it fully. You might say that in the first instance we *hear* music, whereas in the second we *listen to* music.

Let us consider some differences in both of these experiences. First, *hearing* is one of the five basic senses. Often we hear sounds without consciously identifying what they are: birds chirping, wind moving through trees, rustling leaves, and so on. In a crowd we may hear a lot of talking without distinguishing any particular words or meanings. On the other hand, *listening* requires aural skills that include focusing attention on the sound source, remembering sounds, perceiving phenomena unique to sounds, and responding. A baby hears sound but must be taught to listen. Many a parent has said, "My child hears me when I speak, but doesn't want to listen." Listening to music requires focusing attention on its unique qualities. This takes energy and self-discipline; if our minds wander, we lose the meaning of what we are hearing.

A listening experience is very different from a visual experience. After viewing a picture, we can look out the window, leave the room, or think about something else, and when we return, the picture will be in the same place with the same colors, lines, and shapes. In music, however, unless we use a recording, no two performances are ever exactly the same. Music is also unique in that it passes through time and we hear it both in the present (as it is happening) and in our memory (as it has happened). Memory, then, is an important component of listening, for part of the pleasure derived from a musical experience is in recalling a musical theme, a harmony, or a distinctive tone color.

Children can be taught to listen to the expressive use of elements of music such as melody, rhythm, texture, tone color, dynamics, and formal structure. As they grow in their ability to perceive and understand musical phenomena, they have a greater potential for deeply satisfying aesthetic experiences.

A related outcome of a listening experience is learning how music expresses the time, place, and people who create it. For example, as children study and listen to "America," "Yankee Doodle," and "Chester," they can become more aware of and sensitive to the events surrounding the American Revolution.

Although there are many benefits to developing home listening libraries of music, nothing can really replace the thrill and excitement of attending a live performance. Throughout the United States, countless free concerts are given each year by colleges and universities, public and private schools, museums, churches, and others. Many symphony orchestras sponsor educational concerts for children at a nominal cost. It is important for the classroom teacher to seek out such opportunities so that children can attend live performances of music.

This chapter is designed to provide materials and techniques for preparing students to listen to music. It begins with a discussion of the chain of events in musical expression, followed by sections on sound sources for musical listening, how to guide listening, and integrating listening into the classroom.

The Chain of Events in Musical Expression

Musical expression follows a chain of events that runs from composer to performer to listener.

THE COMPOSER

Music begins with an idea in the mind of a person called a *composer*. The idea may be a melody, a rhythmic motif, or a distinctive tone color. The composer must have the skill to organize these musical ideas in a logical and meaningful fashion that can be perceived and understood by the listener. All composers who have created lasting works of art have been able to achieve a high level of imagination and sensitivity in their works.

THE PERFORMER

Written music must be re-created from the musical score by the *performer*. The quality of the performance depends on (1) the technical skill of the performer, (2) insights into the musical meanings that are expressed, and (3) understanding the musical style of the composer. Although there is always somewhat of a personal stamp on any performance, the goal is to interpret the music as accurately and sensitively as possible according to the directions given by the composer.

THE COMPOSER/PERFORMER

In many kinds of music, such as the oral traditions of Africa and India, as well as American jazz, the performer is often the composer. In such traditions, the musician creates or composes at the instant of performance. That is, the role of composer appears in the improvisations by the performer. These improvisations, while appearing to be spontaneous, are most often based on a catalog of musical ideas that have been stored in the musician's mind over a period of time. During performances the musician must organize both stored and newly created sound materials in logical and imaginative ways.

THE LISTENER

The *listener* is one of the most important links in the chain of events of musical expression. The principal function of the listener is to receive, interpret, and respond to music. Learning to be an effective listener requires early and sustained training.

Sounds Produced by Voices

People around the world produce a large number of different vocal sounds. Some are full and open, whereas others are pinched and nasal. In Western music women's voices are classified as *soprano* and *alto*, and male voices are divided into *tenor* and *bass*. Each of the following compositions can be used to illustrate various classical voice qualities:

- Soprano: Giacomo Puccini, "Un Bel Di" (One Fine Day) from *Madame Butterfly*
- Alto: Felix Mendelssohn, "O Rest in the Lord" from *Elijah*
- Tenor: G. F. Handel, "Comfort Ye" from *Messiah*
- Bass: Jerome Kern, "Old Man River" from *Showboat*

Sounds Produced by Western Orchestral Instruments

Sounds are produced by instruments in a variety of ways. In general, instruments are classified as stringed, wind, or percussion, depending on how their sounds are produced. In addition, some twentieth-century instruments produce their sounds electronically.

STRINGED INSTRUMENTS

Stringed instruments are usually played with a bow drawn across the strings. Placing the fingers of the left hand on the strings along the fingerboard changes the pitch. Each pitch is produced by a different finger position. Stringed instruments can also be plucked (called *pizzicato*). The pitches are still created with fingers on the strings; however, the fingers of the right hand pluck the string instead of using a bow. This same technique of plucking is used when playing the Japanese koto or Indian sitar. Other instruments that can be plucked include the harp and the guitar.

Violin

The *violin* is the soprano of the string family and is capable of a wide range of dynamics and expression. It has four strings, which are tuned by tightening or loosening pegs at the upper end of the instrument. *Musical example:* Mendelssohn, Violin Concerto No. 3 in E Minor, Rondo.

Violin

Viola

The *viola* is the alto of the string family. It is somewhat larger than the violin, and its strings are slightly thicker; therefore, its sound is lower and somewhat richer than the violin's. *Musical example:* Hindemith, *Der Schwanendreher* (The Swan Catcher).

Viola

Cello

The *violoncello* (usually called the *cello*) is the tenor member of the string family. Unlike the violin and viola, which are supported by holding the instruments between the chin and shoulder, the cello is placed upright with a peg at the base of the instrument resting on the floor. The cello's tone is warm and mellow. *Musical example:* Mendelssohn, Sonata No. 1 for Cello and Piano, Op. 45.

Cello

String Bass

The *string bass* (double bass) is the lowest-sounding member of the string family of instruments. Although similar to the cello, the string bass is much larger and players must either stand or sit on a high stool to play it. The sounds of the bass are among the lowest in the orchestra. *Musical example:* Saint-Saëns, *Carnival of the Animals,* "The Elephant."

String bass

Harp

Harp

The *harp* is a large instrument with forty-seven strings. These strings are tuned by pegs across the top of the instrument. A series of pedals on the bottom of the harp enable the player to change keys. *Musical example:* Tchaikovsky, *The Nutcracker,* "Waltz of the Flowers."

WIND INSTRUMENTS

The *wind* instruments are played by blowing into a tube whose length is controlled by covering fingerholes, pressing down valves, or, in the case of a trombone, moving a slide. They are divided into the woodwind family and the brass family.

Woodwinds

The *woodwinds* can be classified into three groups: those without reeds, those with single reeds, and those with double reeds.

The first group of woodwinds are those without reeds. The *flute* is the soprano member of this group. Originally made of wood, it is now usually metal. Its tone in the lower register is warm and smooth, but as it proceeds up the scale the tone becomes brighter. *Musical examples:* Debussy, *Syrinx* (RCD1-7173RE) and Prokofiev, *Peter and the Wolf,* "Bird."

The other member of the reedless group, the *piccolo,* looks like a small flute and sounds an octave higher. Composers use it for unusual effects, since its sound can penetrate heavy masses of orchestral tone. *Musical example:* Sousa, "Stars and Stripes Forever," ending.

The second group of woodwinds are those with a single reed. The *clarinet* is a single-reed instrument whose pitch and tone can vary from a low, dark, sonorous quality to brilliant high pitches. *Musical example:* Prokofiev, *Peter and the Wolf,* "Cat."

Flute

Piccolo

Clarinet

Saxophone

The *saxophone* is another single-reed instrument. It differs from the clarinet in that it is larger and is constructed from metal. Saxophones are found predominantly in bands but are occasionally played in orchestras. They come in several sizes, including alto, tenor, and baritone. *Musical example:* Glazunov, Concerto in E-flat for Saxophone and Orchestra, Op. 109.

The third group of woodwinds are those with a double reed. The *oboe* is a double-reed instrument with a bright tone color and a penetrating quality. *Musical example:* Prokofiev, *Peter and the Wolf,* "Duck."

The *English horn* is larger than the oboe and therefore has a lower pitch and a darker tone color. *Musical example:* Dvořák, *New World Symphony,* second movement.

Oboe

English horn

Bassoon

Contrabassoon

The *bassoon* is a still lower-pitched instrument; it is sometimes described as a tenor-sounding instrument. *Musical example:* Prokofiev, *Peter and the Wolf,* "Grandfather."

The *contrabassoon* is the lowest-sounding member of the woodwind family. It is essentially the same as the bassoon, only larger, and sounds an octave lower. Although it is 16 feet long, the instrument is constructed in coils so that it actually stands about 4 feet tall. *Musical example:* Ravel, *Mother Goose Suite,* "Beauty and the Beast."

Brass

A second group of wind instruments are the *brass,* a name that refers to the material from which the instruments are made. There are four main brass instruments: trumpet, French horn, trombone, and tuba.

The *trumpet* is the soprano of the brass family and has a high, brilliant sound. *Musical example:* Purcell-Clarke, Trumpet Voluntary in D.

Trumpet

French horn

The *French horn* is the alto member of the brass family. Its tone is lower and more mellow than that of the trumpet. *Musical example:* Mozart, Horn Concerto No. 3 in E-flat Major, K. 447.

The *trombone* is the tenor member of the brass family. This instrument consists of a tube about 9 feet long, doubled on itself to about half that length. The performer uses a slide to alter the length of the tube and, therefore, the pitch. *Musical example:* "Bones Trombone," March, by Henry Fillmore (Screamers Circus Marches, Frederick Fennell, Phillips Classics Productions, 1991, CD 125362).

Trombone

Tuba

The *tuba* is the bass member of the brass family and has a low and powerful tone. A special type of tuba, known as the *Sousaphone* (originally made from brass but today also from synthetic materials), is designed in circular fashion so that the instrument can be carried more easily in marching bands. *Musical example:* Tripp, "Tubby the Tuba."

PERCUSSION INSTRUMENTS

A fourth family of instruments, those that are struck or shaken, are known as *percussion*. Instruments that have a definite pitch are timpani, chimes, and xylophone. Instruments of indefinite pitch include the snare drum, bass drum, cymbals, triangle, gong, tambourine, and castanets.

Timpani

The *timpani* (kettledrums) are capable of definite and variable pitch. The player strikes the heads with different types of sticks, from hard to soft, according to the quality of tone required. The drums are tuned for the particular composition. *Musical example:* Prokofiev, *Peter and the Wolf,* "Guns of Hunters."

Chimes

Chimes consist of metal bars suspended on a frame and struck with a mallet. They are tuned to the chromatic scale, and the tone is very bright. *Musical example:* Tchaikovsky, *1812 Festival Overture,* ending.

Sousaphone

Conn Sousaphone. Photo courtesy of United Musical Instruments, U.S.A., Inc.

Timpani

Chimes

Xylophone

The *xylophone* consists of a graduated series of wooden bars suspended on a frame in two rows representing the white and black keys of the piano. It is played with hard mallets. *Musical example:* Saint-Saëns, *Carnival of the Animals,* "Fossils."

Xylophone

Snare drum

Bass drum

Snare Drum

The *snare drum* is a shallow cylinder of brass closed at either end by a membrane under tension. Metal strings (snares) are stretched across the lower head so that, when the drum is struck, they vibrate against the membrane, causing the familiar rattling effect. *Musical example:* Bizet, *Carmen,* "Soldier's Chorus."

Bass Drum

The *bass drum* is made of wood or metal; its pitch is indefinite but very low. It is often used for special rhythmic emphasis. *Musical example:* Verdi, *Requiem,* "Dies Irae."

Cymbals

Cymbals are discs of brass with a depression in the center. They are used in pairs for such rhythmic and tonal effects as keeping the beat and dynamic contrasts. *Musical example:* Ravel, *Mother Goose Suite,* "Laideronette, Empress of the Pagoda."

Triangle

The *triangle* is a steel rod bent into a triangular shape with one angle open. It is suspended on a string and played by striking it with a metal stick. It has a brilliant, tinkling tone. *Musical example:* Verdi, *Il Trovatore,* "Anvil Chorus."

Gong

The *gong* is a large, circular, metallic plate suspended by a cord and struck with a mallet. *Musical example:* Ravel, *Mother Goose Suite,* "Laideronette, Empress of the Pagoda."

Cymbals

Triangle

Gong

Tambourine

The *tambourine* is a miniature drum with a single head. In the rim of wood are small metal discs that vibrate when the instrument is struck or shaken. *Musical example:* Verdi, *Il Trovatore,* "Anvil Chorus."

Tambourine

Castanets

Castanets

Castanets are hollow shells that are always used in pairs. When clapped together rhythmically, they give a sharp, clacking sound. They are often used with dance music of Spain or Latin America. *Musical example:* Bizet, *Carmen,* "Seguidilla."

KEYBOARD INSTRUMENTS

Four keyboard instruments are the pipe organ, piano, harpsichord, and celesta.

Pipe Organ

The *pipe organ* consists of a set of pipes (one for each key) that sound at different pitches. Stops activate the many pipes (flues, principals, reeds, and strings), and the player can use them to produce an enormous variety of tone colors. The player sits at a console, which may have several keyboards, including one called the pedal (played with the feet). Each one of these keyboards is connected to a division of pipes. These divisions are called *great, swell, positive, choir,* or *solo,* depending on the number of manuals. The organist manipulates stops and expression pedals (to get louder and softer) and selects tone colors from the various divisions to interpret the music. *Musical example:* Ives, Variations on "America."

Pipe organ
St. Andrew's United Presbyterian Church, Olmsted Falls, Ohio

Piano

Piano

The *piano* has eighty-eight notes and a single keyboard. Sounds are produced by hammers that strike strings stretched across the inner framework of the instrument. *Musical example:* Mozart, Variations on "Twinkle, Twinkle, Little Star," K. 265.

Harpsichord

The *harpsichord* resembles a piano but is smaller and may have two keyboards. Instead of hammers striking strings, small plectrums, activated by the keyboard, pluck strings; thus the harpsichord has a much softer sound than the piano and a more limited dynamic range. *Musical example:* Handel, *The Harmonious Blacksmith*.

Harpsichord

Celesta

Celesta

The *celesta* looks like a small piano but has only a four-octave keyboard. When the keys are pressed, small hammers strike bell-metal bars. The sounds of this instrument are characterized by a light, bell-like quality. *Musical example:* Tchaikovsky, *The Nutcracker*, "Dance of the Sugar Plum Fairy."

Early synthesizer

ELECTRONIC INSTRUMENTS

Many acoustic instruments, such as the piano and guitar, can be electrified. Much popular music today is performed on these electronic instruments.

Another form of electronic instrument is the *synthesizer*. It can perform tasks beyond the capability of traditional instruments. For example, a composer can use a synthesizer to create melodies and rhythms extending beyond the pitch range of a traditional instrument or faster than could be created by a human being. Synthesizers create new sounds and forms of music. *Musical example:* Babbitt, Ensembles for Synthesizer.

Performing Ensembles

Both instruments and voices are often grouped into large ensembles such as orchestras, bands, and choruses. Sometimes the ensembles are much smaller, such as duets (two performers), trios (three performers), and quartets (four performers).

ORCHESTRA

The Western symphony orchestra is a large ensemble comprising stringed, brass, woodwind, and percussion instruments. The principal instruments of the orchestra are given in the accompanying table. Figure 7.1 shows a typical seating arrangement.

Instruments of the orchestra are often studied in terms of their general classification (strings, woodwinds, brasses) and their pitch ranges. Thus there are "soprano," "alto," "tenor," and "bass" instruments, as shown below.

Principal Orchestra Instruments

Range	Strings	Brass	Woodwind
Soprano	Violin	Trumpet	Flute
Alto	Viola	French horn	Clarinet/oboe
Tenor	Cello	Trombone	Bassoon
Bass	String bass (double bass)	Tuba	Contrabassoon

In addition to the instruments listed in the table, orchestras have a variety of pitched and nonpitched percussion instruments with ranges from high to low. Often some keyboard instruments (such as celesta and piano) are also included in the orchestral ensemble.

The Cleveland Orchestra with its conductor, Christoph von Dohnányi

Figure 7.1. A seating plan of the Cleveland Orchestra

Suggestions for Lessons

1. Listen to and watch the video *The Orchestra* with Peter Ustinov.* You may wish to teach the instruments over several days, since the video has three parts to it.

   Part one includes (a) feelings about music, and (b) the composer. Part two includes (a) the string family and (b) the woodwind family. Part three includes (a) the brass family, (b) the woodwind family, (c) special instruments, and (d) the conductor.

2. Listen to Benjamin Britten's *The Young Person's Guide to the Orchestra,* subtitled *Variations and Fugue on a Theme of Purcell* (Purcell was an English composer, 1659–1695). This composition features individual instruments and sections of the orchestra. Place the following diagram on a transparency or on the chalkboard and call out the number as each event occurs:

---

1. **Purcell theme played by the entire orchestra**

2. **Woodwinds play theme**

3. **Brasses play theme**

4. **Strings play theme**

5. **Percussion**

6. **Entire orchestra plays theme**

7. **Variations on the theme, each featuring a different instrument or instrument group as follows:**

   a. Woodwinds
   Piccolo and flutes
   Oboes
   Clarinets
   Bassoons

   b. Strings
   Violins
   Violas
   Cellos
   Double basses
   Harp

   c. Brasses
   Horns
   Trumpets
   Trombones and tuba

   d. Percussion
   Kettledrums
   Bass drum and cymbals
   Tambourine and triangle
   Snare drum and Chinese block (brightly painted, wooden percussion instrument)
   Xylophone
   Castanets and gong
   Whip
   All percussion instruments together

8. **A fugue, in which the theme is played by instruments entering one after the other, follows:**

   a. Piccolo
   b. Flute
   c. Oboe
   d. Clarinet
   e. Bassoons
   f. Violins
   g. Violas
   h. Cellos
   i. Double basses
   j. Harp
   k. Horns
   l. Trumpets
   m. Trombone and tuba

9. **Brass instruments play the Purcell theme in a slow tempo, while remaining instruments continue with the fugal style.**

---

* VHS 646 from Mark Rubin Productions, Inc. 1990. Available from Friendship House, 29313 Clemens Rd., Suite 2G, Box 450978, Westlake, OH 44145-0623; 1-800-791-9876.

BAND

In contrast to the large stringed instrument sections of the orchestra, a *band* has a large woodwind section consisting of clarinets, saxophones, flutes, piccolos, oboes, English horn(s), and bassoons. Brass instruments of the band include trumpets, French horns, trombones, and tubas. In addition there are many different percussion instruments, particularly bass drum and snare drums. Listen to the sound of a band in Sousa's "Stars and Stripes Forever."

The Shaker Middle School Band

CHORUS

A *chorus* is composed of many voices singing together. Large choruses, made up of soprano, alto, tenor, and bass voices, frequently perform works with an orchestra. Listen to the sound of a chorus in Handel's *Messiah,* "Hallelujah Chorus."

The Burleigh (Wisconsin) Elementary Choir

By permission of the Burleigh (Wisconsin) Elementary Choir, Maria Zellmer, director.

How to Guide Listening

A teacher must have knowledge about the musical components of a piece of music. He or she needs to decide on the focus of the listening experience, choose materials appropriate to a given maturity level, and develop sequential and imaginative procedures. It is important for teachers to design listening lessons that are multisensory; that is, students need to hear music, see a visual that helps give meaning to the aural experience, be physically involved through movement, and develop skill in verbally describing a musical experience.

LEVELS OF LISTENING

As you explore students' musical needs, it will be helpful to describe four levels of listening, each of which might occur (in differing degrees of complexity) at a given grade level.

1. *What do I hear?* At this most basic level, the student simply hears sounds, which might be created by a voice, an environmental source, or an instrument. No processing of the sounds occurs and no value judgments are made.

2. *How are sounds organized?* Sounds may be organized as melody, rhythm, texture (harmony), timbre (tone color), and form. They may be organized with a distinctive quality, which may be identified as Japanese, or jazz, or medieval; or possibly the sounds will reflect the style of a particular composer, such as George Gershwin or Leonard Bernstein. At this level the listener processes sounds in very general categories and identifies the sounds he or she hears.

3. *What do sounds express?* At this level the listener processes the sounds heard and both analyzes and judges the effectiveness of the musical components. Thus a melody may be smooth, have a stepwise motion, have a narrow range, be performed with little dynamic change, or be soothing to the listener. On the other hand, a melody may be jagged, have a wide range, contain different meter patterns, and create a feeling of great excitement. The listener makes a value judgment on the degree to which a composer has effectively expressed an idea or a feeling, and how he or she has done so.

4. *What does listening to music do for me?* How can the quality of my life be enhanced by learning to listen to all kinds of music? This is an affective result of a cognitive process. Knowing and understanding how a composer expresses ideas through musical elements and interacting with them can lead to a change in the listener. It may be a feeling of well-being, or it may result in an increased enjoyment of the music. Whatever happens, the listener should feel pleasure and satisfaction as a result of the experience.

THE TEACHER'S ROLE

When you teach a listening lesson, you are actually sharing a piece of music with students—something that was unknown to them before. A piece of music may be familiar to some students. If so, the objective in the lesson could be to further their knowledge or understanding of the music. The same piece might be taught for different reasons at various grade levels. This is known as a "spiral" approach to teaching. Each time students should grow in their understanding and interaction with the piece. Much, of course, depends on the music, for only music that bears repeating and is rich in musical information can be reexperienced with increasing satisfaction and enjoyment.

As you begin to organize and create listening lessons, it is important to keep in mind the following:

1. Have cognitive understanding of the music, such as: Does the melody repeat exactly or repeat with variation? Are the rhythm patterns the same or different?

2. Understand how the music is expressive. For example, is the meaning found simply in the sound and construction of the melody, rhythm, and harmony, or is the composer trying to express an outside meaning as well? An example of the latter might be how the composer Paul Dukas expresses, through musical sound, the story of *The Sorcerer's Apprentice* (see page 285).

3. Write clear objectives that enable students to focus on specific musical concepts or ideas.

4. Carefully and creatively plan steps that will contribute to learning.

5. Develop and implement evaluation tools that will determine whether the objectives have been met.

Guidelines for Planning Listening Lessons

The following suggestions reflect a basic philosophy: Listening to music is *active* listening. The student must focus, concentrate, listen, and respond.

- Get students' attention. Intrigue them. Provide an exciting and stimulating beginning. Use pictures, charts, puppets, games, or creative experiences.

- Introduce the music. Remember, once you get students' attention, they want to hear this music that you are excited about. So don't talk forever. Part of teaching is pacing— knowing when to present an idea and when to hold back another idea.

- Listen to music with the students. Avoid looking out the window or deciding what you are going to do next. Your interest and enthusiasm will help keep them focused on the music.

- Get students involved physically and mentally. Ask them to respond in some way. They may clap the beat, trace the melody in the air, stand up or sit down on the verse or chorus, and so on. Repeat the music as necessary; one time is seldom enough.

- Keep the listening examples relatively short. Give specific directions about the kind of a response you are seeking, such as, "Place the arrows on the chalkboard to indicate the direction of the melody."

- Encourage spontaneous responses to music, such as swaying and finger tapping. Try to channel this behavior into desirable musical responses.

- Use only background information that contributes to musical understanding and is meaningful or important to the listener.

- Encourage students to listen to the music and not to you. Don't talk when you expect students to listen to music. Use the pause button if you must talk while playing a listening selection.

- Sensitivity develops gradually through repeated hearings; don't try to expose students to new music each week. You will probably be providing the first hearing of a piece for many students. You don't want it to be the last. Let them want to hear their "favorite pieces."

■ A class mirrors you. If you show interest and enthusiasm for the music, students are more likely to show interest. If you show insecurity, nervousness, and dislike of the music, they will often begin to talk, exhibit boredom, and perhaps become discipline problems.

■ Fill the room with music. Be certain that students in all parts of the room are hearing a "near live" performance.

■ When explaining a musical element such as form to students, compare it to familiar things. Metaphors such as blueprints, patterns in fabrics, and recipes can often help students understand musical form.

Techniques for Teaching Students to Listen to Music

There are many techniques for guiding perceptive listening. Some of these include (1) using visual representations, (2) using written listening guides, (3) learning a familiar song that is found in a composition, (4) moving to music, and (5) playing instruments.

VISUAL REPRESENTATIONS

Visual representations are often highly effective in helping students follow events as they occur in music. For example:

1. *AB or ABA form:* Use familiar objects to diagram form.

A	B		A	B	A
Cube	Sphere	*or*	Ping Pong ball	Tennis ball	Ping Pong ball

2. *Duple meter or triple meter:* Create patterns of shapes or colors and place them on a chalkboard or bulletin board:

Duple meter   *or*   Triple meter

3. *Tone color:* Create cutouts of animals or instruments and mount them on tongue depressors (readily available from a drugstore or pharmacy). Use stick puppets to identify animals/instruments in selected compositions, such as *Carnival of the Animals* and *Peter and the Wolf.*

Mapping Experiences

Mapping involves developing linear icons for events in a piece of music.

1. Figure 7.2 shows a musical map for Mozart's *Eine Kleine Nachtmusik*, third movement. Place this map on a transparency. You may wish to use different colors to illustrate contrasting sections in the music.

2. As you listen to the piece, ask students to move their right hands in the air as they follow the outline. You should guide the movement by using a pencil to follow the outline on the transparency.

Figure 7.2.
Mozart: Eine Kleine Nachtmusik, *third movement*

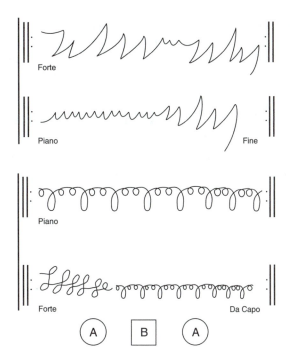

3. After students learn to follow the outline easily, call attention to the repetition, contrast, and then the larger ABA design by placing letters and geometrical shapes on the board.

Integrated Experiences

For an integrated experience, you could incorporate a variety of activities. For example:

1. Read the story of *The Sorcerer's Apprentice:*

   A sorcerer (magician) lives in a giant castle above the Rhine River. He spends most of his days preparing magic potions. His secrets are kept in a large book, which is placed in a locked box in his bookcase.

   As the sorcerer's work increases, he decides that he needs an apprentice to help him. He hires a boy primarily to carry water from the river up to the castle. The boy has interest in becoming a magician himself but is somewhat lazy. He would rather sit along the river, play his flute, and stroke the sorcerer's cat.

   One day the sorcerer has to be away from the castle on an important mission. He leaves his apprentice to look after things. When he is alone, the boy decides to investigate the magic book. He climbs up the ladder, opens the box, and removes the book. As he thumbs through the pages, he murmurs several of the magic words from the text, and suddenly there is a loud clap of sound that causes him to fall off the ladder. As he lies on the floor, the apprentice suddenly realizes that he has unleashed the magical powers of the book. He looks across the room and, as his eyes catch a glimpse of the broom, he has an idea. He quickly says the words "Abrah cadabrah," commanding the broom to pick up the pail and begin bringing water from the river up to the castle.

   The broom obeys and begins to haul water. The apprentice is delighted and frolics around the castle while the broom continues to work. Everything is fine until suddenly the apprentice realizes that enough water has been brought to fill the huge tub but the broom has not stopped its work. The boy repeats all the magic words but is unable to stop the rising water. He becomes frantic and grabs an axe, chopping the broom in half. To his enormous surprise, each of the resulting splinters of wood becomes a broom, picking up a pail and bringing more and more water.

The situation is now truly frantic, with everything in the castle afloat. All seems lost until the sorcerer suddenly reappears and, seeing the terrible mess, commands the water to recede. The castle is devastated and the angry sorcerer gives his apprentice a sharp spank. The boy is sad but wiser, now realizing that his laziness and his opening of the magic book without the magician's approval have led to his predicament.

2. Identify the main events in the story:

   a. Mysterious castle

   b. Apprentice

   c. Brooms

   d. Water rising

   e. Sorcerer

   f. Water receding

   g. "Kick in the pants"

3. Discuss how the composer might express these ideas in music, such as:

   a. Mysterious castle—soft strings and woodwinds

   b. Apprentice—loud, active melodies

   c. Brooms—melody played on bassoon, clarinet

   d. Water rising—louder, higher

   e. Sorcerer—trumpets and horns, loud chorus

   f. Water receding—softer, lower, thinner

   g. "Kick in the pants"—sudden loud chord

4. Show the video "The Sorcerer's Apprentice" from Disney's *Fantasia* and have students match the pictures in figure 7.3 with the music.

WRITTEN LISTENING GUIDES

Another effective way of helping students follow events in a musical composition is through a written listening guide. Here are some suggestions for creating a written guide for listening to theme-and-variation form in Franz Joseph Haydn's Symphony No. 94 *(Surprise)*, second movement.

1. Listen several times to the second movement of Haydn's Symphony No. 94 *(Surprise)*, each time focusing on particular musical elements.

   a. *Melody:* What are some characteristics of the melody (theme) (moves by steps or skips, major or minor)?

   b. *Rhythm:* What are characteristics of the rhythm (duple or triple meter, repeated patterns)?

   c. *Tone color (or timbre):* What types of instrumental sounds are heard (strings, brass, woodwinds)?

1. Mysterious castle: Soft strings and woodwinds

2. Apprentice: Loud, active melodies

3. Broom: Melody played on bassoon

4. Water rises: Texture thickens

5. Water rises: Dynamics louder; texture thickens

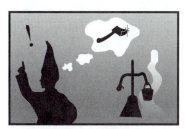

6. Apprentice thinks: Music stops; two brooms: bassoon and clarinet

7. Water rises: Louder; higher; thicker

8. Water rises: Louder; higher; thicker texture

9. Water rises: Louder; higher; thicker

10. Sorcerer: Trumpets herald his return

11. Sorcerer's magic words: Softer; lower; thinner

12. Water recedes; apprentice disciplined: Solo string; softer

13. Sorcerer kicks apprentice: Sudden loud chord

Figure 7.3. Images to accompany **The Sorcerer's Apprentice**

    d. *Dynamics:* What types of dynamic changes occur?

    e. *Form:* How is the piece of music put together (e.g., theme with four variations)? How does the composer create each variation (add a second melody, change the tonality, add repeated notes, change the meter)?

2. From the analysis and discussion, list on the chalkboard the characteristics of each element as it applies to each variation.

3. Construct a listening guide such as the following:

Call Number	Musical Event
1. Theme	Main theme: mostly skips, repeated softly, played staccato
2. Variation 1	Countermelody in the high strings, stepwise melody, legato; contrasts with skips in the main theme
3. Variation 2	Melody changes from major key to minor key
4.	Countermelody added
5. Variation 3	Each melody note repeated as sixteenths; countermelody played by flute
6.	Returns to single-note melody
7. Variation 4	Full orchestra plays main melody; contrasts with ornamented melody (notes above and below the pitches of the main melody)
8.	Ending (coda), sudden pause
	Return of main theme played by woodwinds

4. Place the guide on a transparency or chart.

5. Select a student to point to the events that will be used to guide students' listening experience.

6. Listen to the piece and follow the guide.

7. Provide each student with an evaluation chart; ask them to circle the appropriate response as they listen to the piece again. Example:

Theme	Melody moves mostly by steps Melody is played staccato	Melody moves mostly by skips Melody is played legato
Variation 1	Countermelody Many skips	No countermelody Mostly stepwise
Variation 2	Major key	Minor key
Variation 3	Melody repeated with sixteenth notes	Melody as at the beginning
Variation 4	No ornamentation of melody	Much ornamentation of melody

THE FAMILIAR SONG IN A MUSICAL COMPOSITION

One of the most effective ways to guide listening is to teach a song that is used by a composer in a musical composition (see pages 293 through 295). As the student learns to sing the melody, it becomes easier to hear it in a larger context.

GOULD'S "AMERICAN SALUTE"

Grades: 5–6

Activity: Listening to a piece of music as played by an orchestra; singing a song

Concepts: Theme-and-variation
Familiar song in larger musical composition

When Johnny Comes Marching Home

Key: E minor
Starting pitch: E
Meter: 6/8, begins on 6

Words and Music by Patrick S. Gilmore

When Johnny comes marching home again, Hurrah! Hurrah! We'll give him a hearty
Get ready for the Jubilee, Hurrah! Hurrah! We'll give the hero

welcome then, Hurrah! Hurrah! The men will cheer, the boys will shout, The
three times three, Hurrah! Hurrah! The laurel wreath is ready now to

ladies they will all turn out, And we'll all be glad When Johnny comes marching home.
place upon his loyal brow, and we'll all be glad When Johnny comes marching home.

Objectives

Students will:

1. Sing the song "When Johnny Comes Marching Home" with accurate pitches and rhythms.

2. Identify the song as popular during the Civil War.

3. Identify the song as a march.

4. Identify the meanings of *jubilee*, *three times three*, and *laurel wreath*.

5. Exhibit an understanding of form (theme-and-variation).

Materials

- Musical score for "When Johnny Comes Marching Home"

- Pictures of Civil War

- Chart with words *march*, *jubilee*, *three times three*, and *laurel wreath*

- Keyboard, guitar, Omnichord (Q chord), or Autoharp

- Blank 8½ × 11–inch white or colored paper

- Crayons or markers

- Chalkboard

- Examples of augmentation, diminution, fragmentation, accelerando, and syncopation on charts

Procedures

1. Teach the song "When Johnny Comes Marching Home."

2. Show pictures from the Civil War and discuss the role (if any) of your state. Make students aware that the Civil War was between "brothers" in our country. "When Johnny Comes Marching Home" was one of the most popular songs to come out of the Civil War (along with "Dixie" and "Battle Hymn of the Republic"). The words were written by Patrick S. Gilmore, a bandmaster attached to General Benjamin Butler's command in New Orleans. It is a march with a strong beat.

3. Discuss the meanings of words used in the text.

   a. Most soldiers were from small towns where they were well known.

   b. The village church also served as a meeting house and place of assembly for the community, so the use of the church bell celebrated special events. We still ring bells for national celebrations.

   c. *Jubilee* is another word for celebration.

   d. *Three times three* = "Hip, Hip, Hurray! Hip, Hip, Hurray! Hip, Hip, Hurray!"

   e. The laurel wreath was placed on the heads of victorious athletes in the ancient Greek games. It is made of woven leaves.

4. Sing both verses of the song, accompanied by guitar, keyboard, Omnichord (Q chord), or Autoharp.

5. Explore the concept of theme-and-variation:

   a. How many different ways could you "draw" the first letter of your last name?
   For example:

   Place examples on chalkboard.

   b. How many ways could you draw a circle? For example:

   Place examples on chalkboard.

   c. Using the "white sound" *chooo* held for five seconds, how many different ways could you alter it? For example:

   Staccato: *choo, choo, choo, choo,* etc.

   Scoop:

   d. How many different ways could you alter the melody of "When Johnny Comes Marching Home"? Examples: faster, slower, higher, lower, different voices, fragments. Experiment by playing the first phrase in different ways on the piano, melody bells, or recorder.

e. Explain musical terms:

Augmentation: Stretching out, for example, ♩ ♩ ♩ becomes 𝅗𝅥 𝅗𝅥 𝅗𝅥

Diminution: Squeezing together, for example, 𝅗𝅥 𝅗𝅥 𝅗𝅥 becomes ♩ ♩ ♩

Fragmentation: Breaking up the melody into small pieces

Accelerando: Getting faster

Syncopation: Emphasizing a weak beat

Closure

1. Listen to Morton Gould's *American Salute.* Follow the listening guide below. You can use individual guides, a transparency, or a large chart. Have a student identify each musical event by pointing to it as it occurs.

Listening Guide: Morton Gould, *American Salute*, "When Johnny Comes Marching Home"

Call Number	Musical Event	Call Number	Musical Event
1.	Introduction is based on rhythmic fragments	9.	Melody: Use of rhythmic syncopation
2.	Melody: Bassoon and bass clarinet	10.	Bridge: Meter changes from 3/4 to 4/4
3.	Bridge: Rhythmic fragments	11.	Part one, melody: Trumpets and trombones (augmentation)
4.	Melody: English horn	12.	Repeats: Pianissimo
5.	Melody: Strings	13.	Part two, melody: Woodwinds (diminution)
6.	Bridge: Brass and timpani play rhythmic fragments	14.	Coda: Fragments of theme in imitation
7.	Melody: High woodwinds (ornamentation)	15.	Coda: Accelerando (gets faster)
8.	Bridge: Woodwinds and strings play a crescendo		

2. For students with special needs such as a learning or hearing challenge: Use pictures of the instruments as a listening guide rather than asking the student to read words.

Assessment

1. Listen to *American Salute.* Ask students what *jubilee, three times three,* and *laurel wreath* mean.

2. Ask students how the composer creates each variation (fragments of the melody, faster, slower, changes in instruments, changes in meter, and so on).

MOVING TO MUSIC

Although chapter 8 is devoted to techniques for teaching music to students through movement, here are several suggestions for the teacher wishing to use movement as part of the listening experience. Young children in particular are in constant motion. They walk, run, jump, fidget, bounce, mimic, skip, and dance. As teachers you can capitalize on this desire to move.

Suggestions for Lessons

1. Listen to the Rondo from Mozart's Horn Concerto No. 3 in E-flat Major (third movement). Divide students into pairs and ask each pair to create a movement for A, B, or C. Be sure each pair keeps a steady beat. Practice the movement until students are comfortable with it and then have them perform with the recording. You may assist by pointing to shapes placed on the chalkboard.

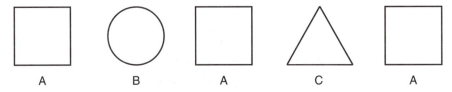

2. Invite children to respond physically to such directions as: "Walk and change direction when you hear a new melody" (grades 4–6); "Pretend you are a rosebud opening as the music gets louder" (grades K–3); "Change partners when you hear a different meter or tonality" (grades 4–6).

PLAYING INSTRUMENTS

Playing classroom instruments is a popular activity with children of all ages.

Suggestions for Lessons

1. Create an ensemble by combining several instruments. Orff instruments (designed by the German music educator Carl Orff) such as xylophones, drums, and glockenspiels can be used by either a few or many students to interpret larger musical compositions. For example, you may wish to use drums and triangles (or glockenspiels) to interpret the "Anvil Chorus" from the opera *Il Trovatore* by Giuseppe Verdi.

   You may wish to alternate between the opening section when all students can play and the "anvil" section where only a few students play selected instruments.

2. A second composition that lends itself to use of instruments is *Pictures at an Exhibition* by Modest Moussorgsky (orchestrated by Maurice Ravel). Students may select classroom percussion instruments that reflect the mood of each of the pictures. For example, heavier instruments such as drums and bass metallophones might be used for the "Promenade" theme. Other parts of this piece that might be selected for use with instruments include:

   ■ Gnomes (a bandy-legged dwarf)   ■ Bydlo (a heavy ox-drawn cart)

   ■ The Old Castle   ■ Ballet of Chicks in Their Shells

   ■ Tuileries (famous gardens in Paris)   ■ The Great Gate of Kiev

Songs Used in Larger Musical Compositions

Song	Composer	Composition*
"America" ("God Save the King") (American hymn)	Ludwig van Beethoven	*Wellington's Victory*
	Ludwig van Beethoven	Variations on "God Save the King"
	Claude Debussy	*Preludes*, Book II, No. 9
	Charles Ives	Variations on "America"
	Max Reger	Variations on "God Save the King"
	Niccolò Paganini	Variations on "God Save the King"
Austrian Hymn (Austrian national anthem)	Franz Joseph Haydn	String Quartet, Opus 76, No. 3
	John Knowles Paine	Variations on "Austria"
"The Bear Went over the Mountain" ("For He's a Jolly Good Fellow")	Ludwig van Beethoven	*Wellington's Victory*
	Virgil Thomson	*Symphony on a Hymn Tune*
	Virgil Thomson	Suite from *The River*, fourth movement
"The Birch Tree" (Russian folk song)	Peter Tchaikovsky	Symphony No. 4, fourth movement
"Camptown Races" (Civil War square dance)	Aaron Copland	*A Lincoln Portrait*
	Charles Ives	Symphony No. 2, third movement
"Chester" (American Revolution)	William Schuman	*New England Triptych*, third movement
"Columbia, the Gem of the Ocean" (American Revolution)	Charles Ives	Symphony No. 2, third movement
	Charles Ives	*The Fourth of July*
"Dixie" (Civil War/minstrel song)	Ernest Bloch	*America*
"The Farmer in the Dell" (play song)	Edwin Franko Goldman	*Children's March*
	Alec Templeton	Variations on "The Farmer in the Dell"
"Frère Jacques" ("Are You Sleeping?") (French round)	Gustav Mahler	Symphony No. 1, third movement
"Gaudeamus Igitur" (German student song)	Johannes Brahms	*Academic Festival Overture*
"Git Along Little Dogies" (American West)	Aaron Copland	*Billy the Kid*
"Goin' Home" (American folk song)	Antonín Dvořák	Symphony No. 9 (*New World*)
"Goodbye, Old Paint" (American West)	Aaron Copland	*Billy the Kid*
"Greensleeves" (English folk song)	Ralph Vaughan Williams	Fantasia on "Greensleeves"
	Buryl Red	*Greensleeves*

---

* Current recordings, listed in the *Schwann Catalog,* are available in most record stores and public libraries. They are also available on the Internet at *www.amazon.com* and *www.cdnow.com.*

Songs Used in Larger Musical Compositions (continued)

Song	Composer	Composition
"Hail, Columbia" (American Revolution)	Ernest Bloch	*America*
	Charles Ives	"Putnam's Camp" from *Three Places in New England*
"Happy Birthday" (American)	Igor Stravinsky	*Greeting Prelude*
"Hatikvah" (Israeli national anthem)	Bedřich Smetana	*The Moldau*
"Irish Washerwoman" (Irish folk song)	LeRoy Anderson	*Irish Suite,* first movement
"Jesu, Joy of Man's Desiring" (German chorale)	J. S. Bach	Cantata No. 147
	Walter Carlos	*Switched-on Bach*
"Joy to the World" (English carol)	Charles Ives	Symphony No. 2, fifth movement
"Land of Hope and Glory" (English)	Edward Elgar	*Pomp and Circumstance,* No. 1
"London Bridge" (English)	Edwin Franko Goldman	*Children's March*
"Londonderry Air" (English)	Percy Grainger	*Irish Tune from County Derry*
"Mack, the Knife" (German opera)	Kurt Weill	*The Threepenny Opera*
	Andre Previn and J. J. Johnson	"Mack, the Knife"
	Louis Armstrong	"Mack, the Knife"
"March of the Three Kings" (French opera)	Georges Bizet	"Farandole" from *L'Arlésienne Suite,* No. 2
"The Marseillaise" (French national anthem)	Robert Schumann	*The Two Grenadiers*
	Peter Tchaikovsky	*1812 Festival Overture*
	Hector Berlioz	*La Marseillaise*
"Mary Had a Little Lamb" (American)	Edwin Franko Goldman	*Children's March*
"The Metronome" (German)	Ludwig van Beethoven	Symphony No. 8, second movement
"A Mighty Fortress Is Our God" (German chorale)	J. S. Bach	Cantata No. 80
	Felix Mendelssohn	Symphony No. 5 *(Reformation)*
"Ode to Joy" ("Joyful, Joyful") (German)	Ludwig van Beethoven	Symphony No. 9, fourth movement
"Old Chisholm Trail" (American West)	Aaron Copland	*Billy the Kid*
"Old Hundredth" ("The Doxology") (fifteenth-century chorale)	J. S. Bach	Cantata No. 130
	Ernest Bloch	*America*
	Henry Purcell-Clarke	Voluntary on "Old Hundredth"

Songs Used in Larger Musical Compositions (continued)

Song	Composer	Composition
"On Springfield Mountain" (American folk song)	Aaron Copland	*A Lincoln Portrait*
"O, Susanna" (Civil War square dance)	Ferde Grofé	*Death Valley Suite*
"Pop, Goes the Weasel" (English)		
	Ernest Bloch	*America*
	Lucien Cailliet	Variations on "Pop, Goes the Weasel"
	Leo Sowerby	Variations on "Pop, Goes the Weasel"
"Sakura" ("Cherry Blossoms") (Japanese)	Eto	Variations on "Sakura"
"Simple Gifts" (Shaker hymn)		
"The Star-Spangled Banner" (U.S. national anthem)	Aaron Copland	*Appalachian Spring*
	Edwin Bagley	*National Emblem March*
	Charles Ives	"Putnam's Camp" from *Three Places in New England*
"Streets of Laredo" (American West)	Roy Harris	*Folksong Symphony*
	Virgil Thomson	*The Plow That Broke the Plains*, cattle movement
"Toreador" (opera)		
"Twinkle, Twinkle Little Star" (German-French)	Georges Bizet	Overture to *Carmen*
	Erno Dohnányi	Variations on a Nursery Song
	Wolfgang Mozart	Variations on "Ah, vous dirai-je Maman"
	Camille Saint-Saëns	*Carnival of the Animals*, "Fossils"
"When Johnny Comes Marching Home" (Civil War)	Morton Gould Roy Harris	*American Salute Overture*, "When Johnny Comes Marching Home"
"Yankee Doodle" (American Revolution)	Ernest Bloch	*America*
	James Hewitt	"Yankee Doodle" with Variations
	Charles Ives	*The Fourth of July*
	Charles Ives	"Putnam's Camp" from *Three Places in New England*
	Roger Sessions	Symphony No. 2, second movement

SAMPLE LESSON PLANS

The following sample lessons and teaching ideas are presented for use with primary-age students.

PALMER'S "PARADE OF COLORS"

Activity: Listening and moving to music

Grade: Kindergarten

Concepts: Steady beat
Individual response versus all responding together

Objectives

Students will:

1. Respond with proper color.

2. March to a steady beat.

3. Distinguish between individual responses to a single color and entire class marching.

Materials

- Recording: Palmer, "Parade of Colors" (*Learning Basic Skills Through Music*, Educational Activities, Inc., Freeport, N.Y., vol. II AR 522, cassette)

- Colored flags (may be made from remnants; be sure to sew a plastic ring onto one corner to enable physically challenged students to participate more fully)

- Two drums, for a student and a teacher

- Paper and markers or crayons to make hats

Plastic ring

Flag

Fold

Making a paper hat   Turn up

Procedures

1. Review colors. Help the students make hats to match colors of flags. Print name of its color on each hat.

2. Play a recording of "Parade of Colors" and invite the students to march to the steady beat of the music. Follow the directions in the song—that is, green stand up, yellow sit down, and so on. All march on the chorus "This is the parade of colors."

3. Play the recording again, asking a selected student to be the leader of the parade and to play the drum to a steady beat. Ask students to march as in a parade by raising their feet off the floor for each step.

Assessment

1. Ask students the difference between "skipping" music and "marching" music.

2. Ask students what colors were used in the "Parade of Colors."

3. Ask students what words indicate the chorus. ("This is the parade of colors")

BERRY'S "JOHNNY B. GOODE"

Activity: Listening to music

Grade: 3

Concepts: Form: AB (verse/chorus)
Meter: Duple

Objectives

Students will:

1. Distinguish between the verse and chorus (AB) of Chuck Berry's "Johnny B. Goode" with creative responses.

2. Identify and respond physically and cognitively to duple meter.

Materials

- Recording: "Johnny B. Goode" (Chuck Berry, *His Best*, vol. 1, UNI/Chess Records Asin B000005KQI)
- Geometric forms ■ ●
- Basketball and football
- Cards with the letters *A* and *B*
- Chart with the words of the verse and chorus
- Twelve flashlights with colored transparencies (six red and six green) or other contrasting colors mounted over light bulb

Procedures

1. Divide the class in half. Label one group A and the other B. Assign a drum and player for A and another drum and player for B.

2. Divide A into three sections, one for each verse.

3. Give green flashlights to six selected students in B.

4. Give red flashlights to six selected students in A. It is important that three people in A are the leaders for each verse; thus, two will have flashlights for each verse with one a designated leader.

5. Play "Johnny B. Goode." Ask section 1 of A to follow the word rhythms on the ceiling with flashlights. Drums will play the duple meter ♩ ♩ | ♩ ♩ ♩ :‖ with accents on 1. Drums only are used on the introduction and interlude.

6. On the chorus, ask section 2 of B to follow the word rhythms on the ceiling with green flashlights. The tambourine plays in duple meter with accents on 1. Only the tambourine is used on the introduction and interlude. ♩ ♩ | ♩ ♩ ‖

7. Continue alternation of activity with verse and chorus. Drums and tambourine fade out at end.

8. Use the basketball as a label for one group and the football as the label for the other group. Repeat steps 5 through 7 but play only two verses.

9. Use the shapes A = ■, B = ● to label the two groups. Repeat but play only two verses.

10. Review the concept of verses and chorus: The verses (A) have the same melody but the words change; the chorus (B) has the same melody and words.

Closure

Play "Johnny B. Goode." Combine all activities: pointing to balls, letters, and shapes and flashing flashlights. Students who do not have an assignment should clap the duple meter.

Assessment

1. Ask students what AB form in music means.

2. Ask students how contrast was created.

BINARY FORM

Activity: Listening to binary form
Grades: K–2
Concepts: Binary form (AB)
            Contrasting musical idea

Objectives

Students will:

1. Identify AB as being different.

2. Identify like sounds and different sounds.

3. Identify melodies that are the same and melodies that are different.

4. Identify AB as the form of Herb Alpert's "Spanish Flea," Bach's "Aria" from Suite No. 3 in D Major, and Berry's "Johnny B. Goode."

Materials

■ Pictures showing two contrasting ideas, such as winter/spring; boy/girl; red/green; square/circle

■ Cutout letters *A* and *B* to mount on chalkboard

■ Classroom instruments: wooden and jingling types

■ Recordings: "Spanish Flea" (Herb Alpert and the Tijuana Brass Greatest Hits, A&M CD-3267); "Johnny B. Goode" (Chuck Berry, *His Best,* vol. 1, UNI/Chess Records Asin B000005KQI); Bach, Suite No. 3 in D Major (London CD-430378)

Procedures

1. Show two contrasting pictures. Discuss how they are the same and yet different.

2. Show the letters *A* and *B*. Place them on chalkboard.

3. Assign jingling instruments to five students and wooden instruments to a second group of five students.

4. Ask one group to play (either by ear if in K–1, or from a chart if in grade 2) the following:

5. Select two children to be machines for A and two others to be machines for B. Children face each other and create a movement that will match the rhythm patterns.

Closure

Combine instruments and movement to illustrate the A and B sections for each of the following:

- Alpert, "Spanish Flea"
- Bach, "Aria" from Suite No. 3 in D Major
- Berry, "Johnny B. Goode"

Assessment

1. Ask what AB form means.

2. Ask students to name techniques used in class for identifying each of the A and B sections.

TERNARY FORM

Activity: Listening to ternary form

Grade: 3

Concepts: Form: Ternary (ABA)
Repetition and contrast

Objectives

Students will:

1. Identify the repetition of a musical idea.

2. Identify ABA (ternary) form.

3. Use classroom instruments to create a short piece in ABA form.

4. Identify ABA sections in Josquin's "El Grillo"; Chopin's Op. 66, "Fantasie Impromptu"; and "We Wish You a Merry Christmas."

Materials

- Recordings: Josquin's "El Grillo" (Josquin des Prez: Adieu Mes Amours/Other Songs, Harmonia Mundi [FRA] 901279); Chopin's Op. 66, "Fantasie Impromptu"
- Score of "We Wish You a Merry Christmas" (page 73)
- Rhythm instruments (jingle sticks, drums)
- Rhythm charts

- Marked spoons (red = A, blue = B)

Procedures

1. Clap the A rhythm and ask students to echo until they tire of it. Discuss why they got bored. (same thing over and over)

2. Clap the B rhythm.

3. Perform three measures as ABA.

4. Choose rhythm instruments for each measure and play—for example, jingle sticks play A and drums play B.

5. Play "We Wish You a Merry Christmas." (Students without instruments should sing.) Discuss whether it is in AB form or ABA form. Does anything repeat?

6. Select two students to create a movement for A and another two students to create a movement for B. Match the movement to the rhythms. Perform together with instruments.

Closure

1. Listen to each of the listening examples and raise spoons colored red for the A section and spoons colored blue for the contrasting section.

2. Ask students to diagram the ABA form or ternary form as they listen.

Assessment

1. Discuss the meaning of ABA form. Ask selected students to create an example of ABA form using mouthed sounds or to rearrange materials in the room to reflect this concept.

2. Ask students the difference between AB and ABA form.

3. Ask students to identify a song in ABA form from the basal music series used in your school.

Integrating Listening Experiences into the Classroom

MUSIC AND DRAMA: OPERA

An *opera is* a story set to music. It incorporates staging, lighting, costumes, and scenery. In opera the dialogue between the characters is sung (in contrast to an *operetta,* wherein some of the dialogue is spoken). There are contrasts not only in the character roles but also in the types of music each sings. Some of the most significant musical sections are arias (or songs), which are accompanied by the orchestra. A favorite opera of children is Gian-Carlo Menotti's *Amahl and the Night Visitors,* an opera that was written for television.

MENOTTI'S *AMAHL AND THE NIGHT VISITORS*

Activity: Listening to an opera

Grades: 4–6 (This lesson should extend over two days)

Concepts: Melody: Direction, legato/staccato, range
Rhythm: Tempo, meter, rubato
Tone color: Female soprano (mother), boy soprano (Amahl), male trio (kings)

Objectives

Students will:

1. Exhibit an understanding of opera by dramatizing the story.

2. Identify techniques used by the composer to portray musical events:

   a. Descending musical line when Amahl goes to the door

   b. Slower tempo when mother goes to the door

   c. Use of trio when three kings sing

   d. Duple meter and brass instruments in "March"

   e. Contrast between legato and staccato, loud and soft, high and low

Materials

- Recording: *Amahl and the Night Visitors* by Menotti (Original, 1951 RCA 6485-2-RG or Jay Records [UK] 1303)

- Chart with words *descending, ascending, staccato, legato, fast, slow*

- Stick or hand puppets: Amahl, mother, kings (Balthasar, Melchior, Kaspar), page, assistants

Procedures

1. Tell the story of *Amahl and the Night Visitors:*

   Amahl, a poor shepherd boy who cannot walk without assistance, lives with his mother in a small, sparsely furnished house. He has a wonderful imagination and likes to tell wild make-believe stories. As the story opens, Amahl is seated outside the

Staging **Amahl and the Night Visitors**

house, playing his flute and looking at the sky. After calling him several times, Amahl's mother becomes very angry and demands that he come into the house. Using his crutch, Amahl enters the house and, upon questioning by his mother, tells of seeing an enormous star. She doesn't believe him and tells him to go to bed. During the night Amahl hears singing and goes to the window. Looking out, he sees a procession in the distance. Soon there is a knock at his door. His mother tells him to go and see who it is. Amahl goes to the door, looks startled, and returns to tell his mother that there is a king outside. Again she doesn't believe him and sends him back. After two more trips to the door, he tells her there are three kings. When Amahl's mother looks for herself, she is greeted by the three kings and their page.

She invites them into the house and soon leaves to find food and bring other shepherds to visit. Amahl asks questions of the kings—Balthasar, Melchior, and Kaspar. After the shepherds return with their gifts of food for the kings, two entertain with a dance. Later, while the kings are asleep, the mother tries to steal the gold for her child. A fight ensues between the mother and the page, who catches her in the act. The kings, however, tell her to keep the gold, for they are on their way to visit the Christ Child and He really won't need their gold. Amahl announces that he would like to go also, but that he has no other gift to give but his crutch. As he offers his crutch, Amahl is miraculously cured and runs and jumps in excitement. The opera closes as the mother waves to Amahl, who joins the kings on their journey.

2. Use hand or stick puppets to dramatize this scene.

3. Play the opening section of the opera, through where the mother becomes impatient with Amahl and threatens to spank him.

4. Discuss what is different about this kind of conversation (it is all sung).

5. Point out that in an opera, the story is sung rather than spoken and that an orchestra provides the accompaniment.

6. Play the scene where Amahl is going to the door to see the kings. Students should identify musical events:

   a. Descending melody to the door, ascending melody on return

   b. Staccato

   c. Repetition of "Mother, mother, mother come with me" text and melody

   d. Contrast of slower, legato, heavier sound when the mother goes to the door

   e. Smooth, legato singing in harmony by the three kings

7. Play the scene where Amahl is asking the kings questions. Compare the musical answers of each king:

Balthasar: Long melodic lines, smooth (bass)

Melchior: Long, melodic lines, smooth (bass)

Kaspar (who cannot hear): Fast, much repetition (tenor)

8. Create a procession of kings, page, and assistants carrying gifts. Play the "March" and identify the types of instruments used: trumpets, drums, woodwinds. Discuss the use of duple meter and staccato sounds.

9. The entire opera may be performed in 50 minutes. You will want to play a few scenes each day. Keep the students' interest with this continued story.

Closure

Play a recording of the opera and dramatize the events.

Assessment

1. Ask the meaning of the word *opera*.

2. Review the story of Amahl and ask students to point out the high voice of the boy soprano Amahl.

3. Ask students what musical techniques were used by the composer to tell the story (direction of melody, speed, legato, staccato, type of instruments used).

MUSIC AND DRAMA: ORATORIO

An *oratorio* is also a large dramatic work, but it is performed in a concert hall without staging, costumes, or scenery. It is always based on a religious text and contains recitatives, arias, and choruses. One of the most famous oratorios is *Messiah* by George Frideric Handel.

HANDEL'S *MESSIAH*

Activity: Listening to music

Grades: 5–6

Concepts: Recitative
Aria
Chorus
Text (word) painting
Homophonic and polyphonic texture
Jagged/smooth melody

Objectives

Students will:

1. Identify a recitative.

2. Exhibit an understanding of word painting in the aria "Every Valley Shall Be Exalted."

3. Distinguish between homophonic and polyphonic sections of the "Hallelujah Chorus."

Materials

- Recording of *Messiah* (many are available)
- Chart with the words *aria, recitative, chorus,* and *word painting*
- Graphic listening guide

Procedures

1. Explain to students that in an opera or oratorio most of the conversation or story is sung. Experiment with ideas, letting students create their own recitatives. Notice that there is very little accompaniment.

2. Listen to the recitative "Then Shall the Eyes of the Blind" from *Messiah*. Notice that it is very short and has little accompaniment.

3. The word *aria* means "song." Handel liked to use musical sounds to express the meaning of certain words. Thus in "Every Valley Shall Be Exalted," the word *crooked* is written with a jagged melody, whereas *exalted* is a long phrase with many repeated patterns. *Plain* is expressed with a sustained single-note melody:

Write the words *crooked, exalted,* and *plain* on the chalkboard.

4. Listen to the aria "Every Valley Shall Be Exalted." Students should follow the musical line with their hands.

5. Play a game in which children follow a leader, all doing the same motion at the same time. Count 1 2 3 4 and create four measures of activity. For example:

   ■ Slap thighs, slap thighs, clap, clap (1 2 3 4)

   ■ Tap shoulders (two times), tap top of head (two times) (1 2 3 4)

   Next, have one group do the first activity, and on the count of 3 a second group begin the second activity. Perform in the same fashion as a round. Point out that composers do the same thing with music. Sometimes all of the instruments play the same rhythm at once, and sometimes a melody "chases" after another melody.

6. Listen to the first part of Handel's "Hallelujah Chorus." Decide which performance of the motions would be appropriate, for example, when all do the same thing at the same time.

7. Continue the "Hallelujah Chorus" until the parts "chase one another." Diagram as follows:

Closure

Listen to the entire composition and complete a map of the sounds. For example:

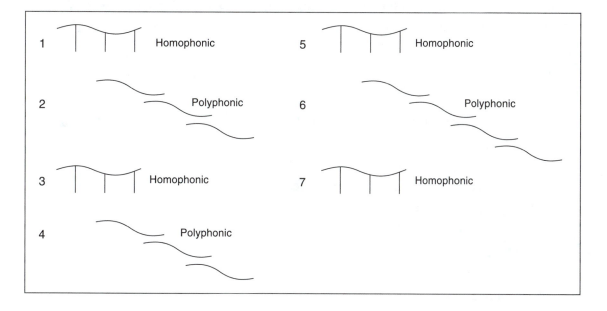

Assessment

1. What do the terms *recitative, aria, chorus, text painting, homophonic,* and *polyphonic* mean?

2. Can you give an example of a jagged melody? A smooth melody?

3. On which words in "Every Valley Shall Be Exalted" would you use a jagged melody, and on which words would you use a smooth melody? Give a reason for your choice.

MUSIC AND DANCE: BALLET

Music and dance are combined in the art form called *ballet.* Even though the music is written for a specific function, it is also exciting to listen to without the visual dimension. As with program music, knowledge of the story adds to the listener's enjoyment.

COPLAND'S "HOE-DOWN"

Activity: Listening to music and dancing a square dance

Grades: 4–6

Concepts: Syncopation
Rests
Contrasting tone colors
Different phrase lengths

Background Information

Rodeo by the American composer Aaron Copland is a ballet whose story centers on a rodeo in the West. The dancers portray cowboys and cowgirls. In one scene a champion roper displays his roping talents. Another of the principal scenes is a Saturday-night dance that the cowboys and cowgirls attend in their finest attire.

Objectives

Students will:

1. Identify accents, syncopation, and use of pauses to express a square dance in "Hoe-Down."

2. Identify contrasting instruments such as trumpets, piano, and xylophone.

3. Identify repeated patterns that give the piece unity.

4. Identify different-length phrases used to create a "jerky" motion.

Materials

■ Pictures of rodeos

■ Xylophone

■ Recording of Copland, *Rodeo,* "Hoe-Down"

■ Cards with terms: *accent, syncopation, pause, repeated pattern, loud, fast,* and *slow*

Procedures

1. Show pictures of a rodeo. Discuss some of the activities, such as cattle roping, steer riding, and chuckwagon races. Use a xylophone to create patterns of sound expressive of these events (wide skips, fast tempo, pauses—rider falls off horse). Help students create some syncopated patterns.

2. Form eight selected students into partners for a square dance. Have the rest of the class clap a steady beat as the dancers go through some simple motions.

   a. Head couple and foot couple: forward and bow; back to place

   b. Side couples forward and bow

   c. Face partners, right-arm swing

   d. Face partners, left-arm swing

   e. Couples one and three exchange partners; couples two and four exchange partners

   f. Repeat dance

3. Point out that Copland wrote a piece of music, called *Rodeo*, for a ballet, in which men and women wear costumes and dance. One of the sections is called "Hoe-Down." Review examples of accents, syncopation, pauses, and repeated patterns. Play "Hoe-Down" and place these terms, along with others such as *loud, fast,* and *slow,* on cards.

4. Play "Hoe-Down" a second time. Have students select the terms and place them on a chart as they hear the piece. Any student may choose a card at any time, or you may wish to create a competitive game with two teams alternating.

5. Play "Hoe-Down" a third time and make any necessary changes in the cards.

Closure

Listen to "Hoe-Down" from *Rodeo* and choose cards from the chalkboard that are appropriate to the music as it is played (for example, syncopation, fast, slow, pauses, and so on).

Assessment

1. Ask what is meant by the following terms:

   a. Accent

   b. Syncopation

   c. Patterns

2. What are some contrasting instruments?

3. Can you identify any melodic or rhythmic patterns that repeat?

4. Are the phrases of the same length?

PROGRAM MUSIC

SAINT-SAËNS'S *CARNIVAL OF THE ANIMALS*

Activity: Listening to program music

Grades: 2–4

Concepts: Identification of low strings, high strings, woodwinds, and brass
Low, high; fast, slow
Wide skips, stepwise melody
Steady beat
Dynamics: Loud, soft

Objectives

Students will:

1. Identify the sound of instruments with an appropriate animal, such as elephant, birds, and swan.

2. Identify sounds that are low or high, fast or slow, loud or soft.

3. Identify wide skips, range of melody, steady beat, and dynamics and associate them with appropriate animals.

4. Integrate the study of *Carnival of the Animals* with language arts and visual art.

Materials

- Recording: Saint-Saëns, *Carnival of the Animals*

- Pictures or puppets of the animals described, such as elephant, birds, cuckoo, swan, and fish

- Pictures of the orchestral instruments used in the composition, such as piccolo, string bass, trumpet, oboe, xylophone, and violins

- Chalkboard or bulletin board

- Cards with words *low, high, fast, slow, thick, thin, strings,* and *brass*

- Cassette and tape recorder

Procedures

1. Play the selection "The Elephant" from *Carnival of the Animals.* Show a picture of an elephant and discuss its characteristics (big, lumbering, thick skin, large trunk, and so on).

2. Use a puppet of an elephant to show children how to move as an elephant might (slowly, with big steps).

3. Show pictures of instruments: piccolo, string bass, trumpet, oboe. Play recordings illustrating each. Discuss which instrument the composer might use to portray an elephant (string bass). Place the following words on the chalkboard:

low   high

fast   slow

thick   thin

string   brass

Play the selection "The Elephant" again. Have children choose appropriate words and place them on a chart with a picture of an elephant at the top.

4. Integrate the lesson with language arts by having children write a poem or paragraph describing an elephant. Integrate it with visual art by having children draw pictures of elephants.

5. Follow this procedure for other animals represented in the work, for example:

   ■ Lions: Low, fast, rise and fall to the melody, punctuates the pacing (steady) beat of the lions' walk, low strings, piano

   ■ Kangaroo: Wide range, staccato (jumpy), many skips, accents, crescendo and diminuendo, suddenly loud, suddenly soft

   ■ Fish: Smooth, harp, glissando, celesta represents rippling water, mostly steps

6. View the video *Carnival of the Animals* (Marionette production by Jim Gamble*)

Closure

Make a cassette tape on which you feature five short "animal" pieces from the larger work. Place five pictures of animals in the front of the room. Divide the class into two teams. Affix all the words to the chalkboard. As each selection is played, have team members decide on the words that best describe the music. One of the team members places them under the proper pictures. The total number of points possible is determined by the number of musical events you have identified.

Additional compositions about animals include:

■ Copland, *The Cat and the Mouse*

■ Debussy, *The Children's Corner Suite*, "Jimbo's Lullaby"

■ Griffes, *The White Peacock*

■ Hovhaness, *And God Created Great Whales*

■ Messiaen, *Oiseaux Exotiques* (Exotic Birds, for piano and orchestra)

■ Moussorgsky, *The Flea*

■ Prokofiev, *Peter and the Wolf*

■ Rimsky-Korsakov, "Flight of the Bumble Bee"

Assessment

1. Review the composer's use of instruments to represent animals. Discuss ways the composer uses these sounds to represent the animal.

2. Play at random three animal themes from *Carnival of the Animals*. Ask students to identify the instruments used, how they are used, and what animals the music represents.

---

* The video *Carnival of the Animals* from *Introduction to Great Music* is available from Friendship House, 29313 Clemens Rd., Suite 2G, Box 450978, Westlake, OH 44145-0623; 1-800-791-9876; *www.friendshiphouse.com*.

VIVALDI'S "SPRING" FROM *THE SEASONS*

Activity: Listening to program music

Grades: 4–6

Concepts: Melody: Repeated patterns, narrow range
Rhythm: Repeated patterns, steady beat, duple meter
Dynamics: Loud and soft, echo effects
Tone color: Strings
Form: Concerto grosso (small group of solo instruments alternates with the orchestra)

Objectives

Students will:

1. Identify techniques the composer uses to express nature.

2. Identify the contrasting sections of the concerto grosso (small group of instruments and all instruments).

3. Identify different techniques used by string instruments.

Materials

- Poems about spring: birds, flowers, sun

- Paper and markers to draw pictures of budding flowers

- Charts: concerto grosso

- Listening guide

- Recording: Vivaldi's *The Seasons,* "Spring"

Procedures

1. Read poems about spring: birds, flowers, the sun. Discuss how nature, which has been dormant all winter, comes to life again.

2. Draw pictures showing the budding process in trees to full leaf.

3. Point out the delicate colors of spring (light green leaves, pink dogwood).

4. Read the musical events found in the listening guide on page 461. Discuss any that are vague or unknown to the students.

5. Listen to Vivaldi's "Spring" from *The Seasons.* Follow the listening guide (page 461). Additional compositions about the seasons include:

- Haydn's *The Seasons,* "With Verdure Clad"

- Vivaldi's *The Seasons,* "Summer," "Fall," and "Winter"

Closure

Compare another season (summer, fall, winter) with "Spring." Discuss the different techniques that the composer might use. How does the music sound different?

Assessment

Create an evaluation chart from the listening guide. You may wish to include other musical information that you have learned.

HONEGGER'S "PACIFIC 231"

Grades: 1–4

Suggestions for Lessons

1. Show pictures of locomotives. Ask students whether they have ever ridden on a train or whether they have toy trains. Discuss the characteristics of a locomotive: run by coal, begins slowly with a *choo, choo* sound, and so on.

2. For young students, play a game with a leader as locomotive and other students as cars attached behind. They can move their arms as if they are the wheels. Ask one child to be the whistle. Consider how the train might move when going up a hill, down a hill, starting out from the station, and coming in to the station.

3. Select classroom percussion instruments and accompany the dramatization.

4. Read the story *The Little Engine That Could* by Watty Piper.* Discuss the use of tempo in reading the story with expression.

5. For older students, listen to Honegger's "Pacific 231."† Follow this listening guide:

Listening Guide

1. Strings, woodwinds, brass; soft; train starting up

2. Woodwinds and strings joined by low brass; speed increases; becomes louder

3. Steady beat; staccato; imitation; becomes louder

4. Steady beat; staccato; clarinet, bassoon, horn, strings, trumpet, and full orchestra

5. Long theme: staccato, bassoon

6. Orchestra staccato; gradually gets louder

7. Staccato theme with imitation in orchestra

8. Contrasting melody played by clarinet, followed by strings

9. Brass instruments play staccato theme; gradually gets louder

10. Strings play sweeping, contrasting melody; clarinet plays soft running notes

11. Orchestra gradually gets louder; driving beat; imitation

12. Orchestra plays loudly; horns and trumpets play high theme above orchestra melody

13. Gradually slows down as train approaches stop

Additional compositions about machines include:

- Anderson, "The Typewriter"

- "Orange Blossom Special"

- Brubeck, "Cable Car" from *Time Changes*

- Schuller, "The Twittering Machine" from *Seven Studies by Paul Klee* (Mercury Living Presence, CD 434329)

---

* Watty Piper, *The Little Engine That Could* (New York: Platt & Monk, 1980).

† Silver Burdett Ginn, *The Music Connection* 4 (2000), pp. 142–143 (CD 6-5).

GROFÉ'S "CLOUDBURST" FROM *GRAND CANYON SUITE*

Grades: 5–6

Suggestions for Lessons

1. Show pictures of the Grand Canyon. Discuss where it is located and its type of climate. Ask students who have visited this "wonder of the world" to describe it to classmates.

2. Discuss what is meant by the word *cloudburst*. Consider ways that a composer might describe such an event through instruments (lightning—loud, crashing cymbals; thunder—roll of drums). Use classroom percussion instruments to create a musical composition that describes a cloudburst. Write an original poem about a cloudburst and draw pictures that express this phenomenon in nature.

3. Listen to Grofé's "Cloudburst" from *Grand Canyon Suite*. Follow this listening guide:

Listening Guide

1. Lyrical melody played softly by strings (canyons with huge rock formations bask in calmness of clear, sunny day)

2. Oboe and strings play lyrical melody with harp accompaniment; crescendo

3. Low strings play long lyrical melody

4. Woodwinds play ornamental melody

5. Full orchestra, strings play melody; crescendo

6. Strings decrescendo; cellos play slow, soft melody; repetition of short, melodic fragments

7. Loud splashes of orchestral sound; strings and piano go up and down; rumbling of timpani represents thunder reverberating through canyons, rain splashing against rocks, and lightning

8. Brass build in tempo and dynamic level as orchestra expresses fury of storm

9. Storm ends with decrease in dynamics and a slower tempo

Additional compositions about nature include:

- Beethoven, Symphony No. 6 *(Pastorale)*
- Debussy, *La Mer* (The Sea)
- Smetana, *The Moldau* (a river in Czechoslovakia)

WILLIAMS'S *STAR WARS*

Grades: 4–5

Suggestions for Lessons

1. Show the beginning of the motion picture *Star Wars* (available on video).

2. Discuss the music of the film and consider the demands made on the composer (e.g., music reflecting the characters and interplanetary travel).

3. Listen to a recording of the main theme of composer John Williams's *Star Wars* and follow this listening guide:

Listening Guide

1. Introduction: full orchestra
2. Main theme: High brass accompanied by strings, low brass, and percussion
3. Theme 2: Strings, legato, followed by crescendo in brass
4. Main theme: Low brass, joined by strings and high brass
5. Bridge: Rhythmic and melodic fragments; ascending melody
6. Ritard (slow down): Solo violin
7. Crescendo: Repeated rhythmic fragments; brass and percussion; ritard
8. Faster: Steady beat in percussion; block chords in high brass
9. Strings: Short melodic patterns played fast
10. Main theme: Low brass; block chords in high brass; main theme repeats
11. Theme 2: Strings
12. Main theme: Low brass, block chords in strings and high brass
13. Theme 3: Low strings, legato, softer; high strings play countermelody
14. Accelerando to main theme: High brass, repeats
15. Theme 2: Altered; strings play ascending melody
16. Block chords in high brass accompanied by strings, percussion; ascending melodies
17. Block chords repeated by violins; slower, softer
18. Full brass, percussion; crescendo; closing loud chords, ends with sustained low strings

Additional compositions about outer space include:

- Holst, *The Planets*
- Perrey-Kingsley, *The In Sound Way Out*, "The Little Man from Mars," "Spooks in Space," "Visa to the Stars" (CD 79222-2)
- John Williams, *Return of the Jedi*, *E.T.*, *Close Encounters of the Third Kind*, *Empire Strikes Back*, *Star Trek*
- John Williams, *John Williams Plays John Williams*, "The Star Wars Trilogy" (Sony/classical CD/SK 45947)

TCHAIKOVSKY'S *1812 FESTIVAL OVERTURE*

Grades: 4–6

Suggestions for Lessons

1. Read the following background information to the class:

The *1812 Festival Overture* by Peter Tchaikovsky was written to dramatize and commemorate the withdrawal from Russia of the French troops under Napoleon in 1812. Originally, the music was to be performed by an enormous orchestra in a public square in Moscow. Arrangements were made for cannon to be included in the percussion section. A large programmatic work, it begins with the Russian hymn "God, Preserve Thy People." A realistic musical description of the Battle of Borodino includes the French national anthem "The Marseillaise" and the czarist Russian national anthem "God Save the Czar." Chimes and carillon, and bells along with cannon (where possible) provide a fitting climax to the Russian victory.

2. Play the last four or five minutes (including the cannon) of the *1812 Festival Overture*. Discuss with students various sounds they hear (cannon, bells ringing, large orchestra, and so on).

3. Discuss events for which a cannon might be fired or many bells rung (for example, a battle, a victory, a special national event).

4. Play the last four or five minutes of the piece again. Ask students to identify instrumental sounds (strings, brass, percussion).

5. After reviewing the background information in 1 above, play or sing the Russian national hymn and the French national anthem.

God, Preserve Thy People

Russian Hymn

The Marseillaise

Rouget de Lisle

Ye sons of France, a-wake to glo — ry! Hark, hark what myr-iads bid you
Al - lons, en - fants de la Pa - tri - e, Le jour de gloire est ar - ri-

rise! Your chil-dren, wives and grand-sires___ hoar-y: Be-hold their tears, and hear their___
vé, Con - tre nous, de la ty-ran-ni-e, L'é - ten - dard san-glant est le-

cries, Be-hold their tears,___ and hear their___ cries! Shall hate-ful ty-rants mis-chief___
vé, L'é - ten - dard___ san-glant est le - vé. En - ten-dez - vous,___ dans les cam-

breed - ing, With hire-ling hosts,___ a ruf-fian___ band, Af - fright and des-o-late the
pa - gnes, Mu - gir ces fé-ro-ces sol - dats? Ils vien - nent jus-que dans nos

land,_____ While_____ peace and lib - er - ty be bleed - ing? To arms,_____ to arms ye
bras, _____ **É - gor - ger** _____ **nos fils, nos com - pa - gnes!** **Aux ar - mes, Ci - toy-**

brave, Th'a - veng - ing sword un - sheathe! March on, march on,
ens, **For - mez** _____ **vos ba - tail - lons!** **Mar - chons, mar - chons,**

all hearts re - solved On vic - to - ry or death!
Qu'un sang im - pur A - breu - ve nos sil - lons!

6. Play the composition up through the French national anthem.

7. Show a photograph of the painting *Liberty Leading the People* by Eugène Delacroix. Discuss what the artist does to create the feeling of power and victory (focus on female figure in center, upraised arms, mixture of people, many diagonal lines creating movement). Apply these principles of analysis to music. Ask students such questions as the following:

    a. Can you describe what musical ideas would express an army approaching from a distance? (soft to loud—crescendo)

    b. What types of percussion instrument might be used for the clatter of guns? (snare drum)

8. Play sections of the *1812 Festival Overture.* Each time, discuss with students the musical ideas that express the nationalistic event.

9. Play the entire composition. Ask students to choose from the following cards and place them on the chalkboard in the order they hear the corresponding music. (Some may repeat—provide multiple cards.)

Dynamics	Tone Color	Melodies	Tempo	Range
Soft	Strings	Smooth	Faster	Gets higher
Loud	Brass	"The Marseillaise"	Slower	Lower
Accents	Snare drum	Legato	(Ritard)	
Louder	French horns	"The Marseillaise" (fragments)		
Softer	Tambourine	Long descending melody		
	Timpani	"God, Preserve Thy People"		
	Triangle			
	Drum roll			
	Cannon			
	Bells			

Additional compositions about historical events include:

- Alford, *Colonel Bogey March* (theme from the film *Bridge over the River Kwai*)
- Beethoven, *Wellington's Victory*
- Ives, *The Fourth of July*
- Ives, *Memorial Day*
- Rodgers (arranged by Robert Russell Bennett), *Victory at Sea*, "Guadalcanal March"

COPLAND'S *A LINCOLN PORTRAIT*

Suggestions for Lessons

1. Show pictures of the Lincoln Memorial in Washington, D.C.
2. Play performances of "Battle Hymn of the Republic." Have the class sing the song and discuss its use during the Civil War.
3. Teach the songs "On Springfield Mountain" and "Camptown Races." Discuss the difference in text and style of music (e.g., quiet, lively).

On Springfield Mountain

American Folk Song

Key: G
Starting pitch: D
Meter: 3/4, begins on "and" of 2

On Spring-field Moun-tain there did dwell A love-ly youth, I knew him well. Too roo-de-nay too roo-de-noo, Too roo-de-nay too roo-de-noo.

Camptown Races

Key: E♭
Starting pitch: B♭
Meter: 2/4, begins on 4

Stephen C. Foster

With humor

1. The Camp-town la-dies sing this song, do-da, do-da! The Camp-town race track five miles long, Oh, do-da-day. Oh, see those hors-es round the bend, do-da, do-da! Guess that race will nev-er end. Oh, do-da-day.

Chorus

Going to run all night, going to run all day, I'll bet my mon-ey on the bob-tail nag, Some-bod-y bet on the bay.

4. Play part one of *A Lincoln Portrait.* Ask students to identify the musical means by which Copland expresses Lincoln's early life (soft dynamic level, open harmony, large skips in the melody, thin texture).

5. Review social activities during the middle of the nineteenth century (square dances, Saturday-night "military post" parties).

6. Play part two of *A Lincoln Portrait.* Ask students to raise their hands when they hear the fragments of "Camptown Races" in the music. Discuss other ways the composer portrays a Saturday-night dance (strong rhythmic beat, use of "fiddles," much syncopation).

7. Play parts one and two. Discuss in what ways they are the same and in what ways different.

8. Ask students to read the excerpts from Lincoln's speeches that are heard in the composition:

This is what Lincoln said:

"Fellow citizens we cannot escape history. We of this Congress and this administration will be remembered in spite of ourselves. No personal significance or insignificance can spare one or another of us. The fiery trials through which we pass will light us down in honor or dishonor to the latest generation.

"We even, we here, hold the power and bear the responsibility.

"The dogmas of the quiet past are inadequate to the stormy present. The occasion is piled high with difficulty, and we must rise with the occasion. As our case is new so we must think anew, and act anew. We must disenthrall ourselves, and then we shall save our country.

"It is the eternal struggle between two principles, right and wrong, throughout the world. It is the same spirit that says 'you toil and work and earn bread, and I'll eat it.' No matter in what shape it comes. Whether from the mouth of a king who seeks to bestride the people of his own nation and live by the fruit of their labor, or from one race of men as an apology for enslaving another race, it is the same tyrannical principle.

"As I would not be a slave, so I would not be a master. This expresses my idea of democracy. Whatever differs from this, to the extent of the difference is no democracy."

Abraham Lincoln, sixteenth president of these United States, is everlasting in the memory of his countrymen. For on the battleground at Gettysburg, this is what he said:

"That from these honored dead, we take increased devotion to that cause for which they gave the last full measure of devotion. That we here highly resolve that these dead shall not have died in vain. That this nation under God, shall have a new birth of freedom, and that government of the people, by the people, and for the people shall not perish from the earth."

Listening Guide (Part One)

1. Introduction: Short melodic fragment (brass; woodwinds; strings)
2. Texture gets thicker and dynamics louder
3. Melody: "On Springfield Mountain" (clarinet)
4. Melody: "On Springfield Mountain" (oboe and strings)
   Melody: "On Springfield Mountain" (trumpet)
5. Fragments of "Camptown Races"; faster, lighter (clarinet and oboe alternate with melody)
6. Fragments of "Camptown Races" (trumpets)
7. Melody: "On Springfield Mountain" (fragment) (trumpets and other brass)
8. Melody: "On Springfield Mountain," in imitation between low brass and high brass; strings play a high descant above

Preparing Students to Attend a Concert

Many communities throughout the United States offer educational concerts for students in grades 4, 5, and 6. These concerts may be performed by such professional orchestras as the Cleveland Orchestra, the New York Philharmonic, or the Philadelphia Orchestra. In smaller communities, local orchestras and college or university ensembles fulfill this function. The cost is usually defrayed by funding from corporations, and sometimes students pay a token ticket charge. Some larger communities provide "docents"—volunteers who visit schools to prepare students for what they will hear; most schools, however, rely on the classroom teacher, who may or may not have received audiovisual materials from the orchestra's educational department.

It is not the purpose of these lessons to suggest proper behavior or attire; instead, it provides three minilessons based on what students might see and hear at a concert.

SAMPLE CONCERT

■ Slavonic Dance No. 1 in C Major	Antonín Dvořák
■ Violin Concerto No. 3 in E Minor, Op. 64	Felix Mendelssohn
■ "Trumpeter's Lullaby"	Leroy Anderson
■ "Syncopated Clock"	Leroy Anderson
■ "Triplets" (xylophone and three marimbas)	George Hamilton Green
■ "The Little White Donkey," Histoires for Piano	Jacques Ibert
■ "The Entertainer"	Scott Joplin
■ "Hoe-Down," Rodeo	Aaron Copland

ANDERSON'S "TRUMPETER'S LULLABY"

Activity: Listening to music

Grade: 4

Concepts: Instruments of the orchestra: Strings, brass, woodwinds, percussion, keyboards
Placement of the musicians
Role of the conductor
Role of the concertmaster

Objectives

Students will:

1. Identify by sight and sound instruments of the orchestra.

2. Define the role of the conductor.

3. Define the role of the concertmaster.

Materials

- 16mm film: *Toot, Whistle, Plunk, Boom* (available from Kent State University Media Library Catalog: *www.kent.edu*)
- Projector
- Basal music series instruments of orchestras (pictures and recordings)
- Recording: Anderson's "Trumpeter's Lullaby"
- Small cards with words, such as *soft, loud,* and *smooth*
- Large card with title "Trumpeter's Lullaby"

Procedures

1. Show the film *Toot, Whistle, Plunk, Boom* (Disney c. 1953 [10 minutes]—a cartoon that traces the origin and development of the four families of instruments, as well as the piano, in the modern symphony orchestra).

2. Discuss the characteristics of each instrument and reinforce them with pictures from the basal music series books or large charts showing instrument families.

3. Play the composition "Trumpeter's Lullaby" by Leroy Anderson and ask students to choose the solo instrument either from the book or the chart.

4. Discuss possible reasons for naming the piece a *trumpeter's lullaby* (such as soft, smooth, quiet). Write the descriptive terms on cards and place them on the board under the title of the composition.

5. Show a picture of a large symphony orchestra and ask students to identify the various "families" of instruments. Which sections have the most instruments? Which have the fewest?

6. Ask students to sing a familiar song, such as "Row, Row, Row Your Boat." Do not give any indication of pitch, tempo, or dynamics. Discuss some of the problems they encountered (they didn't sing together, little or no dynamic change, couldn't decide on how fast to sing, and so on).

7. Perform the song again, but this time invite one student to conduct the performance. Point out that the role of a conductor is important because the conductor controls how the music is played.

8. Invite the students to sing, whistle, or speak "Row, Row, Row Your Boat" whenever they like. The result will be cacophony. Now appoint a student to be the "concertmaster" and give the starting pitch. Have everyone in the class tune to (or match) that pitch. After the leader is sure of the pitch, ask the conductor to lead the performance.

9. Dramatize the members of the orchestra and trumpeter playing "Trumpeter's Lullaby."

Closure

Play "Trumpeter's Lullaby" in its entirety.

Assessment

1. What is the role of the conductor?

2. What is the role of the concertmaster?

3. How many "families" are there in the Western orchestra? What are they?

4. What "family" in the Western orchestra has more instruments than any other?

5. What is the name of this piece?

6. What instrument does it feature as a solo?

MENDELSSOHNS'S VIOLIN CONCERTO NO. 3 IN E MINOR (RONDO)

Grade: 4

Concepts: The orchestra concert
        The string family

Objectives

Students will:

1. Identify the violin as the solo instrument in Mendelssohn's Violin Concerto No. 3 in E Minor (Rondo).

2. Identify characteristics of the violin: can play a wide range; can play very loud and very soft; can play staccato or legato; does not have any frets; has only four strings.

Materials

- Recording: Itzhak Perlman playing Mendelssohn's Violin Concerto No. 3 in E Minor

- Pictures of violin, viola, cello, and bass

- Basal music series instruments of orchestra

- Video: *The Orchestra* (Peter Ustinov, narrator), strings only*

Procedures

1. Show pictures of violin, viola, cello, and bass. Discuss their differences in appearance.

2. Play examples of each.

3. Show and discuss pictures of a violin, including fingerboard, bow, mute, and lack of frets.

4. Indicate that in a concerto, the solo instrument plays both with the orchestra and alone.

5. Play a recording of Perlman playing Mendelssohn's Violin Concerto No. 3 in E Minor (Rondo). Ask students to diagram the form on the chalkboard (A B A C, etc.).

---

* The video *The Orchestra,* narrated by Peter Ustinov, is available from Friendship House: 1-800-791-9876 or *www.friendshiphouse.com.*

6. Discuss the relationship of Perlman's talent to his physical challenges due to polio, a disease that affects the nervous system.

Closure

Play "Rondo" and ask students to raise their hands when they hear the main melody.

Assessment

1. What instrument is featured as a solo?

2. What are some parts of the violin? (fingerboard, bow)

3. What is the form of the rondo that you heard? (A B A C A)

4. What is a concerto?

IBERT'S "THE LITTLE WHITE DONKEY"

Activity: Listening to music

Grade: 5–6

Concepts: Program music
Mechanism of piano
Jagged melody
Thick chords

Objectives

Students will:

1. Identify the piano as a keyboard instrument and name the mechanical parts that differentiate it from other keyboard instruments.

2. Identify the programmatic qualities of the piano piece "The Little White Donkey" and describe how the composer expresses these qualities in sound.

Materials

- Recording of "The Little White Donkey" from Histoires for Piano by Jacques Ibert (MCAD-25969)

- Pictures of the piano and its mechanism

- Small cards and letters *A, B, A* for chalkboard or bulletin board

- Large card with title "The Little White Donkey"

Procedures

1. Play the video *Anatomy of a Piano.** Discuss the characteristics: such as pedals (damper, sustaining, soft), hammers, size and function of strings, and keyboard.

2. Point out that some music has a story. The piano composition is "The Little White Donkey" from a collection called Histoires for Piano by the French composer Jacques

_____

* The video *Anatomy of a Piano* (grades 5 and up) is available from Friendship House: 1-800-791-9876 or *www.friendshiphouse.com.*

Ibert. In this little piece, a donkey is walking along a railroad track when suddenly he hears a train. He gets off the track safely and listens to the whistle warning of the approaching train. After it goes by, he resumes his walk down the track.

3. Play the recording of "The Little White Donkey" and ask students to listen for the composer's musical expression of a train and also of the donkey walking down the tracks. Place the title card of the piece on the board and then place labels that describe the piece under it (such as steady beat = donkey; thick chords in upper register = train).

Closure

Play "The Little White Donkey." Ask students how the composer creates program music.

Assessment

1. Ask students what the various parts of the piano mechanism are.

2. Ask students what program music is. Give an example for piano.

3. What is meant by "expressing something outside the music"?

4. What are some of the musical techniques used by the composer of "The Little White Donkey"?

For Your Journal

In your journal or portfolio, make a section on listening to music, which might include:

- Musical instruments and ensembles
- Guidelines for planning listening lessons
- Techniques for teaching students to listen to music
- Several sample listening lessons that you have prepared

Teaching Music Through Movement

RHYTHM IS ONE OF THE MOST BASIC ELEMENTS OF MUSIC. Nature has innumerable rhythmic patterns to which we respond (night and day, changing seasons, ebb and flow of tides); our physical system is subject to rhythm (heartbeat, respiration, digestive system, sleep patterns); and everyday activities require a sense of rhythm (walking, jogging, playing tennis, throwing or catching a ball). Thus rhythm seems to be a widespread phenomenon and an integral part of our human existence.

Children exhibit simple rhythmic movements from infancy. Newborn babies move within their own time and space as they stretch their arms and fingers and kick their legs. Later, as children learn to organize their movements, they walk, run, and jump. With maturation they develop more-complex rhythmic movements for swimming, dancing, playing basketball, or performing on a musical instrument.

This chapter focuses on the use of movement to (1) develop body awareness in space, (2) express musical concepts, (3) interpret musical ideas, and (4) develop skill in folk dancing. It is based on the premise that a child's body, mind, and emotions are integrated into natural rhythmic expression and that through guided experiences involving movement children will learn to identify what they hear with what they do, thus stimulating their interest in and developing their skill with every facet of musical learning.

Teachers often ask, "How do I begin?" The following guidelines will help you generate ideas and techniques for musical learning experiences through rhythmic bodily response activities.

- Encourage the child's natural inclination to move.

- Encourage the natural use of speech, gesture, and body language to express thoughts and emotions.

- Encourage the use of various levels of energy (dynamics) and timing in movement, speech, and gesture (for example, hurried but forceful speech).

- Allow children to explore and find ways to "live" particular elements of the music in movement (such as with an ascending melody).

- Identify elements, concepts, or other aspects of music that children should experience (such as repetition or contrast in music).

- Pay attention to children's individual responses. Sometimes a child's response is so imaginative that it is worth having the whole class try it.

- Allow children freedom and opportunities to express music with their bodies in spontaneous ways.

- Encourage the completion of structured tasks that will, in turn, result in musical learning.

- Choose music for rhythmic activities that causes children to respond instinctively, by, for example, tapping a foot (Sousa, "Stars and Stripes Forever") or bouncing and catching a ball ("This Old Man").

- Use a variety of music (jazz, popular, folk, classical, Hispanic, African American, Native American). Begin early to find music you like and make a list of possible ways to move to it.

Developing Body Awareness in Space[*]

Some basic tasks involving children with music and movement include (1) developing body awareness, which will enable the child to move freely in space, and (2) developing the rhythmic ability to feel and move to a beat. When children can use their bodies expressively in space and can successfully feel and move to a beat, they are ready to experience movement in more-complex musical settings.

In developing the body awareness that allows them to move freely in space, without inhibition, children should be involved in both locomotor and nonlocomotor activities. *Locomotor* means to move from one place to another, whereas *nonlocomotor* means to move within a stationary position. The four stages in developing body awareness are (1) movement as an expression of problem solving, (2) movement as an expression of imagery, (3) movement with no external beat, and (4) movement to a beat with a sense of timing.

MOVEMENT AS AN EXPRESSION OF PROBLEM SOLVING

Expressive movement may be used as a response to challenging statements, questions, or situations. These activities can also reinforce visual/aural awareness.

---

[*] This material is based on the work of Phyllis Weikart in developing rhythmic and spatial concepts for teaching rhythm. See Phyllis S. Weikart, *Teaching Movement and Dance* (Ypsilanti, Mich.: The High/Scope Press, 1982), pp. 31–42.

Suggestions for Lessons

1. Ask the student to respond to such questions as:
   - How can your hand move?
   - How can your foot move?
   - How can your whole body move?

2. Invite students to imitate a leader:
   - My hand can go up or down.
   - My hand can go over and under.
   - My hand can go fast and slow.

3. Draw expressive responses with such statements as:
   - Lift your arm slowly.
   - Lower your arm quickly.
   - Draw a square with one foot.
   - Make an S with your whole body.

4. Play the game "Simon Says." Create interesting and expressive movements.

5. Play music on a radio and turn the volume down to stop the music. Ask the students to move creatively when they hear the music and "freeze" when it stops.

6. Improvise sounds on the strings of the piano (tap, pluck, glissando). Ask students to respond by moving their hands, feet, bodies, and heads creatively.

7. Using only the black keys on the piano or other keyboard instrument, improvise in the low, middle, and high registers. Ask the students to express the concepts of high and low by moving their bodies.

MOVEMENT AS AN EXPRESSION OF IMAGERY

In movement associated with imagery, the student's imagination is challenged by activities related to something previously experienced. Responses are limited only by the student's frame of reference; thus, "Show me how a snowman melts to the ground" assumes that the student has seen a snowman and has a mental picture of how slowly it melts away.

Suggestions for Lessons

1. Ask students to express the following:
   - Show how a turtle moves.
   - How would you move if you had to carry a heavy pack on your back?
   - How would you move your hand if you (a) touched a warm stove, (b) touched a hot stove, (c) touched a sizzling-hot stove?

2. Using musical examples such as the following, ask students to move creatively:

   a. Rimsky-Korsakov, "Flight of the Bumble Bee" (fast)

   Ideas for movements: Move hands in circular motion; fingers "run" across tabletop.

   b. Debussy, "Jimbo's Lullaby" from *The Children's Corner Suite*

   Ideas for movement: Stretch from one side to another, walk slowly with heavy steps, swing arms from side to side.

    c. "Orange Blossom Special" (bluegrass)

    Ideas for movement: Rapid circular motion of arms (as for wheels of train), vertical raising of arms to "pull train whistle."

    d. Perrey-Kingsley, "Spooks in Space" from *The In Sound Way Out* (Vanguard CD-79222-2)

    Ideas for movement: Short, choppy hand movements, alternating with long sweeping motions of hands and arms overhead. Vertical wave motions with hands for "ghost sounds."

    e. Copland, "Hoe-Down" from *Rodeo* (fast, slow, pause)

    Ideas for movement: Clap a fast beat, walk slowly, lift knees high, "freeze" on pause with both arms outstretched.

    f. "Navaho Gift Dance Song" or "Hopi Basket Dance"*

    Ideas for movement: Short, choppy movement with drum and bells; legato movements such as making body and hands both high or low to match melody.

3. Sing "The People on the Bus" and have students create appropriate motions that express the words. Create your own verses and additional motions.

---

* Available on *Authentic Music of the American Indian* (Legacy International, Box 6999, Beverly Hills, CA 90212).

The People on the Bus

United States

Key: G
Starting pitch: D
Meter: 4/4, begins on 4

4. Sing "Little Tommy Tinker" and do the motions of raising hands high into the air on "Oh, Ma."

5. Sing "Eency, Weency Spider." The words of the song suggest movements that children might do. For example, the motion of the spider can be represented by touching the tip of the index finger on one hand to the tip of the thumb on the other, alternating hands as the "spider" goes up the water spout. Both hands, palms down, are lowered for "down came the rain." Have students create movements for the rest of the words.

Little Tommy Tinker

Key: D
Starting pitch: D
Meter: 4/4, begins on 1

Nursery Rhyme

Eency, Weency Spider

Key: G
Starting pitch: G
Meter: 6/8, starts on 1

Action Song

MOVEMENT WITH NO EXTERNAL BEAT

A third type of movement requires the students to move from one space to another freely and successfully according to their own beat or tempo.

Suggestions for Lessons

1. Ask students to walk to the other side of the room as if walking a straight line. Play repeated chords on keyboard, Autoharp, or Omnichord (Q chord).

2. Ask students to walk to the other side of the room as if walking a jagged line. Play black keys of the piano only—any series of skips.

3. Ask students to walk and, on your signal, change directions (walk backward, walk sideways, and so on). Follow this same procedure when playing "Spanish Flea" by Herb Alpert and the Tijuana Brass. For example, every time the first melody repeats, return to the original way of walking.

4. Vary intensity and affect. Play or sing "We Wish You a Merry Christmas" and ask students to walk "happy." Play or sing "When Moses Was" and ask students to walk "sad." Play or sing "I've Been Working on the Railroad (Dinah)"; ask students to walk and let their head and arms be happy.

MOVEMENT TO A BEAT WITH A SENSE OF TIMING*

In developing a sense of timing and the ability to move to a beat, it is first necessary to concentrate on the use of a single motion, such as patting the head. Use language as an organizer of movement and concentrate on bilateral motions (such as "Both hands pat your head, both hands tap your shoulders"). Begin with body parts and create other activities. Sitting rather than standing contributes to a child's sense of security and confidence.

Suggestions for Lessons

1. Perform the following simple movements and ask the children to echo them.

   TEACHER (says): "Head," points to head with both hands.

   STUDENTS (say): "Head," point to head with both hands.

   TEACHER (says and does): "Pat, pat, pat head."

   STUDENTS (say and do): "Pat, pat, pat head."

   TEACHER (whispers and does): "Pat, pat, pat head."

   STUDENTS (whisper and do): "Pat, pat, pat head."

   TEACHER (silently): "Pat, pat, pat head."

   STUDENTS (silently): "Pat, pat, pat head."

2. After many experiences with bilateral motions, add a drumbeat to a song or musical composition that has a strong and steady beat. Good examples include the recordings *Grease* (RSO Records, Inc.), "Saturday Night Fever Medley," *Saturday Night Fiedler* (Boston Pops, Midsong International Records, Inc.), "Turkey in the Straw" (Roy Clark,

---

* Based on the four-step language process developed by Phyllis S. Weikart, *Teaching Music and Dance* (Ypsilanti, Mich.: The High/Scope Press, 1982), pp. 17–19, 24–27.

A Festival of Golden Country Instrumentals, Readers Digest, 1980), and the songs "It's a Small World" (page 121) and "This Land Is Your Land" (page 379).

3. As perceptual-motor skills become more developed, create rhythmic sequences from the following more complex sequences of movement.

   ■ Alternate motions: One hand or the other; one foot or the other

   ■ Double alternate motions: Both hands alternate with both feet; two foot taps alternate with two shoulder taps

   ■ Combined double alternate motions: Right hand to head/left hand to head; both hands to waist; left foot tap, right foot tap/both hands clap

4. Use such motions to express form as in the following example. Phrases of eight or sixteen beats and clear repetition of sections help students discriminate among their movements.

   ■ *Musical example:* Scott Joplin, "The Entertainer" (4/4 meter, quasi-rondo: ABACA)

   ■ Main theme, A: Pat head, tap shoulders

   ■ Contrasting melody, B: Slap thighs, clap hands

   ■ Contrasting melody, C: Tap chest, clap hands

5. Sing "The Little Shoemaker" and ask half the class to tap a steady beat throughout. The other half of the class should tap the word rhythms.

The Little Shoemaker

Key: F
Starting pitch: A
Meter: 4/4, begins on 4

Words by Janet Gaynor
Music by Alice Riley

Brightly

1. There's a lit - tle, wee man in a lit - tle wee house, Lives o - ver the way, you see. And he sits at the win - dow and sews all day, Mak - ing shoes for you and me. A-rap - a - tap - tap, a - rap - a - tap - tap. Hear the ham - mer's tit - tat - tee. A-rap - a - tap - tap, a - rap - a - tap - tap, Mak - ing shoes for you and me.

Expressing Musical Concepts Through Movement: The Dalcroze Approach

Émile Jaques-Dalcroze (1865–1950) was a well-known Swiss educator and a pioneer in teaching music based on the premise that rhythm is the primary element. His approach to teaching music consisted of three parts: eurhythmics (rhythmic movement), solfège (ear training), and improvisation. Through his teaching Dalcroze advocated developing the whole child, which he saw as involving physical and muscular control, mental awareness, social consciousness, and emotional health.

The system known as *eurhythmics* (meaning "good rhythm") focuses on developing the child's rhythmic potential through the use of his or her own body. Through experiences with natural movement, eurhythmics offers opportunities for developing keener hearing, concentration, mental alertness to musical elements, rhythmic control, coordination, flexibility, recognition and understanding of musical symbols, and appreciation of expressive qualities of music. Students are also asked to improvise rhythm patterns on a pitch or pitches and to improvise melodies, rondos, and moods using percussion instruments. The study of eurhythmics is based on the following concepts:

1. The use of the whole body, involving the larger muscle groups, ensures a more vivid realization of rhythmic experience than does the more customary use of the extremities, such as the hands in clapping and the feet in tapping.

2. The physical coordinations developed in the well-directed rhythm class give the individual power to control his or her movements in related activities. This is especially true in regard to instrumental skills, where coordination is difficult and specialized.

3. Bodily movement acts as a reference for the interpretation of rhythm symbols, which become truly significant when learned as the result of a vital rhythmic experience.

4. Children develop habits of listening in the process of identifying what they *hear* with what they *do*.

5. Body, mind, and emotion are integrated in rhythmic expression.

6. The freedom of expression that is a cardinal principle in eurhythmics stimulates the creative impulse in every department of musical learning.*

The following section includes some basic concepts of rhythm, with specific suggestions for presentation to students according to Dalcroze's ideas.

CONCEPT: BEAT/METER

As students' perceptions of music are developed, their attention should be focused on the steady beat in music. A *beat* is a regularly recurring pulse in music, which may be strong, with heavy accents, or weak, with little or no accent. Grouping beats according to accents creates *meter*, which may be in groups of twos or threes or in combinations of four, five, six, seven, and so on.

---

* Elsa Findlay, *Rhythm and Movement* (Easton, Ill.: Summy-Birchard, 1971), p. 2.

Suggestions for Lessons

1. Feeling the beat: Set a pendulum (or metronome) in motion. Have students say the word *swing* as they move to it. Vary the speed. Add something as simple as a finger cymbal or two pitches on a xylophone for each swing. Use familiar music with a strong beat, and encourage students to speak, chant, swing their arms, and move their whole body to the beat.

2. Feeling accents:

   a. Sing or play the songs "Yankee Doodle," "I'd Like to Teach the World to Sing," and "Chim Chim Cheree" (from *Mary Poppins*). Put a gentle push or weight on the first beat of every measure. Ask students to listen and respond by "lifting a low-hanging cloud back up into the sky" when they feel the music "lift."

   b. Sing or play "76 Trombones" from *The Music Man* by Meredith Willson, or the song "Bicycle Built for Two." Give balloons to small groups of four or five children. Ask them to "lift" the balloons when the music seems to say "lift" (on the accent).

3. Feeling meter:

   a. Use balls for developing coordination and discovering a feeling for beat. Individually or with partners, have students bounce a ball on the accent and then catch it. (You could play beats on drums or chords on piano; caution students not to bounce the ball indiscriminately.) As the students say "One" on the accented beat, they will develop a feeling for groupings of twos and threes.

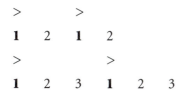

After students can feel duple and triple meter, ask them to bounce the ball to changing meters. Have them say "Bounce, catch" (duple), or "Bounce, catch, hold" (triple).

```
      >        >          >              >
  1     2    1     2     1    2    3    1    2    3
```

   b. Have students use their arms and upper bodies to find a swing in twos (two beats), then find a swing in threes.

   c. Have students find the accent and move their bodies or bounce balls to the following meters:

   - *Duple meter:* Current rock, country-western, and such songs as "Consider Yourself at Home" (from *Oliver*), "It's a Small World" (page 121), "This Land Is Your Land" (page 379), "I'd Like to Teach the World to Sing" (page 334), and "The Candy Man."

   - *Triple meter:* Songs such as "Edelweiss" (from *The Sound of Music*), "Roll On, Columbia" (page 156), "Silver Bells" (page 335), and "Did You Ever See a Lassie?" (page 120).

I'd Like to Teach the World to Sing (In Perfect Harmony)

Key: F
Starting pitch: D
Meter: 4/4, starts on "and" of 4

Words and Music by B. Backer, B. Davis, R. Cook, and R. Greenaway

Silver Bells

Words and Music by Jay Livingston and Ray Evans

Key: B♭
Starting pitch: B♭
Meter: 3/4, begins on 3

CONCEPT: FAST, SLOW, GETTING FASTER, GETTING SLOWER

Suggestions for Lessons: Grades K–3

1. Play "The Little Shepherd" from *The Children's Corner Suite* by Debussy. Ask students to respond with small and larger movements of hands, arms, and bodies as the music varies from slow to fast. Explore other types of physical expression, such as walking fast and then slowly as the music changes. Use fingers to do the walking or running over the desktop.

2. Play "Little Train of the Caipira" by Villa-Lobos. Ask the students to sit in a circle. Pass a large yarn ball to the right when the music gets faster and to the left when the music gets slower.

3. Play a recording of "Kee-Chee" (Silver Burdett Ginn *World of Music* 2, CD-2-23, or Silver Burdett Ginn *The Music Connection* 2 (2000), p. 56, track 22). Ask students to show the beat by tapping it on their knees. Have students indicate when the music gets faster or slower. Ask students to sit in a circle on the floor and pat their knees one at a time (each quarter note) through the words of the fourth line—"kae ay-na." Then, on the rest at the end of the fourth line, ask students to cross their hands to the opposite knees with one pat for each measure. Have them resume motions with the beginning of the song.

Kee-Chee

Game from Zaire

Reprinted by permission from *Girl Scout Pocket Songbook*. Copyright 1956, Girl Scouts of the United States of America.

4. Try similar experiences with the following pieces:
   - Saint-Saëns, "The Elephant" from *Carnival of the Animals* (slow)
   - Rimsky-Korsakov, "Flight of the Bumble Bee" (fast)
   - Chopin, Valse in D-flat Major, Op. 64, No. 1 (fast)
   - Ibert, "The Little White Donkey" from Histoires for Piano (slow, fast, slow)
   - Grieg, "In the Hall of the Mountain King" from *Peer Gynt Suite,* Op. 46, No. 1 (slow, becoming fast)
   - "Kalinka" (slow, becomes faster)

Suggestions for Lessons: Grades 4–6

1. Play sections of "Pacific 231" by Honegger. As the tempo changes from slow to fast to slow, ask students to respond by raising or lowering their arms. Point out the tension at both slow and fast tempos.

2. Dramatize the opening train scene from the musical *The Music Man.* Students should illustrate through their movements a train starting slowly, becoming fast, and then slowing down.

3. Many other musical compositions use tempo to express a mood, idea, or feeling. Encourage students to improvise free, creative movements as expressions of slow, fast, or slow-fast-slow, using the following pieces:
   - Chopin, "Fantasie Impromptu," Op. 66 (fast-slow-fast)
   - Prokofiev, Sonata No. 7 (III) (fast)
   - Mozart, Clarinet Concerto in E-flat (II) (slow)
   - Tchaikovsky, "Arabian Dance" from *The Nutcracker* (slow)

CONCEPT: ACCENTS

Many musical compositions use *accents* as an expressive device. Encourage students to use free, creative movements to express accents as they occur in music.

Suggestions for Lessons: Grades K–3

1. Play the following rhythms on a drum. Ask students to sit in a circle and raise or lower yarn balls as accents are played.

2. Play "Golliwog's Cakewalk" from *The Children's Corner Suite* by Debussy. Ask the students to make tight fists, then open their hands suddenly as they hear accents. Then have them stand and relax their bodies, with arms hanging loosely at the sides, and tighten their muscles for the accents.

Suggestions for Lessons: Grades 4–6

1. Invite students to create a designated movement on the accents in each of the following:

2. Apply movements denoting proper accents to any of the following pieces:

- Stravinsky, "Dance of the Adolescents" from *Rite of Spring*
- Bernstein, "America" from *West Side Story*
- Bruch, Violin Concerto in G Minor, Op. 26, No. 1 (III—Rondo)

CONCEPT: DYNAMICS

The body is an important means by which a child can be made aware of the role of *dynamics* in music. Movement experiences should include quiet, slow movements as well as sudden and gradual changes in energy levels.

Suggestions for Lessons: Grades K–3

1. Ask students to draw a big circle when the sound is loud and a small circle when the sound is soft. Play an echo game with movement as the response.

2. Listen to the song "Frosty the Snowman." Discuss how music gets softer when expressing the words *but he waved good-bye.* Have students pretend to be snowmen and melt to the ground as the music gets softer.

Suggestions for Lessons: Grades 4–6

1. Play portions of Beethoven's "The Storm" from Symphony No. 6 *(Pastorale),* or Grofé's "Cloudburst" from *Grand Canyon Suite.* Ask students to decide how to move in their own space in such a way that they show more energy as the storm intensifies and less energy as the storm recedes. Follow up this activity with a discussion about how students decided on the amount of energy to use, when to change it, and what in the music caused the change (dynamics: loud/soft/accents).

2. Listen to Debussy's "The Sunken Cathedral" from *Preludes* Book I. It begins softly as the mystical cathedral rises through the mist. The music gets louder as the cathedral comes into full view with its bells tolling, and then gradually gets softer as the cathedral vanishes from view. Ask students to interpret the dynamics of this piece with their bodies. You might begin by having them lie on the floor, curled up tightly to represent the soft dynamics of the beginning. As they stretch and expand their bodies with larger

motions, they may express louder dynamics. Returning to the still, quiet position on the floor signifies the return of the cathedral to the hidden depths of the imagination and the soft dynamics of the ending.

CONCEPT: RHYTHM PATTERNS

When long and short sounds are put together and then repeated, a rhythm pattern results. If this pattern is placed in a melody, melodic rhythm is created. For example: ♩♩ ♩ is a melodic rhythm in the song "Jingle Bells."

Suggestions for Lessons: Grades K–3

1. Use children's names or seasonal words to put note values together.

   Examples: Spring fever

   Daffodils, jonquils

   Rain! o or

   Let children respond aurally and physically before they are shown the patterns. Then put patterns together in various combinations.

2. Step characteristic rhythm patterns as students learn songs. The more precisely students can step a pattern fully with their bodies, the better they feel it in preparation for visual and intellectual understanding.

   Examples: "Jingle Bells"

   "Yankee Doodle"

   "Got a Mule"

3. Make up word patterns. Practice stepping, clapping, and speaking the patterns, then remove the words and speak the patterns with rhythm syllables.

   Examples: Ice-cream cone

   May I have some ice cream?

   George Washington

   Abraham Lincoln

4. A ﹀ is a *rest,* which is a silent pause in music. Help children feel the rest with their bodies but without a sound. An idea for small children is to clap on "walk" and to touch temples gently on the rest.

   walk,   walk,   walk,   rest

5. Start a beat ♩ ♩ ♩ ♩ and then add words to help you remember the following patterns. Locate the patterns in familiar songs.

   corn   cobs   ap - ri - cot   dou - ble trou - ble   straw - ber - ry   piz - za pie

Suggestions for Lessons: Grades 4–6

1. Present the song "Erie Canal" (page 63) on a transparency. In part one of the song, ask students to circle the following repeated pattern: ♪ ♩. Count the number of times this pattern occurs (nine). Perform part one of the song for students. Ask them to create a motion for the ♪ ♩ (syncopation).

2. Present part two of "Erie Canal" on a transparency. Ask students to circle the following repeated rhythmic pattern: ♩. ♪. Count the number of times it occurs (15). Perform part two of the song for students. Ask them to create a different motion for the rhythmic pattern ♩. ♪ (the motion will need to be short).

3. Divide the class in half. Perform the song again and ask half the class to do the motion for ♪ ♩ and the other half to do the second motion for ♩. ♪.

4. Perform the song with the class singing (without the motions), then perform the song with motions.

CONCEPT: MELODIC CONTOUR

Movement can be a major activity in learning the melody of a song. Moving their hands or "mapping the melody" helps students feel when the melody moves up or down.

Suggestions for Lessons: Grades K–3

1. Ask students to apply movement to the phrase "Oh, Ma" in "Little Tommy Tinker" (page 329). Notice how students can use their head voices better and sing high to low.

2. Ask students to place their hands on feet, ankles, knees, waist, shoulders, jaw, eyes, and top of head as they sing the song "Do-Re-Mi" from *The Sound of Music.*

Interpreting Musical Ideas Through Movement

Interpreting musical ideas through movement focuses on the simple expressiveness of musical elements, text, or programmatic ideas in music. The bodily movement may be free and creative or carefully planned and either abstract or dramatic. Essential to this type of expression is skill and comfort in using the body in a spatial environment. Many techniques for exploring the use of the body in space are explored in "Developing Body Awareness in Space" earlier in this chapter. Children will find increased pleasure and satisfaction in musical experiences as they become comfortable with physical movement to music and are no longer self-conscious.

WHAT INSPIRES INTERPRETATIVE MOVEMENT?

Inspiration for creating movement patterns or expressiveness comes from the musical elements inherent in the piece of music. Questions to be asked by the teacher include:

1. What is the rhythm (beat, meter, syncopation)?

2. What is the tempo?

3. What kinds of rhythm patterns are used?

4. What is the text about? Are there programmatic ideas in the music?

General Guidelines for Planning Movement Experiences

- Keep movement within the skills and capabilities of the student (for example, use bilateral motions for young children). These movements may range from very simple to highly complex.

- Choose musical compositions that lend themselves through text or programmatic ideas to interpretative movement. Be careful not to impose a story meaning on a simple melody.

- Plan movements so that they flow freely from one to the other.

- Plan movements carefully. Sometimes children will improvise movement as a part of the learning process, whereas at other times you will want them to follow a planned pattern of movements.

- Ask children to help decide on appropriate interpretative movements and chart them with stick figures and captions that give specific directions, along with the text of the song (if there is one).

- Make sure children learn each movement well; children must concentrate on the interpretation and not on "what do I do next?"

- Be sensitive to the children's ages. Do not choose a movement that will be awkward or embarrassing to them.

- For performance experiences, you may wish to use simple costumes.

- Emphasize important words or syllables. You may choose to do the movement on a strong beat or on a particular word.

- Enhance the rhythm of the song with coordinated movement (that is, everyone doing the same thing at the same time).

5. What are the characteristics of the melody/melodies (steps, skips, up, down, legato, staccato, phrase length)?

6. What is the form (AB, ABA, rondo, theme-and-variation)?

7. How would you describe the dynamics (loud, soft, gradually getting louder, softer)?

As you study and analyze the qualities of a musical composition, you need to decide how you will use such basic rhythmic activities as walking, marching, clapping, slapping, snapping, stretching, bending, and swaying.

One type of interpretative movement is free and creative, in which students are encouraged to respond in an appropriate way to a given musical composition. Music may contain programmatic ideas to which children relate, or it may be abstract.

- *Music examples (programmatic):* Moussorgsky's "Ballet of the Chicks in Their Shells" from *Pictures at an Exhibition;* Sondheim's "Send in the Clowns" from *A Little Night Music;* Grofé's "Sunrise" from *Grand Canyon Suite*

- *Music examples (abstract):* Chopin's "Fantasie Impromptu," Op. 66; Prokofiev's Classical Symphony, Gavotte; J. S. Bach's "Jesu, Joy of Man's Desiring"

A second type of movement is structured, as determined by the students, the teacher, or both together. The movements are the same from performance to performance and are done together. Structured movement may be abstract or dramatic. In the former, basic rhythmic activities, such as snapping, clapping, and swaying, dominate the interpretation, whereas in the latter, movements are determined by a literal interpretation of the text or programmatic idea. Songs are popular sources for structured movement. The following general guidelines will help you use movement to involve students in experiencing music.

ABSTRACT INTERPRETATIVE MOVEMENT

"ROCK-A MY SOUL"

Activity: Slapping, clapping, and snapping fingers to music

Grades: 4–6

Concepts: Rhythm: Beat, syncopation, melodic rhythm
              Form: ABA

Procedures

1. Sing "Rock-a My Soul" (page 254).

2. Say the text out loud to feel the beat and develop ideas for movement.

3. Determine the form (ABA) and create two sets of contrasting rhythmic motions as follows:

Measures	Movements
A Section	
Measures 1–8	Slap thighs on beats 1 and 3; clap hands on beats 2 and 4
B Section	
Measures 9–10	Snap fingers on beats 2 and 4, arms in front
Measures 11–12	Snap fingers on beats 2 and 4, arms left
Measures 13–14	Snap fingers on beats 2 and 4, arms right
Measure 15	Arms at side
Measure 16	Clap hands on beats 2 and 3
A Section	
Measures 1–8	Repeat motions for measures 1–7; end with two claps on measure 8

"I'M GONNA SING WHEN THE SPIRIT SAYS SING"

Activity: Stretching, crossing arms, clapping

Grades: 4–6

Concepts: Rhythm: Beat, accent, melodic rhythm

I'm Gonna Sing When the Spirit Says Sing

Key: G
Starting pitch: D
Meter: 4/4, begins on "and" of 3

Spiritual

Procedures

1. Sing the song.

2. Create movements that follow the text, such as:

   - *I'm gonna*   Hands and arms in ready position
   - *sing*   Both hands and arms stretch out and up
   - *spirit*   Both hands cross chest
   - *o-bey*   Clap
   - *Lord*   Both hands and arms outstretched in front; palms up

3. Chart the movements with stick figures to help students remember them.

DRAMATIC INTERPRETATIVE MOVEMENT

Most children enjoy creative dramatics. They like to be something or someone else and experience great pleasure in acting out a song. Adding some visuals, costumes, and movement can generate a tremendous amount of excitement in the classroom, and, because children have vivid imaginations, the teacher's role is minimized. Although dramatic movement can be added to any song, songs that lend themselves especially well to such treatment are those that (1) tell a story (ballad or multiple verses), (2) have contrasting phrases or sections, (3) feature a particular event or time in history, or (4) portray a strong human emotion or action.

In the following songs, ideas for dramatic interpretative movement can be found in the text or musical concepts.

"LITTLE MARIONETTES"

Activity: Staccato finger movements, clapping, smooth hand motions

Grades: K–2

Concepts: Tempo: Quick

Melody: Staccato, short phrases, skips

Rhythm: Steady beat, duple meter

Little Marionettes

Key: G
Starting pitch: G
Meter: 2/4, begins on 1

French Nursery Song

♩=84

Danc - ing, danc - ing   fin - gers,   Ti - ny mar - io - nettes are danc - ing.

Danc - ing, danc - ing   fin - gers,   Clap, clap, clap, and   three times 'round.

From *Music for Early Childhood* © 1952 Silver Burdett Company. Reprinted by permission.

Procedures

1. Have students pretend that their fingers are marionettes on strings. Have students dance, stressing the first beat until the words "clap, clap, clap," when they should clap hands.

2. Have students circle one hand with the other at the words "three times 'round."

"I WISH I WERE A WINDMILL"

Activity: Swaying, moving arms up and down

Grades: K–2

Concepts: Rhythm: Steady beat, duple meter

Text: Windmill, move my arms like this

I Wish I Were a Windmill

Play Song

Key: F
Starting pitch: C
Meter: 4/4, begins on 4

I wish I were a wind-mill, a wind-mill, a wind-mill; I wish I were a

wind-mill, I know what I would do. I'd move my arms like this,_____ like

this,_____ like this;_____ I'd move my arms like this,_____ That's what I would do.

Procedures

1. Have students choose partners and face each other.

2. Each should clasp the right and left hands of his or her partner and raise them overhead to form the "blades" of the windmill.

3. Have each pair move their arms up and down, swaying right and left with the beat.

"AIZU LULLABY"

Activity: Rocking, swaying

Grades: K–3

Concepts: Rhythm: Steady beat, duple meter

Tempo: Slow

Melody: Legato

Text: Rocks her/his sweet little baby

Aizu Lullaby (Aizu Komori Uta)

Key: D
Starting pitch: B
Meter: 4/4, begins on 1

1. Hi ya!___ Go to___ sleep,_____ ba - by,___ Hi ya!___ Go to___ sleep._____
Hō ra___ nei ro___ nen_____ nei - ro,___ Ho ra nei ro___ ya.
2. Moth - er___ rocks her___ sweet lit - tle ba - by,___ Hi ya!___ Go to___ sleep._____
3. Dad - dy___ rocks his___ sweet lit - tle ba - by,___ Hi ya!___ Go to___ sleep._____

Go to___ sleep my___ sweet_____ ba - by,___ Hi ya!___ Go to___ sleep._____
Nēn _____ nei ro nen ___ nei ro,___ Ho ra nei ro___ ya.

Betty Warner Dietz and Thomas Choonbai Park, *Folk Songs of China, Japan, and Korea.* © 1964. By permission of Betty Warner Dietz.

Procedures

1. Students take turns rocking a baby doll to sleep.

2. Have them follow the quadruple meter and sway right and left on beats 1 and 3.

More-complex movements can be used to interpret an entire composition. The following movements can be performed either as a classroom activity or on stage for a school program.

"CATCH A FALLING STAR"

Activity: Dramatization, snapping fingers

Grades: 5–6

Concepts: Rhythm:

Accents:

Catch a Falling Star

Words and Music by Paul Vance and Lee Pockriss

Key: B♭
Starting pitch: D
Meter: 4/4, begins on 1

Procedures

1. Practice the rhythm of the song and then decide on appropriate dramatic movements that will express the words.

2. A few students may create a rhythmic ostinato movement while another group of students may dramatize the text.

3. Reinforce learning by asking a select group of students to play the ostinato on percussion instruments.

"DREAM A DREAM"

Activity: Walking, stretching, holding hands

Grades: 5–6

Concepts: Melody: Phrases, contour, legato

Text: Dream, hope, brighter day, find a way, make it happen

Dream a Dream

Key: B♭
Starting pitch: D
Meter: 4/4, begins on 4

Ed Robertson (Studio Recordings)

Dream a dream of a new to-mor-row when the
Dream a dream of a world u-nit-ed when the

peo-ple learn to love their fel-low man. Dare to hope for a
na-tions choose to lay their wea-pons down. Dare to hope for a

peace-ful morn-ing when we've learned to walk to-geth-er hand in hand. If we
day of glad-ness when the world can let a smile re-place a frown.

all will dare to dream dreams of a new and bright-er day, if we work to make them come true, we will sure-ly find a way. ___

Dream a dream, ___ dare to hope, - may-be we ___ can make it hap-pen. Dream a

dream of a new to-mor-row; may-be some-day we can see our dreams come true.

Procedures

1. Sing the song.

2. Create movements that follow text, such as:

"Dream a dream of a new tomorrow"	Two steps forward, hands gradually raised, right hand sweeps in arch above head, eyes follow
"when the people learn to love their fellow man."	Stop, cross arms over chest, face front
"Dare to hope for a peaceful morning"	Two steps DS* right, turn, left hand gestures with palm up, body faces L
"when we've learned to walk together hand in hand."	All join hands and step forward
"If we all will dare to dream dreams"	Drop hands, turn to each other in pairs—point to each other; on the word "dreams," outer hand of partners sweeps upward
"of a new and brighter day,"	Face front, left hand out with palm up on "new," right hand out with palm up on "brighter"
"if we work to make them come true"	All step four steps DSR
"we will surely find a way."	On "surely" turn, face front, both hands front in form of fist
"Dream a dream,"	Right hand upper sweep
"dare to hope,"	Left hand upper sweep
"maybe we can make it happen."	Face partner—join hands in pairs
"Dream a dream of a new tomorrow;"	Drop hands, stand as beginning—take two steps forward, gradually raise arms, right hand sweep, eyes follow
"maybe someday we can see our dreams come true."	Stop, face front, and cross arms over chest

---

* Stage directions: DS = Downstage—toward the audience; US = Upstage—away from audience; R = Right; L = Left; C = Center

"BROTHER, CAN YOU SPARE A DIME?"

Activity: Walking, marching, stretching, slapping

Grades: 5–6

Concepts: Text, tempo

This song depicts a railroad man who has become a victim of the Great Depression in the United States during the 1930s and is now waiting in a breadline.

Procedures

1. Select a boy to sing the song as a solo. Dress him in ragged clothing.

2. Create movements that follow the text, such as:

"Once I built a railroad, made it run,"	Marches forward; hands form wheel, turn on "made it run"
"Made it race against time."	Hand straight out in arch "against time"
"Once I built a railroad,"	Walks downstage (toward audience)
"Now it's done."	Hand motions across right, palm down
"Brother, can you spare a dime?"	Pantomimes holding up tin cup for a handout
"Once I built a tower, to the sun:"	Right hand sweeps upward toward sun
"Brick and rivet and lime,"	"Brick," slaps hand; "rivet," pantomimes staccato riveting; "lime," smooths hand on other hand as if on brick
"Once I built a tower,"	Right hand sweeps upward
"Now it's done."	Repeat of earlier motion: hand sweeps across, palm down
"Brother, can you spare a dime?"	Pantomimes holding up tin cup
"Once in khaki suits, Gee! we looked swell,"	Marches and swings arms vigorously
"Full of that Yankee Doodle de-dum."	Stops and salutes
"Half a million boots went sloggin' through Hell,"	Marches as if through mud
"I was the kid with the drum."	Pantomimes playing of drum with drumstick (bass drum)
"Say, don't you remember, they called me Al"	Turns to audience and points to himself with thumb
"It was Al all the time?"	Points to audience, shakes head, takes
"Say, don't you remember I'm your Pal?!"	two steps, turns, points to himself . . .
(Sings slowly as he sinks to his knees)	
"Buddy, can you spare a dime?"	Holds up tin cup.

Brother, Can You Spare a Dime?

Key: C minor
Starting pitch: C
Meter: 4/4, begins on 1

Music by Jay Gorney
Words by E. Y. Harburg

Playing Singing Games and Dancing

One of the most enjoyable ways of involving students in moving to music is through singing games and dances. Learning to coordinate body movements and music provides an excellent way for students to improve their listening skills.

Following are some popular singing games and folk dances for various grade levels. Although some are accompanied by recorded music, most have songs that are to be sung by the students as they participate in the movement. It is suggested that students learn to sing the songs well before adding appropriate movements.

"CHICKEN DANCE" ("QUA, QUA")

Recorded

Grades: 3–6

Procedures

1. Have students stand in several circles (according to the size of the class, but no more than eight students per circle).

2. Play the first two verses of "Chicken Dance" (*Drew's Famous Party Music* 1994 [cassette], Turn Up the Music, Inc., band 17).

3. Show the motions for the A section:

   a. Pat head four times.

   b. Move arms like a chicken four times.

   c. Weave body to the ground on four counts.

   d. Stand and clap hands four times.

   (You or a student can play a percussion instrument on the clapping of hands.)

4. Ask students to imitate you from their standing positions.

5. Show the movements for the B section:

   a. Form a star with other people in the group and walk four steps clockwise.

   b. Drop hands and reverse direction (counterclockwise) four more steps.

6. Ask students to imitate you.

7. Ask students to follow you in a performance of the piece. Be sure that they change when the music does (they are listening to the A section and then the B section).

"OBWISANA"

Grades: K–1

Procedures

1. Play a recording of "Obwisana" (Silver Burdett Ginn, *World of Music* 2, CD 2-12). The African words mean "Oh, Gramma, I just hurt my finger on a rock."

2. Ask students to choose any small object and then bring it with them as you ask them to sit in a circle on the floor. Each child should place the object in front of him or her.

3. As the song is performed on a recording or sung, students should move their object over to their right one person on the first beat of the measure and lay it down on the second beat of the measure. Students continue alternating motions as long as they hear the music.

"DID YOU EVER SEE A LASSIE?"

The music for "Did You Ever See a Lassie?" is on page 120.

Grades:　K–3

Procedures

1. Students form a circle, alternating boys and girls, with hands joined; one student is placed in the center.

2. As the students sing each phrase of the song, have them perform the corresponding action:

   - "Did you ever see a lassie, a lassie, a lassie,"

     Students move to the left four steps in time to the music

   - "Did you ever see a lassie do this way and that?"

     Students move to the right four steps in time to the music

   - "Do this way and that way, do this way and that way,"

     Student in center makes some movements while those in the circle stand still

   - "Did you ever see a lassie do this way and that?"

     Students in circle imitate movements of student in the center

   While the students are performing the last phrase, the student in the center points to a student in the circle, who will change places with him or her at the end of the phrase. Then the song and dance repeat.

"WILD BIRD"

Grades:　K–2

Procedures

1. Play a recording of the song "Wild Bird" (Silver Burdett Ginn, *World of Music*, CD 2–4).

2. Teach the song.

3. Experiment with listening to various voices to determine who belongs to them. (*Examples:* Jimmy has a low, throaty voice; Yolanda has a high, thin voice.)

4. Have students form a circle or "cage" for the bird. (Face inward, hands joined.) One child (the bird) sits in the center with eyes closed. As students in the circle move to the left, they stop when they sing "free." A single student who is directly behind the bird sings or says the rest of the song as a solo. The student who is sitting in the middle then tries to identify the singer (or speaker). If the student in the center is correct, they change places and play the game again. Otherwise, the student in the center remains the bird.

5. Play the game and ask the children who are not the bird to sing.

Wild Bird (Kagome)

Key: C
Starting pitch: A
Meter: 2/4, begins on 1

Singing Game from Japan

Round, round, the wild birds fly,
Ka - go - me, Ka - go - me,
kah - goh - meh kah - goh - meh

Poor lit - tle bird in a cage, don't___ cry!
Ka - go - no na - ka - no to - ri - wa,
kah - goh - noh nah - kah - noh taw - ree

Hide your eyes and soon you'll___ be
I - tsu, i - tsu de - ya - ru?
ee - tsoo ee - tsoo day - yah - roo

With the wild birds, fly - ing free.
Yo - a - ke - no ba - n - ni,
yoh - ah - kay - noh bah - nee

Solo

Who's stand - ing back of you, can you___ say?
Tsu - ru to ka - me to sub - be - ta.
tsoo - roo toh kah - meh toh soob - beh - tah

If you guess the name you can fly a - way!
U - shi - ro - no sho - men da - re?
oo - shee roh - noh shoh - mehm dah - reh

"THE MULBERRY BUSH"

Grades: K–1

The Mulberry Bush

Key: G
Starting pitch: G
Meter: 6/8, begins on 1

England

Here we go 'round the mul-ber-ry bush, the mul-ber-ry bush, the mul-ber-ry bush.

Here we go 'round the mul-ber-ry bush, so ear-ly in the morn - ing.

Procedures

1. Have students form a circle, facing inward, with hands joined.

2. As students sing, have them perform the indicated actions or movements:

"Here we go 'round the mulberry bush, the mulberry bush, the mulberry bush. Here we go 'round the mulberry bush, so early in the morning." — Students move counterclockwise in time to the music

"This is the way we wash our hands, wash our hands, wash our hands. This is the way we wash our hands, so early in the morning." — Students pantomime each verse of the song

(Repeat first verse above.)

"This is the way we brush our teeth, brush our teeth, brush our teeth. This is the way we brush our teeth, so early in the morning."

(Repeat first verse.)

"This is the way we comb our hair, comb our hair, comb our hair. This is the way we comb our hair, so early in the morning."

(Repeat first verse.)

"This is the way we sweep the floor,
sweep the floor, sweep the floor.
This is the way we sweep the floor,
so early in the morning."

(Repeat first verse.)

"THE FARMER IN THE DELL"

The music for "The Farmer in the Dell" is on page 218.

Grades: K–1

Procedures

1. Have students form a circle, facing inward. Boys alternate with girls and join hands. Select one student to be the farmer; he or she stands in the center of the circle.

2. As students sing, have them perform the indicated actions or movements:

"The farmer in the dell,
The farmer in the dell,
Hi! ho! the derry oh,
The farmer in the dell."

Students walk to right in time to music

"The farmer takes a wife,
The farmer takes a wife,
Hi! ho! the derry oh,
The farmer in the dell."

Students walk to right in time to music;
"farmer" moves to the circle and takes a "wife";
farmer and wife return to center of circle

"The wife takes the child,
The wife takes the child,
Hi! ho! the derry oh,
The farmer in the dell."

Students walk to right in time to music;
"wife" moves to the circle and takes a "child";
wife and child return to center of circle

"The child takes the nurse,
The child takes the nurse,
Hi! ho! the derry oh,
The farmer in the dell."

Students walk to right in time to music;
"child" moves to the circle and takes a "nurse";
child and nurse return to center of circle

"The nurse takes the dog,
The nurse takes the dog,
Hi! ho! the derry oh,
The farmer in the dell."

Students walk to right in time to music;
"nurse" moves to the circle and takes a "dog";
nurse and dog return to center of circle

"The dog takes the cat,
The dog takes the cat,
Hi! ho! the derry oh,
The farmer in the dell."

Students walk to right in time to music;
"dog" moves to the circle and takes a "cat";
dog and cat return to center of circle

"The cat takes the rat,
The cat takes the rat,
Hi! ho! the derry oh,
The farmer in the dell."

Students walk to right in time to music;
"cat" moves to the circle and takes a "rat";
cat and rat return to center of circle

"The rat takes the cheese,
The rat takes the cheese,
Hi! ho! the derry oh,
The farmer in the dell."

Students walk to right in time to music;
"rat" moves to the circle and takes a "cheese";
rat and cheese return to center of circle

"The cheese stands alone,
The cheese stands alone,
Hi! ho! the derry oh,
The farmer in the dell."

Everyone returns to the circle except the
"cheese"; all stand still facing the cheese

3. The above steps can be repeated, with the "cheese" becoming the "farmer."

"THE HOKEY POKEY"

Grades: K–1

The Hokey Pokey

Key: G
Starting pitch: D
Meter: 4/4, begins on "and" of 3

American Folk Song

Procedures

1. Have students form a circle facing inward.

2. Play a recording of the song "The Hokey Pokey" (*Drew's Famous Party Music* 1994 [cassette], Turn Up the Music, Inc., band 18),* or have the students sing. Have them pantomime words for each verse, performing the refrain as follows:

"And then you do the hokey pokey   Both hands wave over head
And you turn yourself about;   Keep both hands up and turn around
And that's what it's all about.
Hey!"   Drop hands and return to circle

---

* Other dances on the same recording are: "Jailhouse Rock," "The Conga," "Born to Be Alive," "La Bamba," and "Hands Up."

"SHOEMAKER'S DANCE"

Grades: K–2

Shoemaker's Dance

Key: F
Starting pitch: C
Meter: 2/4, Begins on 1

Danish Folk Song

Wind and wind the thread and wind and wind the thread And pull, pull, tap, tap, tap.

Tra la la la la la, la   Tra - la la, la, la, la, la

Procedures

1. Have students form two circles, with boys on the inside and girls on the outside; have partners face each other.

2. As students sing, have them perform the indicated actions or movements:

"Wind and wind the thread and,"	Students pantomime by making fists, which they roll forward around each other four times
"wind and wind the thread,	Reverse fist movement, now backward four times
And pull, pull,	Pull twice with both hands as if pulling up shoelaces
tap, tap, tap." (Repeat.)	Tap fists together three times
"Tra, la, la, la, la, la, la,	Boys' right hands join with girls' left hands;
Tra, la, la, la, la, la, la,	partners skip counterclockwise around
Tra, la, la, la, la, la, la,	the circle in time to the music
Tra, la, la, la, la, la, la."	

"ROUND AND ROUND THE VILLAGE"

Grades: 1–3

Round and Round the Village

United States

Key: F
Starting pitch: A
Meter: 2/2, begins on "and" of 2

1. Go 'round and 'round the vil - lage, Go 'round and 'round the vil - lage, Go
2. Go in and out the win - dows, Go in and out the win - dows, Go
3. Now kneel and say "Good morn - ing," Now kneel and say "Good morn - ing," Now
4. Now fol - low me to Lon - don, Now fol - low me to Lon - don, Now
5. Shake hands be - fore you leave her, Shake hands be - fore you leave her, Shake

'round and 'round the vil - lage,
in and out the win - dows,
kneel and say "Good morn - ing,"   As we have done be - fore.
fol - low me to Lon - don,
hands be - fore you leave her,

Procedures

1. Have most of the students form a circle, alternating boys and girls with hands joined; a few students stand in a line outside the circle.

2. As students sing, have them perform the indicated actions or movements:

"Go 'round and 'round the village, Go 'round and 'round the village, Go 'round and 'round the village, As we have done before."	Students on outside of circle move counterclockwise around the circle; students in circle slap hands to beat
"Go in and out the windows, Go in and out the windows, Go in and out the windows, As we have done before."	Students in circle join hands and raise arms to form windows; students on outside go *in* and *out* of the windows; at the end they should be *inside* the circle
"Now kneel and say 'Good morning,' Now kneel and say 'Good morning,' Now kneel and say 'Good morning,' As we have done before."	Students on inside of circle kneel facing students in the outer circle (this is where the new partner is chosen)
"Now follow me to London, Now follow me to London, Now follow me to London, As we have done before."	Students inside of circle skip counterclockwise (followed by new partners)
"Shake hands before you leave her, Shake hands before you leave her, Shake hands before you leave her, As we have done before."	Each student in inside circle shakes hands with new partner, followed by changing places with each other; inside circle thus returns to outside circle as the dance is repeated

"POP, GOES THE WEASEL"

Legend tells us that this song originally did not refer to an animal but to a tool used by London hatters and tailors called a "weasel," which they would pawn, or "pop," when they were short of funds and needed money to tide them over.

Grades: 1–3

Pop, Goes the Weasel

Key: C
Starting pitch: C
Meter: 6/8, begins on 1

England

1. All a-round the cob-bler's bench, the mon-key chased the wea-sel; mon-key thought 'twas

all__ in fun, Pop, goes the wea-sel. Pen-ny for a spool__ of thread,

Pen-ny for a nee-dle, That's the way the mon-ey goes, Pop, goes the wea-sel.

Procedures

1. Have children form two lines facing each other.

2. As students sing, have them perform the indicated actions or movements:

"All around the cobbler's bench,"	Head couple join hands and slide to foot of row
"the monkey chased the weasel; monkey thought 'twas all in fun,"	Return to original position Head couple slides down the row a second time
"*Pop*, goes the weasel.	All clap hands on "Pop"
Penny for a spool of thread,	From this position, head couple peel off to
Penny for a needle,	right and left; rest of students follow;
That's the way the money goes,"	head couple return to head of line and continue down row, becoming new "foot couple"

"*Pop*, goes the weasel."

Game begins again with a new head couple.

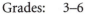

"O SUSANNA"

Grades: 3–6

O Susanna

Key: F
Starting pitch: F
Meter: 2/4, begins on "and" of 2

Stephen C. Foster

1. I___ came from Al - a - bam - a with my ban - jo on my knee, I'm___
2. It___ rained all night the day I left, the weath - er, it was dry; The___

going to Lou' - si - an - a my___ true love for to see.
sun so hot I froze to death, Su - san - na don't you cry.

Chorus
O Su - san - na, O don't you cry for me, For I've

come from Al - a - bam - a with my ban - jo on my knee.

Procedures

1. Have students form a circle, alternating boys and girls, facing inward.

2. As students sing, have them perform the indicated actions or movements:

"I came from Alabama with my"	In time to the music, girls move four steps into the circle; boys clap beat
"banjo on my knee,"	Girls move four steps back to their original place in the circle; boys clap beat
"I'm going to Lou'siana my"	Boys move four steps into the circle; girls clap beat
"true love for to see."	Boys move four steps back to their original place in the circle; girls clap beat

"It rained all night
the day I left, the
weather, it was dry;"

"The sun so hot I
froze to death,
Susanna don't you cry."

"O Susanna, O don't you
cry for me,
For I've come from
Alabama with my banjo
on my knee."

Grand right and left: Boys face clockwise,
girls face counterclockwise, join right hands
and move around circle, alternating left and
right hands; on "me," take new partners

New partners promenade eight walking steps
counterclockwise; on the last beat, everyone
faces inward ready to repeat the dance again

"LA CUCARACHA"

Grades: 4–6

Key: G
Starting pitch: D
Meter: 3/4, begins on "and" of 2

Mexico

Chorus

La cu - ca - ra - cha, la cu - ca - ra - cha.   ya no quie - re ca - mi -

nar,   Por - que no tie - ne, por - que le fal - ta   di - ne - ro pa - ra gas - tar.

Verse

U - na cu - ca - ra - cha pin - ta   La di - jo a u - na co - lo - ra - da

D.C. al Fine

Va - mo - nos pa - ra mi tie - rra   A pa - ser la tem - po - ra - da.

Procedures

1. Have students form two circles, boys on the inside and girls on the outside. Students face counterclockwise; boys put their hands on their hips, girls hold their skirts with left hand and castanets in right hand.

2. As students sing, have them perform the indicated actions or movements:

"La cucaracha, la cucaracha,"	Partners move sideways one step away from each other and back
"Ya no quiere caminar,"	Partners take six running steps forward, clap on rest
"Porque no tiene, porque le falta" "dinero para gastar."	Repeat side steps Repeat running steps and clap
"Una cucaracha pinta La dijo a una colorada,"	Partners face each other, left hand behind back, right hand over head; boy circles left, girl stands still and clicks castanets for twelve counts
"Vamonos para mi tierra A pasar la temporada"	Boy changes direction, circles right; girl clicks castanets for twelve counts
(Repeat chorus.)	Repeat actions for chorus

"HAHVAH NAHGEELAH"

Grades: 5–6

Hahvah Nahgeelah

Jewish Folk Song

Key: G minor
Starting pitch: D
Meter: 4/4, begins on 1

Hah - vah nah - gee - lah, hah - vah nah - gee - lah, hah - vah nah - gee - lah vuh - nis - muh' kh - hah.

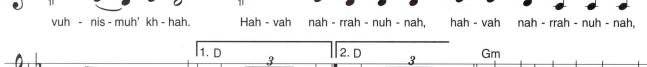

vuh - nis - muh' kh - hah. Hah - vah nah - rrah - nuh - nah, hah - vah nah - rrah - nuh - nah,

hah - vah nah - rrah - nuh - nah vuh - nis - muh' kh - hah vuh - nis - muh' kh - hah. Oo - roo, oo - roo ah'kh - heem,

oo - roo - ah'kh - heem buh - lev sah - meh - ah'kh, or - roo ah'kh - heem buh - lev sah meh - ah'kh,

oo - roo ah'kh - heem buh - lev sah - meh - ah'kh, oo - roo ah'kh - heem buh - lev sah - meh - ah'kh;

oo - roo ah'kh - heem, oo - roo ah'kh - heem b'lev sah - meh - ah'kh.

Procedures

1. Have students form a circle, alternating boys and girls, facing toward the center, hands joined.

2. Everyone follows these directions:

   a. Move left foot one step to the left; step on right foot crossing behind left foot.

   b. Move left foot one step to the left; hop on left foot while swinging the right foot across the front of the left foot.

   c. Move right foot one step to the right; hop on right foot while swinging the left foot across the front of the right foot.

   d. Repeat movements.

"IRISH JIG"

Grades: 5–6

Galway Piper

Traditional Irish Folk Song

Key: D
Starting pitch: D
Meter: 4/4, begins on 1

Ev - 'ry per - son in the na - tion,___ Of a great or hum - ble sta - tion,___

Holds in high - est es - ti - ma - tion, Pip - ing___ Tim___ of___ Gal - way. Loud - ly___ he can play or low.

He can___move you fast or slow, Touch your___hearts or stir your toe, Pip - ing___Tim of Gal - way.

Procedures

1. Have students form two lines, boys in one and girls in the other, with partners facing each other and hands on hips.

2. As students sing, have them perform the indicated actions or movements:

"Every person in the nation,
Of a great or humble station,
Holds in highest estimation,
Piping Tim of Galway."

Partners skip four steps forward toward
each other, then skip four steps backward
from each other, returning to places
in line (repeat)

"Loudly he can play or low."

Each student hops four times on left foot
while at the same time tapping the right
toe on the floor (forward, side, back, close)

"He can move you fast or slow,"

Repeat with the right foot while tapping the
left toe on the floor (forward, side, back, close)

"Touch your hearts or stir your toe,"
"Piping Tim of Galway."

Repeat four hops on left foot as above
Repeat four hops on right foot as above;
add a clap on last beat

3. Repeat dance for second verse.

"CIELITO LINDO"

Grades: 4–6

Cielito Lindo

Mexican Folk Song

Key: A
Starting pitch: A
Meter: 3/4, begins on 1

De la Sie - rra Mo - re - na, Cie - li - to Lin - do vie - nen ba - jan - do.
From Si - er - ra Mo - re - na Cie - li - to Lin - do comes soft - ly steal - ing

Un par de o - ji - tos ne - gros Cie - li - to Lin - do, de con - tra - ban - do.
Laugh-ing eyes, black and ro - guish Cie - li - to Lin - do, Beau - ty re - veal - ing

CHORUS

Ay, ay, ay, ay, Can - ta y no llo - res. Por - que can - tan -
Sing ban - ish sor - row To pass the hours

- do se a - le - gran, Cie - li - to Lin - do, los co - ra - zo - nes.
light - ly sing - ing Cie - li - to Lin - do glad - dens the mor - row.

From *Heritage Songster* by Leon and Lynn Dallin, 2nd ed. (Dubuque, Iowa: Wm. C. Brown, Co., 1980).

Procedures

1. Have students form a circle and join hands.

2. As students sing, have them perform the indicated actions or movements:

"De la Sierra Morena, Cielito Lindo vienen bajando." — Join hands and walk counterclockwise seven steps; on step eight, change direction

"Un par de ojitos negros Cielito Lindo, de contrabando." — Walk clockwise seven steps; stop on step eight and face center of circle

"Ay, ay, ay, ay," — Take four steps to center, raising arms high

"Canta y no llores." — Take four steps backward, lowering arms

"Porque cantando se alegran," — Four (two boys, two girls) join right hands and circle four steps to right:

"Cielito Lindo, los corazones." — Change hands (left hands); circle four steps to left

3. Repeat dance.

ADDITIONAL SINGING GAMES AND DANCES APPEARING IN OTHER AREAS OF THIS BOOK

- African game song "Tue, Tue" (page 406)

- African game song "Kye, Kye Kule" (page 403)

- African dance "Salamatu Bansa" (page 406)

- Native American song "Mos', Mos'!" and Round Dance (page 434)

- American square dance (page 440)

- Greek dance (page 428)

- Spanish dance to "La Raspa" (page 442)

For Your Journal

In your journal or portfolio, make a section on movement to music. Drawing on ideas in this chapter, specifically comment on some types of movement to music experiences you might design for children.

Creative
Experiences
with Music

CREATING MUSIC CAN BE AN EXCITING AND REWARDING EXPERIENCE for students, because it is a personal expression of their own feelings and ideas. Being involved in the creative process requires self-discipline, imagination, sensitivity, an understanding of the functions and possibilities of sounds, and the ability to organize materials into logical form. As students explore the realm of sound and focus their efforts on creating a musical work, they experience pleasure and satisfaction in having achieved a goal. Creating a musical composition requires that students use their current musical skills and may motivate them to learn new ones.

As in all creative effort, *a musical composition must begin with an idea.* This may be generated out of a student's interest in innovative ways of creating sounds, mixing instrumental or vocal sounds with environmental ones, writing a poem and setting it to music, creating a percussion accompaniment for a song, or expressing a dramatic idea or event. The teacher needs to encourage this type of creativity and at the same time set parameters for the musical effort being undertaken.

For instance, after being given an example of playing a drum by tapping the rim, students might be asked to explore three other ways of playing the drum (such as playing in the center of the drum with a drumstick, tapping the drum with fingers, or scratching the drumhead with fingernails). When students are given the opportunity to be creative, their activity has a focus. This is far more desirable than saying, "You have five minutes to play these instruments. Do anything you want to." With such a procedure, chaos is sure to result. Without some sort of direction, it is impossible, for instance, for students to be successful in writing a song. They simply do not know where to begin.

This chapter is directed toward developing skills for creative musical experiences. Students need to (1) have many opportunities to develop techniques for improvising and organizing sounds; (2) produce and use a rich variety of sounds: vocal, instrumental, environmental, body, and recorded; and (3) create songs, song accompaniments, and musical compositions that express feelings and ideas. The following materials and suggestions may be adapted to planning creative musical experiences for students in grades K–6.

The Orff Approach[*]

Carl Orff (1895–1982) was a German composer/educator who believed that it is important from the very beginning that students *physically* experience beat, meter, and rhythm and that they express these elements by dancing and playing instruments. Orff agreed with Jaques-Dalcroze's belief that rhythm is a foundation of musical growth, and he developed an approach that begins with speech rhythms already known to the child, such as names and familiar words. These rhythms are used to create original pieces and accompaniment patterns. Orff believed that the study of traditional musical instruments should begin only when the learner can perform simple rhythms on percussion instruments or sing basic tonal patterns and intervals.

The pentatonic (five-note) scale was popular with Orff, because it always gave a pleasant sound and students could not make any mistakes. In the Orff system, students are asked to create melodies or accompaniments in major or minor tonalities only after they have learned to create melodies and accompaniments within the pentatonic scale.

Orff advocated asking students to create introductions, codas, and accompaniments for folk songs within the student's ethnic tradition. He designed percussion instruments of high quality to form an ensemble. Some of these instruments are the glockenspiel (soprano and alto), xylophones (soprano, alto, bass), metallophones (soprano, alto, bass), and various assorted drums, jingle bells, and jingle sticks.

The word *process* is paramount in Orff's system, and the keys to this process are *exploration* and *experience.* Students are encouraged to explore space, sound, form, and creativity. The most important instrument in the Orff approach is the body, followed by the voice. The Orff process at every maturity level includes movement, voice and instruments, and improvisation.

Improvising and Organizing Sounds

Improvising involves creating something spontaneously at a given moment. Experiences in improvising rhythms, melodies, and musical forms contribute to a student's confidence and skill in singing, playing instruments, and moving to music, as well as to greater perception and understanding of music created by others. It is essential that the teacher lead students carefully from simple to more complex experiences and provide them with many opportunities to explore sounds (e.g., high/low, fast/slow). Guidelines for improvisation activities include providing a framework for the activity (*examples:* given a steady beat, students will improvise rhythm

---

[*] The material in this section is based on Lois Choksy, Robert Abramson, Avon Gillespie, and David Woods, *Teaching Music in the Twentieth Century* (Englewood Cliffs, N.J.: Prentice-Hall, 1986), pp. 96–103. For more information see American Orff-Schulwerk Association Web site *(www.aosa.org)*, Jane Frazee and Kent Kreuter, *Discovering Orff: A Curriculum for Music Teachers* (Mainz/London: Schott, 1987), and Arvida Steen, *Exploring Orff: A Teacher's Guide* (New York: Schott, 1992).

patterns; using only the black keys of the piano, students will improvise a melody). As students gain confidence in improvising with their voices and playing instruments, they will expand their understanding of music and find increased satisfaction and pleasure in the creative process. Following are some techniques for encouraging early experiences with improvisation.

1. Improvise rhythm patterns.

    a. Students keep a steady meter beat in duple meter:

    Pat knees or clap: 1 2 | 1 2 | 1 2 |

    Teacher claps: ♩ ♩ | ♩ ♩ to reinforce meter beat.

    As students maintain a steady beat, teacher improvises a different rhythm, such as

    b. Individual students improvise their own rhythm pattern as other students keep a steady beat, such as

    c. Repeat these procedures in triple meter.

2. Select a student to keep the steady beat on a drum. Ask individual students to improvise rhythm patterns on classroom instruments.

RHYTHM IN SPEECH

An excellent way to introduce children to rhythm is through speech patterns.

Suggestions for Lessons

1. Create word phrases and clap them in rhythm, then ask children to imitate.
   For example:

   Teacher:

   Students imitate.

   Teacher:

   Students imitate.

2. Ask students to create other word phrases that fit a pattern. The pattern may be played by the teacher or a student. For example:

   Leader:

   Student word rhythms:

3. Ask students to create a short speech pattern and then a rhythm to go with it. For example:

Squeak, squeak, squeak, went the lit - tle mouse

Bark, bark, bark, went the dog.

4. Experiment with changing the number of beats in a measure according to a speech pattern:

I want to go swim - ming, swim - ming in the pool, in the pool.

5. Play a game in which one student says his or her name and a second student plays the rhythm on a percussion instrument. For example:

Tim - o - thy An - der - son

Vic - to - ri - a Smith, Vic - to - ri - a Smith

Rich - ard Mil - ler

RHYTHM SPEECH CANONS

A *canon* is a repeating form in which the same thing is sung or said at a precise interval of time.

Suggestions for Lessons

1. In the following short "geographic" canon, have half the class begin and the second half enter one measure later. Speak the example as a rhythmic speech canon.

Geographic canon

New York, I - da - ho, Mass - a - chu - setts, Maine.

2. Try other types of canons, such as the following winter and spring canons. You might wish to make up your own. Experiment with using instruments instead of your voice and try various types of movement for each measure.

Winter canon

Snow and ice,   win-ter's here,   ski-ing, sled-ding,   slip-ping, slid-ing,   cold, cold,   freez-ing cold.

Spring canon

Rain-drops   pat-ter on the   win-dow   pane,   Pud-dles, pud-dles, pud-dles in the

street.   Splish, splash, splish, splash,   Yuk,   Yuk.

IMPROVISING MELODIES

To improvise a melody, begin improvising using only two notes, such as *sol-mi,* or G-E (scale: C D E G A). Create a rap based on these two notes and a set rhythm, such as ♩ ♩ ♩ ♩:

sol   mi

Improvise on "We are going to school today" or another phrase of your choice. The music may be different each time. For example:

We   are   go-ing   to   school   to - day

We   are   go-ing   to   school   to - day

Try improvising on a three-note scale—*sol-mi-la* (G E A):

We   are   go-ing   to   school   to - day

Next, using a five-note scale (pentatonic), ask students to improvise a melody to a speech pattern or speech canon they have composed.

do   re   mi   sol   la

Play the song on any pitch, but perform to a prescribed rhythm. Any combination of pitches will sound pleasing. For older students, add a freely composed rhythmic accompaniment on classroom percussion instruments. Be sure to keep a steady beat on some instrument, preferably a drum.

OSTINATO PATTERNS (RHYTHMIC AND MELODIC)

An *ostinato* is a melodic or rhythm pattern that is repeated throughout a song or larger musical composition.

Suggestions for Lessons

1. Following are some examples of simple ostinato patterns to "This Old Man." Combine several and play them on classroom instruments, thus creating a small ensemble (appropriate for grades K–2).

This Old Man

Key: F
Starting pitch: C
Meter: 2/4, begins on 1

Ostinato: xylophone

Glockenspiel/bells

Drum

2. Following are some ostinati accompaniments on a variety of instruments that can be used to accompany the song "Swing Low, Sweet Chariot." Try these accompaniments and then ask students to create their own ostinati for familiar songs. (This material can be adapted for grades 3–6.)

Swing Low, Sweet Chariot

Key: F
Starting pitch: A
Meter: 4/4, begins on 4

Spiritual

Swing low, sweet char - i - ot ___ com - ing for to car - ry me home. Swing ___

low, sweet char - i - ot ___ com - ing for to car - ry me home.
1. I
2. If
3. I'm

looked o - ver Jor - dan, and what did I see, ___ com - ing for to car - ry me home? A
you get there be - fore I do, com - ing for to car - ry me home, tell
some - times up and some - times down, com - ing for to car - ry me home, but

band of an - gels com - ing af - ter me, ___ com - ing for to car - ry me home.
all my friends I'm com - ing, too, com - ing for to car - ry me home.
still my soul feels heav - en - ly bound, com - ing for to car - ry me home.

Laura Wheeler and Lois Raebeck, *Orff and Kodaly Adapted for the Elementary School,* 3rd ed. (Dubuque, Iowa: Wm. C. Brown, 1985), p. 272.

IMPROVISING AN ACCOMPANIMENT TO A SONG

Suggestions for Lessons: Grades 3–6

1. Play or sing the chorus of "This Land Is Your Land."

   Tap or clap the beat:

2. Play or sing the song and have students clap the following pattern:

3. Ask students to create other patterns that fit the song. Direct them to stay with the beat. Experiment with several patterns while singing the chorus. For example:

etc.

4. Explore the sound possibilities of playing these rhythms on classroom percussion instruments. Select a single instrument for the refrain and a second instrument for the verse. Have the class sing the song and students improvise a rhythmic accompaniment.

This Land Is Your Land

Key: F
Starting pitch: F
Meter: Cut time, begins on "and" of 1

Words and Music by Woody Guthrie

IMPROVISING RHYTHMS WITH CLASSROOM INSTRUMENTS

Suggestions for Lessons: Grades K–2

1. Ask students to choose and demonstrate the sounds of classroom percussion instruments by playing simple rhythm patterns, such as:

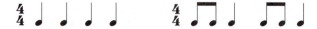

2. Determine instruments that can sustain a sound (such as tambourine and triangle) and those that cannot (such as woodblock and rhythm sticks).

3. Divide the class into two groups. Assign group 1 nonsustaining instruments; assign group 2 sustaining instruments.

4. Ask individual students in group 1 to improvise a rhythm while keeping a steady beat. Give all students a chance to play. Repeat the procedure for group 2.

5. Create a duet by selecting students from each group to improvise a rhythm together. For example:

6. Experiment with rhythm in duple and triple meter. Have students who are not playing keep a steady beat, such as:

   Duple meter: Pat knees, clap

   Triple meter: Pat knees, clap, clap

7. As students sing familiar songs, take turns improvising rhythm patterns.

Creative Experiences with Vocal Sounds

Perhaps the most personal and individual sound is the human voice. We can make our voices sound high, low, nasal, or guttural. We can sing any pitch within a one- to two-octave range, and intervals from eighth or quarter tones to skips of an octave or tenth. We can make our voice wail like a siren, bark like a dog, and sigh like the wind, and we can click, cluck, buzz, chirp, pop, and hiss. Almost unlimited vocal possibilities exist within our imaginations.

Suggestions for Lessons: Grades 4–6

1. Have students list the sounds that can be made by the human voice and perform them. Vary the pitch from high to low and the speed from fast to slow (tempo). Some suggestions:

   - Sighing
   - Whispering
   - Sneezing
   - Gurgling
   - Screaming

2. Have students use their voices to imitate or express an idea, such as:

- We're going to the circus tomorrow, and I can hardly wait.

- I'm a Martian from outer space.

- Tonight's the night of Halloween. Boo!

3. Have students write a sentence and explore ways of saying it using different sounds. Possibilities for different sounds include:

- Whisper, shout

- Shorten a word

- Lengthen a word

- Use a different pitch for each word

- Accent selected words

- Raise the pitch at the end of a sentence

- Begin the sentence on a high pitch and end the sentence on a low pitch

4. Introduce a *whoop* sound, along with suggested notation, such as ⌢⌢. Ask students to create other ways of saying "whoop" and devise appropriate notation. Continue with other sounds, such as boom, tongue clicks, hiss, and whistle.

5. Use four contrasting sounds that can be performed in a variety of ways, such as a high-pitched sound on "whoop" (may be said/sung on a pitch with a swoop upward—siren effect); a low, heavy sound (*poom-poom* or *boom-boom*); tongue clicks with a variety of pitch levels; or hissing sounds (both short and long). Have students organize each set of sounds into a short pattern and perform it. Create symbols expressive of the sounds and use as notation. For example:

- Whoop

- Whistle

- Siren (*whoo*)

- Boom

- Tongue clicks   × × ×

- Hiss   Sss

Creative Experiences with Instrumental Sounds

Exploring instrumental sounds involves not only traditional ways of creating sounds (such as playing the keys of a piano or blowing a horn) but also imaginative and nontraditional ways (such as plucking the strings of a piano). You may use not only Western instruments but also such instruments as the synthesizer, guitar, ukelele, banjo, and dulcimer. If available, explore the sounds of non-Western instruments (Japanese koto, African dono drum, agogo bells or shekere rattle, or Indian sitar and tabla). Encourage students to experiment with a variety of instrumental sounds and to create their own melodies, rhythms, textures, tone colors, and musical forms.

Suggestions for Lessons: Grades 3–6

1. Ask students to explore ways of playing the piano, such as strumming strings with a plastic card, an eraser, fingers, or finger picks; tapping strings with hard and soft mallets; or placing metallic objects (paper clips) underneath the hammers and sliding a finger along a string.

Follow the Leader

Here are some icons that might be used with the voice in creating a round.

There are 4 counts to a block, 16 to a line. Divide the class into four groups. Group 1 begins on line 1. When group 1 begins line 2, group 2 starts line 1; when group 1 begins line 3 and group 2 line 2, group 3 begins line 1, and so on.

Line 1 (16 counts)	Whoop, whoop, whistle	Whoop, whoop, whistle	Siren	Whoop, whoop, whoop, pause
Line 2 (16 counts)	Boom Boom Boom, Boom boom boom boom, boom boom boom, boom boom	BOOM BOOM BOOM BOOM	Boom Boom Boom Boom Boom Boom Boom Boom Boom Boom	BOOM BOOM BOOM BOOM
Line 3 (16 counts)	Tongue clicks (high/low at random)	Two high clicks, two low clicks	Tongue clicks	High clicks, low clicks
Line 4 (16 counts)	Sssss— Hiss............	SsSsSs Hiss Hiss Hiss	Sssss— Hiss............	SsSsSs Hiss Hiss Hiss
Rhythm pulse:	1 2 3 4	1 2 3 4	1 2 3 4	1 2 3 4

Group 1 performs lines 1–4 two times.
Group 2 performs lines 1–4, then repeats 1–3.
Group 3 performs lines 1–4, then repeats 1–2.
Group 4 performs lines 1–4 once only.

2. Divide the class into small groups. Assign an instrument (such as Omnichord, drums, xylophone, and keyboard) to each group. Ask students to experiment with producing at least four different sounds on each instrument. Decide which sounds are similar among the instruments (if any) and which are the most contrasting. Organize the sounds into duple or triple rhythmic patterns and perform in a sequence, alternating timbre and meter.

First Sound	*Second Sound*	*Third Sound*	*Fourth Sound*
Omnichord	Drums	Xylophone	Keyboard

3. Divide students into small groups and assign to each a class of instruments (tambourines, jingle sticks; rhythm sticks, woodblocks; bongo drums, hand drums; maracas, castanets). Tell them to discover at least three ways of creating short sounds and three ways of creating long sounds. Ask each group to demonstrate for the class.

4. Have students explore ways of creating new sounds on the piano (plucking strings, tapping strings with hand in both upper and lower register, using a pencil to "zip" up or down the strings). Play "The Banshee" by Henry Cowell* and ask students to describe some of the unusual sounds.

5. Have students create a musical composition in the form of a rondo: ABACA. Be sure to keep a steady beat and strong sense of rhythm. For example:

■ **Section A:**

Piano swoops (ad lib)

Continues throughout section A

* "The Banshee" can be found in *Music and You* (Macmillan Grade 3, Record 2). It is also available on Smithsonian Folkways, CD SF40801.

■ **Section B:** Improvise from musical materials such as plucking strings, tapping strings with hand or mallet, or "zipping" up or down strings with pencil. Keep a steady beat, alternating tone colors and texture (thick/thin). Continue for eight beats.

■ **Section A** repeats.

■ **Section C:** Improvise from the musical materials but confine sounds to the low register of the piano or keyboard. Hold pedal down on piano to create blurred sounds. Continue for eight beats.

■ **Section A** repeats and gradually gets softer as piece ends.

Creative Experiences with Environmental Sounds

The raw material of music is *sound*. Sounds in our environment often go unnoticed; yet, if we pause to listen, there are many, each with a tone quality and rhythm all its own. Increasing perception of environmental sounds and how they can be used to create a musical composition can be a significant and enriching experience for students.

Suggestions for Lessons: Grades 4–6

1. Ask the class to be completely silent and listen to the sounds around them (clock ticking, a locker door slamming, bird chirping, jet airplane, car engine, coins dropping on the floor, animal sounds). Discuss which of these sounds are long, short, high, low, legato, staccato, loud, and soft.

2. Ask students to bring in a written description of the area they pass through on their way to school, along with sound-producing materials to express appropriate sounds—for example, a factory district: whistle, machinery sounds (metal pipes), car horn (see the following example). Discuss differences between sounds produced and heard in the morning and those in the afternoon.

3. Decide on sounds and sound materials you wish to use in the musical composition. Create picture notation for each sound. Place all sounds into a time frame of four beats (see example).

Creative Experiences with Body Sounds

Another category of sounds are those produced through body percussion. These include such sounds as clapping, tapping, patting, pounding, stamping, and snapping. Sometimes, when only the hands are used, body percussion is referred to as "hand jive." Many times body sounds are used in combination with vocal sounds or in combination with movement. Thus, students might walk in a circle and then stand still and clap a rhythm.

Factory District in Sound

Rhonda Williams

A few blocks from my house are a lot of big factories. They are in operation all day and all night. The early-morning and late-evening hours are quiet. There is always a light motor hum heard in the morning. After a while, the people begin to come to work. At first there are just a few, then more and more report for work. Occasionally, you hear a car horn blow in the parking lot, and greetings of one to another. As the morning continues, the sounds from the factory become louder and more intense, spreading from section to section. In addition, there are sounds of people in the street. At the end of the day, there is a whistle signifying the end of one shift and the beginning of another. Then there is a gradual slowing down of machinery in the factory, since not as many workers are employed on the evening shift. Gradually, the parking lot empties of cars, and the factory sounds return to the quiet hum of evening.

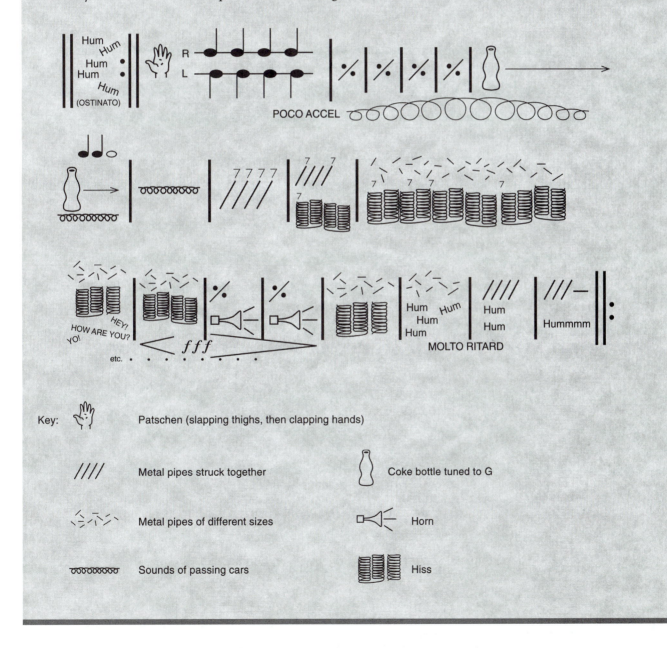

CREATING A MUSICAL VIDEO

Suggestions for Lessons: Grades 3–6

1. Listen to the first four variations of Pachelbel's Canon in D Major.*

2. Decide how the composer created each variation—a high part (called a descant), broken chords in the bass, and so on.

3. Listen to the first four variations again and ask students which variation they would like to be.

4. Divide the class into four groups, each with a tape recorder and a cassette of their chosen variation. There should be no more than five students in each group. If the class is large, you may want to have more groups and cassette tapes.

5. Assign an activity to each group (group 1, hands or fingers walking; group 2, using string; group 3, feet; group 4, sunflowers; and so on).

6. Ask each group to go into a separate corner of the room or into another space, such as the hall or a vacant room. Each group of five students should listen to its segment and then create a movement that matches the musical variation.

7. Each group should determine what props it needs and bring them the next day.

8. Each group practices the particular variation using the props and activities it has decided on.

9. After each group practices the selected variation, bring students back together and make a sample videotape using a camcorder. Show the tape and allow the groups time to make any changes.

10. Make a final videotape using a new tape and an *experienced* camcorder operator. Students like to view their creation.

Caution: This project takes time and cannot be hurried. Often there is organized confusion. Allow at least two weeks (a half-hour per day) to make the musical video. Although this project is time-consuming, it is well worth the effort.

CREATING A PERCUSSION ACCOMPANIMENT TO A SONG

It is essential in rhythmic experiences to establish the *tempo* (speed of the beat). Early on, students must feel and be able to clap (or move) to a steady beat. As students create rhythm patterns to accompany songs, they will need to develop techniques for playing and notating the rhythms.

Suggestions for Lessons: Grades 3–6

Try the following experiences with the African folk song "Tue, Tue" (page 406):

1. Teach the song "Tue, Tue."

2. Have students tap their knees and clap the beats (duple meter: 1 2 1 2).

3. Decide on an instrument to play the beats, and notate. For example:

---

* *The Pachelbel Canon,* RCA Victor 65468-2-RC (there are also many others to choose from).

4. Explore rhythms that might fit the duple meter and play them on a variety of instruments. Make your choice and notate. For example:

Write as a percussion score:

CREATING A PERCUSSION COMPOSITION

Suggestions for Lessons: Grades 4–6

1. Ask students to improvise a variety of rhythmic patterns in duple or triple meter.

2. Select four different patterns for use in the composition.

3. Discuss how you can extend a composition by repeating an idea or provide interest and variety with a contrasting idea. For example:

4. Have students practice clapping each pattern.

5. Decide on instruments to be used for each pattern. For example:

(add maracas on repeat)

(add temple blocks on repeat)

Conga drum:

(add finger cymbals on repeat)

Bongo drums:

(alternate lower and higher pitch)

6. Begin with one instrument and add the rest one by one for a cumulative effect.

7. Discuss ways of creating a contrasting section, such as slower, different meter, or different instruments. For example:

Conga drum   Tambourine   Woodblock   Tambourine

Sand blocks   Sand blocks   Tambourine   Conga drum

8. On the repeat of the contrasting section, ask one student to play a pattern in 3/4 meter, thus creating a polyrhythmic effect. Use a high-sounding instrument such as a high-pitched temple block:

9. Add a closing section (coda) with elements of each section:

Claves/woodblock   Tambourine

Tambourine   Conga drum   All_____   tamb. (struck)

Creative Experiences with Writing Melodies or Songs

Writing an original melody or song involves students in synthesizing their total response to music. It is a major means for developing concepts about melody, rhythm, meter, harmony, and form, as well as for providing opportunities for creating expressive and formal relationships between words and music. All children create melodies. Just listen to them at play and you will hear them sing many chants and short melodic phrases.

As students create melodies or songs, they become involved as composers, performers, and listeners. Musical growth occurs as they become aware of possibilities for sound exploration and pattern development and use these in expressive ways. Although the process of composing is most important, the student should also be guided to achieve as expressive a product as possible.

WHAT MAKES AN INTERESING MELODY?

Essentially, two elements contribute to a successful and interesting melody: repetition and contrast. A melody must also have a sense of coming to a rest or close. This discussion focuses on writing a song melody, but the guiding principles may be used for writing instrumental melodies as well.

The use of repetition can extend the length of a melody, emphasize certain words, create rhythmic interest, and provide unity. Contrast can be achieved by such techniques as alternating melodic skips and steps, changing the direction of the melodic line, changing rhythms, and creating contrasting sections. If a melody is to be sung, one must also consider the range and its appropriateness for a given maturity level.

PREPARING STUDENTS TO WRITE MELODIES OR SONGS

Suggestions for Lessons: Grades 3–6

1. Have students sing many songs and play classroom instruments to develop a feeling for tonality, rhythm patterns, tone color, and pitch.

2. Help students develop a sense of tonality and beat. Students in grades 4–6 should be encouraged to write out their responses in rhythm notation.

3. Sing or play a short phrase. Ask students to improvise a second phrase in the same meter, ending on the tonic (keynote of the scale). Explore in several keys, such as G, D, and F. For example:

4. Sing or play melody patterns and ask students to repeat exactly and then as a sequence (beginning on different pitches). For example:

5. Sing or play rhythms and ask students to improvise a response. For example:

6. Sing or play a familiar melody and ask students to create ways of changing it, such as repeating a phrase, adding notes, or changing the rhythm. For example:

Original melody (phrase):

Adding notes, changing rhythm:

Adding notes above and below:

Changing the meter from duple to triple:

Changing the tonality from major to minor:

WRITING A MELODY USING A PENTATONIC SCALE

It is easy to write a melody based on the pentatonic (five-note) scale, because every combination will be satisfying to the ear. Some melodies, however, will be more interesting than others.

Suggestions for Lessons: Grades 4–6

1. Have students select a rhythm pattern and improvise a melody, then have them place the notation on a staff. It might look something like this (black keys only):

2. Help students explore the tonal possibilities of other pentatonic scales, such as:

3. Add rhythms appropriate to grade level, such as:

WRITING A MELODY USING A SEVEN-NOTE SCALE (MAJOR/MINOR)

1. Prepare a handout with (1) a staff showing the C major scale and (2) a staff with a rhythm pattern above it.

2. Tell students to begin on the first note of the C scale (C) and end on the last note (C). Use each pitch only once and place the pitches beneath the rhythm pattern. For example:

3. Choose a label (syllable, number, or letter) and name each note.

4. Play or sing the four-measure melodies of several students. Discuss the most interesting ones.

5. Experiment with a variety of rhythms for the melodies. Repeat a pitch when necessary to make the melody "fit" the rhythm.

6. Transpose the four-measure melody into different keys, both minor and major. For example:

7. Review melodies previously learned (see the standard forms on page 395) for ideas of what other composers have done.

8. Create a melody of eight measures. Measures 1–4 should end on the dominant (fifth tone of the scale), and measures 5–8 should end on the tonic (first tone of the scale). For example:

9. Add chords (C, F, G₇) and accompany on a keyboard instrument. Sing melody on "doo-be-doo" or play on recorders. Explore the possibilities of creating an AB or ABA form by adding a contrasting melody.

SETTING A POEM TO MUSIC

Students in grades 4–6 will enjoy creating original music to a short poem. The procedure is outlined as follows.

Suggestions for Lessons: Grades 4–6

1. Select a favorite poem of the students and explore some rhythm possibilities suggested by the text. For example:

*Firefly**

A little light is going by,
Is going up to see the sky,
A little light with wings.

I never could have thought of it,
To have a little bug all lit,
And made to go on wings.

---

* Elizabeth Madox Roberts, *Under the Tree* (New York: Viking Press, 1950). Reprinted by permission.

2. Using either duple or triple meter, explore some other rhythm ideas using the same poem.

3. Reread the text of the poem. Consider the following:

   a. Appropriate directions for the melody

   b. Words or phrases that might be repeated

4. Use melody bells and ask students to explore various pitch and rhythm combinations of the pentatonic scale for each phrase assigned. Suggest that they might repeat words or add more than one note per syllable. Limit the range of the melody to one octave. For example:

Pentatonic scale used in the song "Firefly"

   Let the meaning of the words, the rhythm patterns, and the concepts of repetition and contrast be your guide.

5. Divide the class into groups and provide each with a transparency with a music staff on it. Have them write the words beneath the staff and then the corresponding pitches and rhythms above. Each group performs a phrase for the class. Students should make changes in the melody or rhythm of each phrase until they are satisfied with their song.

6. Place the entire song on the transparency and sing.

7. Use the same procedure to explore other types of tonal organization (for example, major, minor); be sure, however, that these songs end on the tonic (keynote of the scale).

8. After the song has been completed, add a percussion accompaniment. You may want to create a short introduction and a closing section (coda) to extend the composition. For example:

Alto xylophone

Introduction: Begin with xylophone (two measures), add woodblock (two measures), and triangle (two measures).

Coda: All three instruments join in (two measures), then woodblock and triangle (two measures), then just triangle (one measure).

Firefly

Key: Pentatonic
Starting pitch: F
Meter: 4/4, begins on "and" of 4

Music by Joy E. Lawrence
Words by Elizabeth Madox Roberts

A lit-tle light___ is go-ing by,___ is go-ing by,___ is go-ing by,___ is

go-ing up___ to see the sky, A lit-tle light___with___ wings. I nev-er could have

thought of it.___ To have a lit - tle bug all lit___ And made to go___ on___ wings.

WRITING AN ORIGINAL POEM AND SETTING IT TO MUSIC

Suggestions for Lessons: Grades 4–6

1. Choose a subject for a poem, such as nature, an event, an idea, or a person. Be sure that it has a strong rhythmic pulse. Following is an example of a poem (later set to music) by a fifth- and sixth-grade class:*

   We're America's children, and we're here to celebrate.
   Living, learning and growing in a land that's really great.
   Our land consists of different people, each unique in his own way,
   It matters not if you're short or tall, black or white, great or small—

---

* Written for the eightieth birthday celebration of the Cleveland Heights–University Heights School System, Ohio, 1982.

Standard Melody Forms

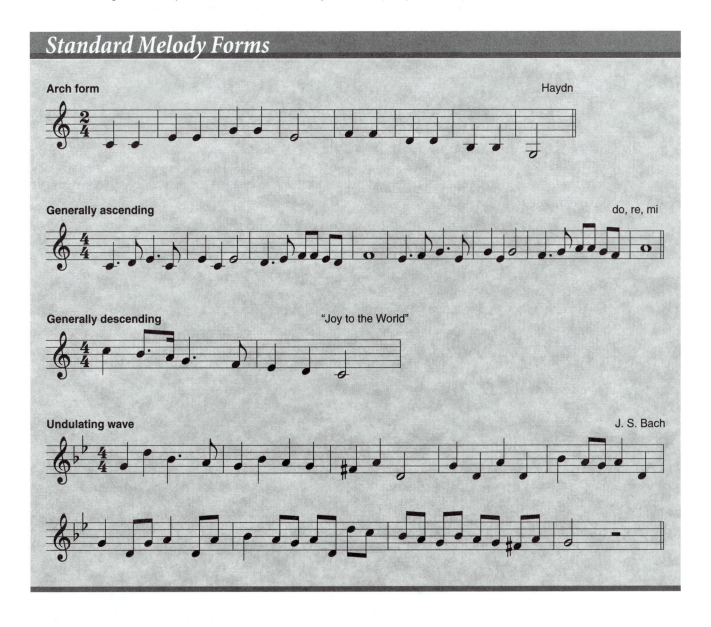

We're America's children, and we're here to celebrate.
Living, learning and growing in a land that's really great.
We all have a chance, you see, to be the best that we can be.
Sing it loud, sing it proud, really great, celebrate.
America, we love you.

2. After you have written a poem, mark the rhythmic pulses above the text. If necessary, adapt or change the text to fit this pulse:

We're A-mer-i-ca's | chil-dren, and we're | here to cel-e- | brate. |

Liv-ing, learn-ing and | grow-ing in a | land that's real-ly | great, Our|

land con-sists of dif-f'rent | people, each u-|nique in his own | way, It |

mat-ters not if you're | short or tall, | black or white, | great or | small— |

We're A-mer-i-ca's | chil-dren, and we're | here to cel-e-| brate |

Liv-ing, learn-ing and | grow-ing in a | land that's real-ly | great. We|

all have a | chance, you see, to | be the best that | we can be.|

Sing it loud, | sing it proud, | real-ly great, | cel-e-brate.|

A-mer-i-ca, | we love | you. |

3. Before you begin composing the melody, note the repeated phrases (such as "We're America's children, and we're here to celebrate. Living, learning and growing in a land that's really great."). You will want to use the same melody for each.

4. Select a key (such as the key of C) and write the pitches on the chalkboard.

5. Experiment with different rhythm patterns within the two-pulse tempo beat and then notate your choice:

6. Using the pitches of your chosen scale, explore various tonal patterns and create a melody for each phrase. For example:

7. When you have completed the song, add accompaniment. Simple chords played on a keyboard instrument or guitar might be appropriate, or perhaps a music teacher could arrange a piano accompaniment.

We're America's Children

Key: C
Starting pitch: C
Meter: 4/4, begins on 1

Dolores Blackburn
Taylor School
5–6 Grade Classes of 1982

We're A - mer - i - ca's chil - dren, and we're here to cel - e - brate.

Liv - ing, learn - ing and grow - ing in a land that's real - ly great. Our

land con - sists of dif - f'rent peo - ple, each u - nique in his own way, It

mat - ters not if you're short or tall, black or white, great or small

We're A - mer - i - ca's chil - dren, and we're here to cel - e - brate.

Liv - ing, learn - ing and grow - ing in a land that's real - ly great. We

all have a chance, you see, to be the best that we can be.

Sing it loud, sing it proud, real - ly great, cel - e - brate. A -

mer - i - ca, we love you.

For Your Journal

In your journal or portfolio, make a section on creative experience in music. Drawing on ideas in this chapter, specifically comment on some types of creative musical experiences you might design for children.

*I*ntegrating Music with the Study of Peoples, Places, and Cultures

STUDENTS TODAY ARE TRULY LIVING IN AN INTERNATIONAL AGE. Almost every day, they encounter cultures from other areas of the world through television, radio, movies, books, magazines, and now the Web. Through new technology in communications satellites and the Internet, a single part of our globe can be in instant contact with another. In many regions of our country, children are also coming to know large numbers of foreign peoples who now permanently reside in the United States. From its beginnings, our country has been a refuge for peoples from throughout the world; and demographic surveys of the United States today quickly reveal that while we are indeed one nation, we comprise many cultures.

American schools traditionally have encouraged the study and appreciation of different cultural groups. Social studies, geography, and history curricula have directed attention to the contributions of many peoples of the world, and teachers at every grade level have sought to bring multicultural viewpoints to their classrooms. Reflecting this concern for keeping in touch with the international age in which we live, teachers have increasingly endeavored to present a greater variety of music representative of many different cultural groups. This trend has paralleled the work of music scholars, who have documented that music is a worldwide phenomenon occurring among all peoples.

We now know that our planet contains a number of highly developed musical systems of which the European-American classical tradition is just one. Such findings have clearly challenged many traditionally held views. Today it is evident that although music is an international phenomenon, it most certainly is not an international "language." Musical systems in other areas of the world are often constructed in very different ways from our own. If we wish to understand these musics, we must learn how they are constructed. Thus, one of the primary objectives in studying a variety of musics is *to help students understand that there are many different but equally logical ways for organizing sonic events.*

This chapter is devoted to providing musical experiences for the classroom from selected places or cultures of the world. We begin in Africa, move to Asia and Europe, and then to the Americas. For each of these geographic areas, musical examples and teaching strategies are provided. The experiences suggested may serve as a basis for musical study alone; however, the intent is to help children perceive music as interrelated with other aspects of culture. Thus as students study some examples of traditional Japanese music, they will also study other aspects of Japanese life and culture. Children enjoy learning about other peoples of the world, their customs and crafts, their architecture, dance, literature, painting, sculpture, and music. Through an integrated study of many aspects of a culture, children develop new and important understandings of other peoples. They begin to realize the integral place of the arts in other societies. Many teachers have also found that a combined study showing the interrelationships of culture and arts significantly enhances a child's interest in investigating and performing music.

Some Suggested Classroom Experiences

Along with studying the musics of various ethnic groups, you may wish to introduce the cultural backgrounds through the following:

1. Prepare a bulletin board on each country studied. Place a map on the board and have students use pins to mark the major cities, mountains, rivers, deserts, and so on. Have students look for pictures of people, examples of the visual arts (architecture, sculpture, painting, dance, puppet theater), and photos of musicians. Arrange them in an attractive design on the board.

2. Have students search the World Wide Web for pictures, information on, and sounds of music of various cultures.*

3. Invite guests from various countries and ethnic groups to speak to the class. Ask them to bring cultural items (especially musical instruments) to show to the students.

4. Show videos on different peoples and cultures.

5. Take a field trip to a museum to see examples of the visual arts of various cultural groups.

6. Investigate the beliefs of various groups. For example, Buddhism is a major religion in China and Japan. Have the class explore the topic *What does it mean to be a Buddhist?*

7. Ask the physical education teacher to assist you in teaching dances from various cultures.

8. Have students look for stories from the various areas being studied. Read them in class and perhaps plan short dramatizations.

9. Plan imaginary trips to different countries. Make an itinerary of things you hope to see and do.

10. Have your school plan a multicultural or international festival. Include dress, dance, visual arts, food, and music.

---

* A good teacher resource for materials on various music cultures is found at World Music Press *(www.worldmusicpress.com).* Of particular interest at this Web site are "A Checklist for Evaluating Multicultural Materials" and a link to a number of other companies publishing multicultural materials.

Music of African Peoples

BACKGROUND INFORMATION FOR THE CLASS

Africa is the second largest continent in the world (see figure 10.1), with a land mass stretching approximately 3,500 miles from north to south and almost 2,000 miles from east to west, an area approximately equal to Europe, China, and the United States combined.

The continent contains some of the most diverse land in the world. Its vast stretches of terrain contain the world's largest desert (the Sahara) and longest waterway (the Nile). Dense rain forests, receiving up to 8 feet of precipitation each year, result in vegetation so lush that the sun is almost totally obscured; whereas in bitterly cold regions, such as the mountain peaks of the Atlas and Ruwenzori Ranges, snow falls for most of the year.

Africa is characterized by enormous ethnic diversity, which is clearly evident in the many countries and languages on the continent. Some ethnic groups, such as the Bantu, who reside in a number of countries south of the equator, primarily raise cattle and cultivate the land. Other groups, such as the Sudanese living between the equator and the Sahara, have built large metropolitan areas. One of the most powerful influences to affect the continent resulted from the development of Islam and the migration of Arab peoples along the northern and eastern areas of the continent.

Figure 10.1. Africa

SOME GENERAL CHARACTERISTICS OF AFRICAN MUSIC

A great variety of music is found throughout the African continent. Music is a part of almost every aspect of life from birth to death. It is closely tied to festivals, work, politics, courtship, and recreation. Multiart productions involving music, dance, and drama (with the latter two often involving brilliant visual effects in costuming and masks) frequently occur throughout the continent.

Because of the vast geographical and cultural differences on the continent, one can expect a considerable amount of diversity in music. The following general outline identifies some basic characteristics of much African music south of the Sahara and provides a resource for organizing a study of music for the classroom.

- Much music is communal and functional; it is often associated with dance and games. Although there are some exceptions, the emphasis is on group rather than solo performance.

- Melodies are often short; longer melodies are often composed of short phrase units. A variety of scales are found: four-, five-, and seven-note scales occur, although pentatonic are most common; intervals are predominantly seconds and thirds. Melodies tend to be syllabic (one syllable of text per note), and "resultant melodies" occur with pitches contributed by several individuals.

- There is a strong beat in much music. Particularly in West Africa, there is often a driving, pulsating beat with steady tempo throughout. Polyrhythms and syncopation are frequent. Repeated rhythmic patterns are common.

- Texture is monophonic (one musical line), heterophonic (simultaneous variations on a single musical line), and polyphonic (many musical lines). Harmony occurs in thirds, fourths, fifths, and sixths, although thirds are the most common. Both stratification of melodic and rhythmic lines and imitation are common.

- Form is often related to function (e.g., game songs, work songs); the call-and-response form is prevalent. The use of ostinato (repetition of melodies and rhythms) is common.

- Timbre is characterized by a wide variety of tone colors in the voice, but generally there is an open, relaxed quality in singing. Many percussion, stringed, and wind instruments are used; percussion instruments predominate. Music is often dominated by a percussive quality (e.g., individual tones are attacked strongly; many plucked stringed instruments). An important xylophone tradition is also present. A "buzzy" quality is created on some instruments (e.g., on xylophones through gourd resonators with spiderweb membranes placed over holes, and buttonlike rattles added to the mbira).

TEACHING AFRICAN MUSIC: SUGGESTIONS FOR LESSONS*

The overall goal of the suggestions for lessons on African music that follow is to acquaint students with some of the many types of vocal and instrumental music present on the continent and to have them study these types in terms of the elements of music: melody, rhythm, texture, timbre, and form. Objectives are given for each of the sample lessons, along with performance and listening suggestions, some of which are coordinated with dance.

A number of songs are included in the lessons, and it is suggested that they be taught by rote. Teachers will need to practice the pronunciation of texts before presenting the pieces to the class.

African instruments, such as the mbira, can be purchased in a number of music stores. Where authentic instruments are not available, suggestions for substitutes are given. Teachers and students may also wish to make some instruments, such as drums.

---

* In designing lessons for different school settings, you may wish to rearrange the order of materials and teaching strategies given.

"KYE, KYE KULE" AND "TWA-MU-SANGA"

Grades: 1–2

Kye, Kye Kule

Starting pitch: F
Meter: 4/4, begins on 1

Ghana

Leader | Response | L. | R.

Kye Kye Ku - le   Kye Kye Ku - le   Kye Kye Ko - fi Nsa   Kye Kye Ko - fi Nsa
(chay chay koo - lay)   (chay chay koe - fee nsa)

L. | R. | L. | R.

Ko - fi sa lan - ga   Ko - fi sa lan - ga   Ke - te Kyi lan - ga   Ke - te Kyi lan - ga
(Koe - fee sa lahn - ga)   (Kay - tay chee lahn - ga)

L. | R. | All

Kum   a - den - de   Kum   a - den - de   Kum   a - den - de   Hey!
(Koom a - den - day)   (Kum   a - den - de   Hey!)

Mona Lowe, *Singing Games from Ghana*, © 1970. By permission of MM Publications, 19603 Jacob, Cerritos, California.

Starting pitch: D
Meter: 2/4, begins on 1

Uganda

Twa - mu - sa - nga ng'a - zi - na;   twa - mu - sa - nga ng'a - lo - ga!

(Twah - moo - sah - ngah ngah - zee - nah   Twah - moo - sah - ngah ngah - loh - gah)

repeat 6 times

Joseph Kyagambiddwa, *African Music from the Source of the Nile* (New York: Frederick Praeger, 1955), p. 107.

Objectives

Students will:

1. Be introduced to some geographical characteristics of the continent of Africa.

2. Perform the song "Kye, Kye Kule," add dance movements, and identify the following musical characteristics: short melodic phrases, five-tone or pentatonic scale, syncopation, and call-and-response form.

3. Perform the song "Twa-Mu-Sanga" and identify its musical characteristics: short phrases, "undulating" shape of melody, medium range, syllabic nature of melody, and ostinato.

Materials

■ Globe or map of the world

■ Rattle or shekere (pronounced "shā-kǎ-rāy")

Procedures

1. Using a globe or map, have students find the continent of Africa; then have them locate various countries on the continent, including Ghana. Have them compare the countries in size with one another and with the United States.

2. Have the class perform "Kye, Kye Kule."

   a. Sing the song in call-and-response style, with the leader singing the first portion of the melody and the group providing the response. This is especially good in teaching tone-matching skills.

   b. This song generally accompanies dance. Use the following gestures to accompany the dance: Hands placed on top of the head ("Kye, Kye Kule"), hands placed on top of the shoulders ("Kye, Kye Kofi Nsa"), hands on the waist ("Kofi sa langa"), hands on the knees ("Kete Kyi langa"), hands on the ankles ("Kum adende"). Students should let their bodies sway in time to the music.

   c. Call attention to some of the important musical characteristics:

      ■ Short melodic phrases passed back and forth in call-and-response form

■ Five-tone, or pentatonic, scale:

■ Syncopation (third measure):

Shekere

3. Have students sing "Twa-Mu-Sanga," a short song from Uganda.

   a. Clap the beat as you sing.

   b. Follow the beat with a rattle. If you do not have an African rattle (shekere), use a maraca or make your own rattle.

   c. Notice how the song you are singing repeats over and over. This repeating melody is known as an *ostinato*.

   d. This is a dance song. Make up some repetitive movement to accompany the music.

   e. While singing ask the students to move their arms in an arch to indicate the two phrases in the piece. Are the phrases short or long?

   Length of phrases

   f. Have students draw an "outline" of the melody. Then ask them to look at these melodic shapes and choose one that most closely matches their drawings:

   Melodic shapes

   Undulating   Arched   Terraced   Descending

   g. Ask students: "What is the range of the melody? In your drawing did you move a large distance or a small distance between the lowest and highest points?"

   Ranges

   Narrow range   Medium range   Wide range

h. Have the class sing the song again, particularly noticing the relationship between notes and text.

Many notes to one syllable

or

(circle one)

One note per syllable

Assessment

Have the class list characteristics of African music they have learned in this lesson.

"SALAMATU BANSA" AND "TUE, TUE"

Grades: 3–4

Salamatu Bansa

Starting pitch: G
Meter: 2/4, begins on "and" of 2

Kwasi Aduonum

Sa - la - ma   tu, Sa - la - ma tu   ban - sa, Sa - la - ma   tu,   Sa - la - ma tu   ban - sa.
(Sah - lah - mah   too, Sah - lah - mah too   bahn - sah)

Tue, Tue

Starting pitch: C
Meter: 4/4, begins on 1

Ghana

Tu - e Tu - e   ba - ri - ma   tu - e tu - e   Tu - e tu - e   ba - ri - ma
(Too - ay Too - ay   ba - ree - ma   too - ay too - ay   Too - ay too - ay   ba - ri - ma)

tu - e tu - e   A - bo - fra   ba A - ma da - wa da - wa   tu - e tu - e   A - bo - fra
(too - ay too - ay   A - boe - fra   bah Ah - mah dah - wah dah - wah   too - ay too - ay   A - boe - fra)

ba A - ma da - wa da - wa   tu - e tu - e Hai ba - ri - ma   tu - e tu - e Hai ba - ri - ma
(bah Ah - mah dah - wah dah - wah   too - ay too - ay Hey ba - ree - ma   too - ay too - ay Hey ba - ree - ma)

Mona Lowe, *Singing Games from Ghana,* © 1970. By permission of MM Publications, 19603 Jacob, Cerritos, California.

Objectives

Students will:

1. Sing the song "Salamatu Bansa," add dance movements, and identify the following musical characteristics: strong feeling for the beat, call-and-response, and ostinato.

2. Perform the song "Tue, Tue," add a rattle accompaniment and body percussion, and identify the following musical characteristics: strong beat, syllabic melody, and pentatonic scale.

Materials

■ Rattle or shekere

Procedures

1. Make a "Characteristics of African Music" chart on the chalkboard or bulletin board. As you study each piece of music, list the predominant characteristics under each musical element (melody, rhythm, and so on).

2. Have the class sing the African song "Salamatu Bansa" in call-and-response style. The teacher either acts as the leader and sings the first phrase ("call"), with the class responding in unison on the second phrase ("response"), or divides the class, having one half sing the first phrase and the other half sing the second phrase.

   a. The song repeats over and over in ostinato style. Have students follow the beat by clapping as they sing.

   b. As you sing, have students perform the following dance:

   ■ Form a circle, facing forward.

   ■ Bend your knees and let your shoulders and arms hang forward.

   ■ Move in a circle in time to the beat. Let your body rhythmically sway as you clap and move to the beat.

   ■ For variety, as you move in the circle, form a chain by placing your hands on the shoulders of the person in front of you.

3. Have the class sing the song "Tue, Tue," a singing game song from Ghana.

   a. While singing, have the group keep track of the beat by clapping. Notice the strong feeling for the beat.

   b. Keep the beat with a rattle (African shekere rattle [gourd covered with beads] or a substitute, such as a maraca).

   c. Add body percussion to the piece. Have the class divide into pairs. Place two pairs together and have them clap in the following manner: Clap partner's hands on beats 1 and 2; hands against the thighs on beats 3 and 4; repeat the pattern for measure 2; change partners for measure 3 and, as before, clap hands on beats 1 and 2 and then against thighs on beats 3 and 4; in measure 4 repeat the pattern of measure 3.

   d. Draw attention to the fact that every syllable in the text of the song has one note. This gives a percussive effect to the music.

e. Have students write out the pitches present in the song. Because there are five pitches, the scale is described as pentatonic.

Assessment

Have the class list characteristics of African music they have learned in this lesson.

"MA LO WE"

Grades: 5–6

Starting pitch: A
Meter: 4/4, begins on 1

Adesanya Adeyeye

Ma lo we l'o-kun mo___ Ma lo we l'o-kun mo___ Ma lo we l'o-kun mo o on-gbe won lo
(Mah lō way lō-koon mo___ mah lo way lo-koon mo___ Mah lō way lo kŏon mo ō ŏon-bā won lo)

Objectives

Students will:

1. Sing the song "Ma Lo We" and identify the following musical characteristics: strong feeling for the beat, repetitive melody (ostinato), five-tone scale, and syncopation.

2. Play "Ma Lo We" on the mbira.

3. Perform an example of African polyrhythm.

4. Identify polyrhythm in a recorded musical example.

Materials*

- Mbira (also known as kalimba or sanza), a plucked percussion instrument
- Agogo (also known as gankogui) bells, two sizes
- Shekere rattle
- Large and small drums

Procedures

1. Have the students sing "Ma Lo We."

   a. Students learn the song by rote.

   b. Students clap the beat.

   c. Students can also keep the beat by playing a rattle.

---

* African instruments may be purchased from The House of Musical Tradition, 7040 Carroll Avenue, Takoma Park, Maryland 20912; *www.hmtrad.com*.

Instruments for African music

Conga drums

Agogo bells

Shekere

Mbira

d. Point out the general characteristics in the song:

- Strong feeling for the beat

- Syllabic melody

- Repetitive melody; ostinato

- Five-tone scale:

- Syncopation:

2. Have students play "Ma Lo We" on the mbira.

a. Students should practice finding the different notes on the instrument.

b. Have the class sing the song slowly while one student plays the melody. As the melody becomes more familiar, the tempo of the piece can be increased.

c. Call attention to the percussive quality created by plucking the mbira.

3. Have students count each line of the following set of numbers, clapping on the boldface characters. Practice until the class can perform the entire example correctly, keeping a steady tempo throughout. Practice the example at several tempos: slow, medium, and fast.

1	2	**3**	4	**5**	**6**	7	**8**	9	**10**	11	**12**
1	**2**	3	**4**	**5**	6	**7**	8	**9**	10	**11**	12
1	2	**3**	4	**5**	**6**	**7**	**8**	**9**	**10**	**11**	**12**
1	2	**3**	**4**	5	**6**	**7**	8	**9**	**10**	11	**12**
1	2	**3**	4	**5**	6	**7**	8	**9**	10	**11**	12

4. Divide the class into five sections and have each section clap one line over and over in ostinato fashion. When all sections are combined, the class is performing polyrhythm.

5. Following is an example of the above rhythm in Western notation. Ask the class to clap the five lines one at a time; then divide the class into sections and have each section clap a line at the same time. The students can hear and see the polyrhythm.

6. Play the following example with instruments.

   a. The first line is played on the metal percussion instrument known as an *agogo* ("ah-go-go") or *gankogui* ("ghăn-ko-gwee"). This instrument has two bell-shaped projections (one producing a lower pitch and the other a high pitch), which are struck with a stick to produce the sound.

   b. The second line of music is played on a larger and, therefore, lower-sounding agogo.

   c. The third line is played with a shekere. The agogo and shekere may be purchased in the United States, but teachers and students may wish to create their own instruments (see page 258).

   d. Lines 4 and 5 are played with small and large drums, respectively.

Bruno Nettl, *Folk and Traditional Music of Western Continents*, 2nd ed., © 1973. By permission of Prentice-Hall, Inc., Englewood Cliffs, New Jersey.

7. Perform the entire polyrhythm example several times, giving different students a chance to play the instruments. Other students in the class can clap along on a part while the instruments are being played. Perform the example at different tempos; each tempo must be consistently maintained throughout.

8. Listen to an example of polyrhythm (*Mustapha Tettey Addy: Master Drummer from Ghana,* Lyrichord, LLCT 7250, selection 3 ["Ewe Atsimevu"]). Also available on *Music Resources for Multicultural Perspectives* (MENC: The National Association for Music Education, 1806 Robert Fulton Drive, Reston, VA 20191, 1-800-336-3768), selection 12.

    a. This is music that accompanies the Agbeko ("Ahg-bek-o") dance of the Ewe ("ā-wāy") people of Ghana. You will hear a master drum, a supporting drum, and an agogo.

    b. As the students listen to the music, have them clap the rhythm played on the agogo:

Assessment

Have the class list characteristics of African music they have learned in this lesson.

THE MUSIC OF GHANA

Grades: 5–6

Objectives

Students will:

1. View the video *Discovering the Music of Africa.*

2. Describe the instruments, their sounds, and how they are used.

3. Identify characteristics of African music.

Materials

■ Video *Discovering the Music of Africa**

Procedures

1. The 22-minute video is on the music of Ghana. Have the students find Ghana on a map of Africa.

2. Show the video, particularly noticing the drums, bells (gankogui), and rattles (shekere) and the distinctive singing style and dance.

---

*The video *Discovering the Music of Africa* is available from West Music Company, P.O. Box 552, Coralville, Iowa 52241.

3. On the chalkboard place the following characteristics of African music as seen in the film:
   - Emphasis on percussion instruments and sounds
   - Call-and-response form
   - Open, relaxed quality of singing
   - Singing in harmony
   - Polyrhythm
   - Ostinato

Assessment

Have the class list characteristics of African music they have learned in the three lessons presented here.

Music of Asian Peoples: China and Japan

BACKGROUND INFORMATION FOR THE CLASS

Among the largest and smallest countries of Asia are China and Japan, respectively (see figure 10.2). China extends 2,700 miles from east to west and 2,600 miles from north to south, encompassing approximately the land mass of the United States and Mexico together. Within its borders live more than 1.25 billion people—more than in any other country in the world and four times the population of the United States. In contrast, the islands of Japan stretch 1,250 miles from north to south, but in total land area encompass only approximately that of Iowa and Minnesota. Within this relatively small land mass live more than 125 million people.

China and Japan have rich historical traditions, and over many centuries their peoples have made major contributions to the world. The Chinese invented paper and printing and have given the world silk, porcelain, and the compass, whereas the Japanese have increasingly demonstrated their technological accomplishments in the electronic and manufacturing industries.

Many aspects of life in China and Japan have been subtly affected by the religions and philosophies of their peoples. Particularly evident in the arts have been (1) the Buddhist emphasis on simplicity of lifestyle, contemplation, peace, and tranquillity; (2) the rules of order and personal conduct stemming from the philosopher Confucius; and (3) the religions of Taoism and Shintoism, which have stressed the importance of humans being in communion with nature. The tangible outcomes of these beliefs are present in several major thematic emphases in the arts.

One of the most persistent themes is *nature*. From the very earliest times, artists have sought to put themselves and their audiences in harmony with the "spiritual qualities" of the natural world. The theme of nature is evident in Asian architectural settings and building designs; in the visual arts of painting, sculpture, and flower arranging; in literature; and in music.

Another common tenet in both Chinese and Japanese arts is an emphasis on *understatement*. Artists seem to be directed toward simplicity, disciplined control, and attention to detail. In paintings bare outlines are often used to depict such natural objects as mountains and trees. Muted, pastel colors complement the delicacy and simplicity of the lines, and there are many blank, open spaces that viewers are left to fill in with their minds. It seems clear that many Chinese and Japanese artists wish to "suggest" through understatement with the hope of achieving maximum effect with minimal materials.

Figure 10.2. A portion of Asia

SOME GENERAL CHARACTERISTICS OF CHINESE AND JAPANESE MUSIC

Music has been an important part of Chinese and Japanese life from the beginnings of their recorded history. Several highly developed systems of traditional music are present today and are represented in a number of vocal and instrumental forms. Some general characteristics of these forms of music are as follows:

■ There is much use of pentatonic scales, although six- and seven-tone scales occur. Melodic lines often contain subtle ornamentation.

■ Meter is predominantly duple.

■ Monophonic (one-line) and heterophonic (simultaneous variations on a single line) textures occur frequently. There is much emphasis on distinct, delicate lines of music, unlike the thick, homogenous sounds of much Western orchestral music. Some harmony is present, however.

■ Both loud and soft dynamic levels are found. Loud, dynamic levels occur, for example, in Beijing opera music. Because much music is composed for small ensembles, however, dynamic levels are often soft. The predominant use of soft and medium dynamic levels reflects a general tendency toward understatement and delicate refinement in many types of traditional music. Within any single performance group, however, a full range of dynamic levels, from soft to loud, is present.

■ A variety of instrumental and vocal tone colors are present. These include stringed, percussion, and wind instruments, with stringed instruments predominating. The tone color of singers sometimes has a pinched, nasal quality.

■ Many compositions are programmatic. Theme-and-variation and ternary forms are common.

TEACHING CHINESE AND JAPANESE MUSIC: SUGGESTIONS FOR LESSONS

The overall goal of the sample lessons that follow is to acquaint students with some of the many types of Chinese and Japanese music and to have them study these in terms of the elements of music: melody, rhythm, texture, timbre, and form.

Several songs are included and are given in the native languages as well as in English. Children should be encouraged to use the native languages, because by doing so they will more closely identify with the people. It is also suggested that the songs will be learned most quickly by rote.

For the listening selections, children should have a chance to see and discuss the instruments before listening to them. Listening guides are given with each selection to help students follow the musical events. These may be duplicated for each student or may be placed on a transparency for the entire class to see.

In addition to the music selections given here, you may also wish to consult the current music series for other examples from these cultures.

Chinese Music

"COLORFUL BOATS"

Grades: 4–6

Colorful Boats

Starting pitch: A
Meter: 2/4

Melody Collected by William Anderson

English words by Carol Kerr, in Silver Burdett *Music* 4, © 1981. Reprinted by permission.

Chinese zheng

Chinese xiao

Objectives

Students will:

1. Be introduced to China, its geography, and its culture.

2. Sing the song "Colorful Boats" and identify the following characteristics in the song: pentatonic melody, duple meter, monophonic texture.

3. Listen to the instrumental selection "Winter Birds [Ravens] Flying over the Water," played on the zheng and xiao; identify the instruments by sight; identify the instruments by sound; classify the instruments (stringed or wind); describe the meter (duple); and describe the programmatic effects in the music.

Materials

- Globe or map of the world
- Pictures of the instruments (zheng and xiao)
- Melody bells or xylophone
- Recording of "Winter Birds [Ravens] Flying over the Water" (*China's Instrumental Heritage,* Lyrichord, LLRCD-792 [LLCT 792]). Also available on *Music Resources for Multicultural Perspectives* (MENC: The National Association for Music Education, 1806 Robert Fulton Drive, Reston, VA 20191, 1-800-336-3768), selection 21.

Procedures

1. Have students locate China on the globe or map. Compare its size to that of the United States (approximates the size of the United States and Mexico). Then compare China's population with that of the United States (1.25 billion versus 275 million). Ask students to locate some of the main cities (Beijing, Shanghai, Canton).

2. Make a "Characteristics of Chinese Music" chart on the chalkboard or bulletin board. As each piece of music is studied, list the important musical characteristics learned.

3. Sing the Chinese song "Colorful Boats," about colorfully decorated boats at a New Year's celebration. Lead a discussion about Chinese New Year (see page 179). The date for Chinese New Year varies each year, occurring between January 21 and February 19. The exact date is determined according to the lunar calendar, falling on the second new moon after the winter solstice. Each new year is designated by one of the animals of the Chinese zodiac: rat, ox, tiger, hare, dragon, serpent, horse, sheep, monkey, rooster, dog, and boar. (Children may wish to draw the animal of the particular new year.) The Chinese New Year is a time of great celebration, often involving fireworks and paper dragons being carried through the streets.*

a. Have students sing the song in both Chinese and English.

b. As students sing, have them keep track of the rhythm by clapping hands together on beat 1 and waving hands outward on beat 2. They should be able to feel and see the duple meter.

c. Write in scale fashion the pitches used in the song:

d. As students sing the song, note that there is only *one* line of music (even though many people are singing it). This music is described as *monophonic* (*mono* = one, *phonic* = sound).

4. Play a recording of the piece "Winter Birds [Ravens] Flying over the Water," played on the *zheng* (also spelled *cheng*, and pronounced "zhung") and *xiao* (also spelled *hsiao*, and pronounced "she-ao").

a. Show pictures and describe the zheng and xiao. The zheng is a plucked stringed instrument. It normally has sixteen strings, which are tuned to a pentatonic scale. Note how the performer plucks the strings with his or her right-hand thumb and fingers and how the left-hand fingers glide along the strings to produce different pitches. The xiao is a wind instrument made from bamboo. Point out the notch at the upper end of the instrument, across which the performer blows air to produce the sound. Point out that there are no keys on the instrument.

b. Have students listen to the tone qualities of each instrument (clear, plucked string sound of zheng and breathy, wind sound of xiao).

c. Have the students keep track of the beat and follow the duple meter by clapping lightly on beat 1 and waving on beat 2.

d. Call attention to the nature theme in the title of the composition. This is programmatic music. Discuss how the music reflects this theme (sweeping melodic lines played on the zheng symbolize birds flying over water).

Assessment

Have the class list characteristics of Chinese music they have learned in this lesson.

_____

*Encyclopedia Americana, 1992, vol. 6, p. 597.

"OLD MONK SWEEPING THE BUDDHIST TEMPLE"
"THE HERO'S DEFEAT"

Grades: 4–6

Objectives

Students will:

1. Explore tone color and texture in Chinese music by listening to the sheng composition "Old Monk Sweeping the Buddhist Temple."

2. Identify the sheng by sight and sound and classify the sheng as a wind instrument.

3. Compare the free reed structure of the sheng and the Western harmonica (its distant relative) and identify the distinctive harmonic texture produced on the instrument.

4. Listen to "The Hero's Defeat" played on the pipa and identify the pipa by sight and sound.

5. Classify the pipa as a stringed instrument.

6. Dramatize the programmatic ideas of "The Hero's Defeat."

Materials

■ Pictures of instruments (sheng and pipa)

■ Recordings of "Old Monk Sweeping the Buddhist Temple" (*China's Instrumental Heritage,* Lyrichord LLRCD-792 [LLCT 792]) and "The Hero's Defeat" (Chinese pipa composition; available on *Music Resources for Multicultural Perspectives* [MENC: The National Association for Music Education, 1806 Robert Fulton Drive, Reston, VA 20191, 1-800-336-3768], selection 23.)

■ Harmonica

Chinese sheng

Chinese pipa

Procedures

1. Have students listen to the recording of "Old Monk Sweeping the Buddhist Temple" played on the *sheng* (pronounced "shung").

   a. Show a picture of the sheng and describe how the instrument is constructed. The sheng consists of a bowl-shaped base into which are inserted bamboo reed pipes, each designed to produce a different pitch. Within each pipe is a small reed, which vibrates to produce the sound as air moves through the pipe.

   b. Bring a harmonica to class. Show the reeds in the instrument. (They may be seen by looking carefully into the instrument; it may be possible to remove the upper or lower sections of the instrument to see the reeds clearly.)

   c. Play the harmonica. Notice that sound can be produced both by exhaling air into the instrument and by inhaling air from the instrument. Thus, one can produce *continuous* sound on the harmonica. The same is true for the sheng. Also, point out that one can produce several pitches at the same time on the harmonica, thus creating harmony. This is also true for the sheng.

   d. Have students listen to the distinctive tone color produced by the sheng.

   e. Point out the distinctive harmonic sounds that are often produced on the sheng.

2. Have students listen to the recording of "The Hero's Defeat" played on the *pipa* (pronounced "pee-pah").

   a. Show a picture of the pipa and describe how it is constructed and played. The pipa is a plucked stringed instrument somewhat similar in shape to the Western guitar. Point out the characteristic manner in which it is held upright as it is played. The strings are plucked with the fingernails of the right hand. Among the most characteristic sounds of the instrument are rapidly repeated notes in the melody executed by the quickly moving fingers of the right hand.

   b. This piece is programmatic, depicting a battle between the kingdoms of Han and Chu. Have students listen to the manner in which the music depicts soldiers marching back and forth and the battle sounds of clashing swords.

   c. Plan dramatic movement to accompany the music.

Assessment

Have the class list characteristics of Chinese music they have learned in this lesson.

- *Instruments:* Sheng—wind instrument with reeds activated by air; pipa—plucked stringed instrument
- *Texture:* Distinctive harmonic texture produced on the sheng
- *Melody:* Rapidly repeating notes produced by the pipa
- *Form:* Programmatic ideas of the music

Japanese Music

"SAKURA"

Grades: 3–4

Sakura

Starting pitch: A
Meter: 2/4, begins on 1

Trans. Joy E. Lawrence

SA - KU - RA	SA - KU - RA	YA - YO - I - NO	SO - RA___ WA,	MI - WA -
Sah - koo - rah	*sah - koo - rah*	*yah - yoh - i - noh*	*so - rah - wah*	*mee wah*
Sa - ku - ra	Sa - ku - ra	cher - ry blooms are	eve - ry - where	clouds of

TA - SU KA - GI___ RI,	KA - SU - MI KA	KU - MO___ KA	NI - O - I - ZO
Tah - soo kah - gee - ree	*kah - soo - mi kah*	*koo - moh___ kah*	*ni - o - i - zoh*
glo - ry fill the___ air.	Mist of beau - ty	in the___ sky	Love - ly col - ors

I - ZU___ RU.	I - ZA - YA,	I - ZA - YA	ME NI YU - KA - N.
i - zoo - roo	*i - zah - yah*	*i - zah - yah*	*me ni yoo - kah n.*
float - ing___ by.	Sa - ku - ra,	Sa - ku - ra	Let us come___ and see.

John M. Kelly, Folk Music Festival in Hawaii. Copyright 1965. By permission of the Boston Music Company, 172 Tremont St., Boston, MA 02111.

Objectives

Students will:

1. Be introduced to the geography and some cultural characteristics of Japan.

2. Sing the song "Sakura" (Cherry Blooms) in both Japanese and English, and identify the pentatonic scale and the duple meter.

3. Listen to Variations on Sakura played on the koto; identify the koto by sight and sound and explain how the koto is constructed and played.

4. Identify the theme-and-variation form.

Materials

- Globe or map of the world
- Picture of koto
- Melody bells
- Japanese props, such as kimono, fan, or parasol
- Recording of Variations on Sakura (*Art of the Koto: The Music of Japan*, Elektra Records, CD 70234)

Procedures

1. Using a globe, have students locate Japan. Compare its size to that of the United States. (Japan's total land area is approximately equal to that of the states of Iowa and Minnesota combined, yet it has approximately half the population of the United States.) Japan is an island country; have students find the four main islands: Hokkaido, Honshu, Shikoku, and Kyushu. Also have the class locate some of the major cities: Tokyo, Yokohama, Nagoya, Kyoto, and Osaka.

2. Have students sing the song "Sakura," one of the most popular folk songs in Japan. The song celebrates the national flower of Japan—the cherry blossom—which in springtime provides a profusion of pink-and-white blossoms throughout the country. Have them sing in both Japanese and English.

3. Call attention to the theme of nature. Ask students to identify the words (in English) that refer to nature (cherry blooms, clouds, air, mist, sky).

4. Have students write out, from low to high, the different pitches in the song:

Because there are five notes, this is a pentatonic scale. Play the scale on melody bells, then sing it on the syllable "loo." Notice the particular sound quality of the pentatonic scale.

5. Dramatize "Sakura" by creating stylized movements that express ideas in the song and by adding a kimono, Japanese parasol, fan, and so on.

6. Show students a picture of the koto. The *koto* is one of the most important Japanese stringed instruments; it has a position in Japanese homes comparable to the piano in our own country. The instrument is approximately 6 feet long, 13 inches wide, and 2 inches thick. It has thirteen strings, which extend the length of the body and are tuned to the pentatonic scale by movable bridges inserted between the body of the instrument and the strings. The instrument is played with plectrums, which are attached to the right-hand thumb, index, and middle fingers. A variety of pitches and subtly executed ornamentation can be produced by the left hand pressing and pulling strings.

7. Play the recording of Variations on Sakura played on the koto. Have students follow the outline of this form on the board.
   - *Theme:* "Sakura"
   - *Variation 1:* "Sakura" theme played with added melodic figures; fast tempo
   - *Variation 2:* "Sakura" theme played at a slow tempo
   - *Variation 3:* "Sakura" theme played with many "running figures"; fast tempo

   Plan dramatic movement to portray the changes in tempo.

Japanese koto

Japanese shakuhachi

Assessment

Summarize the lesson by having the students make a list of "Characteristics of Japanese Music" on the chalkboard or bulletin board: pentatonic melody, duple meter, monophonic texture, theme-and-variation form, nature theme.

"DEER CALLING TO EACH OTHER IN THE DISTANCE"

Grades: 5–6

Objectives

Students will:

1. Listen to the composition "Deer Calling to Each Other in the Distance" played on the shakuhachi and identify (a) the shakuhachi by sight and sound; (b) the programmatic theme of nature, in which two shakuhachi players imitate deer calling to each other; and (c) how the sense of understatement is created through the slow tempo, soft dynamic level, and monophonic texture.

2. Show sections devoted to the koto and shakuhachi on the video *Discovering the Music of Japan*. Note the following characteristics of Japanese traditional music: pentatonic scales, duple meter, tendency toward soft dynamic levels, programmatic nature of pieces, sense of understatement—creation of maximum effect from minimal materials.

Materials

- Picture of shakuhachi
- Recording of "Shika no Tome" ("Deer Calling to Each Other in the Distance"), Elektra/Nonesuch CD 72076, track 4
- Video *Discovering the Music of Japan**

---

* The video *Discovering the Music of Japan* is available from West Music Company, P.O. Box 552, Coralville, Iowa 52241.

Procedures

1. Play the composition "Deer Calling to Each Other in the Distance" ("Shika no Tome") as performed on the shakuhachi.

2. Show a picture of the *shakuhachi.* This instrument is made from bamboo and is approximately 18 inches in length. Sound is produced by blowing across a small notch at the upper end of the instrument.

3. Call attention to the nature theme in the title of the composition. Listen to the manner in which the two shakuhachi players imitate deer calling to each other.

4. Place the following statements on a chart or the chalkboard. As they listen to the composition, have the students circle the appropriate items:

Music is loud	*or*	(Music is soft)
(One line of music)	*or*	Many lines of music
Strong beat in music	*or*	(Weak beat in music)
(Tempo is slow)	*or*	Tempo is fast

   After students have completed this task, call attention to the manner in which understatement is created by each of the items.

5. Show the video *Discovering the Music of Japan.* Three traditional musical instruments are played: the koto (plucked stringed instrument), the shakuhachi (wind instrument), and the shamisen (plucked stringed instrument). A short Japanese dance is also performed. Although you may wish to view the entire video, the first two segments, on the koto and shakuhachi, are suggested here. Before showing the video, review with the class some of the principal characteristics of Japanese music: pentatonic scales, duple meter, tendency toward soft dynamic levels, programmatic nature of pieces, and a sense of understatement—the creation of maximum effect from minimal materials.

6. Call attention to the cultural setting of the music on the video: Beautiful color photography of a home and garden and a Japanese painting combine to create the proper setting (particularly the emphasis on nature) for the music.

Assessment

Conclude the lesson by having students summarize some of the general characteristics of Japanese music as they appear on the chalkboard or bulletin board.

Music of European Peoples

BACKGROUND INFORMATION FOR THE CLASS

The European continent extends from the Mediterranean Sea in the south to the Arctic Ocean in the north, and from the Atlantic Ocean in the west to the Ural Mountains in Russia (see figure 10.3). In total land area, Europe is actually the second-smallest continent (Australia is the smallest), having about one-fifteenth of the world's land area. Its more than 500 million people, however, make up about 10 percent of the world's population.

Figure 10.3. Europe

A great variety of cultural backgrounds and languages are present on the European continent. Some indication of the great ethnic diversity is clearly evidenced in the more than thirty countries into which the continent is divided and the nearly fifty languages spoken.

SOME GENERAL CHARACTERISTICS OF EUROPEAN MUSIC

Because of the large number of cultural groups in Europe, there is considerable variety in the styles of music. Following is a list of general characteristics of European music. It should be understood, however, that not all of these characteristics will be present in music from every region. The attempt here is to provide general guidelines for presenting European music in the classroom.

- Melody is characterized by balanced phrases, particularly in western Europe; phrases of unequal length are sometimes present, particularly in eastern European music. Scales include major, minor, modal, pentatonic, and whole tone. Melodies from western Europe are not generally heavily ornamented; ornamentation is found in some music, however, particularly in eastern Europe.

- Rhythm is characterized by a moderately strong beat, with tempo even and constant. Meter is mostly duple or triple; unequally divided meter (5/4, 7/8, etc.) is found in eastern Europe.

- Homophonic and polyphonic textures are common, along with much use of chordal harmony. "Drone" harmony is present in many areas.

- Timbre is characterized by a variety of vocal and instrumental tone colors. Open, relaxed singing quality predominates. Stringed and wind instrument tone qualities are most frequently found.

- There is much use of form in which a musical idea is stated, followed by contrasting material, which is in turn followed by a return to the first musical idea (ABA).

TEACHING EUROPEAN MUSIC: SUGGESTIONS FOR LESSONS

Following are some sample lessons on European music, designed to introduce students to some of the traditional music of Europe in terms of the elements of melody, rhythm, texture, timbre, and form.

Russian Music

"SONG OF THE VOLGA BOATMEN"

Grades: 4–6

Song of the Volga Boatmen

Russia

Key: A
Starting pitch: A
Meter: 4/4, begins on 1

Āy___ ŭh-nyem   Āy___ ŭh-nyem   yĕhs-chăh rāy-zik   yĕhs-chăh dăh răs
Yo,___ heave ho,   Yo,___ heave ho,   Pull to-geth-er   Yo,___ heave ho.

Rah-zahv yōm___ mē___ bĭr-yō-zū   rah-zahv yōm___ mē dăh kud-ryah-voo
Yon-der birch-es___ on the shore,   We must reach___ them,___ Pull men more

ī-dă-dă ī dă   ī dă-dă ī dă   rah-zahv yom-me dah   Kued___ ryah-vŏo
                              Pull to-geth-er   yo,___ heave ho.

Āy___ ŭh-nyem   Āy___ ŭh-nyem   yehs-chăh ray-zik   yehs-chăh dah răs___
Yo,___heave ho,   Yo,___heave ho,   Pull to-geth-er   Yo,___ heave ho___

Objectives

Students will:

1. Be introduced to the geography and cultures of Europe with special attention to Russia.

2. Sing "Song of the Volga Boatmen" and identify the phrygian scale (F#, G, A, B, C#, D, E), duple meter, and AABCA form.

3. Listen to a Russian folk orchestra featuring the balalaika and correctly identify musical events.

Materials

■ Globe or world map

■ Recording of Russian folk orchestra (*Balalaika Favorites,* Mercury CD 432000-2, track 4 ["Flight of the Bumble-Bee"])

Procedures

1. Using a globe or map, have students find the European continent, individual countries, and some of the largest cities. Discuss with the class how closely many families in the United States are related to people from European countries. Undoubtedly, some students in the class will be from families that originally came from Europe.

2. Have the class sing "Song of the Volga Boatmen" in both Russian and English. Point out that this song is about the Volga River, one of the great waterways of Russia and the longest river in Europe. Have the students find the Volga River on the map.

3. While singing, have some students conduct the 4/4 meter. Point out the four-measure balanced phrases.

4. Write the phrygian scale (F♯, G, A, B, C♯, D, E) on the board and have the students sing it or play it on instruments:

5. Diagram the form of the song:

A A B C A

Russian balalaika

6. Play a recording of a Russian folk orchestra featuring a variety of instruments, including the balalaika (a triangular-shaped, stringed instrument), the domra (a long-necked plucked lute), and the bayan (an accordion-like instrument). The selection is entitled "Flight of the Bumble-Bee" by Rimsky-Korsakov. (Place the outline below on the board without the circled answers.) While listening to the music, ask students to circle the appropriate musical events:

How does this music portray the flight of a bumblebee? (Younger students may wish to dramatize the flight of a bumblebee.)

Assessment

Have the class list characteristics of Russian music they have learned in this lesson.

Greek Music*

KALAMATIANOS

Grades: 4–6

Samiotissa

Key: G
Starting pitch: D
Meter: 7/8

English Version by Stella Phredopoulos
Music by D. A. Vergoni

Sa - mio - tis - sa, Sa - mio - tis - sa, You will re-turn to Sa - mos. Sa -

mio - tis - sa, Sa - mio - tis - sa, Is - land of beau - ty and de - light.

You will come home a - gain to   me, Sa - mio - tis - sa, There's   mu - sic in the sum - mer   night.

You will come home a - gain to   me, Sa - mio - tis - sa, There's   mu - sic in the sum - mer   night.

Students will:

1. Listen to the Greek music that accompanies the Kalamatianos dance. Identify the instruments of the ensemble (fiddle, clarient, laouto [lute], and percussion), and the uneven quality of the 7/8 meter.

2. Perform the Kalamatianos dance.

Materials

■ Recorded Greek dance music, "Kalamatianos"†

---

* Special thanks to Maria Foustalieraki for her assistance with this lesson.

† See *Greek Dances and How to Do Them,* CD 3GT-101, available from Greektown Gift and Music Shop, 330 South Halsted, Chicago, IL 60661; 312-263-6342.

Procedures

1. Listen to Greek music in 7/8 meter performed by fiddle, clarinet, laouto, and percussion, or sing the song "Samiotissa" (about the Greek island Samos).

2. Have the students practice following the 7/8 meter:

   a. Without the music, count from 1 to 7, clapping on 1, 4, and 6; repeat.

   b. Add the music and count from 1 to 7, clapping on 1, 4, and 6; repeat.

   c. Again, without the music, count from 1 to 7, emphasizing 1, 4, and 6 by lightly stamping your feet on the floor; repeat.

3. Repeat the foot movements in 2c, but this time with musical accompaniment.

4. Teach the dance Kalamatianos, which is done in 7/8 meter, with either recorded accompaniment or accompanied by the song "Samiotissa."

   a. Have students form an open circle, facing to the right:

   b. Circle to the right:

   c. Circle to the left:

1–6	Walk to the right, starting with the right foot
7	Step to the right with the right foot
8	Cross left foot over right foot to the right
9	Rock right foot back to position 7
10	Step to the left with the left foot
11	Cross right foot over left foot to the left
12	Rock left foot back to position 10

   Repeat.

   Note that the dancers face (body and head) to the right (direction of the line) for all measures except the last (numbers 10–12), for which they face to the left.

d. Teaching suggestions:

- Say the phrase "strawberry peaches apple"
- Clap the first syllable of each word while speaking:
- Speak and bounce in place (feel this pattern with body):
- Speak and walk the pattern freely in the room, starting with the right foot.
- Do the same with the music (all the above steps).
- Practice the "cross-rock" part to the right and then to the left (steps 7–12) a few times without the music first, then with the music.
- Put the two parts (steps 1–6 and 7–12) together.
- At the beginning it helps to speak the phrase "strawberry peaches apple" while dancing.
- The walking should be bouncy. You actually walk mainly on tiptoes.

Assessment

Have the class list characteristics of Greek music they have learned in this lesson.

Spanish Music

"THERE'S A FIESTA"

Grades: 4–6

There's a Fiesta

Key: G
Starting pitch: G or B
Meter: 3/4, begins on 1

Spain

There's a fi-es-ta to-day, tra la la la,_____ Gui-tars are be-gin-ning to play, tra la la la,_____ Sweet-ly their mu-sic rings out, tra la la la,_____ As ev-'ry-one gath-ers a-bout, tra la la la_____ Cas-ta-nets start keep-ing the beat, Danc-ers be-gin mov-ing their feet, Whirl-ing a-way while ev-'ry-one cries out "O-lé!"

Objectives

Students will:

1. Sing the Spanish song "There's a Fiesta," perform the composition in harmony, and identify the triple meter and the AAB form.

2. Listen to a Spanish guitar composition entitled "Recuerdos de la Alhambra" (Recollections of the Alhambra), which depicts in music the ornamental quality of the Alhambra Palace in Granada, Spain. In particular listen for the rapid, repetitive plucking producing the ornamental melody and the alternating AABBAB form. Compare with pictures of the Alhambra Palace.

Materials

- Paper with letters *A* and *B* or two different geometric shapes
- Castanets, tambourines
- Recording: "Recuerdos de la Alhambra"*
- Pictures of the Alhambra Palace in Granada, Spain†

Procedures

1. Have the students sing "There's a Fiesta." Ask the class what they think the Spanish term *fiesta* means (a celebration or festival).

2. Call attention to the Spanish instruments mentioned in the song (guitars, castanets). Also call attention to the word *dancers;* Spanish music is often accompanied by dance.

3. Have the class sing the song: first just the top melodic line, until the words and tune are learned well; then have the higher voices sing the top line and the lower voices, the lower line.

4. As the students sing, have them clap the triple meter.

5. Using letters or paper of different colors and geometric shapes, have the students outline the form of the piece (AAB).

6. Add castanets or tambourines on the triplets (♩♩♩) to create a Spanish effect.

7. Play the Spanish guitar composition entitled "Recuerdos de la Alhambra," which depicts in music the ornamental quality of the Alhambra Palace in Granada. In particular listen for the rapid, repetitive plucking producing the ornamental melody and compare with the ornamental motifs of the Alhambra Palace. Also follow the alternating AABBAB form (section A in minor; section B in major). Circle the letters as you listen to the music:

   A   A   B   B   A   B   Coda

Assessment

Briefly review some of the things you have learned in this lesson about Spanish music.

---

* *The Segovia Collection* (vol. 3), *Andres Segovia, Guitar, My Favorite Works,* MCA Records, MCAD 42069, track 6 ("Recuerdos de la Alhambra").

† *National Geographic,* vol. 147, no. 6 (June 1975), pp. 834–35, and *National Geographic Traveler,* vol. 4, no. 4 (Winter 1987/88), pp. 98–99.

British Isles Music

BAGPIPE SONGS

Grades: 4–6

Objectives

Students will:

1. Sing the Irish song "Galway Piper" (pp. 235 and 367) and identify the following musical characteristics: balanced four-measure phrases, strong beat, duple meter, and AB form.

2. Listen to a medley of pieces played by a Scotch bagpipe band and identify the following musical characteristics: ornamental melody, drone harmony, loud dynamic level, strong beat, and duple meter.

3. Listen to the Irish bagpipe composition "Rakish Paddy" and identify the following musical characteristics: ornamental melody, duple meter, fast tempo, and drone and chordal harmony.

Materials

- Red and blue paper

- Recorded bagpipe music (*Bagpipe Marches and Music of Scotland,* Legacy CD 386, track 7, or *The Bagpipes and Drums of Scotland,* Laserlight CD 15159, track 5, and *Festival of Irish Folk Music,* Chyme CH-CD 1013, disc 2, track 8)

Procedures

1. Sing the song "Galway Piper." Point out that the song is about a bagpipe player—Piping Tim of Galway.

2. Using two pitches (D and A), have students sing a drone on the sound *Raā,* making it very nasal. Half the class can be bagpipes while the other half sings.

Bagpipe of Scotland

3. Call attention to the repetition in the melodic line (measures 1 and 4 nearly alike; measure 2 like measure 1 except down one step; measures 5 and 6 nearly alike; measures 5 and 7 exactly alike).

4. Have students keep the beat and the duple meter in the song by clapping on the strong beats (1 and 3) and waving outward on beats 2 and 4.

5. Ask students to diagram the overall form of the piece with letters and colored paper:

A (Red)	**B** (Blue)
Measures 1–4	Measures 5–8

6. Listen to Scotch bagpipe music.

7. Show a picture of the Scotch bagpipe. Explain that the bagpipe is one of the oldest and most

widespread instruments in Europe. The instrument consists of several distinct parts: (1) a *pipe* through which the player blows air into (2) the *bag,* a device that acts as a storage reservoir for the air, which makes possible the continuous sound produced on the instrument; (3) the *chanter,* a pipe with fingerholes on which the performer plays melodies; and (4) *drone pipes,* which, like the chanter are activated by air from the bag, but unlike the chanter normally produce only a single pitch.

8. Give students copies of the following listening guide and, as they listen to the music, have them circle the appropriate musical events:

Brass and stringed instruments	*or*	(Wind and percussion instruments)
One line of music	*or*	(Several lines of music)
(Loud)	*or*	Soft
(Rhythm: Strongly felt beat)	*or*	Rhythm: Weakly felt beat
Triple meter	*or*	(Duple meter)

9. Play a recording of Irish bagpipe music. Irish bagpipes differ from Scotch bagpipes: Instead of blowing air through a pipe into the bag, a *bellows,* which is attached under the right elbow of the performer, is pumped to fill the bag with air. In addition, the Irish bagpipes have keys on both the chanter and drones. Through these the performer can produce simple chords.

10. Place the following items on the board or on a handout. As they listen to the music, have students circle the appropriate musical events:

(Wind and stringed instruments)	*or*	Brass instruments
One line of music	*or*	(Many lines of music)
The melody is plain	*or*	(The melody is highly ornamented)
(Fast tempo)	*or*	Slow tempo
(Duple meter)	*or*	Triple meter

Assessment

Summarize the lessons by asking the class to list on the board some of the general characteristics of the music of the British Isles.

American Music

BACKGROUND INFORMATION FOR THE CLASS

America is a huge continental land mass extending almost 9,500 miles from north to south and about 3,000 miles at its widest east-west expanse (see figure 10.4). The continent is generally divided into two principal areas, North and South America, with the narrow intervening strip referred to as Central America.

With more than twenty-five countries present on the American continent, there is considerable ethnic variety both among different countries and within countries. Much of the ethnic diversity

Figure 10.4. The Americas

of the United States results from numerous peoples who immigrated from other parts of the world. Some of the earliest inhabitants, those peoples commonly referred to today as Native Americans, are thought to have come across the Bering Strait from Asia beginning as early as 50,000 years ago. In more-recent times (beginning around A.D. 1000), people from a number of European countries traveled to the Americas. Shortly thereafter, numerous Africans were brought to both North and South America. In the past several hundred years, Asian peoples from a variety of countries have also immigrated to the Americas. It is clear that today many cultural groups now make up the United States and each has its distinctive music.

TEACHING AMERICAN MUSIC: SUGGESTIONS FOR LESSONS

Because of the enormous ethnic diversity caused by migrations of peoples from all over the globe, it is impossible to describe "typical" American music. The following sections outline suggestions for lessons on some representative types of American music.

Native American Music*

"MOS', MOS'!"

Grades: 1–3

Mos', Mos'!

Key: C
Starting pitch: G
Meter: 2/4, begins on 1

Collected by David McAllester

♪=132

Mos', mos', nai - ti - la, mos', mos', nai - ti - la,

Ka - nel - per - kye nai - ti - la, Ka - nel - per - kye nai - ti - la,

Mo - sa! Mo - sa! nya, ya, ya, ya, ya, etc.

Objectives

Students will:

1. Learn the Hopi song "Mos', Mos'!" and the actions that go with it. They will also discuss the background of the song and text to broaden their understanding of the place of music in Native American life and some of the valuable perspectives in the various Native American views of the world.

2. Sing the Apache "Blessing Song," accompanying the song with a steady drumbeat. Diagram the ABA form of the song.

Materials

- ■ Map of the United States
- ■ Videotape of David McAllester teaching the song "Mos', Mos'!" at the MENC Symposium on Multicultural Approaches to Music Education†

---

* Lessons derived from Edwin Schupman (ORBIS Associates, Washington, D.C.) and David P. McAllester, "Teaching the Music of the American Indian," in William M. Anderson, *Teaching Music with a Multicultural Approach* (Reston, VA: MENC, 1991), pp. 39–43.

† *Teaching the Music of the American Indian,* Music Educators National Conference, 1991; available from MENC: The National Association for Music Education, 1806 Robert Fulton Drive, Reston, VA 20191, 800-336-3768; *www.menc.org.*

Procedures

1. Look for pictures and make a bulletin board on Native American culture. An excellent introduction, with maps and pictures, appears in *The World Book Encyclopedia*. Invite a Native American to visit your class.

2. Locate the home of the Hopi tribe of Arizona on a U.S. map. (It can be found on several mesas extending east from Tuba City in western Arizona, east of the Grand Canyon.)

3. Have students learn the song "Mos', Mos'!" by singing along with the videotape.

4. Have the children "sit like a cat," holding up their hands like a cat's paws. They move their paws up and down on each beat, and where the cat says "nya, ya," they accelerate the tempo and pretend to scratch each other.

5. Discuss the role of animals: Native Americans feel a close relationship to the animal world; they believe that animals are creatures that think, feel, and even teach. Animals are our relatives, who share this planet with us and with whom we should learn to live in harmony. This is very different from the common Anglo-American attitude that animals exist for the benefit of humans.

6. Discuss some of the basic features of the song "Mos', Mos'!": paired phrases and three-tone scale.

7. Sing the Apache "Blessing Song." Accompany the song with a drumbeat. Diagram the ABA form of the song. Note that some Native American music, like European American music, uses ABA form.

Blessing Song (My Father's Song)

"Blessing Song" is found in Chesley Goseyun Wilson, Ruth Longcor-Harnisch Wilson, and Bryan Burton, *When the Earth Was Like New: Western Apache Songs and Stories* (Danbury, Conn.: World Music Press, 1994). Book and accompanying recording. Used by permission. World Music Press, P.O. Box 2565, Danbury, CT 06813.

ROUND DANCE

Grades: 3–5

Objectives

Students will:

1. Put Southern Plains music in cultural and geographic perspective.

2. Recognize and be able to perform the distinctive long-short, dotted-eighth/sixteenth rhythm of a Southern Plains round dance.

3. Recognize and be able to perform the accented and unaccented beats of the round-dance dotted rhythm.

4. Understand basic concepts about the importance and significance of being a drummer, singer, or dancer in the Native American culture.

5. Identify both men's and women's voices on the recordings.

6. Perform the Southern Plains–style round dance.

7. Understand the basic significance and symbolism of the circle to Native Americans, as represented in the shape of the round dance.

Materials

- Several hand drums or one bass drum

- Recording: *Powwow Songs: Music of the Plains Indians* (New World Records, CD 80343-2, track 4)

- Map of the United States

Procedures

1. Prepare students by informing them that they are going to listen to a recording of a Native American song and dance style that comes from the tribes who originally inhabited large regions of the Southern Plains. Point out states such as Kansas, Missouri, Oklahoma, Texas, New Mexico, and Arizona. Before Oklahoma was a state, it was known as Indian Territory: It is where most of these tribes now live after being placed there by the U.S. government in the nineteenth century. Some of the names of Southern Plains tribes are Kiowa, Commanche, Pawnee, Otoe, and Ponca.

2. Listen to a recording of a Southern Plains–style round dance. Have students clap with the drum rhythm and say, "round dance, round dance." Note the long/short pattern.

3. Listen to a portion of the recording again. By yourself this time, clap along with the drum, placing a little more emphasis, or clapping a little louder on the first of the two beats (*round* dance, *round* dance, *round* dance). Ask students, "Is one of my claps louder or stronger? Which one? Is that the way the drummers are doing it, too?" Explain that this is known as an *accent*. Have the class clap and say the words again, this time accenting the first beat.

4. Have students play the round-dance drum rhythm on drums. Lay a bass drum flat on the floor. Have students sit around the drum in a circle, each one playing the drum with a single beater. This is similar to Plains Indian–style drumming. Students can play the rhythm on hand drums if no bass drum is available, but students should be told that this is not contextually accurate.

5. Tell students that Native Americans consider their drums and music to be very important to the well-being of the tribe. They treat their drums, their music, and their musicians with respect at all times.

6. Teach students the round dance. Although a social, nonreligious dance, the round dance is important to Native American people. The circle symbolizes the cycles of life, the shape of the earth, unity, and equality—no one person within the circle being distinguished above the others. It is considered a dance of friendship. Visitors to powwows are frequently invited to join in the round dance as an expression of goodwill.

   a. If done in a more formal setting, the round dance is led by the *head man* and *head woman* dancers of the powwow, or sometimes by an armed forces veteran. All dancers face inward and dance sideways. The line of dancers forms a circle, or a spiral if there are many participants, which moves in a clockwise direction.

   Basic rhythm
   (drum beat):

   Foot movement: L   R   L   R   L   R   L   R

   b. *Basic step:* Begin with feet parallel, slightly spread, facing inward. Lead with left foot; right foot follows. Left foot—lift knee slightly, take comfortable step sideways to left. Right foot—with less knee lift, bring foot to parallel position as at beginning. Continue around in a clockwise circle.

   HM = Head man dancer

   HW = Head woman dancer

   X = Other dancers

Assessment

Briefly discuss some of the things you have learned about Native American music in these lessons.

Folk and Country Music

"OLD JOE CLARK"

Grades: 3–6

Old Joe Clark

Starting pitch: G
Meter: 2/4, begins on "and" of 2

Traditional

I used to live on the moun-tain top. Now I live in town. I'm stay-ing at the big ho-tel, Court-ing Bet-sy Brown. **CHORUS** Fare you well, Old Joe Clark, Fare you well, I say. Fare you well, Old Joe Clark. I'm a-goin' a-way.

Jean Ritchie, *The Dulcimer Book* (New York: Oak Publications, 1974), p. 39.

Objectives

Students will:

1. Sing the song "Old Joe Clark" and identify and perform the mixolydian scale (C, D, E, F, G, A, B♭).

2. Accompany the song with a mountain dulcimer.

3. Listen to "Old Joe Clark" being accompanied by the mountain dulcimer.

Materials

- Mountain dulcimer

- Recording of "Old Joe Clark" (*Dulcimer Songs and Solos,* Smithsonian Folkways Recordings [FG 3571], CD or cassette, 800-410-9815, band 2)

Procedures

1. Sing "Old Joe Clark."

2. Place the mixolydian scale on the board and have students sing and/or play it:

Mountain dulcimer

3. Accompany "Old Joe Clark" on the mountain dulcimer. Mountain dulcimers are sold throughout the United States.* The mountain dulcimer has four strings, two placed close together on which the melody is played, and a third and fourth designed to produce a drone sound. The strings are stroked with a plectrum held in the right hand. Different pitches are produced by a small piece of wood, which is held in the left hand and slid along the strings.

4. Practice playing the mixolydian mode. The rest of the class should quietly hum along. Notice the drone harmony produced by the instrument.

5. Slowly sing "Old Joe Clark," accompanying on the dulcimer. Gradually increase the tempo as you develop facility.

6. Play a recording of "Old Joe Clark" being sung and accompanied on the mountain dulcimer.

BLUEGRASS SONGS

Grades: 4–6

Objectives

Students will:

1. Perform a square dance to "The Arkansas Traveler" played on fiddle, banjo, and guitar.

2. Listen to "Foggy Mountain Breakdown" and "Orange Blossom Special" played by a bluegrass ensemble and follow the musical and programmatic events.

Materials

■ Recordings of "The Arkansas Traveler" (*Wade Ward: Uncle Wade—A Memorial to Wade Ward: Old Time Virginia Banjo Picker,* Smithsonian Folkways Recordings [02380, CD or cassette], 800-410-9815), "Foggy Mountain Breakdown," and "Orange Blossom Special" (*The World of Flatt and Scruggs,* Columbia cassette, CGT 31964)

■ Pictures of various kinds of trains

---

* One source is The House of Musical Traditions, 7040 Carroll Avenue, Takoma Park, MD 20912; *www.hmtrad.com.*

Procedures

1. Have students square-dance to a recording of "The Arkansas Traveler," performed by a country stringed group including fiddle, banjo, and guitar.

   a. Form a square of four couples, with the boys on the left side of the girls. Students clap beat when not dancing.

   b. Listen for 4 counts.

   c. Introduction: All clap 16 beats (2 times).

   d. Couples 1 and 3 make 4 steps to center, bow and return.

   e. Couples 2 and 4 make 4 steps to center, bow and return.

   f. Repeat steps d and e.

   g. Each couple swings partner right (8 counts), then left (8 counts).

   h. Repeat g.

   i. Each couple passes shoulders with partner right (8 counts), then left (8 counts).

   j. Repeat i.

   k. Couples promenade counterclockwise and take new positions in square: Couple 1 is now located in couple 2 position, couple 2 is now in couple 3 position, and so on.

   l. Repeat steps c through k as often as needed.

2. Have students listen to "Orange Blossom Special" and "Foggy Mountain Breakdown" played by a bluegrass ensemble. Tell the class that they are going to hear bluegrass music. The name *bluegrass* came from a performing group organized in the 1940s by Bill Monroe in Kentucky, the Bluegrass state. The bluegrass ensemble consists of guitar, fiddle, banjo, mandolin, string bass, and sometimes other instruments.

3. "Orange Blossom Special" is a programmatic composition about a train. Discuss the sounds and movement of various kinds of trains. Show pictures or have children bring in miniature trains. Listen to the manner in which this music imitates the sounds and movement of a train. You will hear a call to board the train, the train whistle, and the chugging, pulsating motion of the engine. The piece is characterized by virtuoso fiddle playing.

4. The words *foggy mountain* in the title "Foggy Mountain Breakdown" allude to the often misty mountains of the Appalachian region. *Breakdown* refers to a piece that breaks down into a number of sections, each featuring a solo instrument. Follow the theme-and-variation form of the piece:

   a. Theme played by banjo with string bass accompaniment

   b. Theme played by fiddle with banjo, guitar, and string bass accompaniment

   c. Theme played by banjo with guitar accompaniment

   d. Theme played by guitar with banjo and string bass accompaniment

   e. Theme played by harmonica with guitar, banjo, and string bass accompaniment

   f. Theme played by banjo with guitar, banjo, and string bass accompaniment

   (You may wish to make a listening chart for "Foggy Mountain Breakdown," using line drawings of instruments.)

Assessment

Briefly discuss some of the characteristics of folk and country music you have learned in these lessons.

Mexican Music

"CIELITO LINDO" AND "LA RASPA"

Grades: 2–5

La Raspa

Key: G
Starting pitch: D
Meter: 4/4, begins on "and" of 4

Mexico

A

Now work of the day is done, And un-der the set-ting sun The
The band plays a live-ly beat, A - mi-gos, a-mi-gas meet, The And

Castanets   Tambourine

mu - sic calls ev - 'ry one To come join in all the fun.
soon sou - ples fill the street With sounds of their danc - ing feet.

Castanets   Tambourine

B

Their voic - es are lift - ed in hap - py song, No - bod - y has a care; And

Maracas   Cast.
Tamb.   Mar.

peo - ple re - joice that the night is long, Laugh - ter is ev - 'ry - where.

(Mar.)   Cast.
Tamb.

Objectives

Students will:

1. Sing "Cielito Lindo" in Spanish and in English.

2. Perform the Mexican song "La Raspa" and add a dance.

Materials

- Castanets
- Tambourines
- Maracas

Procedures

1. Sing "Cielito Lindo" (page 368), first in Spanish, then in English. On the chorus, have students follow the triple meter by tapping against their legs on beat 1, clapping on beat 2, and waving outward on beat 3.

2. Have students sing the song "La Raspa."

3. Add the designated instrumental accompaniment with castanets, tambourines, and maracas.

4. Once students have learned the song well, add the following dance:

    a. Form a circle, alternating boys and girls.

    b. Have the students place their hands on their hips.

    c. Students execute the following movement four times:

    - Hop on left foot and at the same time extend right foot forward with heel down and toe up (beat 1)

    - Hop on right foot and at the same time extend left foot forward with heel down and toe up (beat 2)

    - Feet pause (beat 3); clap (beat 4)

Assessment

Briefly summarize how you would teach a lesson on Mexican music.

African American Music

JAZZ—IMPROVISATION

Grades: 4–6

Objectives

Students will:

1. Listen to several selections of jazz and identify characteristic features.

2. Listen to "Hotter Than That" and identify the Dixieland ensemble, "scat" singing, and improvisatory form.

3. Listen to "Summertime" and identify improvisation in jazz performance.

Materials

- Recordings of "Hotter Than That" (*The Smithsonian Collection of Classic Jazz*, Washington, D.C., CD I, band 16); Gershwin's "Summertime" from *Porgy and Bess* (Phillips CD 115158 or Angel Records CD 263729); and "Summertime" performed by Miles Davis with the Gil Evans Orchestra (*The Smithsonian Collection of Classic Jazz*, Washington, D.C., CD IV, band 12)

Procedures

1. Play a recording of "Hotter Than That" performed by Louis Armstrong and His Hot Five.

2. Point out that Dixieland is the earliest form of jazz. As its name implies, Dixieland began as a musical style of the southern United States before spreading from the South throughout the United States and the world. The Dixieland ensemble in this selection features cornet, trombone, clarinet, piano, banjo, and guitar. The cornet player here is the famous Louis Armstrong, who also improvises with vocal syllables in a style called "scat" singing. One of the distinctive features of the Dixieland style is the emphasis on improvisation.

3. Place this outline on the board for students to follow:

   a. Introduction: cornet and trombone

   b. Cornet improvising: flat-four accompaniment (strongly felt 4-beat measures):

   c. Clarinet improvising: flat-four accompaniment

   d. "Scat" vocal improvisation

   e. Vocal and guitar interlude; flexible rhythm

   f. Trombone improvising: flat-four accompaniment

   g. Cornet and guitar improvising

4. Play a recording of the song "Summertime" from George Gershwin's opera *Porgy and Bess*, having the students follow the words and listen to the melody. Then play Miles Davis's jazz version of "Summertime" with the Gil Evans Orchestra.

5. Provide the following background information:

One of the most important characteristics of jazz is its emphasis on improvisation. Jazz artists develop extraordinary ability to improvise on given melodies. In the jazz version of "Summertime," the trumpeter, Miles Davis, first plays the theme and then improvises using melodic fragments from the theme along with newly created melodic and harmonic ideas. Listen carefully for the familiar segments of the melody and then the newly improvised phrases.

6. Ask the class to search for other jazz recordings (in their homes, school, or public libraries) and identify improvisation in selections. Have them bring their favorite jazz recordings to share with the class.

Assessment

Briefly discuss some of the characteristics of jazz you have learned in this lesson.

BLUES

Grades: 4–6

Traditional Blues

Ain't no-bod-y wants me, and they would-n't be in my shoes, ____

Ain't no-bod-y wants me, and they would-n't be in my shoes, ____

I feel so bad, I got the lone-some rid-er blues. ____

2. If I had a-listened to what my mama said, (2 times)
   I'd be home sleepin' in my nice warm feather bed.

3. River is deep and the river sure is wide, (2 times)
   The woman (man) I love is on the other side.

4. Hey, baby, baby, I treated you so wrong, (2 times)
   Sweet lovin' baby, I'll be missin' you 'fore long.

5. If I mistreat you, I sure don't mean no harm, (2 times)
   'Cause I'm a motherless child, and I don't know right from wrong.

6. You used to be my sugar, but you ain't sweet no more. (2 times)
   You got another baby hangin' 'round your door.

7. I got the blues at midnight, and they don't leave till day, (2 times)
   Got to find another baby to drive those blues away.

8. I woke up this mornin', the blues all in my head. (2 times)
   I rolled back the covers, the blues all in my bed.

9. Sun gonna shine on my back door someday, (2 times)
   Wind gonna rise up and blow my blues away.

"Lonesome Rider Blues," from Will Schmid, *A Tribute to Woodie Guthrie & Leadbelly* (Reston, Virginia: MENC: The National Association for Music Education, 1991). Used by permission.

Objectives

Students will:

1. Sing the "Lonesome Rider Blues" and identify the AAB form.

2. Listen to "Boll Weevil Blues" sung by Leadbelly and identify the twelve-bar blues form.

3. Listen to "Lost Your Head Blues" sung by Bessie Smith. Identify the AAB form and the distinctive melodic characteristics, including "scoops," "slides," and descending melodic contours.

Materials

■ Recordings of "Boll Weevil Blues" (*Negro Folk Songs for Young People*, Smithsonian Folkways Recordings [FC 7533], CD or cassette, 800-410-9815, track 3) and "Lost Your Head Blues" (*The Smithsonian Collection of Classic Jazz*, CD I, band 4)

Procedures

1. Sing the African American "Lonesome Rider Blues." Identify the AAB blues form; diagram on the board.

2. Listen to "Boll Weevil Blues" sung by Leadbelly. In this blues recording, Huddie Ledbetter (better known as Leadbelly), one of the most famous African American singer/songwriters, accompanies himself on the guitar. As implied in the name, the blues were initially pieces in which black people could talk about things that gave them melancholy, "blue" feelings. (Listen to the explanation given by Leadbelly at the beginning of this selection.) In this piece Leadbelly sings of the destruction caused by the boll weevil, an insect that destroys cotton.

   Blues are cast in twelve-bar (or measure) segments. Students can follow this twelve-bar form by quietly counting:

1 2 3 4	**2** 2 3 4	**3** 2 3 4	**4** 2 3 4
5 2 3 4	**6** 2 3 4	**7** 2 3 4	**8** 2 3 4
9 2 3 4	**10** 2 3 4	**11** 2 3 4	**12** 2 3 4

3. Listen to Bessie Smith's "Lost Your Head Blues," following the AAB form. The piece begins with a short instrumental introduction, which leads to:

- Section A: "I was with you, baby, when you did not have a dime."

- Section A repeats: "I was with you, baby, when you did not have a dime."

- Section B: "Now since you got plenty . . . money, you have throwed your good gal down."

(AAB form continues with new segments of text.)

Particularly note the characteristic features of blues melodies: "scopes" and "slides" between notes and descending melodic countours.

4. Have students look for other recordings of the blues (home, library, record store) and bring them to class.

Assessment

Briefly discuss some of the characteristics of the blues you have learned in this lesson.

CALL-AND-RESPONSE MUSIC

Grades: 2–5

Swing Low, Sweet Chariot

Key: F
Starting pitch: A
Meter: 2/4, begins on 1

Spiritual

Objectives

Students will:

1. Perform the spiritual "Swing Low, Sweet Chariot" and identify the solo/chorus (call-and-response) style of performance and the pentatonic melody.

2. Listen to the jazz composition "Jumpin' at the Woodside" and identify the families of instruments (brass, woodwinds, percussion); harmonic texture; pulsating, driving beat; ostinato; and short phrases passed among instruments in call-and-response form.

3. Sing the African composition "Kye, Kye Kule," particularly noticing the short phrases and call-and-response form, and compare it with "Swing Low, Sweet Chariot" and "Jumpin' at the Woodside."

4. Listen to the gospel composition "Don't Knock," particularly the call-and-response style between the soloist and the group.

Materials

- Recording of "Jumpin' at the Woodside" by Count Basie. (*Count Basie: The Complete Decca Recordings,* Decca, GRD-3-611, disc 2, track 14)

- Recording of "Don't Knock" (*World's Greatest Gospel,* vol. 2, HOB Records, HBD 35097)

Procedures

1. Have students sing the spiritual "Swing Low, Sweet Chariot." Spirituals are a very old form of black music in the United States, although they actually contain aspects of both black and white musical styles. Spirituals should be sung in a flexible rhythmic style that permits the full emotional impact of the song. Pay particular attention to the alternating solo-chorus (call-and-response) style of performance, a very common African method of musical performance. Also notice the pentatonic (five-tone) organization of the melody:

2. Listen to "Jumpin' at the Woodside" performed by Count Basie. This type of jazz, known as *swing*, differs from Dixieland in its use of a larger ensemble consisting of families of instruments: Instead of just one of each instrument, there are multiple trumpets, trombones, saxophones, and percussion instruments. With the larger ensemble, it became necessary to have written arrangements in swing jazz. Swing often contains an interesting mixture of European and African traits. Large numbers of instruments playing together with written arrangements and a strongly harmonic musical style are European traits. Some prominent African traits in the music include the pulsating, driving beat, the use of ostinato, and the short phrases passed among instruments in call-and-response form.

3. As students listen to the music, have them follow the outline:

   a. Piano plays "up and down" scale figures; repeats four times; strong, pulsating beat

   b. Full orchestra—short melodic figures passed among instruments in call-and-response form

   c. Saxophone solo with orchestral accompaniment

d. Full orchestra—short melodic figures passed among instruments in call-and-response form

e. Piano solo

f. Full orchestra—short melodic figures passed among instruments in call-and-response form

g. Trumpet solo with orchestral accompaniment

h. Saxophone solo with orchestral accompaniment

i. Clarinet and muted trumpet pass short melodic figures back and forth

j. Clarinet and saxophone improvise and pass melodic figures back and forth

4. Have students sing the African song "Kye, Kye Kule" (page 403) and compare the short phrases passed back and forth in call-and-response form in this selection to the same characteristic found in "Jumpin' at the Woodside."

5. Listen to the gospel composition "Don't Knock." Gospel is one of the most important contemporary African American musical styles. It is performed by a choir with instrumental accompaniment. In this selection follow the ABACA form, in particular noting the call-and-response style in section A.

Assessment

Briefly discuss characteristics of African American music you have learned in this lesson.

PULSATING BEAT, OSTINATO, SYNCOPATION

Grades: 2–5

Objectives

Students will:

1. Sing the song "Twa-Mu-Sanga" (page 404), following the steady, pulsating beat and the repeated melodic/rhythmic phrases (ostinato).

2. Listen to a steel drum ensemble from Trinidad and identify both African and Euro-American traits in the music (African—strong, pulsating beat and short, repetitive phrases [ostinato]; Euro-American—orchestra made up of families of soprano, alto, tenor, and bass instruments).

3. Listen to the jazz composition "Take Five" and follow the steady, pulsating beat, the repeated melodic/rhythmic phrases (ostinato), and the 5/4 meter, and identify the use of syncopation.

Materials

■ Recordings of "High Life" (*Steel Band/Trinidad: The Sound of the Sun,* Elektra/Nonesuch, 72016), Dave Brubeck's "Take Five" (Columbia CD CK 40585), and "Nursery Rhymes" (*Rap Rhymes! Mother Goose on the Loose,* Epic CD, EK 48986)

Procedures

1. Have students sing the African song "Twa-Mu-Sanga." They should clap the steady, pulsating beat as they sing. They can follow the repeated melodic/rhythmic phrases (ostinato) by moving their arms back and forth in the air.

2. Play the steel drum selection "High Life." Steel drums are fashioned from oil drums. Dents are made in the tops of the drums to produce different notes. Today steel drums are designed in a great variety of sizes that are arranged, like a Western orchestra, with soprano instruments ("Ping Pong"), alto instruments ("Guitar Pan"), tenor instruments ("Cello Pan"), and bass instruments ("Boom"). Ensembles can also include other instruments such as rattles (gourds filled with seeds). The title of this selection is derived from African popular music with the same name. Review the following African characteristics in this music:

   a. Strong pulsating beat; have students follow the beat by clapping their hands or tapping the top of their desks with pencils.

   b. Use of ostinato:

   Have students clap this rhythm over and over, first without the music, then as they listen to the music. Call attention to the short, repetitive phrases.

3. Play "Take Five" performed by the Dave Brubeck Quartet.

4. Identify the instruments in the quartet (piano, saxophone, string bass, and drums).

5. Follow the strong, pulsating beat by counting the 5/4 meter and clapping on beats 1 and 4:

6. Clap the repeating ostinato figure. Particularly notice the use of syncopation:

7. Ask students how the saxophone improvises over the repeating ostinato figure (for example, "scoops" and "slides" in the melody).

8. Listen to the rap composition entitled "Nursery Rhymes." Rap, which began in the 1980s, is one of the newest African American musical styles. It features a speaking style of delivery usually with musical accompaniment of electronic "samples" or by guitars and drums. In this selection first listen to the words of the "nursery rhymes." Then focus on African American musical traits, including the strong beat, the syncopation, and the steady, repetitive rhythm.

Assessment

Briefly discuss some of the characteristics of African American music you have learned in this lesson.

For Your Journal

In your journal or portfolio, make a section on integrating music with a study of peoples, places, and cultures. Include the following:

- Why is it important for teachers to present music from a variety of cultures?

- What are some sources in the school and community that a teacher might draw on for planning units of study (including music) on various cultures?

- How would you go about planning a bulletin board around the theme of studying the musics of other cultures?

- Include some specific examples of how you might combine music with social studies and language arts units in studying other cultures.

- How might you as the classroom teacher collaborate with the art teacher, the music teacher, and the physical education teacher to study other cultures?

- What are some ideas you have for planning a multicultural or international festival for your school?

Experiences with Music and Other Arts

THIS CHAPTER IS DEVOTED TO EXPLORING WAYS of combining the study of music with that of other art forms. It is clear that the visual, literary, and musical arts each provide distinct ways for achieving aesthetic experiences. For example, in the visual arts of architecture, sculpture, and painting, ideas and feelings are expressed through such elements as color, line, texture, volume, perspective, and form. It is the skill with which artists manipulate these elements within their choice of media (such as marble, wood, steel, and plate glass in architecture and sculpture; watercolors, oils, fresco, mosaic, and egg tempera in painting) that determines the expressiveness and meaning in a work of art. In the literary arts, writers express ideas and feelings by using words, both for their meaning and for their sound. They use such elements of literature as grammar, figures of speech, rhyme, rhythm, and form. In music, composers express ideas and feelings by organizing sounds in terms of melody, rhythm, texture, tone color, and form. In all of these arts, it is clear that a perception of basic elements is essential to understanding any single art medium.

Although it is evident that music, painting, sculpture, and poetry are separate and discrete art forms, it is possible to go beyond the perception of elements unique to a single art form and draw relationships among various art forms through understanding the characteristics that they share. For example, all art forms share the principles of enlargement through repetition, contrast, unity, and balance. Further, thematic, historical, and cultural ideas often inspire similar expressions in different art forms.

As a classroom teacher, you are in a unique position to help students interrelate their experiences in music with other areas of the school curriculum. Teachers can often enhance an experience with a particular musical artwork by showing students how some of its elements are shared by other art forms. Further, classroom teachers can help students understand how the arts are often closely allied with many other subject areas, such as history. In all experiences, the ultimate goal is to assist students in perceiving relationships among different modes of aesthetic experience and increasing their understanding of how and why the arts are so closely intertwined with people's lives.

There are many ways to organize a study of music and the arts. The sample lessons that follow center on four basic approaches: (1) an analogous-concepts approach; (2) a thematic approach; (3) a historical approach; and (4) a cross-cultural approach. The lessons are designed as a general guide and may need to be modified for use in various settings and with different interests and grade levels. Further, teachers are encouraged to develop other lessons based on the ideas presented here.

Using Analogous Concepts in Relating Music and the Arts

The analogous-concepts approach is based on studying concepts held in common among different art forms. These include such fundamental relationships as repetition and enlargement, contrast, sense of unity, and balance.

SUGGESTIONS FOR LESSONS

REPETITION AND ENLARGEMENT

Grades: 1–3

Objectives

Students will:

1. Create a visual picture that can be enlarged through repetition.

2. Examine poems that feature repetition and create a poem that shows enlargement through repetition.

3. Lengthen a song by repeating or adding verses or rhythm patterns.

4. Identify repetition as a means of enlargement in music and the visual and literary arts.

Materials

- ■ Construction-paper strips
- ■ Reproduction of Warhol's painting *Campbell Soup Cans*
- ■ Rhythm instruments
- ■ Poems: "I Saw a Fish Pond" and "There Was a Crooked Man"

Procedures

1. Create a paper chain by cutting out small strips of paper, forming loops, and linking and stapling them together. Students can make bracelets, necklaces, or even jump ropes by adding loops. Call attention to the use of repetition to enlarge or expand the chain.

2. Bring a Slinky to class and ask students to make a large shape by expanding the Slinky. (Be sure not to stretch it too much or it will not return to its original shape.) Ask students what is repeated to make the large shape (metal circles).

3. Select one student to be a leader. Have other students line up one at a time behind the leader. Notice how the line becomes longer (expands, enlarges).

4. Ask students to bring in soup cans and build a picture or shape based on repetition of these cans.

5. Show students a picture of Andy Warhol's *Campbell Soup Cans.* Discuss how one can build by repeating an idea.

Andy Warhol's **Campbell Soup Cans**

6. Read the nursery rhyme "I Saw a Fish Pond." Call attention to the repetition of the phrase *I saw.*

I Saw a Fish Pond

I saw a fishpond all on fire
I saw a house bow to a squire
I saw a parson twelve feet high
I saw a cottage near the sky
I saw a balloon made of lead
I saw a coffin drop down dead
I saw two sparrows run a race
I saw two horses making lace
I saw a girl just like a cat
I saw a kitten wear a hat
I saw a man who saw these too
And said though strange they all were true.

7. Read the following nursery rhyme and identify the words that are repeated.

There Was a Crooked Man

There was a crooked man, and he went a crooked mile;
He found a crooked sixpence against a crooked stile;
He bought a crooked cat, which caught a crooked mouse,
And all lived together in a little crooked house.

8. Perform "If You're Happy" (page 139). Notice that the song is lengthened by adding verses.

9. Play a simple ostinato pattern on a percussion instrument as students sing "If You're Happy." Note the repetition of the rhythm pattern. You can use this rhythm as an introduction and ending (coda):

10. Play "Tue, Tue" (page 406), an African folk song. Identify the words that are repeated and count the number of times.

Assessment

1. Ask students to identify ways an artist repeats ideas in music, visual art, and poetry.

2. Ask students how repetition can make a work of art larger (or longer).

The Roman Colosseum

MORE REPETITION AND ENLARGEMENT

Grades: 4–6

Objectives

Students will:

1. Identify repetition as a means of enlargement in music, visual art, and poetry.

2. Create a music composition, a visual artwork, and a poem that show enlargement through repetition.

3. Identify repetition in music, visual art, and poetry as a technique in creating a mood or expressing feelings.

Materials

■ Pictures: Vasarely, *Vonal Ksz**

■ Poems: Armour, "Money"; and Reeves, "Slowly"

■ Recording: Ravel, *Bolero*

Procedures

1. Show the picture *Vonal Ksz* by Vasarely. Discuss the various optical illusions created by the repeated rectangles—for example, curved line, looking into a tunnel, looking down into a well.

2. Show students a side view of the Roman Colosseum or the Pisa Cathedral. Ask them to look for repeated lines or shapes (rounded arch, Greek columns). Also ask them to point out how the building is made larger by such repetition.

3. Have students create their own pictures by making use of enlargement through repeating lines, shapes, colors, and so on.

---

* See H. H. Arnason, *History of Modern Art*, 3rd ed. (New York: Harry N. Abrams, 1986), p. 617.

4. Read the following poems and identify the poets' use of repetition. What is its effect?

*Money**

Workers earn it,
Spendthrifts burn it,
Bankers lend it,
Women spend it,
Forgers fake it,
Taxes take it,
Dying leave it,
Heirs receive it,
Thrifty save it,
Misers crave it,
Robbers seize it,
Rich increase it,
Gamblers lose it . . .
I could use it.

Slowly†

Slowly the tide creeps up the sand,
Slowly the shadows cross the land,
Slowly the cart-horse pulls his miles,
Slowly the old man mounts the stile.

Slowly the hands move round the clock,
Slowly the dew dries on the dock.
Slow is the snail—but the slowest of all
The green moss spreads on the old brick wall.

5. Have students make up poems based on enlargement/expansion through repetition.

6. Have students sing "Row, Row, Row Your Boat" (page 68) as a round, first as two-part, then as three-part, and finally as four-part.

    a. Put the following diagram on the board, illustrating the beginning of the singing of the four-part round:

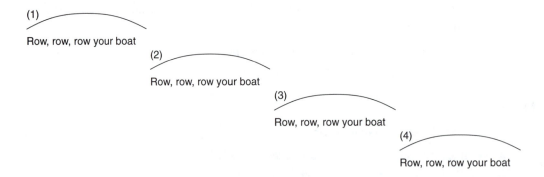

(1)
Row, row, row your boat

(2)
Row, row, row your boat

(3)
Row, row, row your boat

(4)
Row, row, row your boat

    b. Call attention to the organizational principle of enlargement/expansion through repetition.

7. Play a recording of Ravel's *Bolero*. During the first two minutes of the piece, have students softly play the following triple-meter pattern:

$$\frac{3}{4}$$

1	2	3
Drum	Tambourine shake	Tambourine shake

---

* From Richard Armour, *An Armoury of Light Verse*, © Branden Publishing Company. Reprinted by permission of Branden Publishing Company.

† © James Reeves from *Complete Poems for Children* (Heinemann) by James Reeves. Reprinted by permission of the James Reeves Estate.

Have the rest of the class clap the underlying rhythmic motif that repeats throughout the piece:

Assessment

Ask students how moods or feelings can be created through the use of repetition.

CONTRAST

Grades: 1–3

Objectives

Students will:

1. Identify characteristics of contrast in music, visual art, and poetry.

2. Create a sound composition in ABA form for each of the following: dynamics (loud/soft) and tempo (fast/slow).

Materials

- Pictures: Vasarely, *Orion MC*; Miro, *The Moon**; photographs of stained-glass windows at Chartres Cathedral
- Poem: Behn, "This Happy Day"
- Percussion instruments, word cards, colored letters, chalkboard
- Recording: Saint-Saëns, *Carnival of the Animals*

Procedures

1. Place the word *contrast* in different colors on a flannelboard. Emphasize that the word *contrast* refers to things that are different. Have letters cut in different colors, sizes, and shapes. Ask students to create various arrangements of the word on the board.

2. Explore contrast by having the students print their names in at least six different ways (using different sizes, shapes, colors, and so on).

3. Inflate several balloons of varying sizes and colors and arrange them in highly contrasting ways.

4. Ask the students to look for contrast in paintings such as Victor Vasarely's *Orion MC*, Joan Miro's *The Moon*, or stained-glass windows from the Cathedral of Notre Dame at Chartres, France. (They should find contrast in colors, sizes, and shapes.)

5. Encourage students to create their own pictures, making use of contrast in colors, shapes, lines, sizes, and so on.

---

* See Gaston Diehl, *Miro* (New York: Crown, 1979, 1988), p. 71.

Private collection

Victor Vasarely, Orion MC

6. Read the poem "This Happy Day" by Harry Behn and discuss how the poet uses contrast to express his idea of morning and night. What is repeated, and what is different?

This Happy Day*

Every morning when the sun
Comes smiling up on everyone,
It's lots of fun
To say good morning to the sun.
    Good morning, Sun!

Every evening after play
When the sunshine goes away,
It's nice to say,
Thank you for this happy day,
    This happy day!

7. Perform the song "Tinga Layo" (page 94). Use metal percussion instruments to accompany the verse and wooden percussion instruments to accompany the chorus. Discuss how these are "contrasting" sections.

8. Play selections from *Carnival of the Animals* by Saint-Saëns and use cards with words to describe the sounds or expressiveness of various animals (for example, elephant—slow; birds—high and fast).

Assessment

1. Ask students how contrast was used to add interest to selected examples.

2. Create a short rhythm composition in ABA form (twelve measures), in which section B is different (contrasting).

3. Using your composition, experiment with contrasting instruments, contrasting dynamics, and so on.

---

* From *The Little Hill, Poems and Pictures* by Harry Behn. Copyright 1949 by Harry Behn. Copyright renewed 1977 by Alice L. Behn. Reprinted by permission of Marian Reiner.

MORE CONTRAST

Grades: 4–6

Objectives

Students will:

1. Identify characteristics of contrast in music, visual art, and poetry.

2. Create a sound composition in ABA form for each of the following: (a) dynamics (loud, soft); (b) tempo (fast/slow); (c) tessitura (high/low); and (d) texture (thick/thin)

Materials

- Different kinds of balls
- The word *contrast* in different sizes, shapes, and colors
- Rhythm instruments
- Poem: Tippett, "Trucks"
- Pictures: Vasarely, *Orion MC;* or Mondrian, *Broadway Boogie Woogie**
- Recording: Ravel, *Bolero*

Procedures

1. Ask half the class to shout "School's out!" and the other half to whisper "School's out." Discuss the difference (include not only loud and soft but also the vocal mechanisms involved, such as shouting and whispering).

2. Show various kinds of balls, such as a football, basketball, tennis ball, and Ping Pong ball. Discuss how they are different.

3. Place the word *contrast* in many shapes and colors on a chalkboard.

4. Play the following rhythm and ask individual students to respond with a contrasting rhythm in the same meter signature:

Create several different rhythms that contrast with one another. Play these rhythms on contrasting rhythm instruments or sing them at different pitch levels.

5. Ask students to look for contrast in paintings such as Vasarely's *Orion MC* or Mondrian's *Broadway Boogie Woogie.* Ask them to identify contrast in clothing, comic books, textbooks, and magazines.

6. Ask students to look for ways in which contrast is achieved in Tippett's poem "Trucks" (such as contrast in rhyme scheme—ABCB—and in word sounds: *big, rumbling, heavily, little, turning, rushing*).

---

* See H. H. Arnason, *History of Modern Art,* 3rd ed. (New York: Harry N. Abrams, 1986), p. 384.

Trucks*

Big trucks for steel beams
Big trucks for coal,
Rumbling down the broad streets,
Heavily they roll.

Little trucks for groceries
Little trucks for bread,
Turning into every street,
Rushing on ahead.

Big trucks, little trucks,
In never ending lines,
Rumble on and rush ahead
While I read their signs.

7. Play selections from Ravel's *Bolero* and discuss how the composer creates interest through contrast while at the same time repeating the melody and rhythm.

Assessment

1. Ask students to identify how a composer may use contrast in a musical composition to express an idea, mood, or feeling.

2. Create an ABA musical composition using bells, xylophone, or percussion instruments.

UNITY

Unity refers to the process of tying an artwork together through systematically repeating certain elements.

Grades: 5–6

Objectives

Students will:

1. Identify how unity is created in music and in the visual and literary arts.

2. Create artworks that illustrate the concept of unity.

Materials

■ Pictures: Roman Colosseum, Pisa Cathedral; Mondrian, *Broadway Boogie Woogie;* Vasarely, *Orion MC*

■ Recordings: "Spring" from Vivaldi's *The Seasons;* Rondo from Mozart's *Eine Kleine Nachtmusik*

---

* Edna Johnson et al., *Anthology of Children's Literature,* 5th ed. © 1977. By permission of Houghton Mifflin Co.

Procedures

1. Reread the poem "Money" (page 456).

2. Ask students how the word *it* ties the poem together.

3. Call attention to the use of the same number of syllables in the second word of each line *(earn, burn, lend, spend, take, fake).*

4. Ask students which words rhyme, and what effect this technique has on the poem.

5. Have the class create a short poem in which a word or words are repeated to tie the work together and provide a sense of unity.

6. Show pictures of the Roman Colosseum, the Pisa Cathedral, Mondrian's *Broadway Boogie Woogie,* and Vasarely's *Orion MC.* Discuss how items are repeated to provide a sense of unity in these structures and artworks.

7. Have students create their own examples of visual art using repetition of items (shapes, colors, textures, and so on) to provide unity.

8. Listen to "Spring" from Vivaldi's *The Seasons.* This musical work is tied together by repeating the opening section throughout the composition. Follow the chart:

Listening Guide for Vivaldi's **The Seasons**

Section A:	Vigorous, joyful melody—spring has arrived
Section B:	Twittering of birds suggested by high trills in violins
Section A:	Return of a portion of the melody from beginning of piece
Section C:	Gentle breezes and lazy streams of water portrayed by soft, lyrical music
Section A:	Return of a portion of the melody from beginning of piece
Section D:	The sky begins to turn black, and thunder and lightning signal an approaching storm; vividly portrayed by low quivering string sounds followed by passages that sweep upward
Section A:	Return of a portion of the melody from beginning of piece
Section E:	Storm is now over and birds begin to sing, again portrayed by trills and embellishments on violins
Section A:	Return of melody from beginning of piece

9. Ask students to create a listening guide by using red strips of construction paper to indicate the main theme in the Rondo from Mozart's *Eine Kleine Nachtmusik.* Discuss how the repetition of the main theme provides unity to the composition.

Assessment

1. Have students look at various artworks and identify unifying principles.

2. Ask students to identify techniques used by composers to unify their works.

3. Read poems of your choice and discuss how the poet unifies his or her work.

BALANCE

Grades: 5–6

Objectives

Students will:

1. Identify balance in music and in the visual and literary arts.

2. Create artworks that illustrate the concept of balance.

Materials

- Geometric figures (square, circle)

- Red construction paper

- Rhythm pattern chart

- Nursery rhyme: "The Goblin"

- Pictures: Taj Mahal; da Vinci, *The Last Supper*

- Recording of the Rondo from Mozart, *Eine Kleine Nachtmusik*

Procedures

1. Have students balance on one foot, as an ice skater might do, with arms extended in a "swan" position.

2. Have students cut out geometrical figures (square and circle, for example) and place them on a bulletin board so that the square represents a fulcrum and the two circles represent equal weights on each end:

   ![diagram: A — B — A on a fulcrum]

3. Place the following rhythm pattern on the board. Clap the pattern with the class. Ask students to discover balance in the rhythm pattern:

4. Have students read the nursery rhyme "The Goblin" and discover balance (opening words are repeated at end to make an ABA design); compare this structure to the ABA rhythm pattern.

Taj Mahal, Agra, India

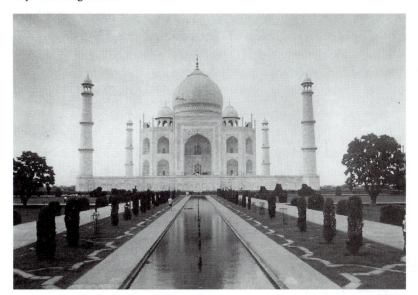

*The Goblin**

A goblin lives in *our* house, in *our* house, in *our* house,
A goblin lives in *our* house all the year round.
He bumps
And he jumps
And he thumps
And he stumps.
He knocks
And he rocks
And he rattles at the locks.
A goblin lives in *our* house, in *our* house, in *our* house,
A goblin lives in *our* house all the year round.

5. Show the students pictures of the Taj Mahal (Agra, India) and *The Last Supper* by Leonardo da Vinci; ask them to identify how balance is achieved in these artworks.

   a. da Vinci: *The Last Supper*

      ■ Christ is the center, with six apostles on either side

      ■ Large window behind Christ has two small windows, one on each side

      ■ Wall area behind apostles has equal sides of wall on left and right

      ■ Table in front of apostles has a center area with equally proportioned sections on either side

   b. Taj Mahal, Agra, India

      ■ Dome area in center has equal portions of building on either side

      ■ Two minarets are on either side of the building

      ■ Large, ogive-shaped door and window opening in center with smaller ogive-shaped window openings on either side

---

* Adapted from *Sugar and Spice*. Edited by Rose Ryleman. Reprinted by permission of Western Publishing Company, Inc.

6. Sing "We Wish You a Merry Christmas" (page 73). Ask students if they hear the same melody in several places in the song (first eight measures and last eight measures). Cut out different geometrical shapes in several colors of construction paper. Place an *A* on two pieces of paper with the same shape and color, and a *B* on a contrasting shape and color. Have students place the construction-paper diagrams on a chalkboard to indicate the form of the piece.

Assessment

1. Ask students to identify techniques used by poets, visual artists, and composers to balance their works of art. Find other songs that show balance.

2. Create a musical composition, poem, or work of visual art that shows balance.

Using a Thematic Approach in Relating Music and the Arts

One of the most frequently used approaches to relating music and other arts is through a common theme. Visual artists, writers, and musicians use a large number of themes in their works, including religion, love, war, freedom, people, machines, nature, stillness, and activity. In organizing units of study in a thematic approach, the intent is to discover how musicians, painters, and poets have been able to express a particular theme using materials that are unique to their art (e.g., sounds in music, words in poetry, and paint in visual art).

In this section suggestions for lessons provide opportunities to explore: (1) the portrayal of nature, (2) the portrayal of stillness, and (3) the portrayal of activity.

SUGGESTIONS FOR LESSONS

NATURE

Grades: 4–6

Objectives

Students will:

1. Identify phenomena of nature, such as storms, flowers, sunrise, sunset, and waterfalls.

2. Identify how nature themes are portrayed in selected examples of music, poetry, and visual arts.

3. Create original works of music, visual art, and poetry that focus on themes of nature.

New York State Historical Association, Cooperstown

Edward Hicks, The Peaceable Kingdom

Materials

- Pictures: Durand, *Scene from Thanatopsis;* Hicks, *The Peaceable Kingdom*
- Poems: Wordsworth, "I Wandered Lonely as a Cloud"; Keats, "On the Grasshopper and Cricket"; Japanese haiku, "Snow Fell Until Dawn"
- Rhythm instruments
- Recordings: Beethoven, "The Storm," Symphony No. 6 (fourth movement); Smetana, *The Moldau;* Britten, "In Freezing Winter Night" from *Ceremony of Carols*

Procedures

(May need to be over several days.)

1. Lead a short discussion on ways we experience nature every day (walk past trees on way to school, see and hear birds, watch fish swim in a pond, and so on).

2. Make a bulletin board titled "Nature." Look for pictures of landscapes, trees, birds, and animals.

3. Show students pictures of Asher Durand's *Scene from Thanatopsis* and Edward Hicks's *The Peaceable Kingdom* and ask them to find evidences of nature in the paintings (river, hills, trees, animals, and so on). Ask students to look for other examples of paintings that have a nature theme.

4. Have students create pictures on themes of nature, such as sunrise, sunset, and waterfall.

The Metropolitan Museum of Art, gift of J. Pierpont Morgan, 1911

Asher B. Durand, **Scene from Thanatopsis**
(formerly known as **Imaginary Landscape***)*

5. Read the following poems. Discuss how the writers portray nature (descriptive words).

a. "I Wandered Lonely as a Cloud," by William Wordsworth. (References to nature: cloud that floats, vales and hills, a host of golden daffodils, lake, trees, breeze, stars that shine and twinkle on the milky way, bay, waves beside them danced, sparkling waves.)

I Wandered Lonely as a Cloud

I wandered lonely as a cloud
    That floats on high o'er vales and hills,
When all at once I saw a crowd,
    A host, of golden daffodils.
Beside the lake, beneath the trees,
    Fluttering and dancing in the breeze.

Continuous as the stars that shine
    And twinkle on the milky way,
They stretched in never-ending line
    Along the margin of a bay:
Ten thousand saw I at a glance,
    Tossing their heads in sprightly dance.

The waves beside them danced, but they
    Outdid the sparkling waves in glee:
A poet could not but be gay,
    In such a jocund company.
I gazed—and gazed—but little thought
    What wealth the show to me had brought:

For oft, when on my couch I lie
    In vacant or in pensive mood,
They flash upon that inward eye
    Which is the bliss of solitude;
And then my heart with pleasure fills,
    And dances with the daffodils.

b. "On the Grasshopper and Cricket," by John Keats. (References to nature: birds, hot sun, cooling trees, hedge, mead, grasshopper, weed, frost, cricket, grassy hills.)

On the Grasshopper and Cricket

The poetry of earth is never dead:
When all the birds are faint with the hot sun,
And hide in cooling trees, a voice will run
From hedge to hedge about the new-mown mead;
That is the Grasshopper's—he takes the lead
In summer luxury—he has never done
With his delights; for when tired out with fun
He rests at ease beneath some pleasant weed.

The poetry of earth is ceasing never:
On a lone winter evening, when the frost
Has wrought a silence, from the stove there shrills
The Cricket's song, in warmth increasing ever,
And seems to one in drowsiness half lost,
The Grasshopper's among some grassy hills.

c. "Snow Fell Until Dawn," Japanese haiku.* (References to nature: snow, twig, grove, sunlight.)

Snow fell until dawn
now every twig in the grove
glitters in sunlight

6. Ask students to compose their own poetry (no more than four lines) based on themes of nature.

7. Ask students to create some of their own examples of music focusing on a theme or themes of nature. For example, using rhythm instruments, they might create a score that expresses the approach, arrival, and departure of a storm.

8. Ask students to listen to the following musical compositions portraying themes of nature and identify what the composer does.

a. Beethoven, Symphony No. 6, movement 4, "The Storm": (1) As the piece begins, the low stringed instruments depict the rumbling of thunder in the distance. (2) The music gets louder and louder, leading to explosive fortissimo sounds portraying thunder and lightning, which are now close. (3) Timpani and brass instruments add to the musical depiction of the fury of the storm. (4) As the movement ends, the storm subsides and the music becomes soft and tranquil.

b. Smetana, *The Moldau:* This composition is a symphonic poem that tells the story of a famous river, the Moldau, which runs through the country of Bohemia (now Czechoslovakia). Follow the "musical trip" of the river: (1) In the shade of the Bohemian forest, two springs bubble, their waves rippling over rocks to form a brook. Active, rippling passages in the woodwinds depict the movement of the water. (2) As the brook winds through the Bohemian countryside, it gradually grows into a mighty river, the Moldau. A long, smooth melody played by the stringed

---

* From *Cricket Songs: Japanese Haiku*, translated by Harry Behn. © 1964 by Harry Behn. © Renewed 1992 Prescott Behn, Pamela Behn Adam, and Peter Behn. Reprinted by permission of Marian Reiner.

instruments portrays the Moldau. (3) The Moldau flows through dense forests in which the sounds of hunting horns, aptly portrayed by brass instruments, are heard. (4) The river flows through a meadow, where a peasant wedding is being celebrated with jubilant dancing. The orchestra plays dance music in 3/4 meter. (5) As night falls, the river flows quietly in mysterious stillness as the moonlight sweeps over its surface. Fortresses and castles, projecting skyward on the surrounding slopes, remain as mute witnesses of the bygone glories and splendors of knighthood. This section is portrayed by slow, soft, lyrical music. (6) Daybreak comes and the Moldau, again depicted by the long flowing melody in the stringed instruments, flows onward through a valley. (7) The river now passes through a rough, rocky area, depicted by loud, turbulent sounds in the orchestra. (8) As the rocky area is passed, the river again flows in majestic peace (portrayed by flowing, lyrical melody) toward Prague (the capital of Czechoslovakia), where it passes another ancient fortress, afterward disappearing beyond the poet's sight.

    c. "In Freezing Winter Night," from *Ceremony of Carols* by Benjamin Britten: Notice the dissonance and repetition of both harp accompaniment and melodies.

Assessment

1. Ask students to identify techniques used by artists to portray events in nature (storm, river, winter).

2. Create a musical composition, poem, or work of visual art that focuses on some aspect of nature.

STILLNESS

Stillness is a state of quietness and calm. The word has many synonyms: *subdued, hushed, peaceful, silent, tranquil, serene.* In artworks a sense of stillness can be achieved in a number of ways: muted colors, horizontal lines, descriptive words *(whisper, sleep)*, soft dynamic levels, slow tempos, and so on.

Grades: 2–3

Objectives
Students will:

1. Identify how stillness is achieved in selected examples of music, visual art, and literature.

2. Create their own artworks portraying stillness.

Materials

- Pictures: Miro, *Blue III;* Tohaku, *Pine Trees in Snow*
- Poems: Livingston, "Whispers"; Sandburg, "Fog"; de la Mare, "Silver"
- Handout: Listening guide for "Ave Maria"
- Recordings: *Gregorian Chant,* Sony Classical CD, SK 53899, track 1; "Shika no Tome" ("Deer Calling to Each Other in the Distance") from *Music for Shakuhachi,* Elektra/Nonesuch 72076; Ives, "Serenity" from *Charles Ives Songs,* vol. 2, Smithsonian Folkways Records, 3345 [CD or cassette], 800-410-9815)
- Classroom instruments

Procedures

(May need to be over several days.)

1. Have students sit perfectly still for one minute and then describe how they feel. Ask for ideas about what causes stillness and quietness.

2. Find pictures of things that are still. Find words that describe things that are still, such as *sleep, quiet, slow, mist,* and *darkness.*

3. Read the following poems with the class, focusing on how the writer has achieved a sense of stillness.

   a. "Whispers" by Myra Cohn Livingston: Call attention to the word *whispers,* which is repeated several times.

   ### Whispers*

   Whispers
      tickle through your ear
      telling things you like to hear.
   Whispers
      are as soft as skin
      letting little words curl in.
   Whispers
      come so they can blow
      secrets others never know.

   b. "Fog" by Carl Sandburg:

   ### Fog†

   The fog comes
   on little cat feet.
   It sits looking
   over harbor and city
   on silent haunches
   and then moves on.

---

* From *Whispers and Other Poems* by Myra Cohn Livingston. © 1958 by Myra Cohn Livingston. © Renewed 1986 by Myra Cohn Livingston. Reprinted by permission of Marian Reiner for the author.

† Excerpt from *Chicago Poems* by Carl Sandburg. Reprinted by permission of Harcourt Brace & Company, Inc.

c. "Silver" by Walter de la Mare: Call attention to the use of the words *slowly, silently, sleeps,* and *moveless;* notice the use of alliteration with many words beginning with *s,* a sound that conveys tranquillity.

Silver*

Slowly, silently, now the moon
Walks the night in her silver shoon;
This way, and that, she peers, and sees
Silver fruit upon silver trees;
One by one the casements catch
Her beams beneath the silvery thatch;
Couched in his kennel, like a log,
With paws of silver sleeps the dog;
From their shadowy cote the white breasts peep
Of doves in a silver-feathered sleep;
A harvest mouse goes scampering by,
With silver claws, and silver eye;
And moveless fish in the water gleam,
By silver reeds in a silver stream.

4. Ask students to write their own poems or phrases using words that create a sense of stillness.

5. Ask the class to draw pictures that convey a sense of stillness. Explore not only stillness as a theme for a picture but also ways for achieving the feeling of stillness or calmness (use of colors such as blue and green, which are more subdued than the active colors of red and orange; use of horizontal lines, and so on).

6. Show pictures of paintings that portray stillness and tranquillity.

a. *Blue III* by Joan Miro.† Ask the class how the elements of line, shape, and color are used in the painting to create a sense of stillness, quiet, and inactivity (open, unobstructed space; color blue; long, curvilinear line; round shapes).

b. *Pine Trees in Snow* by Tohaku.‡ Ask students to point out how the sense of stillness is created through delicate lines depicting this winter scene, by the areas left "open" in the painting, and by the use of subdued colors.

7. Listen to several selections of music that portray stillness and tranquillity.

a. "Ave Maria," Gregorian chant. Have students circle the elements on the listening guide below that help create the sense of stillness/calmness in the music:

(Smooth, stepwise melody)	or	Jagged melody with large skips
Strong beat	or	(Weak beat)
(Slow tempo)	or	Fast tempo
Loud dynamic level	or	(Soft dynamic level)

Discuss the setting of the music and why it needs to convey a sense of calm (performed as part of a religious service; quiet, serene atmosphere of a cathedral).

---

* Edna Johnson, et al., *Anthology of Children's Literature,* 5th ed. (Boston: Houghton Mifflin, 1977). By permission of The Literary Trustees of Walter de la Mare and The Society of Authors as their representative.

† See Gaston Diehl, *Miro* (New York: Crown, 1979, 1988), p. 72.

‡ See Penelope Mason, *History of Japanese Art* (New York: Harry N. Abrams, 1993), p. 267.

b. "Serenity," by Charles Ives. Notice how the sense of stillness and calmness is created in the music to express the text "the silence of eternity" (soft dynamic level, weak feeling for the beat, slow tempo).

c. "Deer Calling to Each Other in the Distance," as performed on the Japanese shakuhachi (wind instrument). Discuss how the soft dynamic level, the flexible rhythm, the slow tempo, the weak feeling for the beat, and the monophonic texture contribute to the sense of stillness, inactivity, and calm in the music.

8. Have students improvise with classroom instruments or their voices to convey a sense of stillness. Discuss how slow tempo, soft dynamic levels, smooth stepwise melodies, flexible rhythm, weak feeling for the beat, and so on help to create a sense of stillness or calm.

9. Ask students to make up movements that express the stillness of the music.

Assessment

1. Ask students to identify techniques used by artists to express stillness in works of art.

2. Ask students to create a musical composition, poem, or work of visual art that shows stillness.

ACTIVITY

Activity involves the state or condition of being energetic, lively, and vigorous.

Grades: 5–6

Objectives

Students will:

1. Describe how artists, poets, and musicians create a sense of activity in their works.

2. Create their own artworks that convey a sense of activity.

Materials

- Picture: Kandinsky, *Sketch I for Composition VII**
- Poem: Morrison, "The Sprinters"
- Recordings: Stravinsky, "Dance of the Adolescents" from *Rite of Spring;* Beethoven, "The Storm" from Symphony No. 6 (fourth movement)
- Handout: Listening guide for "Dance of the Adolescents"
- Classroom instruments

Procedures

(May need to be over several days.)

1. Lead a class discussion of ways in which students see activity in everyday life.

---

* See W. H. Janson, *History of Art,* 4th ed. (New York: Harry N. Abrams, 1991), p. 715.

2. Make a list on the board of words that convey a sense of action.

3. Read the poem "The Sprinters" by Lillian Morrison. Note the sense of action in words such as *explodes, pummeling, pistoning, fly, smash, outpace, runs, streaks, faster, shout, pound,* and *grace-driven stride.*

The Sprinters*

The gun explodes them.
Pummeling, pistoning they fly
In time's face.
A go at the limit
A terrible try
To smash the ticking glass,
Outpace the beat
That runs, that streaks away
Tireless, and faster than they.

Beside ourselves
(It is for us they run!)
We shout and pound the stands
For one to win
Loving him whose hard
Grace-driven stride
Most mocks the clock
And almost breaks the bands
Which lock us in.

4. Ask students to compose their own poems or phrases using action themes and words.

5. Ask students to draw pictures that convey a sense of action. Explore not only action themes (running, playing ball, skating) but also ways for achieving the feeling of action in a painting (sharp, jagged lines; use of active colors, such as red; juxtaposition of strongly contrasting colors).

6. Look for ways in which the sense of action is created in Kandinsky's *Sketch I for Composition VII*. Ask the students to discover what qualities in the painting create the feeling of vigor or activity (warm, active colors of red and orange; contrasts of colors; twisting, swirling lines; diagonal lines).

7. Play "Dance of the Adolescents" from Stravinsky's *Rite of Spring*.

   a. Ask students to listen for ways in which activity is created in the music by circling the correct items:

Weak beat	*or*	(Strong, pulsating beat)
(Strong accents)	*or*	No accents
(Loud dynamic level)	*or*	Soft dynamic level
Smooth, lyrical sounds	*or*	(Short, staccato sounds)
(Jagged, skipping melody)	*or*	Smooth, stepwise melody

   b. Ask the students to make up a set of movements that express the activity of "Dance of the Adolescents."

---

* From *The Ghosts of Jersey City,* T. Y. Crowell Co. Copyright © 1967 by Lillian Morrison.

8. Play "The Storm" from Beethoven's Symphony No. 6. Identify how activity is created by very loud dynamic levels, dramatic contrasts between loud and soft dynamic levels, and moderately fast tempo.

9. Have students improvise with classroom instruments or voices to convey a sense of activity. Discuss how loud dynamic levels, fast tempo, strong accentuation, syncopation, melodies with large skips, and so on help create a sense of action in sound.

Assessment

1. Ask students to identify techniques used by artists to express activity in works of art.

2. Ask students to create a musical composition, poem, or work of visual art that shows activity.

Using a Historical Approach in Relating Music and the Arts

An interesting approach to integrated learning experiences in the classroom involves art experiences that contribute to understanding our past. For example, students discover that events in a particular historical period, such as the American Revolution, are often reflected in sculpture, painting, and music. Through studying the arts in a historical context, students not only learn about aesthetic aspects of the arts but also develop a broader perspective on the people and events in an era.

In addition, dominant philosophical ideas in a period sometimes lead to similar events in different art forms. This is aptly reflected in the lesson The Age of the Knights (medieval period) that follows.

Classroom teachers will find that interaction with examples of architecture, sculpture, painting, literature, and music greatly enhances students' understanding of the past. In effect, multiart presentations help students go beyond the memorization of facts about peoples and places in a particular time period and experience an era through actual examples of its finest artistic products.

The following two lessons are given as sample presentations only; you can use them as models for designing lessons on other historical periods.

SUGGESTIONS FOR LESSONS

THE AGE OF THE KNIGHTS

The age of the knights occurred during the European medieval period, which spanned the years from approximately A.D. 500 to 1400. During this time the Catholic Church was one of the most dominant institutions in Europe, greatly influencing all aspects of life. Many great cathedrals were built throughout Europe. In the latter part of the medieval period, many huge castles were constructed, where kings lived along with their knights. These men often dressed in metal armor to protect themselves in battle.

Grades: 5–6

Objectives

Students will:

1. Identify characteristics of music and visual and literary arts of the European medieval period.

2. Identify how the visual and literary arts and music were closely allied with beliefs of Christianity during the medieval period.

Materials

- Pictures: Medieval cathedrals, such as Notre Dame in Paris, Notre Dame in Chartres, and Canterbury in England; stained-glass windows; diagram of cathedral floor plan; medieval castles; suits of armor; tapestries; map of England

- Stories: Mockler, *King Arthur and His Knights**; *King Arthur and His Knights Sound Recording*†; Chaucer, "The Friar," from the *Canterbury Tales*

- Recordings: *Gregorian Chant* (Sony Classical CD, SK 53899, track 1); motet "Ave Gloriosa Mater—Ave Virgo—Domino" (*A Treasury of Early Music,* vol. 1: Music of the Middle Ages, The Haydn Society [P.O. Box 2338, Hartford, CT], CD ST HSE 7-9100); *Songs and Dances of the Middle Ages,* Dorian Discovery CD, DIS 80109, track 6

- Handout: Listening guide for Gregorian chant

- Video or film: *Discovering the Music of the Middle Ages*‡

Procedures

(May need to be over several days.)

1. Show the students pictures of some of the cathedrals built during the medieval period: Notre Dame (Paris, France), Notre Dame (Chartres, France), and Canterbury (England).

   a. Call attention to the tall spires of the Chartres Cathedral. Ask students why people living during this period might have built such tall spires (to draw attention upward toward heaven).

   b. Show a diagram of the cross on which Jesus died. Call attention to the three upper points of the cross, representing the Trinity ("three") of the church: God as (1) Father, (2) Son, and (3) Holy Ghost. Look at a diagram of the floor plans of the cathedrals, noticing that they are laid out in the form of a cross.

   c. Look at the windows and doorways of the Chartres Cathedral, noticing that they were also built in threes.

   d. Show pictures of the stained-glass windows in the very tall walls of the cathedrals. Note that these pictures are about religious subjects: people from the Bible; rose window with its groups of twelves, representing the twelve disciples.

---

* Anthony Mockler, *King Arthur and His Knights* (New York: Oxford University Press, 1984).

† *King Arthur and His Knights Sound Recording,* as told by Jim Weiss (Benicia, Calif.: Greathall Productions, 1990).

‡ *Discovering the Music of the Middle Ages,* Barr Films, 1982 (available from Audio-Visual Services, Kent State University, P.O. Box 5190, Kent, OH 44242; 800-338-5718; *info@media.kent.edu.*

Medieval architecture

2. In conjunction with showing pictures of the Canterbury Cathedral, have the class plan a hypothetical trip from London to Canterbury. Put a map of England on the bulletin board and highlight the travel route. Discuss that during the medieval period a group of people traveled by foot to the town of Canterbury to see the cathedral and the archbishop. To pass the time on such a long trip, travelers often told stories. Read with the class several selections from the *Canterbury Tales* (such as "The Friar," about a priest who enjoyed having a good time!) by Geoffrey Chaucer, one of the most famous writers of the period.

3. Play recordings of some of the music performed in the church (Gregorian chant, "Ave Maria").

   a. Take the students on a hypothetical trip to a large cathedral during medieval times. Discuss what the mood is as one enters the great building (calm, quietness, peacefulness, tranquillity). Listen to the Gregorian chant. How does this music reflect the setting? Have students circle the appropriate items on the listening-guide handout as they listen to the music:

(Melody is smooth, stepwise)	*or*	Melody has many large skips
Strongly accented beat	*or*	(Weak feeling for the beat)
(One line of music)	*or*	Many lines of music
Women singing	*or*	(Men singing)
(Dynamics soft)	*or*	Dynamics loud

   b. Play the motet "Ave Gloriosa Mater—Ave Virgo—Domino." Note that there are three lines of music, two sung and one played on instruments:

   - Top line: Text, "Hail, Royal Virgin, Mother of Mercy . . ."

   - Middle line: "Hail, Glorious Mother of the Savior . . ."

   - Bottom line: Played on recorder (wind instrument) and viola da gamba (bowed stringed instrument)

   Clap the meter of the piece, noting that it is grouped in threes (triple), symbolizing the Holy Trinity.

4. Show students pictures of some of the great castles built during the medieval period. Discuss how these buildings were fortified to help protect their inhabitants against attack. Show pictures of the armored suits worn by men to protect themselves in battle. Also show pictures of some of the large, multicolored tapestries that were hung on the walls of the castle. Have the students make a bulletin board titled "Life in a Castle."

5. Read with the class stories about King Arthur and the Knights of the Roundtable.

6. Play a popular piece of dance music from the medieval period. Listen for the drum, the shawm (a double-reed instrument), and the recorder. Follow the fast tempo. Make up some dance movements to the music.

7. Show the video *Discovering the Music of the Middle Ages.* It contains selections of vocal and instrumental music. Included are wind instruments such as the krummhorn, recorder, sackbut, the portative organ, and the vielle, a stringed instrument.

8. Discuss contributions that artists of the medieval period have made to the world today. In your community look for examples of medieval-style architecture in churches and stained-glass windows.

THE AGE OF THE AMERICAN REVOLUTION

The age of the American Revolution occurred more than two hundred years ago. At that time the American colonies were seeking freedom from British control. Growing frustration with the British eventually led to the writing of the Declaration of Independence in 1776, which in turn set the stage for the Revolutionary War. In this conflict the thirteen colonies were pitted against the forces of the British Empire. Freedom became a major theme of the period.

During the eighteenth century, the people and arts of ancient Greece and Rome became sources of inspiration for the revolutionary spirit that was under way not only in the American colonies but also in Europe. Leaders such as Napoleon Bonaparte looked to the past for models and found them in such men as Alexander the Great and Julius Caesar. Napoleon, for example, used the eagles of the Roman legions for insignia in the French army and ultimately was crowned with the laurel wreath, an ancient symbol of fame. In the visual arts, Greek and Roman architectural and sculptural ideals greatly influenced innumerable artworks produced in the period.

Grades: 2–5

Objectives
Students will:

1. Design a bulletin board that will include examples of the arts and personalities of the eighteenth century.

2. Identify examples of visual arts from the eighteenth and early-nineteenth centuries and demonstrate an understanding of how they reflect the period.

3. Sing songs that center around themes and personalities related to freedom and independence.

4. Identify the classical qualities of music of eighteenth-century composers.

Materials

■ Pictures: George Washington, Thomas Jefferson, Benjamin Franklin, Wolfgang Amadeus Mozart, Franz Joseph Haydn; colonial Williamsburg; the British flag; Monticello; Trumbull, *The Declaration of Independence;* Greenough's sculpture *George Washington;* Houdon's sculptures of Franklin and Jefferson; Wedgewood pottery

■ Recordings: Mozart, "Ah vous dirai-je, Maman," K. 265 (Deutsche-Grammophone, CD-429808); Michael Haydn, *Toy Symphony,* first movement (Angel 35638)

■ Handout: Listening guide for "Ah vous dirai-je, Maman" (grades 4–5—words; grades 1–3—pictures)

■ Melody bells

Procedures

(May need to be over several days.)

1. Make a bulletin board; include pictures of some of the most outstanding personalities of the eighteenth century: George Washington, Thomas Jefferson, Benjamin Franklin, Wolfgang Amadeus Mozart, and/or Franz Joseph Haydn.

2. Show several pictures or slides of colonial Williamsburg, asking the students to describe how the buildings are different from those built today. Ask if anyone has seen buildings like these. Where? Are there any similar ones in your community? Show a picture of the British flag, which hung (and still hangs) over the capitol building, and ask the students why this flag would be flying in Williamsburg (Britain ruled the American colonies until the American Revolution in the eighteenth century).

The Brooklyn Museum: Dick S. Ramsay and Museum Purchase Funds

Gilbert Stuart, George Washington

3. Draw the students into a brief discussion about events that happened in this country around the year 1775. (Declaration of Independence, Revolutionary War)

4. Look at the painting *The Declaration of Independence* by John Trumbull. Do the students recognize any of the figures? (Benjamin Franklin, Thomas Jefferson, and John Hancock)

5. Read the first two paragraphs of the Declaration of Independence and identify the theme of the document. (emphasis on freedom)

Copyright Yale University Art Gallery

John Trumbull, **The Declaration of Independence**

6. The call for freedom in the Declaration of Independence rallied Americans in the thirteen colonies to go to war against the mighty British Empire. Have students sing the following song from the period to the tune of "America":

> God save the thirteen states,
> Long rule the United States
> God save our states,
> Make us victorious, happy and glorious,
> No tyrants over us
> God save our states.

7. Have students sing "Yankee Doodle," one of the most famous melodies of the period. Notice the reference to Washington, who would become commander of the Continental armies.

8. Show the class pictures of Monticello, Thomas Jefferson's home near Charlottesville, Virginia. Ask students to identify the influences of ancient Greek and Roman architecture: Greek columns (doric), Roman dome over center of building, emphasis on symmetry and balance. Explain that the eighteenth century was called the classical period because of the attention to ideas drawn from classical Greece and Rome. Have students look for pictures of Greek and Roman architecture and place them on the bulletin board beside depictions of Monticello.

9. Show students a picture of Horatio Greenough's sculpture of George Washington. Note that Greenough's Washington is patterned after an ancient Roman figure holding a toga, a one-piece cloth worn by Roman citizens in public. In addition, put on the bulletin

Yankee Doodle

Key: G
Starting pitch: D
Meter: 2/4, begins on "and" of 2

United States

1. O, fath-'r and I went down to camp a - long with Cap - tain Good' - in, And
2. And there we saw a thou - sand men as rich as Squire___ Da - vid, And
3. And there was Cap - tain Wash - ing - ton up - on a slap - ping stal - lion, A -

there we saw the men and boys as thick as hast - y pud - ding!
what they wast - ed ev - 'ry day, I wish it could be sav - ed.
giv - ing or - ders to his men; I guess there were a mil - lion.

Yan - kee Doo - dle, keep it up, Yan - kee Doo - dle Dan - dy.

Mind the mu - sic and the step, and with the girls be han - dy.

Monticello

board pictures of Houdon's sculptures of Franklin and Jefferson and of Wedgewood pottery, much of which was modeled after Greek artifacts (urns, for example).

10. Show a picture of Wolfgang Amadeus Mozart, the famous European musician who lived from 1756 to 1791. Explain that Mozart was considered a child prodigy and that at a very early age he played both the piano and violin. Compare the dress of Americans with that of Mozart. Note that the white powdered wigs, buckled shoes, and long dress were in style both in Europe and America. Discuss reasons for this (Americans had come from Europe seeking freedom here and had brought their culture and traditions with them).

11. Listen to a recording of Mozart's piano composition "Ah vous dirai-je, Maman," K. 265, better known as Variations on "Twinkle, Twinkle, Little Star."

The National Museum of American Art. Transfer from U.S. Capitol.

Horatio Greenough, George Washington

a. Sing and play on melody bells the tune "Twinkle, Twinkle, Little Star."

Twinkle, Twinkle, Little Star

Key: D
Starting pitch: C
Meter: 2/4, begins on 1

Nursery Rhyme

Twin - kle, twin - kle lit - tle star, How I won - der what you are

Up a - bove the world so high Like a dia - mond in the sky.

b. Hand out copies of the following outline to each student (grades 4–5). Play the recording and have students follow the variations and circle each variation number. In each variation encourage students to listen first for the tune and then for ways in which the tune is varied. If time permits, discuss how repeating the "Twinkle, Twinkle" melody unifies the musical composition and how the variations provide

First-grade children dramatizing life during the eighteenth century

contrast so that the piece will be more interesting. For grades 1–3, have students make up movements for each variation.

- *Variation 1:* Melody heard with running melodic line in the right hand
- *Variation 2:* Melody in right hand, running melodic line in left hand
- *Variation 3:* Melody heard in triplet (3's) figure
- *Variation 4:* Melody in right hand, triplets in left hand
- *Variation 5:* Melody with off-beat patterns
- *Variation 6:* Melody in right hand, running melodic line in left hand
- *Variation 7:* Melody heard in running scale patterns in right hand
- *Variation 8:* Melody heard in minor; use of imitation
- *Variation 9:* Melody presented in clear, staccato fashion
- *Variation 10:* Melody in right hand with accompaniment in left hand
- *Variation 11:* Melody in slow, lyrical presentation
- *Variation 12:* Melody in right hand with decoration
- *Variation 13:* Melody with many fast running notes.

12. Play a recording of the first movement of the *Toy Symphony* by Michael Haydn. This is a three-movement work (Allegro, Minuet, Finale [Allegro]) featuring toy instruments, such as one-note trumpet, rattle, triangle, and drum. Call attention to the lighthearted quality of the music and the different bird calls executed by the instruments (twittering of the nightingale and the descending minor third [G, E] of the cuckoo).

13. Ask students to summarize by making a list of some of the things they have learned in this lesson. Put the items on a bulletin board under a general topic heading such as "Eighteenth Century." Group the items into categories (political events, people, dress, music, and so on).

Using a Cross-Cultural Approach in Relating Music and the Arts

In the elementary school curriculum, students learn about other people of the world and the multicultural diversity of American society. They study the geography, history, customs, and beliefs of many peoples. One significant way to help students better understand other cultures is through an examination of the arts. Often basic tenets of a cultural tradition are reflected in the visual, literary, and aural arts.

Following is a suggested lesson on the arts of Japan. The intent of this lesson is to illustrate some fundamental ideas that help students better understand Japanese people. The lesson focuses on (1) the Japanese interest in being in harmony with nature, and (2) their interest in understatement and the achievement of maximum effect with minimal materials.

ARTS OF JAPAN

Grades: 4–6

Objectives

Students will:

1. Identify how the Japanese interest in the surrounding natural world is reflected in visual art, literature, and music.

2. Identify how the Japanese interest in understatement and the achievement of maximum effect with minimal materials is reflected in visual art, literature, and music.

Materials

- Pictures: Japanese countryside, gardens, and buildings (see *The Beauty of Japan**** and Sandoz and Morita, *Kyoto and Nara: The Soul of Japan*[†])

- Arts: see Mason, *History of Japanese Art*[‡]

- Recordings: "Isumi" (*Art of the Koto: The Music of Japan,* Electra Records, CD 70234); "Shika no Tome" ("Deer Calling to Each Other in the Distance," *Music for Shakuhachi,* Elektra-Nonesuch 72076)

- Video: *Discovering the Music of Japan* (available from West Music Co., P.O. Box 552, Coralville, IA 52241)

Procedures

(May need to be over several days.)

1. Ask students to make a bulletin board on Japan, highlighting the scenic natural beauty of the countryside. Discuss how such surroundings might affect the lives of people, particularly the works of painters, writers, and musicians.

---

* *The Beauty of Japan* (Tokyo: Gakken & Co., 1990).

† Philip Sandoz and Toshitaka Morita, *Kyoto and Nara: The Soul of Japan* (Rutland, Vt.: Charles E. Tuttle, 1994).

‡ Penelope Mason, *History of Japanese Art* (New York: Harry N. Abrams, 1993), pp. 267 (*Pine Trees in Snow*); 269 (*White Plum Trees*); and 187 (*Kinkaku [Golden Pavilion] at Kyoto*).

2. Show students pictures of Japanese buildings, calling attention to the emphasis on a natural setting. Notice that the outside surroundings of buildings are often developed into immaculately tailored gardens, which are artistically arranged with rocks, trees, flowers, and ponds to create a kind of microcosm of nature. Japanese buildings themselves often strongly reflect themes of nature. Many are constructed of wood with the natural look preserved through large numbers of unpainted surfaces. Within the buildings, many rooms have a *tokonoma,* a recessed area in the wall containing a print or scroll of a nature scene with a flower arrangement placed in front of it.

3. Show the class examples of Japanese arts: *Pine Trees in Snow, White Plum Trees,* and *Kinkaku (Golden Pavilion) at Kyoto.* Ask students to look for ways in which nature is depicted (pine trees, snow, white plum trees, water surrounding building).

4. Read the class the following Haiku poems.* Ask students to identify references to nature (mountain, skylark, snow, twig, grove, sunlight):

High on a Mountain we heard a skylark singing faintly, far below. — *Basho*	Snow fell until dawn Now every twig in the grove glitters in sunlight — *Rokwa*

5. Sing the song "Sakura" (page 419). Call attention to the references to nature in the words of the song: cherry blooms, flowering, wind, mist, clouds, air, cherry trees.

6. Listen to "Isumi" (A Spring), a composition played on the koto, a popular Japanese stringed instrument. Listen to the running lines of music, which attempt to depict a stream of water gushing from a mountainside.

7. Show the paintings again, calling attention to the manner in which Japanese artists seem to place emphasis on understatement and achievement of maximum effect with minimal materials. Note the emphasis on simplicity and detail. The pictures are composed of a number of delicately drawn lines, which are subtly manipulated to indicate depth and volume. Colors in the pictures seem to complement the delicacy, with their penchant toward subdued, pastel shades. Further, a large number of open-space areas contribute to a sense of understatement and simplicity.

8. Show some pictures of Japanese building interiors, noting how they seem to be directed toward simplicity. Much of the house's interior is left open and uncluttered by a lot of furnishings. The feeling of openness is enhanced by doors that slide back to expose large areas of the house. The walls of rooms are often constructed of simple, unpainted surfaces that are tastefully accented with paintings.

9. Read the haiku poetry again with the students. Call attention to the sense of simplicity and directness. The poems are very short, being composed of just three short lines arranged in groups of five, seven, and five syllables.

---

* From *Cricket Songs: Japanese Haiku,* translated by Harry Behn. © 1964 by Harry Behn. © Renewed 1992 Prescott Behn, Pamela Behn Adam, and Peter Behn. Reprinted by permission of Marian Reiner.

10. Play the recording of "Deer Calling to Each Other in the Distance," performed by two Japanese shakuhachi players. Notice how the sense of understatement is created by monophonic texture (just one line of music), slow tempo, flexible rhythm, and subtly executed ornaments.

11. Show the first two segments on koto and shakuhachi from the video *Discovering the Music of Japan*. Direct particular attention to the emphasis on nature and the sense of simplicity and understatement.

Planning and Presenting a Program

PURPOSE

Planning and presenting a program that integrates many different classroom activities such as music, visual art, language arts, history, geography, and physical education is a common expectation of the classroom teacher. Of course, cognitive learning takes place in the preparation of such a program, but social learning also occurs. For example, students develop responsibility, exercise creativity, exert leadership, and work together. Careful planning by both teacher and students is essential. A primary purpose of such an activity is for students to share with parents, relatives, and friends in the community what they have learned.

PLANNING

The entire class should be involved in the selection of the overall theme so that many activities and ideas can be related to it in meaningful ways. After students have selected a theme, they should begin gathering resource materials for the program. These should include songs, pictures, poems, essays, ideas for dramatic presentation, and so on. As with all such activities, the opening number of the program should be performed especially well and enthusiastically; each subsequent event must be selected with emphasis on variety and interest; and the conclusion should be an upbeat activity that leaves the audience excited about the program and what the students are learning. The following sample programs are for a fifth-grade class, with resources included for each.

REHEARSALS

Rehearsals must occur with enough care and frequency that *nothing* is left to chance. For a thirty-minute program, fifth-grade students would need a minimum of six weeks' preparation (twice a week), with a few more props and special effects added each week. Because this is an integrated program, all students should be involved in the planning and performance, with each student contributing his or her best musical talent and skill.

Program I: A Musical Horn of Plenty (Thanksgiving)

"America the Beautiful"

Introduction: Words of Welcome

Thanksgiving Poem:

Now Thank We All Our God

Now thank we all our God
With hearts and hands and voices,
Who wondrous things has done,
In whom his world rejoices
Who, from our mothers' arms
Has blest us on our way
With countless gifts of love,
And still is ours today.

O may this bounteous God
Through all our life be near us,
With ever joyful hearts
And blessed peace to cheer us,
And keep us in his grace,
And guide us when perplexed,
And free us from all harm
In this world and the next.

(Rinkhart, tr. Winkworth)

Introduction to Rondo

Trumpet Concerto in E-flat Major, Rondo .... Wolfgang A. Mozart

(movement interpretation: ABACA)

Introduction to Theme-and-Variation

Variations on "Simple Gifts" from *Appalachian Spring* .... Aaron Copland

(puppet interpretation)

"Tinga Layo"

(page 94; ostinato accompaniment: claves, bongo drums, maracas)

"Magic Penny"

(page 32; accompaniment: chords on resonator bells)

"Praise and Thanksgiving"

(three-part round)

Thanksgiving Poem: Psalm 150

Praise Ye the Lord

Praise ye the Lord.

Praise God in his sanctuary;
Praise him in the firmament of his power.

Praise him for his mighty acts;
Praise him according to his excellent greatness.

Praise him with the sound of the trumpets;
Praise him with the psaltery and harp.

Praise him with the timbrel and dance;
Praise him with stringed instruments and organs.

Praise him upon the loud cymbals;
Praise him upon the high sounding cymbals.

Let every thing that hath breath
Praise the Lord.

Praise ye the Lord.

"Oh, Be Joyful"

(page 124; descant: vocal; harmony: vocal and xylophone; instrumental interludes and
accompaniment: piano, guitar, xylophone, glockenspiel)
Closure: Words of Thanks and Appreciation

Program II: Liberty

"The Yankee Doodle Boy"

Introduction: Words of Welcome

The Meaning of Freedom (short essay)

How can we define liberty? What is freedom? For the people of East Berlin, 1989 was a time of freedom, when the wall separating East and West Berlin crumbled and people were allowed to move freely between the two sections of the divided city. It was a time when people of Eastern Europe began to experience freedom of choice for the first time. People throughout history have known the value of freedom and paid a price. Who were these people? What price did they pay? What were their rewards? The United States of America was founded on the concept of liberty. Ralph Waldo Emerson, an American poet, expressed the spirit of freedom when he wrote the *Concord Hymn,* first sung at the completion of the Battle Monument at Concord, Massachusetts, on July 4, 1837. This is what he wrote:

Concord Hymn
By the rude bridge that arched the flood,
    Their flag to April's breeze unfurled,
Here once the embattled farmers stood
    And fired the shot heard round the world.

The foe long since in silence slept;
    Alike the conqueror silent sleeps;
And Time the ruined bridge has swept
    Down the dark stream which seaward creeps.

On this green bank, by this soft stream,
    We set to-day a votive stone;
That memory may their deed redeem,
    When, like our sires, our sons are gone.

Spirit, that made those heroes dare
    To die, and leave their children free,
Bid Time and Nature gently spare
    The shaft we raise to them and thee.

(Ralph Waldo Emerson)

Yankee Doodle Boy

Key: G
Starting pitch: B
Meter: 2/4, begins on 1

Words and Music by George M. Cohan

Introduction to "There Are Many Flags in Many Lands"

The United States was founded on freedom from oppression—a nation composed of people from all cultures and religious beliefs, come together as Americans.

"There Are Many Flags"
(Tableau: four or five students with flags of several nations)

There Are Many Flags

Key: A♭
Starting pitch: A♭
Meter: 4/4, begins on 3

Traditional
Words by Mary H. Howliston

There are man-y flags in man-y lands,

There are flags of ev-'ry hue;

But there is no flag, how-ev-er grand,

Like our own Red, White, and Blue.

REFRAIN

Then hur-rah for the flag, our coun-try's flag,

Its stripes and its white stars too,

For there is no flag in an-y land

Like our own Red, White, and Blue.

Introduction to Revolutionary America

"Yankee Doodle"
(page 479; ostinato accompaniment: guitar, drums, rhythm sticks; tableau: three minutemen)

Introduction to War of 1812

"The Star-Spangled Banner"
(page 43; tableau: Francis Scott Key writing song)

Introduction to Civil War

"Dixie"
(accompaniment: harmonica, guitar)

Theme-and-Variation: *American Salute,* Morton Gould
(CD RCA Gold Seal 6806-2RG; movement interpretation)

Introduction to World War I

"Over There"
(*America in Song* 90-3700 Book of the Month Club, side 4, band 5; accompaniment:
snare drum, bass drum; movement interpretation)

Introduction to World War II

"Marine's Hymn"
(*America in Song* 90-3700 Book of the Month Club, side 1, band 4; accompaniment:
snare drum, bass drum; tableau: raising of flag at Iwo Jima)

Introduction to a Fanfare

Fanfare for the Common Man, Aaron Copland
(CBS MY-37257 [record]; MYK-37257 [CD]; listening guide of tone colors—emphasis
on brass and percussion)

Introduction to Gettysburg Address

A Lincoln Portrait (III), Aaron Copland
(CBS MK-42431 [CD]; tableau: Lincoln giving speech at Gettysburg; people listening)

"Battle Hymn of the Republic"
(page 187; audience is invited to join in singing the chorus)

Finale: "You're a Grand Old Flag"

Introduction

There are many symbols of a country; ours is the American flag. It stands for everything that is special about being an American. "The Star-Spangled Banner" is played and the American flag is raised whenever an American wins a gold, silver, or bronze medal in the Olympics.

The American flag is composed of red and white strips representing the original thirteen states, whereas the stars on the field of blue represent the fifty states that make up our country. The American flag is presented to American families when a loved one is killed in battle, and we show our respect for the flag by taking off our hat or facing the flag when it goes by in a parade. In the United States, we honor the American flag on June 14, known as Flag Day.

(entire class sings song and joins in choreographed march)

Closure: Words of Appreciation and Thanks

You're a Grand Old Flag

Key: F
Starting pitch: C
Meter: 2/4, begins on 2

Words and Music by George M. Cohan

You're a grand old flag, you're a high - fly - ing flag;

And for - ev - er in peace may you wave;

You're the em - blem of the land I love,

The home of the free and the brave.

Ev - 'ry heart beats true un - der red, white, and blue,

Where there's nev - er a boast or brag;

But should auld ac - quaint - ance be for - got,

Keep your eye on the grand old flag.

Program III: A Musical Fiesta—South of the Border

Introduction: Words of Welcome

The Meaning of a Fiesta (short essay)

The song "The First of January" is a folk song from Mexico. It features counting from one to seven in Spanish: *uno, dos, tres, cuatro, cinco, seis, siete.* On the seventh of July, people of Spanish origin sing this song, which celebrates the fiesta in honor of the Spanish Saint Fermin. We will sing it in Spanish and then in English. Hand claps, tambourines, and triangles as well as chording instruments (guitar, Autoharp, or Omnichord) provide the accompaniment.

The First of January (Uno de Enero)

Folk Song from Mexico

Key: C
Starting pitch: G
Meter: 6/8, begins on 4

"La Raspa"

(page 441; song and dance)

Dramatics

(a short play with hand puppets or stick puppets featuring an aspect of Mexican life)

"De Colores"

De Colores

Key: C
Starting pitch: G
Meter: 3/4, begins on "and" of 1

Traditional
English Words by Alice Pirgau

Each person is assigned a note; thus, three people play the C chord and four play the G₇ chord (on guitar or Omnichord, resonator bells, xylophone, handbells, or tone chimes)

"La Cucaracha"

(page 364)

A song that is often sung in Mexico is "La Cucaracha." We will sing it today both in Spanish and in English, accompanied by maracas, claves, and chording instruments. The claves and chording instruments will keep a steady beat while the maracas improvise an appropriate rhythm.

"Cielito Lindo"

(page 368)

(recording: *World of Music* CD-4:2, 1991, book 4, p. 63)

A mariachi band or ensemble is composed of street musicians playing guitars, violins, and trumpets, who stroll into restaurants or open-air cafes during the long lunch hour. Sometimes the mariachi ensemble is hired to play for an entire evening. Raise your hands when you hear trumpets, violins, or guitars.

Piñata Ceremony

The piñata is a papier-mâché object filled with candy or nuts and made to look like an animal. The breaking of the piñata is accomplished at the close of the nine days of Christmas celebrations in Mexico. Each child is blindfolded and has a turn with a stick in hopes of breaking the piñata. After it is broken, children gather up their treats. We will first sing "Piñata Song" in Spanish and then in English.

Piñata Song (Al Quebrar la Piñata)

Key: C
Starting pitch: G
Meter: 3/4, begins on 2

Christmas Song from Mexico
English Words by Verne Muñoz

In the hap - py days of Christ - mas,
En las no - ches de po - sa - das,

Sounds of glad - ness fill the air;
La pi - ña - ta_es lo me - jor;

When it's time for the pi - ña - ta,
La ni - ña más re - mil - ga - da

There's ex - cite - ment ev - 'ry - where.
Se_al - bo - ro - ta con ar - dor.

Take a stick and whack it. Be the one to crack it;
Da - le, da - le, da - le, no pier - das el ti - no,

Win pi - ña - ta's trea - sure, Can - dies for your plea - sure.
Que de la dis - tan - cia se pier - de_el ca - mi - no.

Closing: Thank you for coming and we hope that you will join us for refreshments.

COMMITTEES

Students should organize the following committees in the classroom:

1. Program committee

    a. Songs and accompaniments

    b. Instruments needed

    c. Welcome, poems, essays, "connecting" statements, closure

    d. Dramatics

    e. Order of events

2. Classroom decorations committee

    a. Put up decorations

    b. Take down decorations

3. Refreshments committee

4. Table decorations committee

5. Costumes committee

6. Audio-recording committee

7. Video-recording committee

ADDITIONAL IDEAS FOR FESTIVALS OR PROGRAMS

- The Olympics (features song "The Power of a Dream" from Atlanta; movement: clasping hands and swaying)
- Humor in Music
- From Sea to Shining Sea
- America's Songbag
- The World Through Music
- Celebrations
- Seasons
- Transportation
- Style in Music
- Immigrants (Past and Present)

For Your Journal

In your journal of portfolio, make a section on experiences with music and other arts. Include how you would design lessons for lower-elementary (K–3) and upper-elementary (4–6) students. Give examples of (a) analogous concepts of repetition and enlargement, contrast, unity, and balance; (b) a thematic approach; (c) a historical approach; and (d) a cross-cultural approach.

EPILOGUE:

The Continuing Place of Music in the Lives of Children

THIS BOOK HAS FOCUSED on integrating music into the elementary school classroom. You, the classroom teacher, have been given detailed descriptions of ways to assist students in learning to sing, play instruments, listen to music, move to music, and create music. You have been encouraged to integrate music with other areas of the arts and with a study of people and places in the world. There is little doubt that if you carry out the suggestions in this book, your students will receive an excellent introduction to music as a significant phenomenon of human experience.

One of the principal outcomes of music instruction in elementary schools is that children come to value music as an important part of their lives. Because learning experiences in school encompass only a small portion of one's life, it is hoped that students will develop the necessary skills and understanding to want and be able to continue musical study beyond the classroom. It is clear, however, that if teachers wish to foster a continuing place for music in the lives of their students, they will need to lay the foundation for such endeavors in the school music program itself.

A Trip to Buy a Recording

Students should be encouraged to build their own libraries of recorded music, including classical, folk, and popular genres. Such a library might begin by teachers suggesting that students ask for recordings as gifts at birthdays, Christmas, and so on. Teachers should assist students in making lists of their favorite pieces and performers. It is hoped that many of these selections will be those actually studied in school. In addition, however, students will undoubtedly include a number of pieces heard outside the school, either on radio or television or in a live performance.

School librarians should have copies of the *Schwann Spectrum* catalog of compact discs (CDs) and tapes for reference. This catalog lists currently available commercial recordings of musical selections by composer or country. You can help students by suggesting recordings by some of the major orchestras, such as those in Boston, Chicago, Cleveland, New York, Philadelphia, and San Francisco, and well-known artists such as Pavarotti, Perlman, Wild, and so on. Music teachers in your school or in the community can help you decide which are the best performing groups, artists, and recordings.

Below are some general directions to help students in purchasing and organizing a recording collection:

- Is the recording by a well-respected performing ensemble, conductor, or solo performer?
- Is the recording well crafted and engineered?
- Is the recording a good bargain—that is, does it fit within a student's budget?

Invite students to bring recordings from home. These may be organized according to composer, country, or genre (classical, rock, folk, pop), and displays can be made of the cassette or CD packages. The class may wish to make a list on the bulletin board of the best-known conductors and performing artists. If available, you might invite the owner/manager of a record store to visit the class. He or she may speak on a variety of topics, such as how recordings are made (especially the digital process), how owners decide which recordings to stock in the store, and which composers' works seem most popular today. If a record store is near your school, the class may wish to take a trip to the store itself, where they can see how recordings are arranged by type of music, some of the important recording companies, and different price ranges of cassettes and compact discs.

Attending Concerts

One of the principal goals of music instruction in schools is to instill in students a desire to attend live performances of music. There is little substitute for being present as a creative musical performance takes place. The excitement of actually hearing and seeing ensembles and conductors, the virtuoso technical achievements of professional musicians, the distinctive tone colors of voices or instruments, and the acoustical qualities created by the distinctive architecture of a great concert hall all combine to provide truly memorable experiences.

Teachers can do a number of things to help students learn to enjoy and want to attend concerts. Students should carefully study and listen to pieces to be performed. Outlines of pieces to be heard, in terms of the major musical events, are especially important. Students should listen to recorded pieces, following these outlines, until they have least a fundamental grasp of the compositions, thus acquiring some sense of what to listen for in the live performance they will be attending.

Study of musical compositions should also include information about when and where composers lived, types of music they composed, and some of the principal characteristics of each composer's music. Whenever possible, musical information should be placed in a larger framework through comparisons with other events and people of the same period. But though such information is valuable, it should always be secondary to the listening experience itself.

Students should also know something about the performers they will be hearing. This might include information about conductors, featured soloists, and outstanding members of the orchestra. Students will be interested to know of performers who have overcome major challenges to become distinguished performing artists (such as Itzhak Perlman, who contracted polio, and Stevie Wonder, George Shearing, or Ray Charles, who are visually challenged).

Basic understanding of the structure of ensembles should include the number, type, and arrangement of instruments. Diagrams are especially helpful for assisting students in quickly understanding how, for example, an orchestra is seated.

Another important nonmusical item to be considered is proper concert behavior. Students need to be instructed to sit quietly and not to talk or whisper as the music is being performed, not to chew gum or eat candy during a performance, to clap at the end of entire pieces and not between individual sections, and at all times to be courteous with one another.

A number of free children's concerts are offered by professional and college or university orchestras throughout the country. Materials for preparing students to attend such concerts are often provided by the educational departments of the orchestras. In some communities volunteers, called *docents,* visit schools and assist the classroom teacher in such musical preparation.

Performing with Friends

Another principal goal of a school music program is for students to learn to value singing, playing, and creating music so that such experiences can be carried beyond the school itself. Boys and girls should be encouraged to perform either alone or in small groups, with members of their family, in schools, and in the community. Churches and civic organizations are particularly interested in having groups of students perform for various occasions. Many communities have choruses, bands, and orchestras composed of local citizens. Often there are groups for beginning students that provide opportunities for younger performers and act as feeder organizations to adult groups. Many such groups provide scholarships for serious music study. Teachers can encourage student participation in a variety of community ensembles by inviting such groups to perform at the school or by inviting the conductors of such organizations to come to the school to speak with classes.

In addition to participating in formal musical performing groups in the school or the community, children should be encouraged to form their own ensembles and perform together for enjoyment and recreation. Students who play brass instruments, for example, may wish to form an ensemble to play compositions from a number of easy ensemble books currently available commercially. (Easy ensemble materials for woodwind and stringed instruments are also available.) Your school instrumental music teacher will be able to offer suggestions.

Students greatly enjoy playing for social get-togethers, PTA meetings, and meetings of service clubs such as Kiwanis and Rotary. They can have great fun in organizing a "neighborhood circus" in the summertime and providing their own music for various segments of the show, or having a talent show within their class. You should encourage students to think of the many ways they can perform music for all types of occasions, both at school and in the community.

In summary, the ultimate goal of this book is to provide classroom teachers with the knowledge, skill, and confidence for teaching music to children so that they will seek out and participate in musical activities at every opportunity. Such an interest in music is often instilled in the early years of a child's life, and if musical experiences of significant breadth and depth are provided in the elementary schools, it is likely that music will continue to hold a special place in the lives of children, not only during their subsequent school years but as they grow into men and women who value music as an indispensable part of their lives.

Appendix A

Selected Soprano Recorder Fingerings (Baroque System)

Left-hand thumb ○

Left hand:
- 1st finger
- 2nd finger
- 3rd finger

Right hand:
- 1st finger
- 2nd finger
- 3rd finger
- 4th finger

C

C♯ (D♭)

D

D♯ (E♭)

E

F

F♯ (G♭)

G

G♯ (A♭)

A

A♯ (B♭)

B

C

C♯ (D♭)

D

Appendix B

Common Chord Fingerings for the Guitar

Symbols:

X = String not played

0 = Open string

1 = Left index finger

2 = Left middle finger

3 = Left ring finger

4 = Left little finger

R = Root of chord

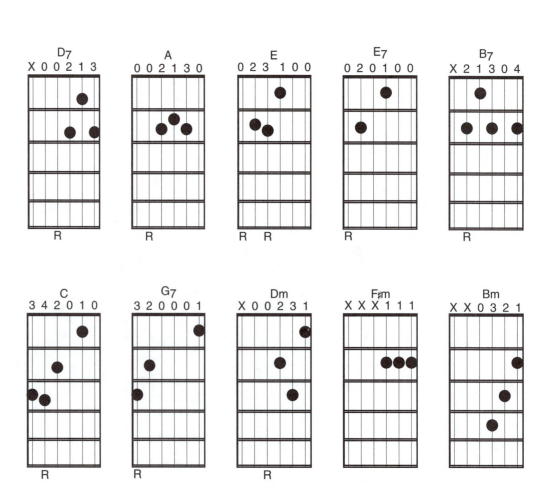

Glossary

a cappella Without instrumental accompaniment. The phrase is Italian for "in chapel style"—that is, in the style of a small place of worship.

accelerando, accel Gradually become faster.

accent Greater emphasis on note or chord. Often indicated by ∧ or > placed above the note or chord.

accidental A sharp (♯), flat (♭), or natural (♮) that appears in the musical score but is not part of the key signature.

adagio Moderately slow tempo.

ad lib, ad libitum A direction indicating that the performer may vary the tempo in a musical composition.

affective Having to do with feeling.

agogo An African percussion instrument consisting of conical metal bells, each having a different pitch.

allargando, allarg Slowing of tempo.

alto The lowest female voice.

analogous concept A concept used in the same way across the arts, such as repetition or contrast.

aria An accompanied song for solo voice.

articulation The way in which musical tones are attacked. It is related to the clarity in vocal or instrumental performance. Legato and staccato are types of articulation.

a tempo A return to the previous tempo.

atonality The lack of a tonal center.

augmentation Presentation of a melody in longer notes.

balalaika A triangular-shaped Russian stringed instrument.

ballad A narrative song.

bar line A vertical line drawn on the staff to divide music into measures.

Baroque music European music from the period between 1600 and 1750.

bass The lowest male voice.

behavioral objective A statement that contains specific skills or behaviors that learners are expected to acquire.

binary form Music composed of two contrasting sections, A and B.

bongo drums Two connected drums of different pitches. The player holds them between the knees and strikes them with his or her hands.

cadence A melodic or harmonic formula that indicates the end of a section or piece.

canon A strict form of imitation in which a melody is stated in one part and is repeated in one or more other "voices."

cantata A sacred or secular choral composition of several movements.

changing meter Frequent changes of meter in a musical composition.

chant   A single, unaccompanied melody.

chord   Three or more tones sounding simultaneously.

chorus   A large group of singers. The term is also used to denote a refrain or a choral segment of an oratorio.

chromatic scale   A scale entirely composed of half steps.

classical music   European music from the period between 1750 and 1825.

clef   A sign placed at the beginning of the musical staff to designate the names of pitches.

coda   A composed ending for a composition.

cognitive   The process of mental learning.

concept   A general term, often applied to a set of ideas that are the same, such as repetition, contrast, or rhythm pattern.

concerto   A composition for solo instrument and orchestra.

concerto grosso   A composition that contrasts more than one solo instrument with the orchestra.

conjunct   A term used to describe melodies that move by stepwise intervals.

contour   The shape of a melody.

cooperative learning   Working together in a group to achieve learning.

countermelody   A melody that is added above or below the main melody.

crescendo   Gradually becoming louder.

cut time   Dividing the meter by two, for example, 4/4 = 2/2 or ¢.

da capo (D.C.)   Go back and repeat from the beginning.

dal segno al fine (D.S. al fine)   Repeat from the sign, and perform until the word *fine,* which means "end."

descant   A countermelody that is always above the main melody.

diminution   The presentation of a melody in shorter note values.

disjunct   A melody in which the intervals are larger than a major second.

dominant   The fifth degree of a scale.

double bar   Two vertical lines that signify the end of a composition.

downbeat   The first beat of a measure.

dulcimer   A name given to several types of American traditional stringed instruments, including the plucked dulcimer and hammered dulcimer.

duple meter   Meter based on two beats or multiples of two.

dynamics   Term indicating degree of loudness or softness in a musical composition.

enharmonic   Descriptive of notes that have the same sound but different names, for example, F♯ = G♭.

fermata   To hold or pause.

fine   The end.

flat (♭)   A musical symbol that lowers the pitch half a step when placed before a note.

form   How a work is designed, its structure.

forte   Loud.

fortissimo   Very loud.

fugue   A musical composition based on imitation. It consists of an exposition, episodes, and reappearance of the subject in different "voices."

grand staff   The G and F clefs joined together.

half step   The interval from one pitch to the next adjacent pitch, ascending or descending.

harmony   The performing of two or more pitches simultaneously.

harpsichord   A stringed keyboard instrument shaped like a modern grand piano but whose strings are plucked rather than hammered to make the sound when the keys are depressed.

homophonic   A musical texture in which a prominent melodic line is supported with an accompaniment.

interval   The distance between two pitches.

key signature   The sharps or flats placed at the beginning of a musical composition to affect the entire composition.

koto   A Japanese stringed instrument that has thirteen strings and movable bridges.

legato   Connecting pitches smoothly.

listening guide   A chart that uses graphics or words to depict various events as they occur in the music.

locomotor movement   Moving the body.

major scale   A seven-tone scale composed of W-W-H-W-W-W-H steps.

mbira   An African instrument consisting of metal or wooden strips of different sizes attached to a resonator (gourd) and played with the thumbs. Also called *kalimba.*

measure   A group of beats between the bar lines on the staff.

melismatic   A melodic passage in which one syllable is sung on several different consecutive pitches.

melodic rhythm   The rhythm of the melody in a musical composition.

melody   An organized succession of pitches.

meter signature   The numbers placed at the beginning of a composition. The upper number indicates the number of beats per measure; the lower number tells what kind of a note will receive one beat.

metronome   An instrument used to indicate a steady tempo.

minor scale   A seven-tone scale composed of W-H-W-W-H-W-W steps.

minuet   A French country dance in triple meter.

mixed voices   A combination of male and female voices.

mode   Scalar arrangements of pitches with distinctive intervals. Common in medieval, Renaissance, and folk music.

modulation   Changing from one key to another within a composition.

notation   A system for writing music that indicates pitch and duration.

note   A musical symbol that may indicate both pitch and duration.

obbligato   A second melodic line that accompanies the main melody.

octave   The interval of an eighth between the lowest pitch and the highest.

opera   A musical drama in which all or most of the dialogue is sung.

operetta   A musical drama in which the dialogue is generally spoken.

ostinato   A repeated melodic or rhythmic pattern that recurs throughout a composition.

partner song   Two songs that are in the same key and have the same length; can be sung together.

patschen   Tapping thighs.

pentatonic scale   A five-note scale.

phrase   A division of a musical line, comparable to a line or sentence in poetry or prose.

pipa   A pear-shaped Chinese stringed instrument that is held upright and plucked by the fingers of the right hand.

pitch   The highness or lowness of a tone.

polyphonic   Music in which there are two or more independent melodies.

polyrhythm   Two or more contrasting rhythms sounding at the same time.

presto   Very fast.

psychomotor learning   Learning through movement.

recitative   A declamatory style of singing.

recorder   A small vertical, flutelike instrument whose pitch is determined by covering and uncovering holes with the fingers.

refrain   A relatively short section that is repeated at the end of each verse of a song.

relative major and minor   The major and minor scales that have identical key signatures; for example, C major = A minor.

Renaissance   The European historical period extending from approximately 1400 to 1600.

repeat sign   Sign indicating that the section should be performed again.

rhythm   The organization of the duration of sound.

romantic period   The European historical period from approximately 1825 to 1900.

rondo   A musical form diagrammed ABACA.

rote   The process of learning a song by imitation.

rote-note   The process of learning a song by imitation and notation.

round   A song in which two or more groups perform the same melody but start at different times.

rubato   Flexibility of tempo.

santouri   A Greek stringed instrument that is played with small hammers.

scale   A succession of ascending and descending tones.

sequence   A melodic pattern that is repeated beginning on another pitch.

shakuhachi   A notched, end-blown Japanese wind instrument.

sharp (♯)   A musical symbol that raises the pitch of a note half a step.

sheng   A Chinese wind instrument made of bamboo reed pipes placed into a bowl-shaped base.

slur   A curved line above or below two or more notes, indicating that they should be performed legato.

solfège   A system for identifying the pitches of the Western scale: *do, re, mi, fa, sol, la, ti, do.*

sonata form   A European musical form that consists of thematic exposition, development, and recapitulation.

soprano   The highest mature female voice.

staccato   Short, detached tones.

staff   A graph of five horizontal lines on which musical notes are placed.

stem   The vertical line attached to a note head.

stepwise   A melodic progression of pitches ascending or descending without skips.

syllabic   Music in which each syllable is sung on one note (pitch).

symphony   An orchestral composition in four movements: fast, slow, moderately fast, and fast.

syncopation   Emphasis on a normally weak beat.

synthesizer   A contemporary instrument that produces sounds electronically.

tempo   The speed of a musical composition.

tenor   The highest mature male voice.

ternary form   A musical form in three sections (ABA).

terraced dynamics   Sudden contrasting dynamic levels.

text painting   Music that describes or enhances the words in the song.

texture   Description of the number of lines of music and the relationships among the lines.

timbre (tone color)   The unique quality of a sound.

tonal center   The key center or home key of a piece.

tonality   How melodic and harmonic elements are organized around a tonal center.

tone matching   Physically singing a pitch that matches that being played or sung by another person.

treble   Another name for the G clef.

triad   A chord of three pitches, arranged in thirds.

triple meter   Meter in threes.

upbeat   One or more notes that occur before the first measure of a musical composition.

verse   A stanza of a poem or song.

vocal techniques   Ways of teaching children to sing.

whole step   An interval formed by two half steps.

xiao   A Chinese wind instrument made from bamboo.

zheng   A plucked stringed instrument from China. The traditional form has sixteen strings; modern versions may have twenty-one strings.

Index of Songs

Songs in **boldface** are included on the accompanying CD.

Partner Songs

Two-Chord Songs

Three-Chord Songs

Songs by Country and Culture

Index of Listening Examples

General Index